VIOLENCE *of* ACTION

The Untold Stories of the 75th Ranger Regiment in the War on Terror

MARTY SKOVLUND, JR.

with LTC Charles Faint & Leo Jenkins
Foreword by Mat Best

BLACKSIDE CONCEPTS

Blackside Concepts
PO Box 63925
Colorado Springs, CO 80962
www.blacksideconcepts.com

ISBN 978-0-9912865-2-2

Cover and Page Design – Lorie DeWorken, MIND*the*MARGINS, LLC

First Edition

Dedication

To the Rangers who made the ultimate sacrifice.
To the wives who will now walk alone.
To the children who will grow up fatherless.
To the parents who will never see their son grow old.
To the families that have an empty seat at the dinner table.
To the nation that lost one of her best.
To the men who must court demons every time they close their eyes.
To the Regiment - past, present and future.

One for the Airborne Ranger in the Sky

"*Violence of Action* is the book about the 75th Ranger Regiment that we've been waiting decades for. While Rangers hit targets night after night throughout the War on Terror, they did it largely in silence and behind the veil of strict Operational Security. While many have written about Special Forces, SEALs, Delta Force, and others, almost nothing is out there about the Regiment's unmatched contribution to the fight in Afghanistan and Iraq, until now. *Violence of Action* pulls back the curtain and allows the reader to finally catch a glimpse of the Rangers in bloody combat."

—Jack Murphy,
New York Times Best Seller and Author of the *Deckard Series*

"As I alternated between chuckling at the humor of the Rangers and gripping the pages with anxiety as I placed myself in their shoes while they fought door to door and leapt rooftop to rooftop, I was blown away by the raw honesty of the book. *Violence of Action* isn't a work about individual accomplishment or chest bumping. Instead, whether in training, in the calm moments before the storm, or in the heat of battle itself, *Violence* shows us that the driving force behind the excellence of the Regiment is every Ranger's biggest fear - to fail the man next to him."

—Nick Palmisciano,
President, Ranger Up

"As a former Delta Force Operator, I always looked forward to conducting joint operations with the Rangers. They were the men that had our backs, and they were the men that would pull us out if we went too deep into the hornet's nest. There is no finer Special Ops infantry in the world, and I would go to hell and back with the U.S. Army Rangers. *Violence of Action* is a must-read for anyone that wants to know what our Rangers are all about and the unsung heroes they really are."

—Dr. Dale Comstock,
Author of *American Badass*

"*Violence of Action* is truly a book like no other ever written. It is a compilation of incredibly impactful stories from individual accounts among some of America's best and brightest—US Army Rangers. While saturated with gripping stories of brave men fighting America's battles abroad, this book is about love, passion, grief, sorrow, and most of all, a brotherhood."

—Kerry Patton,
Author of *Contracted: America's Secret Warriors*

"I salute Ranger Marty Skovlund, Jr. for having produced a book that vividly portrays for us the poignant details and ethos of America's finest Warriors combating the global war on terror. This book is a must read for any young man who thinks he may have the desire and ability to become an elite Ranger. It is even more so for any non-commissioned or commissioned officer who aspires to lead Rangers. The matter-of–fact presentations by the Rangers in this book of actual combat leadership situations are lessons that cannot be taught in any school. These stories underscore their incredible heroism, their uncanny super-human feats under fire borne of intense and continuous training and their ultimate dedication to their Ranger Brotherhood to the degree that they offer their lives willingly to protect their Ranger buddies. This magnificent book accurately captures significant historical data and contributes to the developing legend of the elite 75th Ranger Regiment."

—Gary Dolan,
2011 Ranger Hall of Fame Inductee,
and author of *Of Their Own Accord*

Table of Contents

Foreword

The Global War on Terrorism forever changed the way the world views Special Operations Forces (SOF). The 75th Ranger Regiment is a small but essential part of the elite fraternity of quiet professionals in the Special Operations community who have selflessly dedicated their lives to protecting the freedoms of others through service in the profession of arms.

Throughout their history, the Rangers have demonstrated time and again that they have earned their reputation as one of the most elite light infantry units the world has ever seen. After 9/11 and during the subsequent wars in Afghanistan and Iraq, the Ranger Regiment stepped out of the shadow of more high-profile SOF units and took on the roll as the leader in direct action raids, killing or capturing more high value targets than any other unit. With deliberate and meticulous planning, small numbers, and a great mission set, members of the 75th Ranger Regiment have proven that whether the enemy must be killed from land, sea, or air that they can and will do it, and do it better than anyone else in the world.

When I was approached about writing the foreword for this book about the Ranger Regiment, I was immensely honored that I would even be considered to have a voice in such an amazing piece of history, as the stories in this book are my stories as well. During my time in the military, I was fortunate to serve in the 2nd Ranger Battalion, 75th Ranger Regiment over the course of five combat deployments, working in every position from riflemen to fire team leader and master breacher. I cannot say enough about the men that I served with and the reverence that I have for those still serving in the unit.

Although the accomplishments of the 75th Ranger Regiment have only been recognized in a few media productions, the bravery that emanates from these men on a daily basis more than deserves to be projected to the general public in this manner. I want to thank the humble men that have contributed to this book for sharing their personal stories. Moreover, it humbles me to know that these men are sharing their stories not for social or professional recognition, but rather showing reverence for their fellow Ranger brothers, and enlightening the world to the many sacrifices that occur daily, unknown to so many.

In a normal assertive Ranger manner, may I divulge my conclusion quickly: Thank you Brothers for your selflessness, your humility, and telling your stories – which are a crucial part of modern day history. I am thankful for many things in life, but high on the list was being able to serve with the men of the 75th Ranger Regiment. Godspeed, and Rangers Lead The Way.

In memory of
Staff Sergeant Ricardo Barraza
and Sergeant Dale Brehm

—Mat Best
Former 2/75 Ranger and President of Article 15 Clothing

Preface

*"The more you lose yourself in something bigger than yourself,
the more energy you will have"*

NORMAN PEALE

History is lost if it is not recorded. I have done my best to prevent that from happening to the "GWOT Rangers." This book is homage to these men and the history they made and the impact they had. The 75th Ranger Regiment contributed more to the Global War on Terror than most will ever know; this book is only a small glimpse of those contributions. I had three goals when I set out to write and compile this book:

1. To record the impact the 75th Ranger Regiment had on the global war on terror.

2. To recognize the sacrifices made by Rangers over a decade of sustained war.

3. To inspire future generations of Rangers.

That is what I set out to do, at least. What this book actually became, in true Ranger fashion, far exceeded those goals.

I would like to take a moment to describe exactly what this book is and is not. This book is a collection of real stories written by Rangers who were actually there, and by the men and women that supported those Rangers. I did my best to collect first hand accounts of as many of these events as possible, so as to more accurately record what actually happened during this period of Ranger history.

Writing about true events is a sinister act though. The thing about true events is they encompass real people. People that have real feelings, bleed real blood and weep real tears. So in the pursuit of telling this event I said to these Rangers, "Tell me your story." What I might as well have said was, "Here, take this dull knife and carve your heart out of your chest for me, and then lay it on this nice plate. Oh, and try not to be too messy about it." But what is the alternative? Is it that the story festers within the soul of that person forever? That it dies with that person someday, never to be told again; never to be remembered? Which is the worse fate? I am not sure, but hope I did right by these men and our Regiment. The men and women whose words you see in these pages poured their heart and soul into their work.

As with any firsthand account, it is in the eye of the beholder. Anyone who has been in combat will tell you that everyone involved will remember the same event differently. Although we strived for accuracy, these stories should not be read as official After Action Reports (AARs). Although the Regiment reviewed this book, neither the 75th Ranger Regiment, the U.S. Army, nor the Department of Defense officially endorses what is written.

I spent hours on the phone with some of the writers as we talked about the events described; events that many of them had no desire to remember much less describe in detail. I can assure you that this book does not consist of just mere paper and ink; rather countless sleepless nights, hard liquor, and tears lie within these pages. The common bond that we all saw was the need for this book to happen. The stories needed to be recorded, lest they be forgotten forever.

This is the work of an entire generation of an elite level of the Warrior Caste. This book is presented in chronological order, covering the time period from September 11th, 2001 to September 11th, 2011. Events that happened before or after those dates, while important, are outside the scope of this book. Within that time frame, we did our best to portray both the major and minor events of the period, as well as the transformations the Regiment underwent as a unit. These accounts are not sugarcoated; rather they are raw and told without regard for political correctness, romantic notions of combat, or anyone's feelings on what war "should be." In an attempt to paint a complete picture, we included vignettes from a few people who were not Rangers, but were relevant and very much a part of the Ranger story.

This book is not a political commentary of the events of this time period. We do not have an axe to grind and have no intention of expressing our personal feelings on anything outside the scope of a Ranger mission. This book is not a description of the selection process to get into the Ranger Regiment. This book does not cover the long and storied history of the Ranger lineage; there are a variety of other great books that go into incredible detail about those events. Finally, this book is not a tell-all, an expose, or "the book that the 75th Ranger Regiment does not want you to read." This book was written with paramount attention paid to operational security and personnel security. Many of those who contributed to this book are still out doing the work so few others can or will do. With this in mind, I changed all the names in all of the stories with the exception of public figures and those who explicitly granted permission. I also included the real names of the fallen, so as to ensure their names live on and that their heroic actions are known to everyone who reads this.

This book contains stories that have been told countless times in the barracks room, on the battlefield, and at the backyard barbecue. But they have never been heard by the public before now. As such, this book contains stories that are sometimes critical of other Rangers or members of other units. These stories are not a reflection of the relationship the Regiment has with these units or these men, but rather just a recollection of frustrations that may have happened on those particular missions by those on the ground. It is not my intent to degrade, embarrass, or take away from the accomplishments and contributions of anyone or anything involved in this war. Everyone plays their part, and everyone has had a bad day at some point – the good Lord knows I certainly have! I kept these potentially critical stories in the book though. Without them, it would not be a complete story. I believe that including these deeply personal vignettes, even controversial or critical ones, show that these men are just that – men. Men who volunteered to do extraordinary things. No one understands this better than those of us who have actually worked in this environment.

I knew when I started this book in the fall of 2013 that it was going to be a major undertaking, but it was not until I was months into the project that the gravity of this work hit me. The responsibility to write, collect, organize, and portray previously un-written history is an amazing but worthwhile burden that the contributors to this book and I shouldered. When it is the history of men who have sacrificed life, limb, and emotion to accomplish great feats, the burden is that much more.

Unlike many of the men who contributed to this book, I was not a great Ranger. From the time I arrived at the 75th Ranger Regiment's 1st Ranger Battalion in the spring of 2006, I did anything but thrive in the intense environment that is life as a Ranger. I scraped and clawed my way through nearly five years and five combat deployments, hoping each day the warriors I shared a Scroll with would see fit to let me continue to stand in their ranks. The privilege to walk and fight amongst giants like these is the highest honor any man worthy of the title can have. I am forever indebted to them for that privilege.

With that being said, I don't think I have ever done anything as important as this. I thought the days of making an impact were potentially over when I took the uniform off for the last time in May of 2012, but I see now that I was wrong. This project has grown beyond what I ever imagined it could be, beyond what I believe ANYONE could imagine it would become. These sacred stories will be parables to generations of future warriors; testaments of what courage, leadership, and sacrifice look like. I charge that you have never read anything like this, and are likely to never read anything like it again.

RLTW,
Marty Skovlund, Jr.

Introduction

*"Wherever the Ranger battalion goes,
it is apparent that it is the best"*

GENERAL CREIGHTON ABRAMS

You can't put your finger on it, and you can't quite identify what it is. It is a certain presence that resides permanently around him. He stands straight, the type of posture that is rarely seen in men today. The posture silently screams self-confidence. It is the kind of confidence that comes from going out night after night to hunt other men. Men that hunt back. His back is rounded, shoulders wide. The arms are like leather. The neck thick. A man doesn't get this way by accident. It comes from hours under a ruck, climbing ropes, lifting heavy things, climbing walls, and carrying other full-grown men. Running for miles, endless miles. Miles that make the feet bleed, soaking the white socks red. Miles over road, on gravel, on sand, on dirt, up hills, down hills, upstairs, down stairs . . . Miles that crush a man's soul at the mere thought.

He wears a watch on one wrist, a simple Timex. It is well worn from the hundreds of missions it has been on. The other wrist has a black metal bracelet. It is scratched up, beat up, but never leaves the wrist. It bears the name of a fallen brother. The name of a man who left behind a daughter, a wife, parents. The name of a man who he shared a room with, played Halo with after the mission, drank beer with. The name of a man who received nothing but silence in response to the Sergeant Major beckoning him during that final roll call.

His arms are tattooed. They bear the images of skulls, Spartans, a tattered American flag and flames. There is a weird way in which the ink compliments the blank stare on his face. Almost a slight frown, yet a look of deep thought. His hair is longer than the average soldier, but not too long. He's particular when he explains what he wants at the barber. But then again he is particular about everything in his life.

He pulls his kit out from its cubby in the ready room. It falls over his shoulders in a familiar way. It's weird how the distinctive sound of the Velcro on the cummerbund can be so easily associated with the looming prospect of combat. The Peltors go on, plugged into the radio on his side. He turns them on and turns them up. It just got real loud. The MICH goes on; the NOD's are flipped down and tested. He's paranoid and knows he put fresh batteries in last night, but changes them out again anyway. The amber lenses are dusty, so he takes a red rag and rubs them clear. The helmet is heavy and weighs on a man's neck, but he is used to it. Hours have been spent under the weight of Kevlar, night vision, strobes, Velcro, flashlights . . . He snaps the safety line around his waist, pulls his gloves on, and slips his Oakley's over his ears. You hear a sigh, and then see him do a few squats to make sure everything is on just right. Finally, he grabs his wrist Garmin and his quarterback forearm pad. One goes on each forearm.

He turns the knob on his MBITR and asks for a radio check. He gets a response and is satisfied. Someone yells out that "FMC" will be in five minutes. The others start shuffling away from their cubbies. He grabs his rifle, pulls the charging handle back checking to make sure it is clear, and then releases the bolt. He slides a plastic magazine in and routes the adjustable sling over his shoulder and starts walking for the door. As he walks away you notice that all that heavy gear looks kind of small on his V-shaped torso. He walks with a gait that is swift but quiet.

He floats into the dark, his playground. The air is thin, the moon barely visible. All you hear is the crunch of pea rock under his hiking boots as he walks away toward the flight line. It dawns on you that you just witnessed something few will ever set eyes on. Half the world away, men of a similar age are drinking, playing beer pong, setting new high scores on games. But he is boarding a rotary wing aircraft in the hopes of taking a few more souls off his planet during this period of darkness. Few have seen or done what he has, and fewer still do it with the ferocity that he does.

He is a Ranger. He is the hammer some nights, the scalpel others. His work is carried out with unprecedented speed, surprise, and violence. He does not seek glory, nor recognition of any kind. He lives by a Creed, but for his brothers. He is satisfied knowing that he is doing exactly what needs to be done.

The dirt whipped up from the farm field and pelted the back of the Ranger as the twin rotor helicopter that inserted him and his platoon took back off. The night was dark, no moon to give their position away. The ground was a little damp from the rain that fell earlier in the day, which would make for a silent foot movement. It would be a short walk to the target building tonight, only 1.6 kilometers away. Another day, another dollar, the Ranger thought to himself.

As he walked, he moved his rifle methodically back and forth while using the weapons infrared laser to illuminate any dark areas. No talking, just the occasional radio chatter to keep the platoon updated on the progress of the movement. He listened to the packs of dogs that would bark far off in the distance, always wondering if they could sense what danger crept through the darkness. The Ranger's squad was on primary assault tonight, meaning they would be the first to initiate the breach into the target building. It didn't take long to cover the distance as the platoon settled into a quiet, brisk pace. Before long, the target building was in sight. The platoon started to break down and move to their predetermined areas, almost as if they had been to this very building a hundred times before. A tall courtyard wall surrounded the target building, which was typical of most of the houses they 'hit'. They knew this before even leaving for the mission, and were prepared.

Having carried out this same type of mission hundreds of times before, his squad methodically moved forward and quietly placed a ladder against the courtyard wall and slowly but surely gained entry to the courtyard. The trick to scaling a wall in "full kit" was remaining silent and undetected. It always surprised the Ranger how much junk was just laying around these courtyards, haphazardly strewn about for what must have been years. For that reason, each step was carefully planted being sure not to make a single noise before entry. The green IR lasers flooded the front of the house, checking every crevice to make sure they would not be compromised. The buildings inhabitants appeared to be asleep, and the squad intended to keep it that way for as long as possible. This was his favorite part, the Ranger thought to himself. The mix of adrenaline and anticipation was intoxicating!

The Ranger moved up to the primary entrance while simultaneously assessing it to determine the appropriate method of breaching. The plan was to explosively breach, but as he took a knee and checked the door, he discovered it was unlocked. Perfect. He made the appropriate radio call while he and his team flipped up their night vision devices and prepared to flow into the building. Because the primary breach was unlocked, there was no need to make any noise upon entrance.

3...2...1... the Ranger opened the door and immediately took aggressive steps into the building, wanting to move out of the "fatal funnel" as soon as possible. The lights were all off inside and he made his way through the first room which appeared to be a living area with his team behind. His veins were coursing with adrenaline and his right thumb was firmly planted on the selector switch. Just give me a reason to flick it down, he thought to himself. He cut aggressively into the first bedroom while still maintaining silence. Two adults were lying in a bed, one of which the Ranger assumed was the target. Completely asleep, *they don't even know we are here,* he thought to himself. As the Ranger who flowed into the room with him pulled security on the female, he nudged the sleeping male lightly with the suppressor on the end of his rifle. *This guy is about to have a bad night* the male groggily awoke not realizing the predicament he was in. Then, with eyes suddenly flashing wide he saw the hulking man towering over him with a rifle in his face. Just that quick the Ranger grabbed him by the shirt and violently yanked him out of bed and onto the floor.

By this point the rest of the house had been successfully cleared. Only about twenty seconds from initial breach, without a sound being made. Not a single round fired. Just another night on the job though, not unlike the hundreds of other direct action raids this Ranger had been on in pursuit of high value targets all over Iraq and Afghanistan. This was the "new normal," and he knew Rangers were becoming frighteningly good at the art of surgically applied violence.

Not every night was a sexy, Hollywood firefight. On a vast majority of Ranger missions, nary a single shot was fired. Although this book details some of the major operations that took place during the time period covered by this book, the raid just described was what the majority of missions looked like, especially in Iraq. According to the Regimental website, the 75th Ranger Regiment is a direct-action special operations raid force that conducts forcible entry operations and special operations raids across the entire spectrum of combat. Their official mission is to plan and conduct special missions in support of U.S. policy and objectives.

No other unit in the Department of Defense, whether it be conventional or a special operations force (SOF), has the range of capabilities that the 75th Ranger Regiment brings to the table. The Regiment's four battalions, geographically dispersed throughout the U.S., can deploy anywhere in the world for no-notice missions in high-risk, uncertain, and politically sensitive areas via land, air or sea. Although the direct action raid is the most commonly utilized capability, the unit is also proficient in and capable of airfield seizures, special reconnaissance, counter-terrorism, personnel/ equipment recovery, combat search and rescue, and foreign internal defense – among other things. The platoon is the most common operating size, but the 75th is unique in its capability of working in elements as small as four man teams, all the way up to conducting Regimental operations. This provides the combatant commander a scalable force not found in any other special operations unit, which is one reason the Regiment has been so gainfully employed ever since the onset of combat operations after 9/11.

The 75th Ranger Regiment became the workhorse of the Command during the years following 9/11, executing thousands of raids directed against high value targets every year. Commanders soon found that a Ranger platoon had become one of the most effective and efficient tools to use against the most important targets. Because of that newfound confidence from commanders, the Regiment was doing missions that only a few years prior were considered outside the purview of their capabilities. It is a common misconception that the Regiment is used primarily to support Special Missions Units by pulling security for them. Anyone "in the know" will tell you that rarely is the case. In most instances, Ranger elements work independently, or in some cases side by side in harmony with other Special Mission Units.

Many find it hard to believe that Rangers are working on that level because of their relatively short "pipeline" to get in to the unit compared to other SOF entities. It is hard to explain, but there is something very special about the Regiment. 'The Ranger Standard' is a very proud tradition and possibly the best explanation of why the Regiment has come so far. The standard is excellence in any assigned mission, and because that is the standard, the Regiment WILL BE excellent – they don't know any other way. It doesn't matter if the mission is to move to contact through the mountains of Afghanistan or to do a clandestine special reconnaissance in a denied area. If a Ranger is given a mission, he will not only do it, but also do it better than anyone else would, or could.

If a Ranger does not uphold "The Standard," then he is quickly removed from his position. A seasoned Ranger team leader must fight for a squad leader position, and a squad leader must fight for a platoon – so on and so forth. Rangers are the only special operations unit that will make its leaders go back through selection before moving up, to make sure the standard is being maintained at all levels. Rangers do not have the luxury of having their own branch like many of our SOF brethren; if a Ranger of any rank is not "among the best" when performing their job or moving to the next level of responsibility, they are re-assigned to "the big Army" instead of being shuffled to a different position within the organization. It is an extremely competitive environment day in, and day out. That competitiveness and pursuit of excellence drives "The Ranger Standard," which has in turn propelled the Regiment to heights never before seen.

As you read through this book, you will have an uncanny look at what the modern Ranger has been up to for the first decade following 9/11. This is still only a fleeting glimpse though, as much still remains veiled in secrecy. Nonetheless, I think you will find that the "tip of the iceberg" that we have exposed in this book is quite amazing.

Chapter One

"Cry 'Havoc' and let slip the dogs of War."

WILLIAM SHAKESPEARE

On September 11th, 2001 radical jihadists fundamentally changed our country. They brought war to America's front door through the use of passenger aircraft violently rammed into city buildings and crashed into rural fields. This marked the beginning of a new era for the 75th Ranger Regiment. No longer was it a unit used for short duration missions in trouble spots around the world. When those towers fell, it marked the beginning of a transition to more than a decade of sustained combat. The Rangers didn't know it at the time, but the Regiment would not miss a single day of the long war on terror that was coming.

For the 75th Ranger Regiment, the war started immediately. The Regiment took its first casualties on the night of October 19th, 2001. Specialist Jonn Edmunds and Private First Class Kristofor Stonesifer of 3/75 were killed when the Blackhawk helicopter they were riding in crashed. On the night of Oct. 19th-20th, 2001, A and C Companies of the 3rd Ranger Battalion conducted a combat parachute jump into Objective Rhino, which was located southwest of Kandahar, Afghanistan. This marked the official transition from a largely garrison unit that trained for combat, to a force to be reckoned with that was now at war. Four MC-130s dropped 199 Rangers from the unusually low elevation of 800 feet above ground level with zero illumination present in order to seize a landing strip for use with follow-on forces, provide an aerial refueling point, as well as destroy any Taliban forces present. The mission was also planned in the hope of having a psychological effect on the enemy, proclaiming, "You wanted a fight? Well, here we are!" to those responsible for the terror attack just five weeks prior.

Eleven enemy combatants were reported killed by the ordinance dropped by bombers in preparation of the target ahead of the combat jump, and another nine were reported as fleeing the objective. By the time the Rangers landed and assaulted the objective there was only one enemy fighter remaining, which they handily eliminated. The mission was a success, completed in less than six hours with no American personnel killed and only two wounded in the initial jump.

Although this was the first combat jump of the war, it would not be the last. Not even a month later on November 10th, 2001, the Regimental Reconnaissance Detachment (RRD) Team Three performed a combat military free fall jump onto Wrath Drop Zone in southeastern Afghanistan. The mission was to establish a combat landing strip for follow on forces to land on. The mission was yet another early success for the Regiment.

The next combat jump would come only days later on November 13th, 2001 when two squads of Rangers from B Company, 3rd Ranger Battalion with attached U.S. Air Force Special Tactics personnel performed another combat parachute jump onto a drop zone in the vicinity of Alimarden Kan-E-Bagat, Afghanistan. This small element again jumped with zero illumination, in even colder temperatures (which makes parachutes descend faster), exiting the aircraft from only five hundred feet above ground level. This was dangerously low, as a parachute malfunction from this height would not allow enough time for activation of the reserve parachute.

Upon hitting the ground, almost everyone in the small Ranger assault element sustained injuries. Despite the hard landing, the Rangers were unfazed and continued the mission anyway. After successful completion of their objective, they moved out at a run to make it to the extraction point on time – again using mind over matter to operate while injured.

A week later, RRD Team Three conducted a combat static line jump onto Shiloh Drop Zone in southeastern Afghanistan in order to establish another flight landing strip for follow on forces. Establishing these hubs for aircraft to land on were vitally important to the war effort as Afghanistan is a land locked country inaccessible to naval landings as well as being nearly out of range for rotary wing aircraft to access.

Although the tempo of operations had not yet increased to a sprint, Rangers were involved in the fight early and often as the war on terror picked up steam. No one really knew at that point how long the deployments would last, how many there would be, and what the next decade would have in store for them. At this point, they were taking it one mission at a time.

September 2001
"9/11"

It was evening, and we sat quietly: alone, yet together. I was torn between the two worlds that had become my immediate reality; my head deeply processing the images unfolding in front of me on the small, corner mounted television and my heart reaching for the quiet figure in the hospital bed. Judy sat breathing, watching. The rain was soft as usual and we were alone, together for a rare moment. Years later, I would know it was by design. I looked at her eyes; they were tired and sad, but still somehow beautiful. She was visibly weary, but I still saw the beauty in her that I have fallen in love with in her daughter, Kelly, who I was set to marry in December. I looked back at the television: fire, death, rubble, fears and inside of me, rage cranks like a turbine.

"I can't believe I'm fighting to stay alive in a world like this," her words snatched me back into the room. It wasn't what she said that shocked me; it was the matter of fact delivery. I was back in the present, and in a rare moment unsure of my words, so I said nothing. It is a miserable day, and for Judy, her worst and last birthday.

She was very coherent at this point and said, "Are you going to get involved in this?" I replied, "Yes." She again inquired, "With the guys with the beards, and the big butts?" as she started slipping away again. I laughed. Judy always made me laugh. Her laugh, like that of her daughter, is infectious and captivating. It can light up a room, even one filled with an inescapable and consuming death. I knew who she was referring to, and although I wasn't quite sure about the "big butts part," I gave her a pass in consideration of the chemotherapy and high doses of painkillers running through her body. I managed to reply with a simple, "Yes."

The next day she announced that she was ready to go home, and she did. She and her husband, Lou, had spent over thirty years working in medicine. They knew the end of this story, and so did we. It was, unfortunately, one of only two certainties that the post-9/11 world now had for our 'family'; the second being, 'I was now involved'.

I was a squad leader at the time in 2nd Platoon, A Company, 2/75 Rangers, otherwise known as 'The Blacksheep'. I had grown up there for the past four years and this was my family. We had trained together, fought together, drank together, and lived together. We had waited for our time to close with and destroy the enemies of our country, anytime, anywhere. But not like this. We never imagined an America where thousands of our people would be murdered in our homeland. I felt a pain of responsibility for this, and vowed to avenge this day.

As Rangers, we found ourselves in an odd circumstance, already set to deploy for a routine exercise in Jordan called "Early Victor/Bright Star," where we would train the Jordanian Rangers, even though we were certainly on the brink of a real world deployment. Bags were packed and pallets were already loaded, so we waited. Not knowing if we would still push out to the Middle East or have our training deployment "kanked." We spent our time as we always did, conducting dry fire drills in the house, battle drills on Noble Hill, tape drills in the Quad, PT'ing at a pace that would make most people vomit . . .just another week. Only it wasn't.

SEPTEMBER 17TH, 2001

The week at my fiancé's childhood home proved equally uneventful. Family came in from all over the country as best they could. We went about life as normal as possible considering the circumstances. While I went through the motions at Battalion, Kel spent as much time with her mother lying absently present in her bed; half in this world, halfway home with the Lord. Then it happened, a day of clarity.

Her boy had arrived and Judy sat in her living room and talked to her son Tony, and Lou's parents. She laughed and they reminisced. It was fun. While the day got long, I made two important phone calls: the first to a bishop that I pulled out of the phone book, the second to my Ranger Buddy, "Mike." Now, there are certain things you can always count on with a Ranger. A Ranger is a man of action. A Ranger does not hesitate and he knows when it's time to execute, and a Ranger completes the mission. Another fact about a Ranger is that he never operates alone, so when he gets a random call from another Ranger, you can rest easy knowing that one will become two, two a team, teams into squads and so on in short order. It is engrained into the fabric of our being from day one. It is who we are.

When Mike arrived, the scene was set. A bishop we had never met (and would never see again), a humble altar set up in front of the wall of family photos and memories (one final memory), Judy sitting in her chair with Lou at her arm. Amongst the sadness of the week's events, Kelly was a singular point of beauty—brown hair, and deep eyes to match, standing small with rosy cheeks in a pair of jeans and a t-shirt. We said "I do" and kissed, I knelt beside Judy and asked her if she understood what had happened, she was fading, but a response of "yes" escaped from her. She looked down at me and smiled, I promised I would take care of her little girl for the rest of my life, and she was taken back to bed.

That night Mike and his wife Janice, with baby in tow, took us for a humble honeymoon celebration at the Puyallup Fair. I ate hot dogs, the girls chatted, Mike and I talked about our impending trip...was all of this really happening? It was. Two days later, Judy went home to be with the Lord, and less than a week after that we deployed.

It was a blur. More training (why are we training, there is a war on!), locked down in a camp outside of the city of Amman working with the Jordanians, validating air missions while trying to pinpoint where our sister battalions might be. After a few weeks we were allowed to check our e-mail. I received my turn in the tent and after what seemed like twenty minutes (it was probably more like two . . .Rangers are not a patient breed) of connecting to the Internet, I had a message in my inbox from Kelly. The message read, "you need to call me immediately." I rushed to my platoon sergeant and explained the situation, he fetched me the CO's iridium satellite phone that we used for such special circumstances and as I dialed in, I knew what the rush was about.

We connected, and it was nice to hear my new bride's voice as she jumped right into a conversation I will never forget. Now, if you can agree that a Ranger is a unique beast, you will also understand that a "Ranger Wife" is a wondrous anomaly. She is a strong, intelligent and beautiful creature that is also uniquely gifted with fortitude and a resolve that you rarely see in anyone. These ladies are quite literally our backbone.

"You're not going to believe this . . ." she started.

"You're pregnant," I replied.

"Yup."

I smiled, but a pang shot across my chest. Married, mother recently dead, new husband gone and now pregnant, all in a world on the certain doorstep of all-out conflict. What kind of husband am I? What kind of father am I already? I vowed to never be like mine, but already, I was absent.

October arrived and we sat in a make shift chow hall tent watching our brothers from 3/75 jump into Objective Rhino on Fox News like the rest of our homeland. We felt cheated. Those bastards! The war had started, and we sat impotent watching from what seemed like the closest location our Regiment was positioned. Eventually, we loaded the birds and went home, stopping briefly in Shannon, Ireland for what I would later come to know as the customary "welcome back from a dry region" one-hour alcohol binge.

We were sullen and defeated; we felt like we had missed our opportunity to deploy, and that 3rd Battalion had wronged us. How could they choose 3rd Batt!? We didn't get it back then. We didn't know what we didn't know. We didn't understand that 3rd was no different than 2nd or 1st (sorry brothers, just let it go . . .Ranger truly is Ranger regardless of the Battalion, although it is a blast to see the personality differences per unit). We didn't understand that the "combat dream" we were chasing wasn't real; and most importantly, we didn't understand that the days of the 18-hour hit-it and exfil-style deployments were in the wind like the parachutes over Rio Hato. We would eventually get our chance, and we all would pay for it, some more than others and some with their lives.

It came and went: Objective Rhino, "fixed wing" training, Operation Anaconda, "rotary wing" training, RRF 1 and ranges . . .so many ranges. We rode trucks more now; they wanted us to be more rapidly accessible (I felt like I had been saying that for years . . ."guys, we DO have helicopters!"). We watched the war from home, bitterly awaiting our chance. While all of this raged oversees, Kelly waged a battle of her own: morning sickness and discomfort overshadowed by the pains of loneliness. No mother to comfort her, no husband to help her. When people ask us about our "Ranger Family," how we've been able to stay close for so many years and why we still, to this day, travel to be together every Thanksgiving, it just makes sense to us. All she had were the wives and all I had were my Ranger buddies. Together, yet separate.

I took a squad in 1st Platoon, C Company 2/75 Ranger (The Madslashers) during this time, which added more chaos to my world; more family ripped from me while a new, surprising bond developed. These men would become the Rangers that I would go to war with, hump the Hindu Kush with, fast rope into the Shegal Valley with, jump with and grow with over my three combat rotations. These men became what I think about when I remember my days in the war; the boys I would protect, challenge, and genuinely care for. These were the men who huddled around me as the image of my child materialized in front of me on the CO's laptop in Bagram, Afghanistan.

-BRANDON YOUNG
2/75

OCTOBER 2001
"OBJECTIVE RHINO"

It was October 19th, 2001 and we were all fired up to take the fight to the enemy. I didn't fully understand all of my emotions at the time; however, in retrospect, I know that I was excited because we had been sent to act out the aggression that all of America felt. Most Americans had that sinking, helpless feeling in their gut and wanted to find and kill the ones responsible for the terrible actions on September 11th. I was one of the truly lucky people who were able to do something, to act in an aggressive manner and direct that aggression toward our enemy.

Just like any other jump, we went out to the tarmac about seventeen hours too early and set up all of our gear. My thoughts were on the mission, making sure that my reduced team had all their gear and knew all the important parts of what we would be doing. I had a reduced team due to what I assume is a normal occurrence during any combat jump: the higher-ranking officers wanted in on it. The command and control element for this mission had captains and majors acting as RTOs for other captains and majors. At the time (and still a little to this day) I was pissed. I gave all these "RTOs" the same scowl that I give new Rangers right out of RIP: a look of disgust, anger and disappointment. I was told that if the shit hit the fan all these officers were instructed to fall in with a squad and act as the squad leader saw fit. I was sure that this arrangement was never going to happen. We were going to have to Ranger up and complete the mission short-handed. My anger towards all these officers trying to pad their resume with a combat jump did not get any better when intelligence reports said that there were active anti-aircraft guns on the objective.

A few minutes before the Jump Master Pre-Inspection (JMPI) began, I looked down my chalk and saw the chaplain getting ready for the jump. I am not really a follower of the Good Book, but I did grow up in an Irish Catholic family that taught me to fear the clergy and give nothing but the utmost respect. In the past few months I had a few very brief encounters with the chaplain. He looked like a young captain, but had a combat scroll (I believe from Panama, but not sure). Because of his combat scroll and the fact that he was a man of God, I understood why he would be on the jump.

I was assembling my team for JMPI and glanced over at the chaplain just in time to see him put an M-4 in his case. Now, I do not know all the rules that go into being a military chaplain, however I was pretty sure that I had read somewhere that they never carry weapons. I had never observed a chaplain carrying a weapon during training, at the range, or any other time for that matter. As he walked past me, my curiosity got the best of me. I stammered something to the effect of, "Sir, I see that you are carrying a rifle. Isn't that kind of against your profession?" The chaplain said something to me that has stuck with me to this day. He said with a smile, "My role is to protect my flock during this mission."

I believe that this quick interaction shows the intense sense of duty that makes Rangers special. I came to find out from the chaplain that he was in 2nd Ranger Battalion as a private, and was a bit of a wild child. He told me that he separated from the Army, found God, was ordained, and then came back in. I left the Army and so far have not started looking for God; however, I completely understand the need to re-connect with the people that understand you the best, and help them in any way possible. You can turn a Ranger into a man of God but you can't take the Ranger out of a man! The scroll is a way of life!

–ANDREW HEGGIE
3/75

Chapter Two

"He which hath no stomach to this fight, let him depart;
his passport shall be made."

WILLIAM SHAKESPEARE

As the New Year came and went, 2002 would mark the first full year that American forces and the Ranger Regiment would be deployed for combat operations in southwest Asia. It would also mark the first year that Rangers were killed in combat in the war on terror. Operation Anaconda would prove to be one of the first major operations in pursuit of Usama Bin Laden, the mastermind behind the 9/11 terrorist attacks.

The military had been monitoring enemy forces in the Shah-e-Kot Valley, located high in the mountains of Afghanistan, for well over a month. In February, the Task Force Mountain commander, Major General Hagenback, began planning for Operation Anaconda with the intent of eliminating this pocket of fighters in their high mountain retreat. TF Mountain formed a multi-faceted operation that would incorporate both conventional and special operations forces, along with their Afghan partners. U.S. and Afghan forces in Gardez would push from the west of the valley, causing the enemy to move east into the blocking positions that would be established by soldiers from the 10th Mountain and 101st Airborne Divisions. The operation would last for nearly three weeks and would not go without mistakes and loss of life.

Augmenting TF Mountain would be small reconnaissance elements "Advanced Force Operations," or "AFO" teams, which were drawn from Army, Navy and Air Force special mission units (SMUs). These AFO teams would move to strategic locations where they would establish observation posts (OPs) where they could support the conventional Army Afghan partner units below them. The AFO teams would prove to be extremely effective not only in providing timely intelligence, but also in calling in air strikes on enemy positions.

On March 4th, 2002, one of these AFO teams consisting of Navy SEALs from a Naval Special Warfare SMU and an Air Force Combat Controller were flying towards a 10,000-foot mountaintop of strategic importance called Takur Ghar to establish one of those OP's. As they approached the HLZ, Al Qaeda fighters who were concealed on the mountaintop began engaging their MH-47E helicopter, Razor 03. This caused some of the hydraulic and oil lines to be severed, spraying fluid all over the ramp of the helicopter. Navy SEAL Neil Roberts had prematurely unhooked his safety line, which tethered him to the aircraft, before being knocked off balance by the sudden jerks of the aircraft and slipping on the fluid present on the ramp, falling approximately 5-10 feet onto the snowy ground below. The crew barely escaped the ambush, and managed to perform a controlled crash seven kilometers north of the mountaintop that Roberts had fallen out onto. Roberts was now alone, facing an enemy force that nearly felled the Chinook he was riding in. Another MH-47, Razor 04, had earlier inserted a reconnaissance element nearby and was able to arrive at the crash site within 30 minutes to pick up the SEALs and aircrew. Too heavy to reach altitude in order to attempt an immediate rescue of Roberts, the second MH-47 was forced to return to base in order to drop-off the original flight crew and refuel, before finally returning to Takur Ghar.

At 0500 local time, they approached the original HLZ on Takur Ghar. Again, enemy fire ripped through the bird, but everyone was inserted. They were now in the midst of an intense firefight that resulted in two of the SEALs being seriously wounded and one, Chapman, killed in action. They were outnumbered and taking heavy fire, so they began to break contact and move away.

Back at Bagram, the Ranger quick reaction force (QRF) that was on standby for the mission boarded two Chinooks, one carrying 13 personnel and the other carrying 10, and made their way to the mountaintop with out a briefing on what the situation was on the ground. Due to communications issues while en route to the target, the QRF element never received the instructions to not land on the same HLZ that the previous flights had attempted, nor did they know that the SEALs on the ground had moved away from their original insertion location.

Just after sun up the first of the two helicopters, Razor 01, approaching from the south was hit with effective small arms and RPG fire, with one RPG round impacting on the right side of the helicopter. The helicopter had sustained too much damage to make it off the mountaintop, and thus had to crash land. It impacted in such a way that the nose of the Chinook was pointing up the mountain in the direction of the main enemy bunkers, simultaneously knocking all the Rangers to the floor. The Rangers, CCT personnel, and the eight-man Chinook crew began moving under intense enemy fire in order to get out of the helicopter while also returning fire. During this exchange, Specialist Marc Anderson was killed instantly before he was able to exit the aircraft. Sergeant Bradley Crose and Corporal Matthew Commons survived the initial impact of the crash landing, but then as they exited the rear of the aircraft the barrage of small arms fire felled them.

Pararescueman Jason Cunningham and one of the other medics remained inside the helicopter in order to treat the wounded. Meanwhile, the Rangers quickly maneuvered to cover while simultaneously killing two more combatants to include one of the RPG gunners. The Rangers worked to take the hill, but with the few men they had left were unable to do so. The Air Force Combat Controller had fortunately been working up a fire mission, and within minutes U.S. aircraft were dropping 500lb bombs within 50 meters of their position. This leveled the playing field, and the Rangers were no longer in danger of being overrun by the enemy combatants on the mountaintop.

The second Chinook, who was carrying the Rangers on the other half of the QRF element, had moved to a safe area until further instructions came once Razor 01 had been shot down. Before long, they received orders to insert at a location that was over 2,000 feet below the mountaintop. The Rangers moved for two hours up a 45-70 degree slope, in three feet of snow, weighed down by their weapons, body armor and equipment at an elevation that made breathing difficult. To make matters even worse, they were harassed by intense mortar fire raining down from on top of the mountain. They never hesitated as they moved though, personifying the fifth stanza of the Ranger Creed, "Energetically will I meet the enemies of my country . . ."

By the time they made it to the top, they were physically exhausted but knew they still had a mission to accomplish. They linked up with the Rangers from the crashed Chinook and prepared to assault the enemy bunkers that were a mere fifty meters away. The Air Force Combat Controller called in one more airstrike, two machineguns laid down covering fire, and seven Rangers began the assault on the enemy bunkers. They moved as quickly as they could through knee-deep snow while shooting and throwing grenades in a concert of orchestrated violence. Within minutes, the Rangers killed multiple enemy combatants and overran their entrenched positions.

The Ranger ground force commander then made the decision to move all wounded to the recently acquired hilltop, as it would be easier to defend in case the enemy organized a counter attack. The work was arduous because of the steep terrain and deep snow, but well worth it as they soon began taking fire from a ridgeline that was approximately 400 meters away while still making the move. During this engagement, the medical personnel that were still at the CCP treating the wounded were mortally wounded themselves as they were completely exposed to enemy fire. Both the Rangers and helicopter crewmen maneuvered on the enemy in an attempt to eliminate the threat, while simultaneously risking their lives to pull the wounded to cover behind the nearby rocks. The Combat Controller called in another air strike and the Rangers returned machinegun fire until the enemy fire was finally suppressed. This attack did not go without consequence though, as the enemy claimed the life of Pararescueman Jason Cunningham.

The Rangers consolidated and finished moving their dead and wounded to the top of the hill, while continuing to take sporadic small arms and mortar fire. The situation in the vicinity of Takur Ghar did not make another daylight rescue attempt possible, forcing them to defend their position until nightfall when extraction would be possible.

Finally, at about 2015 local time, four helicopters from the 160th SOAR flew in for both the Rangers on Takur Ghar and the SEALs that were still down on the mountainside. The reconnaissance mission gone wrong followed by the multiple rescue attempts would end up claiming seven American lives, and would mark the most costly day for Rangers since the 1993 battle of Mogadishu.

The mission did not stop after Operation Anaconda. The infrastructure for military operations in Afghanistan was nearly nonexistent in 2002. Bagram, the largest base in Afghanistan today, only consisted of about thirty tents at the time. Because of this, Rangers were one of the few units who had the flexibility to conduct missions, as the conventional Army was still getting its feet on solid ground. Individual Ranger platoons were working out of safe houses, receiving their missions via radio and resupply from the air. Their Ground Mobility Vehicles (GMV's) were not compatible with the terrain at that time, so they had to improvise by moving on foot or using local vehicles. Many units could think of reasons not to conduct operations. The Rangers received missions and figured out a way to complete them, no matter what the obstacles were. Their tenacity, flexibility, and ability to find unconventional solutions allowed coalition forces to continue the mission.

June 2002
"Away at War"

So much happens in nine little months; life is knit together, relationships are forged, love is tested and deployments turn into Operation Enduring Freedom. It was less than a year before we were back
in the hospital, only this time, I am not there. The Iridium phone
was back in my hands while another one of my major life moments
unfolded without me.

I heard her crying and screaming. She felt like a thousand miles
away, and she was. I paced back and forth outside a mud hut that
I think was the gym in Bagram, Afghanistan. Mike checked on me
every now and then; but mainly runs interference on other Rangers
while I burned battery on the satellite phone. I thought to myself,
"If you think you're calling home right now . . .you are sorely mistaken, Ranger . . ." As I listened intently, a bystander to my own life,
I heard him arrive. Jaden Jude was born into the world, and I was
not there.

"You should see him, babe . . .he's so beautiful," the elation in
her voice let me know that her pain is at an end. Her tears are of
joy—mission complete—and this is a relief.

I wanted to feel that joy so much, to reach through the phone
and hold them both, but I can do neither. I felt nothing. I realized
that I have been on the phone for a very long time. Kelly was tired
she handed me off to her father. We finished the call and I went
back to my tent, stopping only to tell Mike and Justin (my roommate
of four years until I got married, a man I considered my brother) that
all is well.

"You ok?"

"Fine, thanks . . ."

I walked off. I was a Father, yet I was not present for the birth of my son. I am a failure, just like my father before me. On this day of joy for our family, a rage was ignited that would consume me for many years, nearly tearing my family apart. Nearly.

-BRANDON YOUNG
2/75

Chapter Three

"Some must be warriors,
that others may live in peace."

MERCEDES LACKEY

The year 2003 brought another war to be fought. On March 19th, 2003 the President of the United States, George W. Bush, announced the commencement of combat operations in Iraq. The opening salvo was a "shock and awe" air campaign, quickly followed by a ground campaign lead by the Army's 3rd Infantry Division pushing forward towards Baghdad.

The 75th Ranger Regiment was tasked with seizing multiple high value targets for the invasion effort. Failure was not an option. On March 23rd, Rangers participated in a high priority raid on the Al Qadisiyah chemical weapons compound. The Rangers were to insert around the building while a SMU searched for the suspected chemical weapons. As the Rangers descended in their MH-60 Blackhawks, they came under fire and one Ranger was wounded immediately. Once the assault force landed they came under heavy fire from positions in the well-protected target building. While the Rangers were in contact, multiple enemy vehicles started speeding towards their positions, only to be neutralized by the hovering gunships in place for such a purpose. Although a fierce firefight, the mission was short lived. They were airborne again within the hour, mission complete. Only two casualties were taken, one Ranger and one of the Night Stalker pilots, both of which received medical treatment. What exactly was found inside the research facility is yet to be disclosed.

On March 24th, Rangers from C Co. 3/75 conducted a combat parachute jump in the vicinity of Al Qaim, Iraq. On March 28th, Rangers from A Co. 3/75 conducted a combat parachute jump onto H-1 airfield. Rangers then went on to take Haditha Dam, which Saddam Hussein was rumored to be threatening to destroy, potentially causing extreme loss of life and a blow to the Iraqi infrastructure. Rangers in a different part of the country also participated in the rescue of Jessica Lynch.

Rangers conducted a combat jump in Afghanistan in February of 2003, before the war in Iraq had begun. At the end of the year, elements of the entire 75th Ranger Regiment were alerted for an operation in Afghanistan called "Winter Strike." From October until January of 2004, the Winter Strike Rangers conducted classic Ranger operations in the most austere terrain in the world. Platoons conducted long movements through the mountains in search of Al Qaida operatives that did not make it out of the country in time. It was one of the worst winters on record for Afghanistan, which in combination with the terrain made for an extremely challenging hunt. Rangers were living off the land, sometimes taking refuge in local Afghans houses, purifying their own water, and setting up patrol bases in the middle of blizzard conditions. Some platoons used civilian Hilux trucks, some used helicopters, and others were on foot the entire time. There were even platoons that stayed out for periods of 30+ days at a time. It was a true testament to the flexibility that the 75th Ranger Regiment brought to the table.

The Rangers were now fighting two wars simultaneously; Captain Russell Rippetoe, Specialist Ryan Long, Staff Sergeant Nino Livaudais, Corporal Andrew Chris, Sergeant Timothy Conneway, and Sergeant Jay Blessing all made the ultimate sacrifice.

FEBRUARY 2003
"THE JUMP"

On February 25th, 2003 a platoon from C Company, 2nd Ranger Battalion, along with attachments from A Company and HHC were streaking through the air to conduct an airborne assault near Chahar Borjak, Nimruz Province, Afghanistan. My boots were laced tight, double knotted and the excess tucked in. The tan suede had been rubbed bald in some places from the hundreds of miles they had traversed in both training and combat. The tread on the bottom was not quite as fresh as it was when I first put them on, but they fit my feet like a fine glove. My legs pushed the Vibram soles into the metal floor of the cramped C-130 aircraft, as I tried to stabilize myself while the bird bumped its way through the air.

I volunteered for this, I thought to myself. I took pride that we did what so few others had the stomach to do. I knew that most did not have what it took to exit an aircraft mid-flight into a foreign hostile country. I knew even fewer could do it with the threat of Iranian jets that were scrambling to intercept us. My calloused hand gripped the yellow fabric that connected me to a steel cable, my lifeline. At the moment the yellow fabric was merely responsible for helping me keep my balance, but in less than ten minutes it would have my life in its proverbial hands. I was staring blankly ahead, quietly saying a short prayer whilst gazing through the customary Ranger face camouflage pattern; dark on the high features, light in the shallow. It was the first and last time we ever "camo'ed" up in Afghanistan. I always thought the pattern made us look like cats, but the enemy saw it differently; "Painted Demons" they called the Rangers in Panama. I thought on this briefly while the lumbering aircraft did evasive maneuvers. It was appropriate, maybe even romantic, since my fellow brothers in arms and I wore the paint in honor of those "Just Cause" Rangers we had grown up worshiping.

I thought about my family back home who did not really know what I did, but told their friends that I, "jump out of planes, or something." Yeah, something like that. I snapped back in to reality as a Ranger NCO approached me, he quickly made sure that my static line was safely routed over my shoulder. I always felt an adrenaline rush when the doors opened, and that day was no different as the afternoon sun flooded into the inside of the aircraft. The mission was to literally scare the enemy out of their hiding spots. Once they start moving, they are easier to hunt. Hunting just happened to be a Ranger specialty.

I quickly touched all of the attachment points on my harness, I knew they were right but did it anyway. For men of our trade, attention to detail is the difference between life and death. "ONE MINUTE" rang from deep within the Jump Masters chest, and we all ceremoniously echoed the command back. My heart started to race in anticipation. My grip tightened, and as the aircraft slowed its pace the entire chalk lurched forward. One foot was in front of the other, and I was doing my best to stay steadfast in my position. You could cut the anticipation in the air with a knife. "THIRTY SECONDS" and the entire column shuffled forward a bit as the first man stepped into the door. I was hunched over under the weight of the ruck hanging from my harness, and wanted nothing more than to slip into the sky and be released from the screaming pain in my shoulders and rounded back. *This is just the beginning,* I told myself, *the real work starts when we hit the ground.*

Right as the ominous red light flicked to green, my cracked lips broke into a smirk. The entire column seemed to be sucked forward by the gravity of the door, men disappearing one by one. The roar of the prop driven engines almost seemed to fade away as I strained for eye contact with the jumpmaster. Then it happened, in almost one fluid motion. I handed the yellow fabric off; turned, and then disappeared out the troop door. I grit my teeth as I waited for the tug of the opening silk. I was now quickly descending into the open, tri-border region of Iran, Afghanistan, and Pakistan. In what only seemed like seconds later, I was on the ground scrambling out of my harness. I released the charging handle on my rifle with a 'clack', and moved expeditiously towards the assembly area. Before long, we were pushing out and securing the airhead line.

It was a successful, but rather uneventful day. The attached Air Force Combat Controllers established a runway and it wasn't much longer before the rest of the platoon and I were extracted from the target in the middle of the night. Was it a successful mission? One can only speculate . . .

-J.M.
2/75

Only days later on March 1st, 2003, Khalid Sheikh Mohammed (KSM) or otherwise known as the "Architect of 9/11," was captured in the town of Rawalpindi, Pakistan. This was a significant leap forward in the war on terror, as well as the pursuit of those directly responsible for the September 11th terrorist attacks. The portly, mustached terrorist is still in custody today.

March 2003
"The Invasion"

It was March of 2003 inside of a filthy 'GP Large' tent somewhere in Saudi Arabia and we waited like anxious kids before Christmas. Our platoon was waiting for a mission, a spin-up, a purpose; we waited for anything. At this point in my first deployment, the Invasion of Iraq hadn't quite turned out to be the intense bloodbath that I thought it was going to be.

Bravo Company, 1st Platoon arrived in the Middle-East ready to deal death as well as endure it if absolutely necessary. As soon as we hit ground, it was constant preparation and walk-through training. The first three weeks of the deployment were some of the most miserable of my life. I could handle the MRE's and a shower every couple of days, but what drove me crazy was the waiting. I sensed that most Rangers felt that way, although you couldn't tell by looking at them. From day to day the mood was stoic, but I knew deep down they were all as tense as I was.

This was my first of four deployments with Ranger Battalion, but my brothers in arms were all house broken in the ways of war from a previous deployment to Afghanistan; that I unfortunately missed due to Ranger School. This probably meant that I was a little more nervous than the rest, but I couldn't have been the only one. The best thing about working with Rangers is that we all met tense situations with a sense of levity. There was no shortage of ball busting, pranks or jokes going around as a coping mechanism for the conditions of war. I guess you have to be a little crazy to compartmentalize everything that happens in war.

Several weeks into our deployment 1st Platoon was still preparing for our main mission. There were mission briefings, static loads, equipment checks and the whole gambit of mission preparation tasks. Amidst the surety that our unit was going to execute this "special mission," we were still shuffling back and forth to the nasty little chow hall that was set up for the US Forces contingent that was in our area. Everybody was still anxious and on edge, day in and day out.

It must have been three weeks in, when the unthinkable happened. We were going about our daily routine and heading to the chow hall for one of the two hot meals we had during the day when we saw a small collection of soldiers from other units gathered around a tent. Several of us popped in to see what the commotion was and up on the TV we saw some American reporters filming what looked like an invasion. It appears that the invasion of Iraq started without us. At some point it was decided that 3rd Infantry Division along with the 1st MEF was to spearhead the main offensive into the inner part of Iraq. From what I gathered on the TV reports, it looks as if the two mechanized units drove through and killed all in their way. Rangers, at least our company, had been essentially taken out of the game. This led us to realize that the several weeks of training we conducted had been wasted, not to mention the several months of training prior to deployment. This was the least desirable outcome for us that I could think of, but deep down in a way I was glad that we lived to fight another day. There were big things on the horizon for B Company, 1st Platoon and I was glad we were all around to see what they were.

-TRISTAN
1/75

In the very early stages of combat in Iraq as the Army's 3rd Infantry Division pushed north towards Baghdad, a wrong turn by the 507th Maintenance Company would result in disaster. The convoy, consisting mainly of support personnel, approached a checkpoint where they were mistakenly told to go in the wrong direction. As fate would have it, they would find themselves in an intense ambush just outside of Nasiriyah, Iraq. It was a costly mistake, and it resulted in eleven soldiers being killed in action, as well seven being captured. One of the captured, Private First Class Jessica Lynch would soon be the focus of the entire nation.

After an intense search effort, the prisoners of war (POW) were determined to be held at a local hospital, and a special operations task force was formed to rescue them. Rangers would naturally play a major role in the first rescue of a POW since the Vietnam War, and the first ever rescue of a female POW. What was truly remarkable about this mission was not the rescue itself though. This mission would be a testament to the leadership found in the Ranger Regiment. This mission was proof that the Ranger Creed, specifically the line "Never shall I fail my comrades" was more than just mere words.

During the rescue, it was discovered that all of the POW's except for Lynch had died, and were recently buried in a field outside of the hospital. The Rangers were not expecting this, and thus were not prepared to dig up bodies. What happened next was truly remarkable. The Ranger NCO's told all of the junior Rangers to go pull security, and they proceeded to dig up the bodies themselves – not wanting the younger Rangers to be exposed to the horrifying task.

One Ranger NCO who was there remembers it as the most gruesome experience he has ever had, "I was digging up a body with my

First Sergeant, and we picked up this girl. She was half wrapped in a bag and all the muscle and tissue came off and slid onto me. I instantly puked again . . . it was bad. You look to the left and right and it was all NCOs. We didn't want to expose the junior Rangers to that shit. Everyone was digging with gloves, we had no shovels or anything like that- everyone was just puking and digging."

Sergeant's stripes are not just something you put on haphazardly in the Regiment. They carry a heavy weight, a weight that is not always convenient or comfortable. It would have been just as easy to consider the task beneath them and assign it to the junior Rangers as they supervised. That is not what they did though, instead they chose to take the hard right and set the example of what REAL leadership is. They set the bar very high, and every leader who is worthy of the name will have to compare themselves to that standard for generations to come.

April 2003
"Jessica Lynch"

As we rolled through our deployment in a period of stasis, we finally received a mission. This was the call we had been waiting for and none of us knew exactly what or where we would be going, nor did we care. We were told that a supply unit's convoy was driving through Nasiriyah, Iraq, and had been ambushed, with some of their soldiers taken hostage. Bravo Company had been effectively nominated to attempt a POW rescue mission as a part of a joint special operations task force. As we received our briefing from the leadership element, I could hear the birds winding up their engines in the background. From the time of the briefing until the time we packed our bags and boarded the C-130's was a blur. I barely remember having a lucid thought. Everything that was running through my head was scenario training playback and solemn contemplation. I was as ready as ever to put any skills I had to the ultimate test, but wished it could be over as fast as possible.

It was barely a matter of hours until we boarded the birds and departed our AO toward our mission staging point near Nasiryah. I have never thrown up on an airplane in my life, but this ride was absolutely terrible. I do not remember how hot it was, but it felt like it could have been 120 degrees. For whatever reason we were in the standard "nut-to-butt" loading formation and I happened to draw the biggest, sweatiest, mongoloid of a human we had in the platoon to sit in front of me. Once this guy got comfortable, I had full force become a recliner to him. Add 260 pounds of sweaty Ranger to hot-ass weather and NAP of the earth movements on a C-130 and I never stood a chance. I don't recall how many vomit bags I filled up, but it was more than a few. Through the flight from hell I was attempting to mentally prepare as much as I could. This was quite a challenge considering my head was spinning.

When we finally landed at our staging area, which appeared to be an old airbase used by the Iraqi Republican Guard, we moved our equipment and gear to an abandoned aircraft hangar. This would be our planning and staging point for the mission. We were met with other Ranger platoons from 1st and 2nd Ranger Battalion to coordinate mission details. I felt some semblance of relief knowing that we had other Ranger brothers watching our six and embarking on this journey with us.

Daytime rolled around and as the last minute planning carried on, I remember one update that was overpowering even to the most 'grizzled' soldiers. It appears that the convoy members who were ambushed had all been executed and buried somewhere in Nasiriyah. I had no idea where they were getting their information, but the situation just became significantly more tense (it was later revealed that the information came from a hospital employee at the facility where Jessica Lynch was being held). Before the briefing was over, one last point was mentioned. It seems that there was one lone survivor who was being kept prisoner in a hospital somewhere in the town. This prisoner, who turned out to be PFC Jessica Lynch, was wounded and immobilized.

As the mission planning started to wind down, the mission gear prep began to propel. We checked and re-checked every piece of equipment we owned. As an M-240 Gunner, I made sure to check every link on my ammo belts and every extra barrel I had. If something was going to happen on this mission, I was going to be the most prepared Ranger out there, as was the mentality of every other Ranger in my unit. One significant low point of this entire experience was when our leadership informed us that we would not be using our normal air wing contingent, the 160th Special Operations Aviation Regiment (SOAR), to conduct the infiltration movement. We were told instead we found the "best Marine pilots that were available on a Tuesday night in Iraq." I remember these words very vividly and I also distinctively remember thinking (and saying aloud) "Shit . . ." I have nothing but a healthy, good-hearted rivalry with my Marine brothers, but I also remember watching a news story about several Marine pilots crashing into each other a few days earlier. I was hoping that I was going to be wrong about the Marine helicopter pilots, but unfortunately I was not.

The CH-46 Sea Knight Helicopters spun as we skimmed over the terrain in a nap of the earth flying formation toward our objective. My bird consisted of my assistant gunner and myself as well as the Battalion Sergeant Major and Commander. As we flew closer to the LZ my heart felt like it was going to rip out of my chest and my adrenaline was pumping in overload. At this point I was completely unaware of what the enemy status was on the objective. I had heard that there was Ba'ath party militia in the area, as well as Fedayeen left behind from the initial invasion. That was OK by me because I had a lot of 7.62 ammo and it was heavy. As it turned out, the hospital where we landed would essentially be empty besides a few civilians.

We were approaching our designated LZ when I remember a flash of light and some over pressure out of the back ramp of the bird. Someone off in the distance had fired an RPG round that exploded sort of close, but not too close, to our bird. Just at that moment, the bird flared downward and directly into several telephone poles and wires. We were still a couple hundred feet above the ground and I thought that this was the end of me. My machine gun had flown out of my hands and I was tossed across the bird. I swear to God my life flashed before my eyes. This was my first mission and I would die before I even got off the bird! Somehow by the grace of God, our helicopter made a hard landing into the literal trash dump which was our LZ and we ran off jostled, but in one piece.

As the platoon was running off and taking up hasty fighting positions behind berms of trash, one of the Rangers from 1st Platoon had tripped over something and immediately injured his ankle. Not quite an admirable combat injury, but it was enough to keep him from walking the rest of the mission. Luckily someone had found a wheelbarrow, although I have no idea to this day where it came from. This particular Ranger would finish out the missing riding in the wheelbarrow like a small child and whining about his sprained ankle.

We started our ground movement towards the hospital down a narrow street. Since it was dark and we were under NVG's, the hospital lights gave an eerie glow making it unmistakable to know exactly where the objective was. Although the patrol was only about a half a mile, it turned out to be somewhat difficult mostly due to the fact that I was wearing a chemical suit and chemical protective mask while carrying 800 rounds of 7.62 ammunition, along with a machine gun and side arm. For those conspiracy theorists that speculated only blanks were carried on the mission and that we knew there was no viable threat, I would invite you to try and hump all that shit in and out of hot ass Iraq while your adrenaline is forcing you to sweat like a whore in church. I was surely losing fluids at an expedited rate.

As we reached the breach point, which happened to be a large concrete wall, the breach team ran up to set a charge while we pulled security along our route. It was strangely quiet in the town, almost like it was empty. That was true, of course, until the blast from what sounded like 10 pounds of C-4 detonated and blew a squad-sized hole into the hospital complex. If the sound of the breach and the helicopters didn't stir up some enemy fire, I wasn't sure what would have. Despite all of our noise, we never received a shot fired towards us while we were inside the hospital perimeter. As the movement preceded, my squad leader, assistant gunner and I moved to set up on our gun position, which is where we would stay for the remainder of the mission. This support by fire position turned out to be the perfect vantage point to see the POW extraction team as well as the soccer field where I would later observe one of the most gruesome scenes of my entire life.

As the rescue mission carried on, we still had not fired a shot, nor taken any enemy fire. We had heard that a Marine contingent at a blocking position some distance away had exchanged some fire, but I cannot personally confirm that was ever the case. From a building top vantage point I saw a fire team from my platoon move through an alley below us to take up another security position for the extraction team's LZ. As the team was moving through this small alley, one of my Ranger buddies knelt down in what looked like a medical refuse pile. This pile of medical waste turned out to be the area where they disposed of lost appendages from surgeries or accidents... They were literally kneeling in human body parts and medical garbage. One Ranger in particular attempted to take a stable shooting position and sat right on a used hypodermic needle. To this day I still tease him about this disgusting accident. Later on back at the staging point, medics would inoculate him with every vaccination known to man. Fortunately for him, I'm pretty sure he didn't catch anything nasty.

The POW exfiltration team came in on MH-6 'Little Birds' and made their breach point at the side of the hospital. We all watched as they flowed into the door and then back out with Jessica Lynch in what seemed like five minutes. I don't know what the actual breach to extraction time was, but it seemed absurdly quick. They certainly earned their money in efficiency that evening. From that point on, we knew the mission was a major success, but it wasn't quite the end for the Rangers.

During the 'infil' and extraction, the leadership element had met up with the hospital employee informant and he had let us know that the remaining soldiers from Jessica Lynch's convoy were buried in a soccer field across the street from the hospital. As previously mentioned, this was the same soccer field we had direct security over. The group that had abducted and killed Jessica Lynch's convoy team managed to bury the remaining members in a very shallow grave, stacked one on top of another. They had been there for a few days so several of their bodies had begun to decompose.

My gun team and I watched in horror as several Rangers from Bravo Company 1/75 (to include a squad from 1st Platoon) began removing these bodies by hand and lifting them out of the hole. Some of the arms and legs of these soldiers had begun to de-glove as they were pulled up from the earth. To this day, including three follow-on deployments to Iraq and Afghanistan, this was the most gruesome sight I have ever witnessed in my life. I felt bad for the soldiers that this was how they were treated in their last days on earth. I also felt bad for my fellow Rangers in having to endure this horrible task. The Ranger creed clearly stated that we shall "never leave a fallen comrade…" and the Rangers on that field performed that task entirely.

As the last few American bodies were extracted from their shallow grave while many of us watched in horror, we prepared for our 'exfil' movement as if this was any other training mission. The squads received their directive and began to peel back towards the landing zone (LZ). The injured Ranger was still in a wheelbarrow and being pushed by fellow Rangers. Although injured and unable to walk, he had turned the wheelbarrow into a personal tactical vehicle, still pulling security with his weapon. We loaded up the helicopters with not a single shot fired from any Ranger on the mission team. We came back with all of our Rangers as well as a few more fallen brothers and sisters . . ..

When we arrived back at the hangars we had chaplain briefings, command briefings and OPSEC briefings thrown at us in true military fashion. We were told that it was the first successful POW rescue mission since Vietnam, but whether or not that was true was beyond me. No shots were fired and no Ranger brothers were lost, hurt, or maimed. Although the tragedy that happened to the 507th Maintenance Company was abysmal, a mission with no lost brothers is a success in my book. At the time nobody thought anything of the mission and after several deployments and hundreds of missions later it was merely an afterthought in my mind. I hardly talk about it or mention it to anybody anymore. It would be too hard to explain to somebody who was not there, the feelings and emotions I had that day. It just so happens that this was my first real combat mission in Ranger Battalion, but certainly not my last.

-TRISTAN
1/75

APRIL 2003
"JESSICA LYNCH AND THE DIG"

It has been eleven years since 2nd Platoon, Bravo Company walked into the back of a Marine Corps CH-46 helicopter. I remember the Regimental Commander telling us Rangers, "You are about to make history men." We had no idea how the POW Jessica Lynch rescue mission would turn into something we never, ever expected though.

After the helicopter took off towards Nasiriyah, I just stared out the back, laughing to myself thinking, *well, sure looks like Christmas in the sky*, and it did as tracers and explosions could be seen everywhere.

The helicopter finally sat down in a field. I ran off the ramp and *BAM!* - Fell flat on my face! We had landed in a bunch of large rocks and the fall fired me up. After we collected ourselves from the cluster-fuck of landing, a squad leader silhouetted himself on the road while shooting an azimuth with his compass to the hospital. I remember my squad leader yelling at him, "you stupid fuck, the whole world can see you!" Our company then began moving to the hospital in road march formation. Resistance was light and besides an RPG going by way over our heads, nobody got any trigger time.

As 1st Squad neared the wall of the hospital, they began moving through a field of water. They sank almost waist deep in this water and soon realized it had human body parts in it as well. 1st Squad moved back and my squad, 2nd, moved around them to place an explosive breaching charge on the hospital wall. The assault force was still rescuing Lynch, so we could not blow the charge yet. We were told to "use your sledge hammers to put in the breach!" I will never forget Adam and I in our MOPP Level 5 suit going crazy on that wall with the sledgehammers. It was like an adrenaline rush from hell. It was only a matter of minutes before we had a sizable opening in the wall.

Meanwhile, the assault force had secured Jessica Lynch and moved with her to a Blackhawk helicopter to exfil from the objective. The call then came in over the radio to blow the breach, but Adam and I were like, 'What the fuck, we already made one?' The squad leader wanted to blow it anyway though! Since someone didn't inform the forward observer of this, the MH-6 Little Bird helicopters in orbit above us had no idea, which resulted in one almost being blown out of the sky when the charge exploded.

The perimeter of the hospital was quickly cleared and the realization that PFC Lynch's fellow soldiers' bodies were not in the hospital morgue had our interpreters questioning the doctors. The doctors informed them, "they are out front in the soccer field; we buried them days ago." My team leader looked at me and said, "Let's go."

I remember walking out to the soccer field and one of the graves had already been opened, and the smell was horrifying. It was so powerful that it was embedded into our clothing and skin for days. The smell was nothing compared to what we did next though. Everyone but a couple of SAW gunners dropped their gear and began to dig. We used the only thing we had.... our hands. Looking down into the mud and seeing your brothers and sisters decaying and falling apart bodies (five males and three females) was infuriating. They did not look human and they did not feel human, some were even falling apart.

Recovering the bodies was an important but difficult job, which was aggravated by a senior NCO who told one Ranger from 3rd Platoon to "pick him up by his arms" to which the Ranger replied, "He doesn't have any fucking arms!" Many of us Rangers remember one squad leader had had enough, yelling, "Shut up and go fuck yourself!" to the NCO that was providing "helpful" advice from the sidelines. I took pleasure in that because hearing "dig faster" was garbage! We continued digging and noticed the female soldiers had

IVs and tourniquets, but the male soldiers were in really bad shape, and it appeared that not all of their wounds were due to combat. Some of them looked like they had been tortured or mutilated pretty badly.

Rangers would dig, get out of the hole, puke, then get back in and keep digging. Curses and the occasional nervous laugh could be heard as Rangers used whatever means they had to adapt, overcome, and keep on digging. I remember one young Ranger sitting at the edge of a grave, not moving but just staring down at the dead decaying Soldier in the ground. I told that Ranger, "get the fuck out of the way and let this country boy dig." The good Lord blessed me with a strong stomach and it thankfully helped me move a lot of dirt that night.

I remember the different emotions I experienced; anger and hatred for the Iraqis, but there was a surreal moment where I was thinking, *God, I am so glad that's not me in that hole.* The eight Soldiers' remains were recovered and returned to their country, which they had died for. We lived the Creed that night! "I will never leave a fallen comrade"

The one thing that has given me peace over the last eleven years, five combat tours, twenty-four surgeries, and nineteen straight months of mental hell in the VA hospital, is the story of Specialist Lori Piestewa. SPC Piestewa was a Hopi Indian who was a member of PFC Lynch's unit, and one of the female Soldiers we recovered that night.

They say the Hopi Indians in Arizona believe that when it snows, it is their ancestors (loved ones) who have passed on, returning to tell them that they love them. The day Hopi Indian SPC Lori Piestewa's body returned to Arizona... it snowed.

-CHRIS BEMISS
1/75

APRIL 2003
"HADITHA DAM"

I remember stepping on to the C-17 cargo jet headed for Iraq feeling incredibly unprepared to be invading another country. The feeling gnawed at me from my inner gut as I stepped foot on the bird that I knew there was no turning away from. It wasn't the same feeling of excitement that I felt leaving Fort Benning, GA with an unknown destination that I assumed to be a Forward Operating Base in preparation for the upcoming war with Saddam Hussein. Now it was real. We were going to war and there was no turning back.

1st Platoon, Bravo Company had cross-loaded two C-17s with attachments from Headquarters Company on a desert airstrip in Saudi Arabia. We had waited on the airstrip, prior to boarding the aircraft, as loadmasters secured our Ground Mobility Vehicles (GMVs), which were armored High Mobility Multipurpose Military Vehicles (HMMMV), sans the armor that left us with a stripped down HMMMV with a stronger engine, chassis, and suspension than regular unarmored HMMMVs. We now filed on to the airplane, shuffling between vehicles wearing Ranger Body Armor (RBA) over our Nuclear, Biological, and Chemical suits (JLIST), carrying our weapons, assault packs, MICH helmets, and in my case, an old MOLLE aid bag. There would be no red cargo net jump seats on this flight - floor space only.

Oddly enough, spreading out on the steel floor of a C-17, especially in full kit, was a lot more comfortable than trying to cram side-by-side with your fellow Rangers on to the folding seats that come complimentary on Air Force flights. Slowly, starting nearest to the nose of the aircraft, Rangers found appropriate floor space and flopped down against their assault packs. We all eventually sat down in spaces between the GMVs and the aisle left between the vehicles and the skin of the C17. Sitting close to me were PFC Matt, PFC Bob, and my Ranger buddy from Anti-Tank (AT) section, PFC Jared.

Jared and I had attended the Ranger Indoctrination Program (RIP) together in July of 2002. Because of our last names, we were alphabetically close on the rosters kept by the Ranger Cadre, and therefore stood next to each other in formations during both hold-over and RIP. Since formations were everything in RIP, the pain and exhaustion that was endured throughout the time required to earn a tan beret was spent together. Jared and I became close friends during those weeks in RIP and following graduation; we were both assigned to 3rd Ranger Battalion, which was deployed in Afghani-stan. Upon assignment, we found ourselves assigned to the compa-nies by our last names and both of us fell into Bravo Company. Less than a year later, we were sitting next to each other on a cargo jet destined for another small desert airstrip in Western Iraq that had been earlier seized by Alpha Company.

B Company 3/75 had been the company sent to Somalia in 1993 during Operation Gothic Serpent and had been on the ground in Mogadishu during the days of Oct 3rd and 4th, in an 18-hour gunfight that would later be immortalized in the book and subsequent film, Black Hawk Down. As such, Bravo Company carried a tremendous amount of unit pride and held itself to a standard that was high by even Ranger expectations.

I looked around at the men to my left and right of the cargo jet as the loadmasters continued their final checks before closing the ramp door. Most of the Rangers on the bird with me that night were already veterans of Afghanistan; however our platoon leader, 1LT Joe was a prior-enlisted Ranger who was also a Somalia veteran that had served as LTC McKnight's RTO on the "lost convoy."

Everyone was quite calm. No one spoke unless required to and even then words were kept to a minimum. We all had taken our places on the floor of the C-17 and awaited departure in a focused silence that was drowned out by the noise of the plane. Finally, the loadmaster signaled to the forward crew and the ramp began to slowly lift off the tarmac. The whine of working hydraulics dominated the inside of the aircraft and drew everyone's attention to the world that disappeared behind the closing door. At last, the ramp closed against the tail of the giant bird with a mechanical thud.

The Air Force crew in the back settled at their stations and the jet engines fired up. The familiar pitch made by turbines overtook all other noise as they worked their way up to idle speed. The engine noise leveled off and the jet began to vibrate as it sat stationary, waiting for takeoff. A large part of me hated to fly, but as we sat there waiting for the pilots to finish their checklist of pre-flight operations; the notion of flying didn't bother me. Nor did the thought of dying necessarily bother me. For the most part, I hadn't even considered my mortality and when I had, I casually brushed it off as something that was uncontrollable and not worth worrying about. Nonetheless, as that C-17 bound for Western Iraq sat there waiting to depart, I was scared and felt extremely unqualified to even be on the bird.

The feeling was a contradiction to all of the training I had received up until that point, but regardless, it was there. It was born out of uncertainty that I had about how well I would perform my job, a job that I literally hadn't signed up for. When I joined the Army, I joined as an infantryman (11B) with an airborne contract. In Airborne School, I volunteered for the Ranger Indoctrination Program (RIP), and upon completion of RIP, I was assigned to 3rd Battalion. Since 3rd Battalion was already deployed, the new privates from our graduating class were left on rear detachment to perform administrative and maintenance duties while the battalion was away. In October, the battalion redeployed back to Fort Benning and the privates in our class were integrated into the line squads. Originally, I had been assigned to 3rd Squad, 1st Platoon, but that soon changed due to a program implemented by the Regimental Surgeon.

Anticipating high casualties during the invasion of Iraq, the Regimental Medical Officers, in conjunction with the three Battalions, formed what was called, the Infantryman Medic Program. The idea revolved around the idea that individual platoon medics would be better prepared to handle multiple casualties if they were augmented with a second, medically proficient Ranger. Since I was the newest Ranger and had not yet integrated into my squad, I was chosen to complete a six-week EMT crash course. Following the EMT course, I was sent to a course in Pre-Hospital Trauma Management, as well as a Combat Trauma Management Course that was taught by the Joint Medical Augmentation Unit (JMAU), a special operations outfit comprised solely of trauma surgeons and other medical officers.

In spite of all of the training I had received, as the jet made its slow start to the end of the runway for takeoff, I did not feel prepared to treat my Ranger buddies should they sustain injuries. Fear of freezing up entered my thoughts. I questioned whether I had the courage to face the adversity that combat would inevitably bring. Would I have the necessary guts to keep moving forward in the face of imminent danger? What if I froze up and my Ranger Buddies paid the price? Uncertainty weighed heavily on me and I was afraid of the unknown.

The C-17 came to a stop after a turn that I assumed was to align the plane with the runway. I sat there and quietly eyed the men around me. No one said a word. Most sat staring at their weapons or equipment, expressionless. I, too, sat expressionless, afraid to show the fear that had crept over me. Suddenly, the jet turbines fired up from idle and inertia thrust us toward the rear of the plane. Facing the tail of the bird, I leaned back to fight the gravitational force pushing me forward. As the cargo jet accelerated, we bounced around next to the GMVs that were strapped down to the floor of the airplane, the suspension of which would rise and fall as the plane sped its way down the airstrip.

Finally, the nose lifted off of the tarmac and we began to gain altitude. Still facing the tail, I had to continue to lean back in order counter against the G's that were trying to push me forward. Seconds later, the pilots retracted the landing gear and we continued our sharp ascent to gain altitude. After a minute or two of altitude gain later, we finally leveled off and the plane banked into its flight path towards Iraqi airspace. I looked around; the expressions of those around me had changed. Eyes had opened up, the hardened scowls of professional warriors lightened, and a sense of excitement filled the plane. As I watched this, I too, noticed a change in my own demeanor. A smile crept over my face while the sense of fear that I had been holding onto began to drain away, as if it had been held to the same laws of gravity that our plane was now breaking.

Bob leaned closer to Matt who had found space in the front seat of a GMV. I could barely hear him shout, however my eyes clearly read his lips exclaiming, "ITS FUCKING ON, DUDE!"

Matt, a casual yet extremely intelligent and physically fit Ranger from Wisconsin, simply smiled in response and settled a little further into the space he occupied in the GMV. As I continued to look around the plane, being in the company of men who were all the best-trained infantrymen our country had to offer eclipsed the thought of failure. Furthermore, we were armed to the teeth with the best weapons and technology our military had access to at the time. Our guns, kit, vehicles, and electronics were more sophisticated than anyone else's in the Regular Army and certainly better than anything the Iraqi Army had to offer. We had the best training, we had the best support, and we had the best men.

This realization motivated and allowed me to bury my earlier feelings of uncertainty. I made a promise to myself that no matter what lie ahead, I would give everything that I had to the guys on my left and right. We had recited the Ranger Creed many times before this moment, making that very promise every time we did, but as I acknowledged that I was a more elite soldier who would never leave a fallen comrade, an entirely new level of determination to live up to that statement solidified within me.

As we neared the Saudi Arabia-Iraq border, the dim white lights on the plane were turned off and red tactical lighting illuminated the fuselage. The red lighting instantly made the flight a radically different experience. It signaled we were in bad guy country, which instantly created an adrenaline buzz throughout the plane. Everybody on the flight showed visible signs of excitement, they all sat a little bit taller, made sure their kit was a little bit straighter, their helmets — a little bit tighter. We continued at cruising altitude for another 40 minutes or so, the plane banking in its flight path every so often until we got the word passed down that we were about to enter into our tactical descent.

All of a sudden the engines powered off and what had moments ago been a very noisy flight had become relatively quiet. Without the noise of the engines, you could hear the suspension of the vehicles as slight turbulence caused the springs to compress and expand. The sound of tie down chains hitting metal as the GMVs rocked back and forth became noticeable. The lack of thrust caused the plane to slow in speed giving us the feeling that we were gently gliding until the pilots dipped the nose of the aircraft and we entered our descent.

The rate at which we dropped in altitude was quite significant. The GMVs lifted up against their shackles and we all held on to our safety lines that had us secured to the floor of the aircraft in case of an emergency. While we weren't experiencing a complete loss of gravity, the decent was as exhilarating as any roller coaster I had ever been on. Other members of the platoon apparently shared this feeling as Bob raised his arms like he was on a ride at Six Flags. One by one, others in the platoon raised their arms until we were all looking around with big grins on our face in anticipation. Without warning, the lights went black, the engines fired back on, and we began to level out. The pilots used the power of the turbines to take control of the rapid descent and moments later we touched down on the bumpy tarmac of the airstrip.

As we had rehearsed many times, we all took a knee and pre-pared to de-link from the plane once it came to a stop. The plane quickly decelerated and we all then fought the inertia in reverse of takeoff. If it weren't for my safety line, I would have gone flying to-wards the front of the plane as it slammed on its brakes. Finally, the plane came to a stop. I double-checked my kit in the dark then flipped down and turned on my Night Vision Goggles (NVGs). In the pitch-black darkness of the C-17, I couldn't see anything and had to feel blindly for the snap link on my safety line. I finally found where it was attached to the plane and unhooked. After triple checking that I had all of my gear, I made my way to the back of SSG Bran-ford's GMV to help unshackle it from the plane. We quickly removed all of the vehicle tie-downs and loaded in the back. As soon as the ramp began to drop, the drivers started their engines and awaited the green light from the loadmasters.

Once the signal was given, each driver released the hand break and we all gently began to roll forward and drive down the ramp out of the back of the C-17. We were finally in Iraq. It was dark with no illumination from the moon. As we drove further and further from the jets, the desert got quieter and quieter. Aside from the infrared (IR) lights on the front grill of the GMVs, it was nearly impossible to see anything surrounding us in the darkness of night. Our column came to a stop near the end of the airfield and linked up with the command element that directed us to a small group of buildings to bed down for the night. Alpha Company had our security so we im-mediately moved to the buildings about 500 meters away.

Upon arriving at our overnight position, we quickly dismount-ed the vehicles, re-cleared the buildings to ensure they were empty, and began priorities of work in order to bed down for the evening. Immediately upon setting up inside for the night, we discovered the rooms were covered with old, petrified goat shit. The decision not to clean it out before implementing the rack plan was more than likely made out of consideration for the little darkness there was left to catch any sleep at all. I certainly didn't argue with anyone when told to pass out. If there was one thing I had learned about sleep in RIP, it was to sleep when told to. I did the best I could to clear the goat feces from around my immediate area, laid down using my assault pack as a pillow, and fell asleep.

The next morning we awoke and began priorities of work in order to be ready to leave at nightfall to begin our 'disruption of enemy forces' mission. Nobody really knew what that meant other than we were going out to close with and destroy whatever enemy we could find. As 3rd Squad began to prepare their equipment, M-203 gunner PFC Tommy fell ill to nausea and vomiting. I assumed it was Gatorade, but nonetheless, I'd never seen puke so fluorescent green before. His vomit reminded me of antifreeze and it was immediately clear he needed medical attention. Without the availability of a hospital or any other medical care outside of what the platoon medic and I had in our aid bags, the options for PFC Tommy were pretty slim. SPC Dave was the platoon medic who I worked under. Dave quickly made the determination that he needed IV fluids and directed me to start a saline lock. After getting permission from our platoon sergeant, SFC Jack, Dave initiated an IV and intravenously gave Tommy the anti-nausea medication Phenergren to fight dehydration and ease the vomiting. The Phenergren kicked in and immediately sedated Tommy, who was left to rest for the remainder of the day.

Shortly after, a Warning Order came down to begin preparing for our first mission. Details were vague, but we were to only be gone from the airfield for 24 hours. Apparently, we were using what we had designated as H-1 as our new FOB. We were told to leave our rucksacks in the buildings, which would be watched by the security element left behind. In addition to our weapons and sensitive items, our packing list was simple: assault packs only. One prepackaged Meal, Ready to Eat (MRE), two power bars, six bottles of water in addition to full Camelbaks and two quart canteens, one extra pair of socks, one extra t-shirt, and a stripped down shave kit that consisted of toothbrush, toothpaste, and a razor. The only optional item not mentioned was Copenhagen or in my case, Marlboros.

Copenhagen had been the tobacco choice of Rangers for generations, although in every platoon there were always a couple of renegade smokers whose habit was regularly ridiculed and put under fire by the dippers who had them significantly outnumbered. Smoking for smokers however was a commitment (nobody likes a quitter!) and when everyone else bought Copenhagen at the makeshift PX in Saudi Arabia, I bought two cartons of 'Cowboy Killers'. This temporarily became an issue when packing my assault pack as I discovered I only had room in my rucksack for one carton of cigarettes. Originally, I was only planning on taking two packs, but since my ruck was full, I had to stuff the 2nd carton in my assault pack that had considerably more free room.

'Better to have and not need, than need and not have,' I told myself as I zipped up my bag after double-checking that I had everything.

As we waited for word on the mission, I periodically checked on Tommy while hanging out with the members of my original squad. 3rd Squad had a lot of experience with all of the privates having at least one deployment and the leaders having two. SPC Plasman, Sergeant Long, and SSG Branford were all from the black beret days prior to the War on Terrorism and had years of Ranger experience. SPC Mike O'Neill had graduated Ranger School a few weeks prior and both PFC Panatela and Matt would probably have been on their way, had it not been for this deployment. Listening to these guys talk about the possibilities that lie ahead for the platoon gave me insight on what to expect, although there was far from a unanimous consensus on what that would be.

Afghanistan had been mostly quiet for 1st Platoon aside from the helicopter crash on the night of the invasion that took the lives of SPC John Edmunds and SPC Kristopher Stonesifer. The prior deployment had been full of stories of long patrols and anticlimactic raids. Would Iraq be the same? Would all of the action go to the Special Mission Units and the Regiment be stuck with objectives that were dry holes? "Surely, not." SPC Plasman reasoned, "We're facing a conventional army out there. The Taliban doesn't compare to the Republican Guard." Sergeant Long thought otherwise, "I bet they just lay down their guns and surrender. Desert Storm all over again. We bomb and they come out waiving their underwear on a stick." "Or we pull security for the SMU's while they kill all the bad guys" Mike added. "Maybe they toss us a squirter every once in awhile."

For a moment the group seemed to consider Mike's suggestion to be the most plausible. After all, that had been B Company's role in Somalia and a good chunk of Afghanistan. I had no idea what to expect and instead of adding my two cents, I sat quietly listening in. To myself, I sided with SPC Plasman, hoping he would be right. On the other hand, we had already been in Iraq for nearly 12 hours and I had yet to hear a gunshot, or a bomb drop. I had half-expected to roll off the back of the plane with guns blazing, but instead, found myself half-rested and listening in on 3rd Squad's debate leaving a question as to whether or not we'd even see real combat.

SSG Branford and SPC Dave finally returned from the operations order with an answer. We had a mission to seize a radio tower that was under control of the Iraqi Army and civilian workers. Details were vague, but we were going with 2nd Platoon and expecting resistance. SPC Dave informed me that I would ride on SSG Branford's vehicle and fall in with the Weapons Squad leader, SSG Shank. A North Carolina native with a thick backwoods accent, we called SSG Shank, 'Gunny', due to the time he spent prior to enlistment in the Army, as a Marine. While Gunny was never officially a Gunnery Sergeant in the Marines, the name fit, as he was the only prior Marine in 3rd Ranger Battalion, if not the entire Regiment.

As late afternoon came, PFC Tommy started to recover from the sedative effects of the Phenergren we had given him for stomach sickness. To my surprise, Tommy felt fine except for a bit of wooziness.

Doc came to the conclusion that he'd either had a temporary bug or might have eaten something in Saudi that hadn't sat right. Regardless, he was good to go and even if he weren't, Tommy probably would have had to be held down in order for us to leave without him. I think everyone had that attitude. In spite of uncertainty or skepticism about what lie ahead, the platoon was primed with anticipation to find out.

Prior to loading our vehicles, the Platoon Sergeant walked up to me and performed a surprise inspection of my packing list and sensitive items. When he got to my assault pack, the first thing he noticed was the carton of cigarettes that had been crammed in there on top of everything else. The Platoon Sergeant was the most vocal of the smoking critics in the platoon. With a visible lump of Copenhagen in the corner of his bottom lip he asked, "Matthews, why do you have a carton of cigarettes for a mission that's only going to last 24 hours?"

I kept my reply as simple as possible "Sarn't, I bought two cartons in Saudi and can only fit one of them in my rucksack." "Well, if you fall out because of the extra weight, your ass is mine . . . I don't wanna hear any excuses." *The actual weight of the carton was a half-pound, max.* "Roger, Sarn't." "You know those things are gonna give you lung cancer, don't ya?" He asked rhetorically as he spit tobacco juice into the sand. "Roger, Sarn't."

He eyed my kit and me for a moment longer. Satisfied, he moved on to quiz others on their awareness of the upcoming mission. I looked at Dave, the second-most vocal antismoking advocate in the platoon who smiled, "Told ya, you should quit, dude."

Shortly before sunset, Bravo Company's 1st and 2nd Platoons loaded our vehicles and left the airfield in a convoy across the desert. An hour after nightfall, we linked up with Charlie Company and picked up 3rd Platoon, along with two sniper teams and Command Sergeant Major (CSM) Birch. CSM Birch's addition immediately boosted morale as word quickly passed that he was armed with an SR-25 sniper rifle and ready for a fight. Our CSM was already a legend amongst the lower enlisted men of 3rd Battalion. A Ranger who had grown up in 2nd Battalion, CSM Birch left battalion in the eighties to join the Army's Special Mission Unit, spending nearly 20 years there before coming to 3rd Battalion, six months prior.

We departed the rendezvous point with Charlie Company, now with three line platoons plus attachments from mortars, snipers, mechanics, and a control element from HHC that included the Battalion Executive Office (XO) and Air Force Joint Terminal Attack Controller (JTAC). Riding in the back of a GMV in full kit is extremely uncomfortable. Every vehicle had four men in the front, four men in the back, and a heavy gunner in the turret, manning either a .50 caliber M2 machine gun or a MK19 automatic grenade launcher. We also had 240B machine guns mounted to swing arms in the back of each vehicle, with PFC Tommy manning ours. Across from Tommy was Matt, whose M-249 SAW was also mounted to a swing arm. Across from me, Sergeant Jonathan, a mechanic from HHC, sat with his M-4 carbine. The four of us did our best to sit outward in spite of the bench seats that faced inward, while scanning the darkness as our convoy moved further and further away from friendly forces. After hours of driving through what seemed like endless desert, we arrived at our Remain Over Day (ROD) site as the sun broke over the horizon. Quickly we sat up security and camouflaged our vehicles in a natural depression prior to performing priorities of work and implementing a rest plan.

Although we had been up driving all night, getting sleep that day was next to impossible. Between rotating out to pull security or radio guard, word had already begun to surface that there was a change in mission and that a FRAGO had been issued. Rumors that we had been diverted to seize a hydroelectric dam began to go around and the persistent detail of that rumor was that Saddam's Republican Guard was holding the dam. By reputation, the Republican Guard was Iraq's best-trained unit who had all taken an oath to defend their homeland to the death. As Rangers, we respected their decision to die for their country and felt happy to oblige them, but the possibility of going up against Iraq's finest stirred up enough excitement to effectively prevent anyone from actually getting any sleep. After four hours of planning, our company commander issued his new operations order, confirming the gossip. Intelligence suggested that Saddam intended to blow up the Haditha Dam and blame it on the Americans. The result would have been disastrous for the Iraqi people and mass flooding would prevent 3rd Infantry Division's push to Baghdad.

The plan consisted of 1st Platoon securing the western side of the dam in order to allow 2nd Platoon to move across the dam, setting up a battle position on the east side of the dam and begin clearing the complex. 3rd Platoon, C Company would move to the south of the dam and secure a power station that would be about 500 meters to the southwest of our position. Instead of assaulting from the south, the CO devised a route to the objective that took us around the western shore of the reservoir, hopefully giving us the advantage of quickly securing the high ground and dam complex with an overwhelming force.

As we had the night before, the assault force loaded our vehicles and left the ROD site just before sunset on a near, twenty-mile journey to the Haditha Dam. A few hours after darkness fell we began hearing bombs exploding in the distance. Ever so slightly, we would see a faint flash on the horizon, followed seconds later by the rumbling of distant thunder. Discomfort quickly settled in as we rode overland to the objective and as it was the two nights before, low illumination from an absent moon made it difficult to see further than 50 yards. Less than a mile from the objective, the column of GMVs came to an abrupt halt. One of the vehicles broke all four bolts to its steering box and was immediately disabled. The mechanics quickly identified the problem and came up with a plan to fix it on the fly. Since the steering box could be secured with only three bolts for the short distance to the target, the mechanics quickly removed one bolt from three other vehicles and secured the steering box, bringing the GMV back up to operational in 20 minutes. Considering the conditions and lack of tools or spare parts, it seemed like everyone in the platoon was amazed at the proficiency of the mechanics and how quickly they got us back up and running.

Before the convoy began moving again, SSG Branford reminded us we were now nearing the objective and to remain alert. I went over my end of the plan again: link up with SSG Shank once we arrive at the objective. With the vehicles loaded, we once again began movement across the desert. We moved slowly, but steadily across the uneven terrain until we arrived at an asphalt road that had just ended in the sand. Once on the hardball, the vehicles sped up and raced toward the upcoming dam structure. We then came to an abrupt halt and everyone immediately dismounted their vehicles. Quietly, the assault force gathered to begin clearing the western flank. I immediately linked up at the side of the road, near a guardrail with SSG Shank who told me to stay within arm's reach.

SFC Jack and 1LT Joe took 1st and 2nd Squads, along with B Team from 3rd Squad to assault a complex of buildings that was located in our AO.

At first, the assault began with no resistance. 2nd Platoon was able to cross the dam to the east side and began making their entry into the complex, itself. 3rd Platoon, C Co. also began making their way down to the power station. Bravo Team, 3rd Squad cleared the first building and set up an over watch on the rooftop with a sniper team. Shortly after clearing the first building, we heard small arms and .50-caliber gunfire to the south. Charlie Company ran into enemy personal at the base of the dam and a quick engagement followed.

As this happened, SFC Jack set in a 240B gun team on another key piece of terrain to cover the movement of 1st and 2nd Squad, as the two squads began to clear the rest of the objective. Building by building, 1st and 2nd Squads began clearing the compound of 12 concrete buildings. Suddenly 1LT Joe called out that enemy soldiers were running in the low ground, about 100 meters from our position, and illuminated their movement with the infrared laser on his rifle. SSG Shank immediately lifted his M-4 and took aim on the runners. Myself, along with Sergeant Pelt joined Gunny and took aim at the squirters alongside him. It was clear they were running to a fighting position.

SSG Shank yelled out, "I got 'em, sir!" I rotated my selector switch from safe to fire, my finger lightly on the trigger as we tracked the moving targets. Before I could finish asking myself whether we were really going to shoot, SSG Shank began firing. My finger contracted several times in rapid succession, each time, my shoulder absorbing the recoil of my M-4. All three figures dropped nearly at once. We stood there for a second, weapons at the high ready, lasers locked on our downed targets waiting for them to resume movement. None of them budged. The realization hit all three of us, at once, but I initially second guessed it. No way, we had just killed those guys. Killing another person was supposed to be difficult.

Everything in life taught me that taking someone's life was supposed to be something that took guts to do, and what we just did was entirely too easy. There was no thinking involved. No moral reasoning as I pulled the trigger while aiming at a moving target. No different than being on a night range at Fort Benning, except that we weren't back home in Georgia. We were in Iraq and the three bodies we were illuminating with our lasers weren't pop-up targets, they were people. Only now, they were dead people.

SSG Shank broke the silence in a disappointed tone, "I just lost my job." He turned as he lowered his weapon, putting it back on safe. Sergeant Pelt responded, "I thought all fighting-aged males were considered hostile?" "They are, but did they even have weapons?"

I glanced back in the direction we'd just fired, "Looked like they were armed to me, Sarn't."

SSG Shank looked at me hard. I could see that he was genuinely worried about whether or not the targets were armed. Behind him, one of our vehicles drove up the hill towards the compound of buildings, its IR light illuminating the concrete structure.

"Yeah, and they were definitely running towards that fighting position." Pelt added. Gunny continued to eye me for a moment and looked to the south where we had just fired. Out of the corner of my eye, the GMV moving up the hill began to turn into the center of the group of buildings. Gunny took a deep breath, which signaled me to let out the one I felt like I'd been holding the entire time. As we both relaxed, a loud concussion caught our attention and what looked like a large roman candle raced out of the low ground towards the buildings 1st and 2nd Squads were clearing. Under night vision, we watched a glowing ball fly just over the rooftop of the building the GMV was in front of, and explode in an airburst that sent a shower of shrapnel everywhere.

Brief silence was followed by an eruption of small arms, machine gun, and RPG fire originating from the base of the hill. In an instant, all hell had broken loose. Rounds began impacting around the buildings that our platoon was maneuvering to take control of. SSG Shank, Sergeant Pelt, and I quickly moved to the support by fire line that was set up along the guardrail twenty meters away.

The support by fire position had already begun returning fire to the Iraqi positions below us. I immediately took up a position next to Bob to begin helping suppress targets. However before I began firing, SSG Branford yelled for me to take a knee back by the vehicle. I looked at SSG Branford with disappointment and he responded to it with, "We can't have the guy helping the medic get shot. Get back to the fucking vehicle!"

The entire fire team was already fully engaged in small arms fire with the enemy making this not the time to argue my case for getting extra marksmanship training. Everybody had a job to do and mine really wasn't to be shooting people. I quickly picked up from my position and fell back to the GMV on the other side of the road. SSG Shank had already begun coordinating fires with the heavy gunners of the GMVs at our position, while SSG Branford directed the support by fire at the guardrail. PFC Panatella laid down 3-5 round bursts on the SAW. Sergeant Long called out targets for Bob to engage with his M-203 40mm grenade launcher, and SPC O'Neill carefully suppressed a fighting position, talking Long and Bob on to a group of Iraqis. In the distance, we saw a flash followed two seconds later by a large airburst explosion over the rooftop that snipers and B-team, 3rd Squad had their positions on.

While I hated the lack of participation that I presently had in the fight, I had a perspective on everything that was going on around me. The position that I was forced to take gave me a nearly unobstructed view of the intense firefight that was now taking place. Bravo Team and the snipers quickly picked up off of the rooftop after an airburst had exploded barely 30 meters away. They quickly set into a covered position on the top of the hill and were immediately engaged by a fighting position at the bottom, about 200 yards away. Matt returned overwhelming suppressive fire with his M-249 SAW, as Tommy engaged with the M-240B that he had dismounted from our vehicle. The combination of automatic fires allowed for the team to gain fire superiority. The engagement was quickly over, leaving five Iraqi soldiers dead and several Rangers to quickly celebrate their first kills before identifying more targets just moments later.

As B Team's initial engagement continued, a rocket from near 1st Squad's position lifted off and began a near vertical gain in elevation towards the reservoir. My first thought was that we had incoming enemy aircraft, but as I watched the rocket climb over the lake, its trajectory made a radical change until the rocket took a nose dive and impacted on an island off in the distance. It donned me that we had just fired a Javelin anti-tank missile at something, but in spite of the secondary explosions, I didn't know at what. All I knew was that even my good buddy Jared was getting in on the action. Even though I had no idea what he had fired at, seeing the secondary explosions afterward let me know he had hit his mark.

Before that realization could really sit in, the distinct and very loud, angry wasp-like buzz only made by that of a McDonald-

Douglass AH-6 Little Bird helicopter filled the fading nighttime sky above us. I looked up and watched two Little Birds momentarily hover a few hundred feet above our position before one of them accelerated forward in what can only be described as a nose dive toward an enemy bunker with their 7.62mm mini gun on full auto, showering us with spent casings that left a second degree burn on exposed skin. As the helicopter pilot neared the end of his gun run, the Little Bird fired its rockets and the bird quickly lifted up to gain altitude. As soon as the first Little Bird cleared the airspace, the pilot of the second Little Bird repeated the same maneuver on a separate enemy target, dropping casings on top of our heads and ending with rockets that lit up the area. This time when the second Little Bird banked, the sky was lit up by anti-aircraft fire from a Russian S60 anti-aircraft (AA) gun. Evading the AA fire, the Little Bird cleared the airspace, while his wingman, already on station, zeroed in on the gun targeting his fellow Night Stalker and swooped in on a second gun run, eliminating it before they could become a factor on the battlefield.

Night was quickly into turning day, and the Little Birds became more vulnerable as more light spilled over the horizon to the east. They ran a couple of more fire missions and were soon called off of the objective. Later we would learn that while one pilot was flying, the co-pilot was engaging enemy soldiers on the ground from the door of the helicopter with an M-4 before manually dropping hand grenades onto Iraqi positions. With day approaching, the company received close air support from Air Force F-16s. The addition of sunlight also made identifying enemy positions much easier. I flipped up my NODs and continued to watch the battle unfold. As it became brighter, the magnitude of everything became clear for the first time. Laying to the south of us for as far as the eye could see was an interconnected trench system cut out of the desert floor, interspersed with enemy fighting positions, bunkers, AA guns, several small buildings, and two large main buildings.

From near the top of the dam, a GMV began speeding down a dirt road but missed its left turn to Charlie Company's position to the southeast, instead driving straight south. I could see that the dirt road led directly between two fighting positions that Alpha Team's support by fire was actively engaging. Bob saw this as well and shouted out, "They missed their turn!"

As the friendly vehicle sped towards enemy positions, SSG Branford called for a cease-fire. Unable to engage for fear of hitting fellow Rangers, Alpha Team lifted fire and watched helplessly as the GMV headed directly for an ambush. The Iraqis noticed the vehicle's approach and got into position on both sides of the dirt road. When the GMV entered the kill zone, small arms and RPG fire opened up from both directions. Several RPGs zipped through the air, all of them missing their target, but we could see small arms impact all over the vehicle. The driver accelerated out of the ambush and pulled a tight U-turn. With no other choice, the Rangers sped back through the kill zone, this time shooting back. The volume of fire that came out of the vehicle on the return route proved to be superior as the rate of enemy fire was far less than the first time. Even so, my gut told me it was impossible for anyone to drive through that and not get hit. There were nine Rangers on a GMV with no armor protection. As the vehicle sped back up the dirt road to the top of hill, I prepared for the inevitable.

The shout came out before the shot up GMV was even two-thirds of the way to the top, "MEDIC!" I grabbed my aid bag. SSG Shank yelled, "Matthews! That's you!" "Roger Sarn't!" I yelled, running past him. Every muscle in my body worked in conjunction to run as fast as possible down the road, towards the edge of the dam. As the vehicle neared the top, I still had 100 feet to run. Immediately my brain was flooded with every scenario that I had ever experienced in training. A sucking chest wound, an upper-leg femoral bleed, and gunshot wound to the head. Everything I had been taught raced through my mind, nearly simultaneously. I arrived at the GMV as Rangers that had gathered at his door were pulling out the driver, Sergeant Aaron. I could immediately see he was in pain and identified him as a casualty. I took a knee next to him and on initial assessment I could see that he was conscious, talking, did not have visible hemorrhaging, but was grabbing at his foot. I ask if anyone else is hit and get a reply that the top gunner had taken several rounds to the back plate of his body armor, but was fine. I turned my attention to the driver.

"Where are you hit?"

"On the foot! Left foot!" I went to the foot next to my left hand, "Other left, dude."

"Sorry."

"It's cool, man . . . It's just the one I'm holding on to feels like it's been smashed with a fucking hammer!"

I told him to hang in there and that I would square him away. I examined his foot and finally noticed what would have otherwise been a tear in the lacing and tongue of the boot, which I quickly removed. With only his black sock on, I still could not see any blood. Once I pulled the sock down around his toes, blood began to pool up in a wound to the top of his foot. Overwhelmed with adrenaline, I exclaimed the obvious, "YOU'VE BEEN SHOT!"

Aaron leans forward to look at his gunshot wound, "That's it? It feels like someone just ran over my foot!"

We both laughed. The reality that it was merely a grazing wound and not a penetrating gunshot had finally sank in. Each of us had been expecting the worst and when we saw that it was nothing more than a flesh wound, we both knew it was going to be ok. I don't think either of us expected to find ourselves laughing in a situation like that, but there really wasn't anything else to do about it.

"Goddamn, it hurts," This time, restating it more out of confusion than anything else. I lean forward to access the Individual Bleeder Control Kit on left side his body armor. Grabbing his Israeli Trauma Dressing and Kerlex I respond, "Roger, Sarn't. Good news though is that I don't think we need to use a tourniquet."

"Thanks, dude."

The size of the actual wound was less than two inches long and about a half inch wide. While his foot had a good number of blood vessels, he wasn't bleeding very heavily and therefore only needed a small amount of gauze and an Israeli Trauma Dressing to wrap and keep pressure on the wound. I had practiced dressing an injury like this at least a hundred times in the past six months and had his foot taken care of in less than a minute. After getting his foot wrapped, the call was made to move him to the platoon casualty collection point (CCP), which had just been newly established in the building 3rd Squad had initially cleared. With help from the other Rangers in his vehicle, we picked him up and supported him under his shoulders as we helped carry him to the building where the CCP was.

Shortly after entering into the room, I quickly began to reassess my casualty. As expected, he was doing well, aside from being in an immense amount of pain. SSG Marcus Muralles, the battalion senior medic arrived moments later. SSG Muralles had heard the call for a medic while he was nearly halfway down the dam and come running to our position. He, too, expected the worst and was relieved to enter the room and discover Aaron with only his foot wrapped. As he caught his breath, SSG Muralles joked that he'd just ran a mile for nothing then began to inspect the dressing and assess the wound. SSG Muralles had been the senior-most medic responsible for training me, and when he went over my work, I became a little nervous that I'd missed something. After undressing and inspecting the injury, Doc Muralles redressed it and told me that I had done a good job.

Positive feedback in the form of 'good job' comes sparingly in Regiment and SSG Muralles telling me that I had done well instantly boosted my confidence as a Ranger. But before I could reflect on the compliment, SFC Jack entered from outside followed by SPC Dave. The two of them had been clearing the compound with 1st and 2nd squads and had heard the call for medic, too. Mike had a noticeable limp as he came in and immediately was looked over by Doc Muralles. While clearing a staircase, Dave took a misstep, sprained his ankle, and nearly fell down a flight of stairs. While they are often an overlooked aspect of the battlefield, sprains, muscle tears, and hyperextensions are common injuries. What happened to Dave could have happened to any one of us, but for now, it meant that he was stuck in the CCP, which required me to accompany the platoon Sergeant around the objective. Before I had time to think, SFC Jack alerted me it was time to go and I immediately picked up and followed him out the door and back outside.

From the top of the hill where the buildings were, I finally had my first real full perspective of the fight that we were in. For one, the dam itself was enormous at nearly two miles in total length. The hill where the buildings were located, occupied the area of a football field. Twelve buildings made a sloppy oval, at the middle of which, a 12 foot stone mural of Saddam Hussein had been erected. Of the buildings, two were bigger administrative buildings and the rest of the smaller buildings appeared to be quarters for the Iraqi soldiers. On the edge of the hilltop, they had previously dug out positions to provide cover for fighting vehicles that were not present when we arrived. SFC Jack immediately directed to bring our vehicles up and use the unoccupied positions to establish converging fires with the heavy guns. With .50 caliber machine guns, MK19 automatic grenade launchers, and M-240B machine guns the platoon instantly utilized the vehicles' firepower to our advantage and gained the complete upper hand.

1LT Joe then began directing fire missions for our 120mm mortars with the Forward Observer, SPC Jameson, while the Air Force ETAC began calling for F-16s to start bombing two main buildings about 500 meters below that the Iraqis were staging counterattacks from. Undeterred, the enemy continued to maneuver in groups of 10-15 through the trench system in the low ground. Meanwhile, isolated groups of Republican Guard occupied bunkers and mortar positions and continued to engage our positions. The anti-tank section led by SPC Eric Carlton engaged enemy positions using the

84mm recoilless rifle, also known as the 'Carl Gustav', or simply 'the goose'. The goose is a remarkably simple weapon system designed by the Swedish military following World War II. Its design allows for the weapon to serve a multipurpose function and has a wide array of rounds for different targets. In this case, enemy personnel were attempting to use a heavy cargo truck as cover in order to engage one of our positions. SPC Carlton recognized this and directed his gunner, PFC Patton, to engage the truck as he loaded a round in the breach. The gunner fired scoring a direct hit, but only partially damaging the truck. Unlike the movies we'd grown up watching, there was no massive fireball, just a black cloud of smoke and debris followed by a concussion from the explosion. With cover still in place, Iraqis began to move back and use it to their advantage. Carlton pulled out another 84mm round, an airburst this time, and set the range. He loaded it into the breach and this time directed the gunner to aim slightly over the truck. The round exploded and killed a few of the Iraqis, but with an effective form of cover, the enemy continued to maneuver and utilize it to their advantage. 1LT Joe and the ETAC noticed this and called for an airstrike on the truck. Moments later a five hundred pound bomb fell from the sky, effectively neutralizing the cargo truck for the duration of the battle.

By midday, our intersecting fires became so effective that we established what began to be referred to as 'No Man's Land'. From the advantage of high ground and good cover, the platoon coordinated fires so well that by mid-morning, we had pushed back the enemy over a half of a kilometer from our hill. At one point, SPC Barron and PFC Cannon spotted a dirt bike in the low ground moving laterally across the battlefield. Had it been headed south, directly away from their sectors of fire, Barron and Cannon probably would not have engaged. However the motorcycle with two Iraqis was moving to the east, into the conflict instead of a way from it. The Iraqis probably thought that being on two wheels would make them harder to target and for a moment, they were correct. Barron and Cannon both engaged with the Mk-19 and a M-240B. The motorcycle evaded the initial volley of fire and looked as if it might make it to safety. Barron ordered Cannon on the M-240B to use the machine gun and give the bike a greater lead then walk the rounds back into it. Cannon adjusted his aim and depressed the trigger of the machine gun letting out a long burst which he raked back toward the motorcycle. It worked. 7.62 ate through the motorcycle and dropped its two passengers. Barron then used the opportunity to walk a burst of 40mm grenades on the bike and surrounding area to make sure no one got up.

After establishing No Man's Land, most of the shooting was relegated to the heavy guns and snipers. For the hours up until midday, snipers had been helping direct small arms fire as well as engaging individuals with their long guns. By noon, their positions in the Eagle's Nest, as they referred to it, became responsible for a quarter of the platoons' fire. By utilizing the highest ground on the dam, snipers called out enemy positions for mortars and air strikes, and used a combination of precision .308 and .50 caliber fires to suppress and prevent the enemy's movement and assembly. Because of this effective fire, the Iraqis relied more and more on their mortar positions to dislodge us. As the targets for the F-16s became smaller, and the indirect fire intensified, the risk of losing a fast mover became greater and the call to pull them off of the objective was made to prevent collision between an aircraft and a mortar round in its airspace. Luckily for the strike force, the Air Force had another platform to provide close air support from. As F-16s went off station, A-10s replaced them.

A-10s are slow flying, one-pilot behemoths of an attack plane. The entire aircraft is designed around a 30mm Gatling-style cannon. It also has numerous hard points for attachment for everything from rocket pods to JDAM munitions. The ETAC would make a call on the radio and the big aircraft would fall from the sky in a tactic similar to the Little Birds, however to a greater effect. When the A-10 would drop in, it would fire two short bursts from its 30mm cannon at a rate of over 3000 rounds per minute. The sound that gun made was unlike anything I'd ever heard before. A mechanically, explosive thundercloud of gun smoke that rained death to those in a 40ft radius of the intended impact area. I'd never seen anything like it. For several minutes, everyone seemed to stop and take notice. It was just the snipers calling targets for the ETAC and the A-10s taking care of the rest. The pilots would circle above like a bird of prey scanning for its next victim. The call would come in and they would swoop down from the sky and engage Iraqi positions with bursts from the cannon, followed by deployment of rockets. Each time they would dive in the Iraqis would return fire, but by the end of the run, their positions would fall silent.

The rest of the afternoon continued like this, snipers and heavy guns engaging long distance targets with the help of 120mm mortars and A-10s. Eventually we began searching the buildings on our hill for intelligence as the small arms fire died out. In the center of the building in front of the Saddam mural, we found an arms room with enough AK47s to arm every Ranger in the platoon, twice. It was reassuring to find backup weapons with enough ammo and grenades to last us for a while. They even had bayonets just in case things got close. We set up the platoon command post (CP) and established it as the future casualty collection point, should we need it. Sergeant Aaron had been moved to the company CCP at the center of the dam and Doc Dave and SSG Muralles joined the command element in this building. With two real medics at the CP, SFC Jack sent me to help 3rd Squad search buildings.

I linked up with Matt, Bob, Tommy, and Panatela to help search the building we had previously had as the CCP. While 3rd Squad had cleared the buildings during the initial assault, a proper search for intelligence hadn't been completed. In the building, we actually found quite a bit of intelligence that the Iraqis had on us. One of the things I found of particular amusement was a poster of coalition military aircraft, mainly that of the United States. Several rows of photos that could have been found on the Internet, depicted American fighter jets, bombers, cargo planes, and even refuel birds along with respective descriptions in Arabic below. There was more than a couple of them so I took one, folded it up, and put it in my cargo pocket. In a file cabinet, someone found files with Iraqi military IDs, presumably of the guys we were fighting below. I grabbed one and looked at it. A black and white photo laminated on cardstock that contained Arabic that I assumed indicated name, rank, and other information. I had not a clue to what anything translated to, but I knew it was a military ID of a man undoubtedly fighting down below us. I wondered if he'd been killed already, or was he still somehow alive? Had this been one of the guys running in the dark that SSG Shank, Jonathan, and I had shot earlier?

I decided that it wasn't the guy who I'd shot. *Couldn't be.* But the thought sat with me as we continued to search for valuable information. Eventually we gathered everything that looked pertinent and stacked it in one corner of the main room. Since this building was the second largest and for the most part out of the way, it became the collection point for everything else found throughout the mission to be eventually taken off of the objective. During the search of another building, I ran into Jared who was in one of the best moods that I'd ever seen him in sober. I finally got to ask him about the Javelin kill from earlier in the morning, "Dude, what were you shooting at earlier?"

"Oh, with the Javelin?"

"Yeah. Out on the lake."

Jared chuckled, "It was a mortar position, dude. Sarn't Santos pointed it out to Sarn't Jack. Could barely see the heat signature with the viewfinder."

"How far was it? I could barely see where it landed . . ."

"Oh, I don't know. Had to be at least 2000 meters. I thought was gonna miss until I saw the secondary explosions." He chuckled again.

"Yeah, you got 'em, alright."

For the first time, I realized that at one point, the enemy had surrounded us on four sides. How no one had been seriously wounded was beyond me. Aside from Sergeant Aaron and the gunner who'd been hit in the back plate of his armor, no one had been hit in over eight hours of sustained combat. As I talked to other guys throughout the afternoon, I learned that everybody had fired their weapon. Some would shrug off whether or not they actually hit anybody, but most guys knew without a doubt. We had all been baptized in fire and everyone's mood was the best it'd been since leaving Georgia. No more the question of whether we'd actually see combat. No more the fear of freezing up or failure to act. We'd all performed like we'd been trained to. We had excelled in the art of war and had set the enemy back more than a kilometer. Someone found Iraqi paper money and pointed out the dam on the Iraq's five hundred dinar bill. I looked across to the dam structure, itself. It was huge, spanning nearly 2 miles in total length and over 14 stories tall. The magnitude and importance of the mission finally sank in. The company had just done something major and everyone in the platoon knew it.

As day turned to night and darkness fell, the line squads began digging into the hill outside of the buildings facing toward the low ground. Doc Dave and I rotated on radio guard with the platoon radio operator (RTO), PFC Wolf, to monitor the platoon net and alert the leadership to any pertinent info or calls from higher up. As a result of being on radio guard, we were indoors for the most part, and did not have to dig positions. This was about the luckiest a private could get. While all of the other privates dug into the night, I smoked cigarettes under the covered entry of the building and watched bombs explode in the distance, while listening to the platoon radio traffic.

Around midnight, Gunny called SFC Jack over the radio. Iraqis were trying to use the cover of darkness to get closer. Using nighttime scopes with thermal imaging, SSG Shank and his gun team leaders spotted the enemy trying to walk up on to our positions.

They were literally walking in a single-file line, weapons slung over their back like they were on a casual stroll in the park. SFC Jack and SSG Shank let the column of would-be attackers get 600 meters out and opened up with intersecting fires and mowed them down. That would be the one and only time they tried to just walk up onto us like that. But for the rest of the night, Iraqis periodically maneuvered small groups who were intercepted by heavy guns once they reached the 600-meter line that had been established. Any further out made it hard to effectively engage at night and since we had been fighting all day, conservation of ammunition became a prime consideration of the platoon leadership.

About an hour later, it was reported that the Iraqis were trying to consolidate once again at the two large buildings about 500 meters out. Earlier in the day, the buildings had been serviced by a couple of 500 pound bombs, but tonight the call came in for a one-ton JDAM to be dropped on each of the buildings to neutralize the enemy that had arrived. A jet made its overpass and moments later a flash illuminated the sky similar to a lightning strike, followed by the loudest thunder I'd ever heard. The concussion was so great that I felt it in my chest as it shook the buildings and ground beneath me. Seconds later, another jet did a flyby followed by a second lightning strike and thunderclap that shook the hill. Rangers celebrated amongst themselves with hushed cheers and high-fives. It wasn't quite a fireworks show, but it sure matched any Fourth of July celebration that I'd ever seen.

Every four hours I would rotate to radio guard for two hours. While off radio guard, I took refuge in the buildings and attempted to sleep. Lying on a concrete floor and trying to fall asleep after a day like we had was next to impossible. In spite of barely sleeping at the ROD site and only a few hours' sleep the night before, I was wide-awake. If I'd get close to dosing off, a burst of machine gun fire or an outgoing 120mm mortar would jolt me out of it. While lying there in the darkness, the memories of the previous 18 hours came flooding back. The Little Birds and A-10s, the support by fire line on the side of the road, everything vivid as if it was still happening. All this time, I'd worried about how I'd handle combat and today I'd discovered war wasn't just exciting, it was fun. I found myself thinking about how different it was from the movies, how much better it was than a video game. I felt like combat was what I'd been waiting for my entire life, that this is what I was meant to do, and it was during these thoughts that I was finally able to drift off to sleep.

I awoke to the sounds of a .50 caliber machine gun engaging a target off in the distance. I didn't feel as if it jolted me awake, rather slowly bringing me back into the world of the Haditha Dam. It almost felt as if I hadn't been asleep, that I'd just mentally checked out for a while. I turned my head to see Doc Dave staring at me from the doorway.

"Morning, sunshine. Get a good night's sleep?'

"Was I asleep?"

Dave chuckled, "Yeah, dude, you were passed out. And now it's my turn because you're on radio guard."

"Awesome."

"Hurry up and get your shit together so you can come relieve me." Dave left the doorway. I checked my watch . . . 0600hrs.

As I started to get up, I realized how tired and slow I felt. I pulled my body armor over my head, cinched it down, and put on my MICH helmet. Grabbing my weapon, I headed to the door and outside to relieve Dave on the radio. By now, it was the morning of the second day on the dam. We had settled into our fighting positions and prepared for another day of defending the high ground. The Iraqis had attempted throughout the night to sneak closer and as the morning stretched on, heavy gunners and mortars pushed them back. Snipers continued to engage, as did our 120mm mortars, and the pilots above us flew coverage dropping death from above whenever called.

Mid-morning, the order came down that we would be holding the dam until relieved. The order didn't specify when that relief would be however. We'd been told the mission would only last 24 hours and we had packed accordingly. The platoon was low on food, water, and ammunition. The order went out to conserve all of our supplies and the squad leaders provided SFC Jack with a list of needs for the future resupply that was growing more needed by the hour.

Brief engagements of sniper fire and heavy guns would periodically fill the air, but for the most part, the morning lacked the feel of excitement and glory the day before had brought. Being physically tired was part of it, but half of me had already become desensitized to the sights and sounds of war. Engagements with the enemy became routine and while big guns would occasionally talk back and forth, the adrenaline rush that came along with it had vanished.

After PFC Wolf took back over the radio for the day, I resumed accompanying SFC Jack every time he left the CP. Mid-day; SSG Santos called in a report of a kayaker off an island near the shore of the reservoir. I followed SFC Jack to a GMV overlooking the reservoir and sure enough, an Iraqi was attempting to paddle away from the island in a kayak.

"I don't believe it." SFC Jack exclaimed.

SSG Santos handed SFC Jack the binoculars, but even without them it was possible to see the kayak a few hundred meters struggling to paddle into the wind.

"He's wearing OD green." SFC Jack remarked. "I don't know, looks hostile to me. Give 'em a warning burst, Carp."

SPC Carp, who was occupying the turret, put a warning burst of .50 cal into the water in front of the kayak. Instead of giving up, the kayaker paddled harder, meeting stiff resistance from the wind.

"Fuck it" SFC Jack said, as he spit tobacco juice. "Sink him, Carp."

SPC Carp shrugged and fired off another burst that tore through the plastic boat. In seconds, it disappeared beneath the surface. SFC Jack sent Bravo Team from 3rd Squad down to the reservoir to search for a survivor. Ten minutes later, Matt and Tommy returned securing a very wet, but unharmed Iraqi. When they got to him to our position, he was searched and SSG Branford found a hand drawn map of our location. We all looked at the Iraqi in amazement. That crazy bastard had paddled in during the night to draw out our positions. Had this gotten into the hands of an artillery crew, it would have made their job very easy to pin point our locations with accurate indirect fire. Fortunately for us, the courageous Iraqi was too impatient to wait until dark to show his artwork to his buddies, making it now ours.

Bravo Team loaded up the detainee in a GMV and quickly took the prisoner to the dam for further interrogation. As they returned from the center of the dam, their vehicle came under fire from a four-barrel ZPU that had gone overlooked. The driver of the GMV accelerated back to our position while the mortar team located the Russian ZPU, taking out its crew with a 120mm HE round. Luckily, the vehicle returned to the group of buildings without getting hit and all of the Rangers on board were unwounded.

The rest of the day continued in the same fashion as the morning and afternoon of the day before. 10-15 Iraqis would build up the gusto to begin maneuvering towards our position, only to be cut down by intersecting machine gun and 40mm grenade fire. It became target practice for whoever was manning the heavy guns, which had become a rotation for everyone on the line. If anyone besides Dave, Wolf, or me had any doubts about their proficiency on the heavy guns, today was the day to erase them.

But as the day progressed, the engagements became fewer and farther between. At this point, no one had shaved since we left Saudi and everyone who could grow facial hair had acquired about four-days of growth. Rangers are known for their high standards of neatness of dress and appearance, making a platoon of unshaven Batt boys quite a unique sight. Unfortunately, that would change before the end of the day. Around sunset, the word came down: everybody must shave. Begrudgingly, Rangers began to pull back from the line and shave. Being only nineteen years old, I had a peach fuzz mustache only a few chin hairs, which made it quite easy to dry shave.

For those who had a near, full beard like 1LT Joe, SSG Shank, and Jared, dry shaving with a Bic razor proved painful and bloody.

Freshly shaven, the platoon was now ready for the sun to go down on our second night on the dam. Since I was the first to pull radio guard the night before, I was the last in the rotation tonight, which meant I had the chance to rack out first. This time, I had no difficulty finding the ability to fall asleep. As soon as I laid my head back against my assault pack, I was unconscious until Dave woke me up four hours later.

Barely awake, I relieved Dave at the radio. I immediately lit up a cigarette to help wake up and lowered my NODS in order to see around me. I checked my watch.

2300hrs.

Two hours to go. If anything important came across the radio, I was to wake up 1LT Joe but for the most part, all was quiet. Occasional updates would come across the net, but the majority of the time was spent chain smoking cigarettes and listening to the sounds of the desert night. Thirty minutes before my shift was due to end, a call came through.

"All elements, be advised. We have just taken casualties, standby for sit rep." A shaken, but calm voice called over the radio.

I quickly woke up the PL and informed him of the report. As he awoke, the second part of the call came through, "We have three KIAs, multiple wounded. Request CASEVAC at our position, immediately"

1LT Joe grabbed the radio and listened to the rest of the transmission. I asked him what was going on after the radio traffic died down a few minutes later. He told me that Alpha Company had been hit a few miles away and that was all he knew. As my guard shift ended, I went inside and woke Wolf, passing on the news as I took a knee next to him.

"What happened?" He asked after the second time of telling him there had been casualties.

"Alpha Company got hit. Three guys dead."

"You know who?"

"No, just that there were three KIAs and a bunch of other guys that got hurt."

Wolf took a moment to let it set in. "Shit's getting real, now."

He was right. I stood up and agreed, "Yep. I'll be outside, man."

I went back outside to where 1LT Joe was on the radio. He put the handset down and looked at me.

"A Co. stopped a vehicle at their checkpoint. A pregnant woman got out and asked for a bottle of water, they went to help her, the car blew up."

"You're kidding me, sir."

"Suicide bomber."

Wolf came outside and asked what happened. 1LT Joe repeated the story to a similar response of disbelief. No one could have imagined this. We'd prepared for almost every type of engagement while training in Georgia, but we never prepared for Iraqis to use pregnant women as decoys. We had never prepared for suicide car bombs and the news of using a woman to initiate one shook everybody to the core.

Wolf shook his head and spit Copenhagen off to the side, "These fucking people."

I went back inside and tried to fall back asleep. Unlike earlier in the night, rest proved elusive, as all I could think about was the situation Alpha Company was dealing with. Three Rangers lost their lives and several others were wounded. I had friends in Alpha and secretly wished that they weren't the ones who'd gotten hurt or died. Reality began to set in that we were not impervious to the risks of war. Rangers could be killed at any moment and Alpha Company had just learned that lesson firsthand.

With morning came news of the names of our fallen brothers. Killed were Captain Russell Rippetoe, SSG Nino Livaudais, and SPC Ryan Long. I didn't know any of them personally, but knew of CPT Rippetoe and remembered that he rode a Harley Davidson that I'd seen around the battalion area in Georgia. The news of their passing spread around the platoon and each of us paid our simple respects. There was nothing we could do, but hold the dam at all costs. They had died at a roadblock that had isolated the objective from reinforcements and it was now our duty to make sure their sacrifices were not in vain.

The assault force was entering into its third day of occupation. The Company CP had received a resupply of ammunition, food, and water in the middle of the night that was brought to our location by the First Sergeant (1SG) around 0900hrs. I hadn't shot but five rounds so only needed resupply on chow and water. As a private without a Ranger tab, I got my pick of the litter from a ransacked box of MREs. I found a Bean and Rice Burrito for breakfast that was better than Beef and Mushrooms or Chicken Teriyaki.

As I ate chow, I noticed how quiet it was. I hadn't heard any of the heavy guns fire or aircraft drop bombs and began to wonder if it was all over. It seemed logical to me as I ate my cold burrito that the Iraqis had given up. It was obvious that we had the dam and weren't giving it up. We had fire superiority in every aspect and there was no way for them to dislodge us from our positions. We'd won. I went outside to smoke a cigarette after eating and looked out on to the battlefield. For the first time, I noticed the number of dogs in the area probably outnumbered the platoon. While, I'd seen one or two and definitely heard a lot of them bark, I hadn't realized the sheer number of feral dogs surrounding the objective. I wasn't the only one to take note. SPC Hamburg sat in the turret of a GMV, smoking a cigarette while surveying his sector.

"Look at the number of dogs, out there." He said in disbelief. "Gotta be at least fifty of them running around." He looked at me while taking a drag and nodded, "Bet they're all out for the bodies lying around. Free food."

I watched a pack of several skinny looking, medium-sized dogs huddled stationary about 200 meters away. I imagined them tearing away at a body, realizing they'd do the same to me if I was lying out there dead.

"Jesus."

Hamburg took another drag, "Yeah, I think out here they call him Mohammed..."

I finished my cigarette and began walking back to the other side of the building towards the CP. As I turned the corner, I heard wind break over my head followed by a loud concussion and an explosion at the base of the dam. That round was different than anything we received so far. The Forward Observer, SPC Jameson declared that it was an artillery round. We waited for another one, taking cover in the entrance of the CP. A call came through from the mortars that they had gotten a back azimuth on where the round came from and air support was sent to investigate. While we waited for an update or the next round to come in, I began to have an urge to make a bowel movement. I quickly decided that now was not the time for me to take my first combat shit, but the nicotine of my last cigarette had already taken effect. I hadn't taken a dump since leaving the airfield, and had only had a couple of MREs and Power Bars since, but after eating breakfast and smoking, my bowels were ready to perform their bodily functions.

War, however, was not pausing for me to drop my drawers. I looked at Dave. The more I thought about it, the worse the pressure in my lower abdomen became. I finally asked him where to go take a dump. He didn't believe me at first, but when he saw I was serious, he told me about the ravine he'd taken one earlier in.

"Just be careful." He said.

I grabbed my M-4 and headed towards the ravine between our hill and the dam that was covered from small arms fire, but completely vulnerable to indirect. I found a spot a third of the way down the hill that allowed for good footing and took off my body armor. The JLIST chemical suit that I'd been wearing was a two-piece that had to be zipped down and nearly taken off in order to facilitate the process of defecating. I finally removed all of the necessary clothing and squatted down. No-shit there I was: chemical-suit around my ankles, brown t-shirt blowing along with everything else in the breeze, with a war going on around me. Details are irrelevant, but eating MREs consecutively for days can lead to a *disappointment of reward versus effort factor*. It was as I was experiencing this moment of dissatisfaction that the *WHOOSH!* of an artillery shell sailing overhead came in and exploded not far away. It was by no means close to hitting me, but nonetheless I instinctively flinched and attempted to crouch lower before I realized that I wasn't in immediate danger. Doing so, I lost my footing on the incline and began to slide down the hill with my pants around my ankles. I caught myself and didn't move for a second to ensure I was done sliding. I looked down and saw my own turd about an inch from my bare thigh. If I slipped any further or forward, I was sure to smear it on my leg. The thought of falling into my own shit trumped the fact that my ass was hanging out so before pulling up my pants, I slowly rolled to my left until I was clear of danger. Satisfied that I wasn't going to come in contact, I pulled up my JLIST around my hips then awkwardly stood up to pull the suit suspender straps over my shoulders and zip it up. I then put kit back on, grabbed my weapon, and returned the CP.

As I got back up to the building, Dave asks if they'd caught me with my pants down. I chuckled and went to my aid bag to grab hand sanitizer. One of the things I definitely hadn't planned for was receiving artillery while taking a dump and I just escaped my first dose of it relatively clean. I couldn't imagine someone knocking on my parent's door to explain how their son died shitting for their freedom.

A few more artillery rounds came in that day and as we sent air support to investigate where the guns were that were firing on us from. As they passed over the actual village of Haditha, the pilots noticed a large group of Iraqi soldiers loading vehicles in an attempt to flee to the south of the dam. After this report and the destruction of the artillery piece that was harassing us, the rest of the day was rather quiet.

That night was uneventful, aside from another resupply that we received from H1. An MH-47 Chinook piloted by the 160th dropped off more food and water, along with ammunition and other supplies at the center of the dam. The First Sergeant decided to wait until daylight to distribute it and so the platoon continued to dig and reinforce their positions with sandbags. Working in shifts, the privates in the platoon would hack away at their positions with E-tools to break up the dry, hard soil enough to fill sandbags. While the platoon dug for the third night in a row, I sat on radio guard taking in the constant *tink, tink, tink* from their shovels hitting hard packed soil and rock. On the horizon to the southwest, lighting flashed in the distance, followed seconds later by the rumble of thunder. I knew it wasn't lightning, but that didn't stop my mind from seeing it any different. Word began to spread that the heavy gunners could see the heat signatures of the dogs fighting over dead Iraqis through the thermal night scopes on the vehicles. Occasionally, we would hear the pack mentality, as they would turn on one of their own. Forced to listen to the cries of the dog being savagely mauled by members of its own social dynamic, I came to appreciate the safety of our positions on the top of the hill more. Never before in my life had I heard dogs turn on each other like that and it was a sound that no one would forget. Eventually I woke up Wolf to relieve me on radio guard. Once back in the room, the sounds of the night were muffled by the walls and rooftop over my head. Lying there in the dark room, I quickly succumbed to exhaustion and fell asleep.

Four hours later, I woke up to Dave gently tapping my boot with his foot. At first, I couldn't understand why he was waking me up.

"Dude. Radio guard." He whispered, "It's time."

"Fucking 'eh . . ."

"I know. Hurry up so I can go take a piss and rack out." I looked at him for a moment, nodded, and he left the room. My watch read 0400 hours. Two hours before the sun came up, so I knew there was no more sleep for the night. I slowly pulled myself together. My arms and legs felt weighted down, motor skills slightly off. At the radio, Dave informed me that nothing had happened since he took over from Wolf and immediately stood up to leave, presumably to go relieve himself. I sat down next to the radio and put the handset to my ear and began the shift of listening to dead air interrupted by brief situation reports. Fatigue made my arms and legs feel numb and useless as I sat, desperately fighting off the urge to lose consciousness. Chain-smoking cigarette after cigarette, my mind wandered freely through memories of the past. Looking out into the night, I wondered what my parents were doing. I figured it was evening at their house and they were both sitting in the living room, watching television. Were they watching news about the war, afraid for their son? I hoped not. Wishing there was a way that I could reach out and let them know that I was ok, I sat listening to a silent radio able to do nothing but put out the Marlboro smoking between my fingers and light up another one.

Eventually the sun began to rise and the platoon slowly began their priorities of work. Shortly after being relieved by Wolf on the radio, the first artillery shell of the day struck about 100 meters from 2nd Platoon's perimeter on the other side of the dam. Within minutes, an artillery gun from the northeast and two heavy mortar positions to the south had dialed in on 2nd Platoon's position, forcing their defensive perimeter to fall back into the dam. 1LT Joe received a call from the CO that gave him the position of the mortar tubes, and SFC Jack directed snipers and heavy guns to begin engaging, while the Forward Observer called in 120mm mortars on the two positions. Within minutes of engaging the positions to our south, our hill began to receive artillery with rounds impacting inside of our perimeter.

During a break from the incoming fire, a call was made to SFC Jack that our previous night's resupply was ready to be picked up at the center of the dam. SFC Jack grabbed SPC Plasman as his driver, as well as Jared, PFC Patton, and I to accompany him to pick up our rations. We loaded up a cargo GMV that wasn't being used on the line and headed to the main structure of the dam. The road leading to the center of the dam was nearly a mile and as we sped down the concrete structure, I was once again amazed at how big everything was. It almost seemed as if we were driving down a long suspension bridge, yet there was no overpass. The dam was a nearly two mile, man-made barrier that was holding back a lake almost the size of one that I grew up near as a kid. The GMV pulled up to the building at the center of the dam and we quickly off-loaded. For the first time since the fighting started, I was actually standing on the structure that the mission revolved around. It was bigger in person than as seen from the hill where our platoon was positioned.

Greeted by Sergeant Donald Buman, or Doc Buma as he was called, I finally had the chance to go inside and take a look around one of the biggest hydroelectric dams in the world. Inside, I was immediately greeted by cooler air. Because the dam generated electricity, the structure itself had power and therefore air conditioning. The change of temperature was refreshing and ever so welcome. Doc Buma led me to the makeshift Company Aid Station where he and the Battalion Physician Assistant, CPT Ray Silver, and a few other Rangers had set up inside.

Located in a big room near the main entrance, the aid station was nothing more than a couple of aid bags set up, with a Ranger guarding two Iraqi soldiers that had been wounded and captured. One Iraqi sat back against the wall with the miserable expression of a man who'd nearly had his jaw blown off. The man looked to be at least fifty, although in reality he was probably younger. He wore the rank of colonel, yet the sad look in his eyes revealed only a man in pain. His face long, he couldn't clench his jaw in order to close his mouth. His bottom mandible hung uncontrollable from the rest of his face as two holes, one on each side, penetrated both cheeks. Slightly balding and overweight, he was dirty with dried blood, sweat, and dust. The second guy lay on the floor with a sandbag over his head. Immediately, I could see that he was dead.

"What's up with this guy?" I asked even though I already knew the answer. Doc Buma looks at him and without taking his hands out of his pocket replies, "Oh, that guy? Yeah, I wouldn't worry about him. I don't think he's going anywhere."

I stared down at the Iraqi while Buma began to dig into his aid bag. Rigor mortis had set in and gave the skin a waxy, dull look. I imagined they had put the sandbag over his face so they wouldn't have to sit there and look at his dead expression, but part of me had wished it wasn't there. A voice inside of me didn't want to believe he was dead, that he was just asleep and still alive, but after a minute of watching and never seeing his chest rise or fall, I knew that my initial suspicion was correct.

Buma walked over to the colonel, holding a small Dixie cup then motioned to the Iraqi officer with a pill in his hand, repeating the Arabic word for medicine. The man indicated that he understood and raised his hands to his cheeks to cover both of the holes in his face. The Colonel gratefully nodded and Buma put the pill on the man's tongue and slowly poured water into his mouth. The Iraqi swallowed twice, water escaping down the sides of his cheeks as he did. Sitting there, watching Doc hand-feed pain pills to another human being took me by surprise. This was the enemy, yet for the first time, I felt compassion towards someone on the other side. The humanity of providing medical aid to the same people we were trying to kill and they us, was a juxtaposition of everything I'd experienced up until this point.

"So what happened?"

"This guy was riding shotgun in a cargo truck yesterday that didn't want to stop for second platoon's roadblock. Sarn't Major Birch smoked him and his battle buddy with the SR-25."

"I guess that explains the sandbag."

Buma shrugged, "Yeah, keeps everything nice and neat."

SFC Jack yelled that we were ready to go so my time with Buma and the wounded Colonel came to an end. Before I walked out the door, Buma stopped me, "You got any Copenhagen?"

I replied that I only had cigarettes. Buma thought about it for a second, "Fuck it, give me one. I ran out of dip yesterday." I pulled out a cigarette and threw it to him as I ran out the door. Back outside, I jogged over to the GMV and jumped in the back with Jared and Patton. We had mostly been resupplied with MREs and water, but as we drove back, I also noticed a couple bags of Twizzler licorice and small cans of Fanta orange soda. I stared at the candy and Fanta with bewilderment. Surely, it must be some kind of joke. Yet, there between our feet were enough eight-ounce cans of Fanta for the entire platoon. Jared shook his head and laughed, "What are we gonna do with orange soda?"

"Drink it." Patton responded as the GMV pulled up to our building. He jumped off the back and Jared and I began handing supplies to him, Salido, and Glassmock who had both come to help unload the vehicle. No sooner than we had gotten the last box of MREs to the building and without warning, the sonic boom of an artillery shell, followed near-instantaneously by a loud explosion shook the hill. A cloud of black smoke and dust lifted into the air. Before anyone could react, several more rounds impacted around the hill. Unlike yesterday, there was no whistling in the air to warn us of an incoming round. Just a loud crack from the 155mm shell breaking the sound barrier, followed immediately by an explosion that would shake the ground where it landed.

All of the Rangers on our hill were either in fortified positions or buildings so the rounds that fell didn't score a direct hit, and no one was wounded on the initial barrage to our position. We could tell by the accuracy of the artillery, however, that the Iraqis now had a forward observer calling fire. SFC Jack quickly ordered over the radio for the snipers to begin scanning for his position. 155mm artillery shells continued to impact on and around our hill, but after nearly three days of digging, our positions were well protected. The Iraqi forward observer must have realized this, as rounds began impacting between our hill and the center of the dam. He must have spotted our 120mm mortar position, because rounds began creeping up the hill towards their position. All of a sudden, a round hit directly on the other side of the retaining wall that the mortarmen were using for cover. One of the Rangers, who was acting as a spotter, was caught by surprise and did not get down in time. From our position in the covered entrance of the CP, we could see him fly up in the air as the round exploded.

Shouts for medic could immediately be heard from the mortars' position. SFC Jack immediately called for SPC Plasman to get back in the driver's seat and Dave and I ran with him to the GMV. Plasman turned the vehicle around and sped to the road leading up to the dam. SFC Jack saw a route around the retaining wall that allowed us to take the strip of dirt between it and the edge of the reservoir. SPC Plasman accelerated down the narrow dirt path. About fifty meters from the mortar's position, the vehicle came to a halt and we all dismounted. Just as we did, another round came in and landed on the other side of the road. The four of us hit the dirt for a quick second then picked up and began sprinting towards the wounded Ranger. We got about halfway and another round came in. We quickly hit the dirt again and then picked back up after the explosion. Mortar crewmembers were huddled next to an unconscious Ranger, trying to get him to wake up when we arrived. It was immediately apparent that he had penetrating head trauma at his right temple. His orbital bones making up the eye sockets had instantly swollen up and turned purple, deforming his upper facial features. The second thing I noticed was that the Ranger was cyanotic and was turning blue at the lips, which meant he wasn't getting oxygen.

Dave and I pulled him off the wall, expecting the worse. I removed his helmet to assess the trauma while Dave felt for a pulse on his neck. Aside from the penetration at his temple and damage to his eyes, there was no other visible trauma. Dave found a pulse and I leaned down to listen for breathing. Faintly, I could hear gurgling in the back of this throat indicating he had an obstructed airway. Dave instructed me to begin suctioning his airway while he prepared for a cricothyrotomy, a surgical procedure that opens the airway by making an incision in the throat and inserting a breathing tube. It was a bold call in any circumstance, but even bolder under the current conditions. However if the suction failed to clear his airway, we would have had no other choice and making the call to begin preparation was the right move to make by Dave. Luckily, I was able to get the suction into the back of the wounded Ranger's mouth and began squeezing the rubber bulb in order to create a vacuum to remove the obstruction. As I squeezed the top of what looked like a large turkey baster, clotted blood and flesh began to be extracted by the suction tube. After about 10 seconds, I stopped pulling up fluid and tissue and removed the suction from his mouth.

Miraculously, he began breathing on his own and color immediately returned to his face.

I asked one of his Ranger buddies, what his name was and they responded, "Feldman!" I called out his name and asked if he could hear me. No response. Dave saw that Feldman had regained breathing and abandoned the cric procedure. He instructed me to secure the casualty's airway with an oropharyngeal tube, which resembled a plastic J. While securing Feldman's airway, the mortar section leader, SFC Smith, pulled one of the mortar's cargo GMVs up on the other side of the wall ordering us to load him up so we could get him to the Company CCP. Knowing it was only a matter of time before the next artillery shell came in and afraid of taking more casualties, we hastily began to lift Feldman up without putting his helmet back on. I had him by the shoulders while a couple of others had him at the legs and waist. SFC Smith and several other Rangers on the other side of the wall waited for us to lift him over the wall. As we did, they grabbed him by the legs and waist. In the chaos, the group on the other side of the wall began to carry him to the vehicle while I still had him by the shoulders. The wall between myself and the other guys prevented me from going any further with Feldman.

I tried to call out and as I did, he fell from my grip, his head smacking the other side of the wall leaving a bloody mark where it had hit. Immediately, my heart sank into my stomach and I knew everything we had just done up until this point to get him breathing was in vain. SFC Smith and the other Rangers quickly picked him up and pulled him into the back of the cargo GMV. I stood there for a moment, shocked, watching them load him up.

"Matthews!" Someone yelled from behind, "Let's go! Get on the fucking vehicle!"

I turned to see SFC Jack yelling at me to get my aid bag and get on the cargo truck. Snapping out of it, I quickly grabbed my bag and M-4 then jumped over the wall and into the back of the GMV, followed closely behind by SPC Dave. As soon as Dave was on board, the driver shifted into drive and sped off towards the center of the dam. Feldman started to regain consciousness, muttering incoherent sentences as we pulled up to the CCP. At once, our vehicle was surrounded by Rangers ready to aid in getting our wounded out of the back. Two of those were Sergeant Buman and CPT Silver, the Battalion Physician's Assistant. Taking his shoulders once more, I was determined not to let Feldman's head so much as touch the ground. He even helped by reaching up and grabbing behind his collar to help keep his head up as we moved him out of the vehicle. The group carried him behind a large concrete wall and set him down. As we lowered him, I squatted down on to both knees so that his head and shoulders would rest elevated on my lap.

Captain Silver and Doc Buma immediately began their assessment and worked to stabilize Feldman for CASEVAC. Buma started a saline lock for an IV, while CPT Silver assessed his head trauma and airway. As they were doing this, SFC Jack and SPC Plasman brought our GMV to the center of the dam to pick up Dave and I. With Feldman's head in my lap, I had to wait for someone to relieve me at elevating his head before I could rejoin the vehicle. Finally, someone took over at his shoulders and after taking one last moment with the wounded Ranger whom I'd never met before today, I ran over and jumped in the back of SFC Jack's GMV. As soon as I sat down, I stared down at the lap of my JLIST suit, which had become saturated in blood from assisting Feldman. I rotated my sleeves and saw they too were covered in blood. As the vehicle pulled off back towards our building on the hill, I looked back one last time to the group of Rangers huddled over Feldman, the thought of his head hitting the wall at the forefront of my mind.

Dave and I sat in silence on the return to buildings. While turning the corner to drive up the last 25 meters to the CP, an artillery round scored a direct hit on the lip of a defilade vehicle position manned by SSG Shank, SPC Hester, and SPC Jameson. The overpressure knocked all three of them from their positions and to the opposite end of the three-sided hole while moving the GMV several feet in the opposite direction. We pulled up to the building as Rangers were helping Gunny and the two others to their feet. Everybody was ok, miraculously, as I had already started going back into response mode.

We all took cover inside the CP building and no one said a word to Dave and I as we passed by covered in blood. I led the way into the center room full of AK-47s. With the lights off, the room was nearly pitch black. Images of Feldman's head smacking the concrete wall like a wet sponge flashed through my mind into the darkness on rapid repeat. A flood of emotion ranging from anger to guilt overcame me and I threw my aid bag to the floor. With nothing else in sight, I stepped forward and kicked the steel door of an AK rack.

Dave grabbed me by the shoulder, not giving much resistance when I pulled away. I knew we'd made a mistake by not putting his helmet back on. I took his helmet off; I should have put it back on before moving him. I should have taken charge of moving him over the wall to prevent him from falling. We'd compounded his injuries

98

and I knew it. He might have regained consciousness, but I knew there was a good chance that we'd pushed shrapnel into his brain by dropping him like that, a complication he might not survive. Expressing this to Dave was impossible. I'd try to begin a sentence and only get a few words out before I'd yell out profanity and start over. My mind was racing, replaying everything over and over.

Not even knowing he was in the room, SSG Muralles let me vent for a moment and then said in a very firm, yet reassuring tone, "Matthews, you did fine. You and Dave got him to the CCP alive; you guys did your job. Now, breathe and relax."

It was just the three of us in the room. Tears swelled up in my eyes, I leaned back against the wall and sat down. Doc Muralles left no room to argue, nor was there any point to. There was nothing more I could do and there was nothing I could say to change what had already happened. A voice inside my head reminded me that I was a Ranger and demanded that I maintain my composure. I began to breathe. As I began to calm down, Dave looked over and said, "Why don't you go smoke a cigarette?"

"You of all people are telling me to smoke?" I half-chuckled.

Dave smiled, "Yeah, man. Get out of here and go smoke."

The thought of a cigarette sounded amazing. Another artillery round impacted in the distance, but I was determined to feed my nicotine habit. I stood up and left the room, heading for the covered entrance of the building. Usually during the day, the leadership wouldn't allow me to smoke close to the entrance, all of them hating the habit, but today no one said a word as I lit up and took my first drag.

Back inside, SFC Jack had finished separating the water and MREs by squad, but he decided the artillery fire was still too heavy to disseminate all of the items, except the cans of Fanta soda. SFC Jack thought the platoon needed a morale boost and orange soda was the way to go about it. He called for 1st and 2nd squads to send guys to the CP to run sodas back to their positions. Gerhart and Hays from 1st Squad joined Salido and Ayman from second. None of the guys could believe it when SFC Jack passed out the junior-size cans of Fanta, almost in complete shock that they had just risked running over for something so trivial. I finished my cigarette as they went back to their positions and SFC Jack asked for two volunteers to run 3rd Squad their sodas. No one wanted to go out and take chances, but Jared volunteered any way.

"Ok, that's one. Jared's gonna need a Ranger buddy. Who's going with him?" SFC Jack asked of the guys taking shelter near the entrance. Nobody spoke up. I looked at Jared standing there and decided that I wasn't going to let him go alone.

"I'll go."

SFC Jack looked at me, I half-expected him to say that I couldn't go. Instead, he nodded and extended his arm with two cans in it. I grabbed them from him and began to load my cargo pockets with as many as I could fit while Jared did the same. With about six cans each, we were ready to head out. I looked at Jared and before I could ask him if he was ready, he took off running towards 3rd Squad's building. Without hesitation, I followed after him, but halfway between the buildings I felt and heard a can fall out of my hip pocket and hit the ground behind me. Part of me didn't want to stop, but I knew I couldn't leave it behind. In an instant, I knew that I was going to die over an orange soda. I reached down and picked it up before pivoting and resuming my mad dash for cover. Luckily, in the thirty seconds that we were exposed, no rounds came in and we both made it alive.

Most of the squad was in the back corner of the building in the same room, taking shelter from the artillery. A few of the guys were in a fortified position on the outside corner of the building. Everyone in the back room was in utter amazement that we just walked in with orange soda. Panatela remarked Fanta was the soda Nazis drank in World War II, but took one any way, while Bob did his version of the Fanta-Fanta song from the commercials. SFC Jack's plan of boosting morale had already worked. Once opened, not even artillery shells impacting outside prevented combat-hardened Rangers from enjoying their sodas. Sporadic impacts from artillery justified hanging out in 3rd Squad's building for a few minutes. While I was there, I passed out about a half pack of cigarettes, dodging questions about the blood all over me. Before we left, I watched from the window as a MH-47 Chinook helicopter flew in and hovered the ramp of the bird over the lip of the dam. In the distance, we could see Rangers load up Feldman into the helicopter, which shortly after took back off and flew away. A radio call came from SFC Jack to SSG Branford for Jared and I to get back to the CP. As I was headed to the entrance, I saw Jared's silhouette in the doorway. I called for him to wait up.

Jared turned and exclaimed, "BET YA I CATCH A ROUND BEFORE YOU DO! WOOHOO!" With that he was off. Barely containing myself in laughter, I followed behind almost determined not to let him win the wager he'd just made. We both sprinted back to the CP, nearly knocking several people over as we stumbled back in. SFC Jack looked at us like we had lost our minds before handing us two sodas for our work. Catching my breath, I found a place out of the way and plopped down, popping the tab of my soda can, instantly smelling orange flavor as carbonation mist escaped the top. I then put the can to my lips and went on to drink the best hot orange soda of my life.

Dave came up and told me they'd evacuated Feldman and he was still alive. He told me the JMAU doctors that had trained me back in the States were on the Chinook that picked him up. Knowing he was in the hands of the best trauma surgeons in the world was reassuring in a number of ways. Feldman was in the best care possible, and I knew for the rest of the mission those doctors would have our backs. As long as we could get our guys to those doctors alive, there was a 99% chance they'd survive. That knowledge reinforced that we were not alone out there. We might be thousands of miles away from home, but our country stood right behind us, providing our company with every asset in her military might, while expending millions of dollars of national treasure to ensure that we could fight on to the Ranger objective and complete the mission.

Pondering this while drinking my Fanta, I realized the value of the decision to include orange soda in our resupply and risk running it to 3rd Squad. When in an environment as corrosive and inhumane as a war-torn battlefield, something as simple as carbonated water and artificial flavoring allow enough of a break from the reality around you to regain the intestinal fortitude needed to overcome adversity.

While the majority of the platoon sat under the cover provided by the buildings during the artillery, a few Rangers were not so fortunate. For most of the day, Matt, Tommy, SPC Barron, and PFC Cannon took up an over watch position on the southeast corner of the hill, using a large pipe that had been exposed by erosion as cover. Without warning, a 155mm shell screamed in over their position so close they could feel the heat of the passing round. It exploded mere feet, uphill from their position, the momentum of the incoming round sending shrapnel away from their position. SPC Barron, a graduate of Ranger school, decided the impact had come too close for comfort and ordered the men to fall back to the buildings and for the next hour, the entire platoon sought refuge under cover provided by their concrete walls and roof. Pinned down in the safety of the buildings, the Iraqi artillery would focus on our position before shifting and concentrating on 2nd Platoon's positions on the other side of the river. Up and down the dam, back and forth between the two platoons, rounds would come in and explode around our perimeter.

The call was eventually made by the command element that the artillery pieces needed to be found and destroyed in order to ensure success of the mission and reduce the risk of further casualties. Our forward observers would generate a back azimuth on the artillery, but by the time the aircraft would fly over the suspected area, the guns would move to another position. We got the word that the 75th Ranger Regiment's Regimental Reconnaissance Detachment (RRD) had been tasked with searching out the artillery and calling air strikes for their destruction. While we waited for RRD to begin their search and destroy mission, the CP building took a direct hit. The overpressure of the round exploding on the rooftop shook the entire structure, kicking up dust and debris everywhere. A few guys were shaken up, but no one was wounded and amazingly, the building was mostly undamaged. Moments later, another direct hit was placed onto the building 2nd Squad was seeking refuge in. As with the CP, the round failed to destroy or heavily damage the building but the two impacts were entirely too close to large groups of Rangers.

Continuing to take direct hits on the buildings risked one of them eventually collapsing which would jeopardize an entire squad and dramatically reduce our combat efficiency. 1LT Joe and SFC Jack called for us to pull out of the buildings and into the ravine where I'd nearly been caught with my pants down the day earlier. Spread out in the ravine, our risk of mass casualties was significantly abated. While we lost the cover, we also lost the risk of the cover collapsing and further complicating the mission with a mass casualty situation. Furthermore, the low ground of the ravine prevented any Iraqi forward observer from being able to pinpoint our location, making it more difficult for him to direct effective fire.

Lying there, spread out as best we could, the platoon waited for the inevitable that never came. CSM Birch walked the line with his sniper rifle slung over his shoulder, passing out Twizzler licorice to the Rangers in the rocky depression, while close air support flew overhead and the sniper team pulled security from an abandoned concrete bunker near the Eagle's Nest. While we had fallen back, security had been maintained, and our hilltop was never in any danger of being maneuvered upon by the enemy. As the sun began to set, the artillery fell silent, and we effectively stopped receiving indirect fire for the night. RRD had used the back azimuths provided by our forward observers and began tracking down and calling for airstrikes on Russian-made 155mm artillery to the northeast. Shortly after nightfall, we pulled out of the ravine and resumed our positions on the line and buildings.

Since the Iraqis had hit our building, 1LT Joe and SFC Jack made the decision to split the CP into separate positions. 1LT Joe, Wolf, and I moved to 3rd Squad's building, while SFC Jack and Dave stayed in the building across from the mural. Wolf and I rotated radio guard all night, which was far from silent as the constant traffic of the search being carried out for enemy artillery continued. The occasional rumble of thunder to the northeast would follow shortly after our comrades in arms found another 155mm.

Morning came and the day reached mid-morning without incident. The CO wanted 3rd Platoon from Charlie Company to clear the power station and begin expanding our lines. 1st Platoon was also tasked with clearing CAS 1 and CAS 2, the two main buildings in the front of our hill. A small contingent was left behind to maintain over watch and security on the hilltop. For the first time, the platoon was being separated into two elements and since I was just an 11B assisting the medic, I didn't accompany the force tasked to clear the buildings, instead remaining with SSG Shank and the over watch.

The platoon loaded up several GMVs and took the dirt road that Iraqis had days earlier ambushed Sergeant Aaron's vehicle on. By radio, I listened as the platoon entered and cleared two buildings that had barely withstood multiple impacts from precision-guided bombs and was mostly rubble. Once inside, the platoon discovered why the Iraqis had been so hell-bent on consolidating there. Inside both buildings were caches of nearly every weapon in their arsenal, along with ammunition and grenades. There was only enough room in the GMVs to clear out the weapons in one of the buildings so the platoon took out what they could and returned to the top of the hill. After their return, those of us waiting at the top heard stories of rooms filled with the stench of death and the site of a desert that was littered with dead bodies beginning to decompose.

Charlie Company elements later seized the power station and had expanded our lines to the south. The day continued quietly and word came that at nightfall the rest of Charlie Company would be en route in a convoy to reinforce our positions. At daybreak, Charlie Company arrived from the southwest and began clearing the town to the south of the dam, Haditha proper. A few hours later, we began receiving indirect fire again, this time from the southeast. As we sent our air support to investigate, the pilots reported a large element of Iraqi T-55 tanks along with cargo trucks en route to our location. The news of enemy tanks generated excitement amongst all of the Rangers on the hill. We began preparing our positions for battle, but word quickly came down that F-16s and A-10s had attacked the convoy and destroyed over two-dozen T-55s. The sheer number of the destroyed armor pieces was a relief to all of us. While we had plenty of ammunition and the advantage of high ground, a fight of that scale would have made for a very long day.

Following the destruction of the column of armor, the battalion commander decided we were going to be relieved from our positions. The call came down and our platoon began preparing to exfil. We were leaving our GMVs in place, but removed all of our gear to take back to H1. 3rd Platoon, B Company would fly in at nightfall and we would leave on the birds they flew in on. Preparing to pull off the dam, I began to realize how exhausted I was. For over a week, I'd received only a few hours of rest a night, and when awake I was consumed with the tasks of combat. Those around me had even less sleep and for some, an even more harrowing experience. Radio guard had been pretty easy compared to digging all night and pulling security all day that the guys in the line squads had endured. While I'd only had the chance to fire five rounds, others had expended hundreds and I felt both fortunate and honored to be in first platoon, having fought alongside those men for that week.

At nightfall, we picked up our positions and fell back to the center of the dam. The battalion commander gave a speech congratulating us on our achievement and assured us that we'd earned our spot in Ranger history. Shortly after his speech, MH-47 Chinooks touched down on the dam and we boarded the helicopters back to H1. After six days of fighting, the assault force had killed at least 230 Iraqi soldiers while destroying twenty-nine tanks, twenty-eight 155mm artillery pieces, twenty-two 82mm mortars, six 60mm mortars, nine S-60's, fourteen AAA pieces, three cargo trucks, two motorcycles, and one kayak. We had also captured eighteen buildings, as well as eight ammo caches.

At the end of it all, the men to my left and right had forged a bond that could never be broken. We had fought and won the longest, sustained ground fight conducted by a single unit since the Vietnam War. Every one of us had given one hundred percent and then some, proving to the world and ourselves that a Ranger is a specially selected and well-trained soldier. We arrived at the cutting edge of battle and energetically met the enemy on the battlefield, defeating him because we were better trained and fought with all of our might. Like the generations that had come before us, and the ones who'd surely come after us, we fought on to the Ranger objective and completed the mission. Rangers Lead The Way!

-ROY MATTHEWS
3/75

JUNE 2003
"INTO THE FRAY"

This mission took place over the course of June 10th, 11th, and 12th of 2003. I don't remember much of what led up to the mission, but I remember being told that the 101st Airborne Division was assigned the mission first. Our chain of command scooped up the mission after the 101st requested more time to prepare. We were stationed at Baghdad International Airport (BIAP) in tents not too far off the tarmac. The objective was a terrorist training camp a few kilometers from Syria, located in a wadi out in the middle of nowhere. We were briefed that there were approximately seventy bad guys living and training there.

I was the Alpha Team leader for 2nd Squad, 1st Platoon, Bravo Company, of the 2nd Ranger Battalion. My team was light on Rangers as we had a knucklehead that we refused take out, since he wasn't ready for missions yet. I had McDonald as my SAW gunner and Working as my grenadier. Both were standup dudes that I knew could take care of themselves, had proven themselves time and again, and that I knew we could trust with our lives. Put simply, they were the shit.

The mission was slated to need at least a company-sized element. I believe that we took the mortars with us and I know that the anti-tank (AT) section went with as well. During the preparation for this target, we pored over imagery of the objective and where all the moving pieces would be going. We did the usual rehearsals and pre-combat inspections (PCIs) before a mission and I remember during these preparations the objective ended up being slipped 24 hours to the right.

It's a blur but the next day was more of the same. We were eventually told the mission was a go. 3rd Platoon left in the afternoon by ground while 1ˢᵗ and 2ⁿᵈ Platoon with attachments took off after dark, divided among Chinook and Blackhawk helicopters.

It was a long ride in the middle of the night. We landed at the forward aerial refueling point (FARP) and waited for the birds to fuel back up for the remainder of the infil. We weren't too far from the objective and while we were waiting for the birds to finish refueling, fast movers (fixed wing jets) were inbound to 'soften' the objective with an aerial bombardment for us in advance. I remember looking off in the distance and seeing the flashes of explosions in the direction of the objective.

I got back on the Chinook with my platoon and headed off for the final leg to the objective. I took one of my earplugs out and placed it in my pocket. We received all the normal time hacks on our way in, "one minute!"

"Thirty seconds!"

At this point I was down the middle of the bird, somewhere near the back. As with any mission, and especially on a Chinook, I loved it when the bird's engine changed sounds and began to flare. You could feel the heavy vibrations on the floor as it reached for the ground. I was on my right knee with one hand on my M-4 as it was seated on my left thigh pointed down. I had my other hand on my snap link on the end of my safety line with the gate open, hooked to the D-ring on the floor of the aircraft, waiting to release it as soon as I felt the bird touch down.

The wheels hit dirt, and the ramp dropped the rest of the way down simultaneously. Quickly moving off the bird's ramp, I peeled to my right, moving to the left side of the bird while the nose of the bird was facing the objective. As my boots hit the dirt, I could see the tracer rounds coming from our support by fire positions (SBF), which had set in moments ahead of the main effort (us) landing. I remember thinking, *Fuck. This is a big one.* We had not been in a major firefight yet, having hit dry hole after dry hole. Not today. These guys were rocking and rolling. We took a knee and waited for the Chinooks and Blackhawks to take back off. Once they cleared out, my platoon moved on line, spreading out and moving towards the objective.

It was flat all around us. We had the SBF positions on both sides of us shooting down into the wadi, thus making it difficult to see through our NODs as we moved forward. There were exchanges of gunfire happening all over in front of us. M-240Bs, AK-47s, PKMs, and RPGs all made their presence known. We had MH-6 'Little Birds' and AC-130 'Spectre' gunships on station and they had been making rocket and gun runs in an attempt to suppress the enemy gunfire.

This caused large fires to start burning, and despite the wadi's large size I remember it being so bright that I was able to see all the way to the other side, even without my NODs. We kept moving forward, when all of a sudden there was a loud explosion and I remember falling straight down to the ground. I had both earplugs out at this point. What I had just heard was a RPG being fired into the sky in an attempt by the bad guys to hit the Little Birds that were doing gun runs on them. The rocket had been fired from inside the wadi, which we still hadn't set eyes on yet, with the exception of the SBF element. I got back up and we inched closer to the wadi as gunfire was erupting all around us, it was very loud.

Another rocket went up in search of a Little Bird. We were now even closer, and it was even louder. Fuck. We inched closer. I already switched on the infrared laser on my rifle and began scouring the edge of the wadi in front of me. I could see fighting positions dug near the edge, but no one in them. I could also see down into some of the wadi, but wasn't about to stick my head over as two rockets had just come up from there.

One of the squads in my platoon had broken off to the left and posted up on a bend in the wadi. I could see that all of their lasers were on and jumping from the recoil of their rifles as those fellas began engaging. Where they were shooting was just to my front, but below me and still out of my line of sight. This was the main effort's spot. My spot, as it was my squad leading point for the main effort. Since I was the Alpha Team leader, I was the point man going into the biggest part of the fight. My thought at the time was, *Fuck, fellas, light them up!* As they were firing, we moved down the draw to our right, which the bad guys had been using as their driveway in and out of the wadi. With rifles at the ready, we began clearing it. I found myself in a draw about ten to fifteen feet deep with steep sidewalls. As I moved forward I saw what was left of their truck, it was a burning hulk. About ten feet back from the entrance to the wadi, my squad leader called for a halt. I remember saying to myself, "Fuck. Now they can see us easy." Vehicles burned bright and it lit up the entire wadi. I thought maybe I should throw some dirt on the fire to try and kill it, but thought better of it. I thought, *One, that won't do shit; and two, any bad guy watching the entrance will know we're there.*

While I was talking to myself and waiting for any target to present itself in front of me, my squad leader was on the radio telling them we were at our release point and asking them, *telling them* to let us MOVE. Here we were just sitting there. Gunfights just around the corner of the entrance we were sitting at. Violence of action. *Let me go!* We're giving these bastards a chance to catch a breath. Violence of action. Keep on the ropes. *Let's go!* I can hear my squad leader yelling into the mic, "We're here. We need to move!"

Finally, the order was given. "Watters! Go!" Up off my knee. Rifle up. Scanning. Hard left. Now into the gunfight. Where are you? Where are you? Scanning, walking, and stumbling. I remember thinking that the ground must have been torn up from the bombs that the fast movers dropped and it made walking a little tougher. That and now I was backlit by that big ass truck on fire and it's whiting out my NOD's and casting weird shadows. Holy shit, I'll never have another adrenaline dump like that one. Bad guys are in here. My boys above were just tearing shit up in here. Scanning. Then from behind me I heard two quick gunshots. I've never grabbed the ground that quick! I don't even remember thinking. Just reacting. Then my squad leader's yell rang out, "You motherfuckers better start double tapping these bodies as we come across 'em!" I would later learn that we hadn't been stumbling on churned up dirt from the bombs. I was actually walking on torsos and limbs. Our part of the objective had been where the tents had been. They dropped ordinance right over these. My squad leader later told me that the two shots I heard were from when he had stepped on a dead combatants arm and the guy jerked it so he fired two rounds right below his feet.

I popped back up after he yelled out to us and yelled back, "I would if I could see shit!" Being all jacked up had me breathing heavy and moving quickly. My eye protection quickly fogged up so I pulled them off and tucked them in my helmet band. I regained my footing and set out again. I could see about twenty meters ahead and I wasn't too worried about what was below me. My job was to find what was in front of us and deal with it. Let them double tap the bodies on the ground. I kept my weapon at the ready and kept scanning with both eyes, as one was naked and the other was behind the PVS-14's. I kept scanning left and right. I now had a sheer cliff wall to my left. I spotted what looked like a dug out fighting position where the wall of the wadi met the floor. I could see something inside and had my infrared laser and floodlight illuminating it. I could make out the shape of something in there but with the firelight behind me it was tough to make out what it was, so I kept scanning to my right.

As my aim moved back to the front of me, I spotted it. Circular glass. My body tensed at spotting something I knew was bad. I had enough time to get *Fuck . . ..* through my head when my world exploded. I remember thousands of orange sparks coming from my lower right front up past my head and left shoulder. I don't remember going airborne but I vaguely remember crashing back to down to earth. Things get fuzzy here. I then remember the most intense pain in my life and screaming my head off. Both my legs hurt and they hurt real fucking bad. I thought, *Ok, they're both just broken. You're okay.* I was on my back now and I lift my head up and I could see my left pant leg in some fire light. I could see that it was shredded mid-leg and there was nothing after that. Even though I was in a shitload of pain, I was just thinking, *Well. That sucks.* I then yelled out, "That son of a bitch shot my shifting leg off! 12 o'clock! 30 meters! Kill that motherfucker!"

I was later told that after I was knocked to the ground by the impact of the RPG explosion, I immediately sat back up and expended nearly an entire magazine towards the combatant who had just shot at me. My squad leader said that he watched me go up and come back down. He said that I sat back up and put my rifle in my shoulder and fired 29 rounds until my rifle broke, as shrapnel had pierced it. He said that when my rifle malfunctioned, I tried doing a mag change but couldn't as my left elbow sustained major wounds, as did my right hand. I remember none of this, which is one of the hardest parts of the entire ordeal. I want the satisfaction of knowing I shot at that motherfucker. I just don't remember it happening. I hit the ground so hard that I scalped the back of my head, pushing all my hair into the size of a fist, even though I had a MICH helmet on. That could be the reason I don't remember firing back.

I'm not a badass, and I give complete credit to my training, which allowed me to focus on the fact that there was a threat that needed to be dealt with. That, and my body taking care of itself by not allowing me to feel all the pain. I was still able to give commands to my team to tell them where the RPG came from. Damn it hurt. I was scared. I remember thinking that I could die right there. I also thought that there was no way that would happen, as I was still too damn coherent. I started to deny that this just happened to me. I thought, *Nope. Fuck you. I'm Matt Watters. This isn't supposed to happen. Not to me. I'm Matt Watters. No!*

I heard my squad leader, who was also a good buddy of mine, yell out "Medic!" The next thing I see is Doc G and he's nothing but 'asses and elbows'. He came in at a full sprint and slid in at my side. I said, "Doc, save my life" and he started going to town. Doc G came to us while we were already in Iraq and from the word "go" he was an absolute stud. He started working on me and my thoughts turned to my wife and little boy. *Fuck. I want to see them. Don't let it end here.* Doc starts talking to me and keeping me with him. "Sing me your ABC'S," he would say.

"Doc. Fuck you. I don't wanna."

"Tell me about Lindsey and Owen" he continued on. I rambled on about them while he worked quickly. McDonald and Working were busy with their own work. I swear to God they were right next to me laying some waste though. Those boys were rocking.

The next thing I heard was "Grenade!" Without hesitating, Doc G laid over top of me. Not a scratch on him at that point, and I was lying there all fucked up, but he was ready to give his life for what was left of mine. I still get misty-eyed to this day when I think about it. I'm not sure if it went off in the marshy area where the cattails were at or if it was a dud. Nothing happened.

Now there was a lull in the fight to the front of us. The Skedco was called up and my boys unrolled it and placed me inside and cinched it up. As per SOP, they put my body armor on top of me as they dragged me away. I wanted it off of me, as I was having a hard time breathing and felt the armor was the reason for that. I flung it off of me, and my platoon sergeant placed my MICH on my chest. I flung that off me as well, as I just wanted to breathe. Some of the boys then had the task of lugging my heavy ass back up the draw. They set me down and began to drag me up. The Skedco started to roll, which would result in me being dragged on my face. I was able to work my right arm free and at this time, I could see that part of my right thumb was severed. I thought, 'Huh. Looks like Pac Man.' I liberated my right arm from the Skedco and placed it on the ground to keep me from rolling onto my face. I yelled out something to the effect of, "You motherfuckers!" These guys had been, and still were getting shot at. I then realized that they were helping me, and called out to them as they lifted my ass up, "I love you guys!"

They hauled me to the CCP and dropped me off. My first sergeant was there. God, it was good to hear his voice. He had also been my platoon sergeant in a previous platoon before I took over as a team leader. I cried out, "First Sergeant! I'm fucked up!" He had called me "Agua" at times, as a play on my name. He told me that I was going to be all right, and he was going to take care of me. He reached into my pocket and retrieved my casualty feeder cards, and while hunched over me using my chest as a desk he began filling them out. I heard several rounds snap right over our heads, and the RTO came running up and yelled, "First Sergeant! We're getting shot at!" Without missing a beat he says, "Fuck it. We'll take care of it in a minute."

A MEDEVAC was called for, and a Chinook came in response. I believe they came under fire as I heard the mini-guns bark a time or two as the bird descended. I was hustled on and strapped in. There were litters on the walls of the bird and I was placed on the floor underneath one of these stacks of litters. I felt the bird power up and take off. I could see one of the crewmembers walking back and forth the length of the bird. I was so damn thirsty. I'd lost a bunch of blood and it felt like I had been chewing on cotton balls for a month. I knew the flight crew always had ice water, as the lucky bastards always seemed to have a fridge or freezer allowing them to have COLD water. I yelled out to him as he passed, but he couldn't hear me. He walked by again, and I was able to reach out and grab his ankle. He bent down and I yelled to him that I wanted water. He walked off to retrieve it, and came back holding a large bottle of water. He held it to my lips for me so that I could drink. He had frozen the water bottle earlier and had been carrying it through the duration of the mission, which resulted in it being half water and half ice. It was the best water I had ever had, or will ever have.

The Chinook landed back at the FARP and the ramp dropped. There was a guy already waiting on a four-wheeler. The aircrew hoisted me up and placed me on the back of it, and the rider took off like a bat out of hell. I thought, *Fuck! We're gonna eat it.* He raced up to the JMAU bird, which was a C-130 all decked out like a flying hospital. The quad driver and medics from the JMAU bird hauled me up the ramp, took me out of the Skedco, and strapped me down to a table on the bird. The white lights were on inside the bird, and I took my first look at myself. My field top and brown t-shirt had already been ripped/cut away. I could see blood all over my torso and arms. I was weak and being strapped down, so I just laid my head back down. At this time I could feel a warm sensation in my butt/crotch area. I was pretty sure I had shit myself and told the medics I thought as much. They gave me an, "Ah! No big deal. That happens when this happens." I vaguely remember the bird taxiing but not taking off. I think that I had been sedated at this point.

The next thing I remember was waking up (sort of) in Kuwait. I was later told that there had been a lull in the fighting as I was being treated. Apparently there had actually been two guys in the fighting position from which the rocket came. They told me that when I sat back up and shot at them, one of the guys got out and ran. The remaining RPG gunner hunkered back down and loaded another round. One of my best friends was on that intermediate support by fire line that was still up on the bend in the wadi. He said that when the RPG gunner popped back up to hit us again, they unloaded on him and in his words, "We sent that motherfucker straight to hell."

-MATT WATTERS
2/75

Chapter Four

"In my dreams I hear again the crash of guns, the rattle of musketry, the strange, mournful mutter of the battlefield."

DOUGLAS MACARTHUR

A s the Regiment progressed into the year 2004, it became apparent to all in the organization that the unit was in a time of transition. The Rangers had been on a sustained rotation of combat deployments since 2001, and were coming off the invasion and first year of combat in Iraq. The mission and operational realities began to reveal the need for change within the Regiment, which raised questions about the unit's identity. Questions such as whether the Regiment identified more with the "Army" or with the Command arose, or were they both? Is that possible? If so, what does that mean?

CSM Gregory Birch, who had spent much of his career at Fort Bragg in the Army's premiere special missions unit, was now the Regimental Sergeant Major bringing a unique mindset that filtered down. The Regiment had previously been primarily relegated to larger raids that encompassed multiple platoons, or supporting the Command's SMUs with security and other tasks. Now, the Regiment had begun to move away from that and into unknown realms that used to only be the purview of the Command's SMUs. It seemed that Regimental leadership was pushing for a "bump up" in the Commands' community, and they were more than proving that they deserved a seat at that table. Rangers were now fully integrating with the Command, carrying out missions independently and of the highest importance. The platoon direct action raid became the 'bread and butter' for the majority of those missions, a transition from working as a company to working as an independent platoon.

There was a palpable shift in mindset from "advanced light infantry" to exclusively "special operations." The Regimental Reconnaissance Detachment (RRD, now 'RRC') became the premiere surveillance asset for the Command. Battalion reconnaissance sections were stood up and validated by the top leadership in the SOCOM community. A fourth week was added on to the Ranger Indoctrination Program that specifically focused on shooting. The training cycle between deployments moved to a close quarters combat, or "Battle Drill 6" focus that had Rangers spending thousands of hours in shoot houses and perfecting breaching techniques. This was the beginning of what would become the most lethal and fierce direct action raid force that the world had ever seen, with some platoons executing over a hundred missions in a single ninety-day deployment.

To visibly illustrate how much this was a time of transition, the traditionally strict adherence to unit Standard Operating Procedures (SOPs) began to loosen. The infamous "high and tight" haircut, which had been a Ranger hallmark, was replaced with a less conspicuous "normal" haircut. The Regiment stood up a "Force Modernization" section, which resulted in a uniform makeover. Rangers ditched the Army-issued MOLLE gear for SOF-peculiar plate carriers and pouches. Rangers traded in their standard issue boots for Oakley S.I. assault boots and Merrell Sawtooths. Even the Oakley ballistic sunglasses, or "Eye Pro," raised eyebrows within the Regiment's NCO Corps.

This time of transition was not without turmoil however. When the Regimental Commander issued Note #2, which repealed the "high and tight" as the standard haircut, there was a lot of pushback. One 3/75 First Sergeant actually ordered the men in his company to keep the "high and tight" as the standard, until he was later overruled. NCOs who were raised with strict adherence to SOPs found themselves at whiteboards drawing what they deemed "the new standard" for haircuts. This may seem like a very insignificant and trivial change to those on the outside, but to those in Regiment at the time, it was just as significant as the change from black to tan berets.

A rift began to form between some senior NCOs and junior NCOs about the direction the Regiment was going in. The younger Rangers fully embraced the new SOF focus, while some in the more senior billets found the changes counter-culture to how they had been raised, and how they viewed the Ranger infantry tradition. The challenge of keeping their identity as Rangers while not sacrificing mission effectiveness was a topic of debate that began in 2004 but would rage for years to come. NCOs who were charged with training their men for real-world combat deployments, found themselves in the peculiar position of making new standards and training for a new way of fighting. It was not uncommon for a Ranger who had just freshly donned their Scroll and Tan Beret to immediately join his new platoon on deployment. Gone were the days of having months of training to prepare, men in this new breed of Rangers often found themselves pulling the trigger overseas before doing their first training mission in garrison.

Although change was in the air, deployments and missions continued at an ever-increasing pace. The global war on terror was not going away, with ten bombs exploding simultaneously on trains carrying commuters in Madrid, Spain killing 190 and injuring 2,000. Usama Bin Laden released multiple videos, confirming that he was still alive and still a threat. Combat operations continued in Afghanistan, with RRD Team 3 performing yet another military free-fall combat jump into Afghanistan in July to emplace tactical surveillance equipment. The priority had shifted to Iraq by this point however. The majority of Rangers found themselves taking part in General McChrystal's increasingly effective head hunting task force that was coming off an important victory with the capture of Saddam Hussein in December 2003.

Despite the fact that Rangers were advancing at a frighteningly lethal pace, it was still war and the year was unfortunately not without sacrifice. On April 22nd, Corporal Patrick Tillman, a former NFL football player who had become a Ranger in 2/75 was accidentally killed by friendly fire in Afghanistan. In addition, three more Rangers would be killed in action in 2004. Private First Class Nathan Stahl, Corporal William Amundson, and Sergeant Michael O'Neill all paid the ultimate sacrifice. The Ranger Regiment was on a roll, but it was now clear they had joined a fight with no end in sight, and were in this for the long haul.

EARLY 2004
"TEAM BAGHDAD"

I served from 2001 to 2005 on active duty. I did three deployments: Afghanistan in the summer of 2002, Iraq from late 2003 to spring 2004, and back to Afghanistan in the fall of 2004. By far the most action packed and intense deployment for me was Iraq. I was 21 years old, and had recently been promoted to corporal. I missed the invasion, as I was in Ranger School at the time. Knowing that I was missing out on the war lit a fire under my ass to push myself and go straight through, which I did. As I pinned on my Ranger Tab, the invasion was winding down, and my platoon was being sent home. All of my peers received a combat star on their jump wings that deployment, so it was bittersweet going straight through Ranger School and still missing out.

That summer training cycle was one of the most intense times of my life. We trained hard, as we knew we were going back. I remember how miserable it was, but the skills I learned and practiced would later manifest themselves as quite literally the difference between life and death.

Just days before the start of 2004, there I was, boots on the ground in Iraq. My platoon was very senior at the time, top heavy with experienced Rangers. We were sent to live in the special operations compound called the "mission staging site" (MSS) on the Tigris River, which was inside the Green Zone in Baghdad. We were supposed to rotate with other platoons, but as the days and weeks wore on, we established a good working relationship with C Squadron of the Army Special Mission Unit we were located with. They requested that we stay put, so there we were going on missions day in, and day out. I remember being shot at via rifle fire or incoming mortar rounds nearly every single day. Most of the time we just ignored it, since we were on the way to go get someone or something and had to carry on the mission uninterrupted. We were a component of the Command's Task Force. We also did some work with the British SAS, U.S. Special Forces, as well as the Polish Special Forces, but for the most part we were with the Brits or the Army SMU.

We went out almost every single night. We were doing real missions, everything I signed up to do. My element was responsible for catching 14 of the most wanted men in Iraq at the time, whose faces were on the famous playing card deck that was published. I even spent four hours standing on top of Chemical Ali, the guy who gassed the Kurds. We didn't have any open seats and had no place better to put him when we hauled him in.

I was a turret gunner; manning the M2 .50 caliber machine gun on the top of the Humvee was my place as I was a gun team leader. Weapons Squad was used to either man the guns or drive. All three members of my gun team were on guns, and I made sure we cleaned them and kept them ready every single day. My commander was happy we did that, although he was sent home early because of some personal things that came up. After that, I spent the rest of the deployment as the platoon sergeant's gunner, as he took over command of the platoon.

There was an accident involving a Pandur armored vehicle at the gates of Baghdad International Airport that took out most of my squad, and we were already short staffed to begin with. It happened roughly halfway through the deployment, although exact dates are fuzzy at this point. The Pandur hit a concrete barricade going at a high rate of speed. I witnessed the whole thing, and it's possible that an IED was involved. Anyway, the vehicle went flipping through the air, end over end. I didn't think there was any way anyone could have survived it. When we ran over to the wreck, the squad leader was on top of the vehicle moaning, obviously concussed. He was still trying to find the men and check sensitive items. Shortly before Ranger

School I attended an EMT course, so I was a squad level medic. I was the only one with advanced medical training, with the others from my vehicle (there were only two vehicles going to BIAP that night) who were RFR qualified.

The turret gunner was my friend Bill; we were close having gone through Basic, Airborne, and RIP together. The top piece of the vehicle landed on top of him. It was roughly a 6' by 12' by 8" thick piece of steel. Somehow my vehicle driver Josh and I pushed the plate off him, and I had Josh pull traction on his neck while I inserted an airway to keep him alive. His neck felt like mush, as he had broken his C-1 vertebrae, which put him in a medically induced coma for months. He eventually recovered enough to function. The other two were privates who were somehow flung right alongside the Pandur, landing next to it. I administered and directed medical care as the platoon sergeant, SFC B, called in the MEDEVAC birds. I rode in the bird with the wounded guys to the hospital to help the medical staff, at the time the hospitals were extremely short staffed.

Everyone survived somehow though. The Pandur was also on fire, with insurgents shooting at us from the overpass a few hundred meters back. I remember almost shooting at the Army Reservists who were gate guards, as they rendered zero aid to us. They were only a hundred meters away. I still have those boots I was wearing, and they still have my squad leader's blood on them. He was really messed up, and ended up with a big steel plate in his face, but made a full recovery. It was the same with the other two privates, Jon and John.

We went into Fallujah on a very regular basis that deployment. The 82nd Airborne had it locked down tight with the brigade-sized element based there. The problems didn't start until it was handed over to the Marines. They decided to hang back to "win hearts and minds," which doesn't really work with Al Qaeda insurgents. The insurgents used the lull to put their men, weapons, and equipment into place in order to take the city. So, at the end of March 2004, a massive storm was brewing. My platoon and others from C Co. 3/75, along with C Squadron from the Army SMU entered Fallujah to conduct another night raid. The Al Qaeda fighters had prepared a massive ambush with RPGs, heavy machine guns, and mortars on the other end of the city. They were setting up on both sides of the road in a massive "Polish" ambush, with crossfire and kill lanes shooting across toward each other, but with the Americans in the middle.

They were hoping to catch a convoy headed into the city from the military base with the intention of killing them all. What they received was a convoy of Rangers and Operators headed from the city to the base, since we were coming back after a mission, by way of Baghdad. I imagine they were a bit confused, but they hit us anyway. I remember seeing green tracers everywhere at the front of the convoy, thinking, *Wow, they're really jacking them up!* Then I remembered that our side didn't have green tracers. I pulled the charging handle on my M2 and joined the fight. I kept my gun thundering as we made our way through the kill zone. There's nothing like shooting a .50 caliber machine gun into a crowd of bad guys, it's a Ranger gun team leader's wet dream.

The firefight was short, but extremely violent. There were targets on both sides of the road. The SAW gunner, Richard, and I engaged as fast as we could acquire targets, and they were everywhere. Thankfully the line team leader, Michael, on my vehicle spent many years in Weapons Squad and knew enough to concentrate his efforts into getting more ammo out and ready to feed my gun. I cleaned my gun every day, and it was now paying off. The whole time my platoon sergeant made sure I stayed on target and helped direct me. I recall the sensation of him grabbing my leg to get my attention and pointing towards more targets. I remember walking my tracers into a bad guy's gun, as he was doing the same to me, the rounds were so close I could feel the heat of the bullets on my neck, but I got him first. Some of the guys who saw it thought I was hit and were grabbing me trying to dress my non-existent wounds when we made it out of the kill zone. I also recall shooting a structure down along with the men inside it not more than 20 feet from me. The close proximity of their muzzle flashes startled me.

The ambush disabled some of our vehicles, so we had to hook them up and tow them out of the kill zone. My friend Jarred, who was on his vehicle's gun, took a round through the neck and it was a miracle that the battalion surgeon happened to be on the vehicle behind him and managed to save his life. An Operator also had his jaw blown off and survived. It was a miracle we didn't have more casualties. There were bullets pinging off my Humvee everywhere.

Video from the AC-130 above us would later reveal that we had multiple near-misses from RPG rockets, but none of them seemed to find their mark. The ambushers were caught off-guard themselves by the lethal and accurate fire given in response, as we killed most of them. When we made it clear of the kill zone, the Little Birds began their runs, taking out most of the survivors. A handful escaped, but were promptly dispatched by the cannons of the AC-130 gunship as they sought shelter from the Little Birds. I had fired most of my rounds, and had to be given more ammunition from other vehicles to continue. I had kept my gun clean and did my job.

This was a prelude to what is considered the first battle of Fallujah. The Al Qaeda elements had arrived in force to retake the city, but we killed them first. The next day a group of Blackwater contractors were killed and hung from a bridge in retaliation. Conventional units went to re-take the city and apprehend the group responsible but were forced to pull back, letting the city fall in the first part of April 2004. As for us, it was time to go home. We were now battle-hardened warriors, and had paved the way for the Ranger Regiment to begin the transition to an increased level of responsibility in the special operations community. Our actions and demeanor while working closely with C Squadron proved that Rangers could hang with the best in Iraq. We were Team Baghdad.

This cauldron brewed the skill-set and experiences that would create the core leaders within C-1 3/75, the elite platoon that Leo Jenkins knew as a medic and featured in his book *Lest We Forget*. I was given a line team leader position and promoted to Sergeant after that deployment. C-1-1 was stood back up (it was disbanded due to lack of manpower) and we became the "Dobermans," a nickname given to us by the first sergeant because of our ferocious demeanor, as we had three of the most squared away and badass sergeants of the Regiment!

-Nick Green
3/75

FALL 2004
"MOSUL"

October 2004 marked my first deployment. It was seven months since I graduated the Ranger Indoctrination Program and arrived at the 3rd Ranger Battalion in Fort Benning, Georgia. I didn't know what to expect, I was just a Private First Class who spent the last seven months being yelled at, getting smoked, training, jumping, being yelled at again, and then smoked some more just because I looked like I could use it.

I was able to do some really great training since I arrive at the unit; ATV and dirt bike operations, nighttime/defensive driving, non-traditional vehicle entry classes, rotary wing exercises in Kentucky, fixed wing exercises, time on the shooting range, and all my radio operator training. I really didn't know how it would play out on deployment since I wasn't assigned to an actual platoon.

I was heading out to Mosul, Iraq, a city in the northern part of the country on the border with the autonomous region of Kurdistan. Our unit would be part of Task Force North, one of the three components that would make up the Command's task force in Iraq (the other two being TF Central and TF West), which oversaw the operation created to track down the only terrorist ranked higher than Usama Bin Laden on the United States' most wanted list, along with the rest of his Al-Qaeda operatives in Iraq.

In late 2004, Iraq was certainly a pretty busy place to be as both the Iraqi insurgency and Al-Qaeda were very active. Although more so in the central areas of Iraq, such as Baghdad, and Fallujah, Mosul had its own al-Qaeda cell, which definitely wasn't on vacation. Just the previous year, an Army Special Mission Unit with the support of the 101st Airborne tracked down and killed Saddam's sons Uday and Qusay in Mosul.

VIOLENCE *of* ACTION

The Ranger assault package being sent to Mosul consisted of a single platoon from Alpha Company and a small support element. There couldn't have been more than fifty of us in total. Once there, we would join an Army SMU element that numbered roughly fifteen men. For the next three to four months, this small force would be responsible for hunting down Al-Qaeda and key members of the insurgency.

We touched down in Mosul in early October. My expectation of what Iraq was like shattered the moment the ramp came down. Mosul was goddamn freezing, it rained the whole time, and the city was gigantic. I think the last time anybody fought in the deserts of Iraq was during Desert Storm. This massive urban sprawl was not what I expected.

Our small force was located on FOB Freedom, later dubbed FOB Courage, a medium-sized coalition base that rested on a hill overlooking the city. This wasn't exactly an ideal location, as insurgents didn't have a hard time visually pinpointing where their mortars and rockets were landing. FOB Freedom was consistently plagued by indirect fire; but the actual chances of a person being hit were incredibly low.

The deployment started off slow, and throughout October, the team went out on maybe 8-10 objectives. To my surprise, I actually went on a handful of them with the force as well. One of which would end up being my first and also last "pulling-a-blocking-position-for-an-SMU" type of objective. That is the type of mission that everybody outside of the Ranger Regiment thinks we do 99% of the time, but in reality, we rarely ever did.

As a junior radio operator that wasn't part of a platoon, it was incredibly rare that I was even allowed on objectives, as almost everybody in my shoes would be put in a watch-and-learn situation their first deployment. I wrapped up that three-month deployment with close to twenty direct action raids. Nothing to brag about whatsoever, but it's twenty more than I was expecting to be on.

October came and went; time flew on deployment. It was mostly uneventful but we did have a couple of casualties in the platoon from a single objective. A Ranger took a round to his leg that severed his femoral artery, but was quickly treated and evacuated by our medics. A second Ranger had taken a round near his armpit, which he didn't notice until he was back on base. He was a hard son of a bitch.

We did have one death in mid-October; my friend Bill Amundson was a mortarman assigned to one of the platoons in Afghanistan when his vehicle rolled over during a combat patrol. We had gone out in downtown Columbus together a few days before flying out. A bunch of drunken dancing fools, hard to believe it's been a decade since.

But things were definitely heating up in Iraq. The Marines were gearing up to enter Fallujah for the second time after the coalition failed to hold the city back in May of 2004 following the First Battle of Fallujah. And now 10,000 U.S. Marines were about a week away from assaulting the city. Everybody with a television knew about it, it was plastered all over the news networks. Hell, that's how I found out about it.

A couple of days later Task Force North discovered something that wasn't being shown on CNN. Dozens upon dozens of trucks filled with armed insurgents were spotted by surveillance platforms to be leaving Fallujah and heading north. Hundreds, possibly even a thousand enemy fighters were making the five-hour drive north for Mosul. This was a smart choice on their part considering that U.S. forces in that area of operations were fewer than 2,000 strong.

On November 7th, the U.S. Marines invaded Fallujah, and we all crowded around the television watching the news footage. The Second Battle of Fallujah had begun. On November 8th the convoy of insurgents reached Mosul, marking the start of the Battle of Mosul.

Mosul, a city of almost two million people, ironically had a disproportionately small U.S. presence compared to the other large areas in Iraq; this is due largely to our reliance on the well-funded and well-trained Kurdish Peshmerga forces that could reach Mosul at the drop of a hat. The 25th Infantry Division was the largest unit in the area, and an entire battalion drove south to join the U.S. Marines in their fight. Sometimes I wonder if the 25th ID Stryker convoy and the insurgent truck convoy from Fallujah passed each other on the highway. I laugh just thinking about it.

When I tell you that the insurgents almost took the entire city on November 8th, please do not think I am exaggerating. In a well-coordinated attack they assaulted numerous Iraqi police stations killing dozens and making off with heavy weapons, RPGs, and flak jackets. In the coming days, 1,500 Iraqi security forces personnel would abandon the city. Mosul would not have a police force for another month.

Our small special operations task force didn't play a huge part in the first couple of days of the assault on Mosul. We were assigned to hunt down the insurgent and al-Qaeda leadership. What could seventy men do to retake a city of two million? That task was given to the 25th Infantry Division, and we would play a supporting role as needed.

The next morning, on November 9th, I looked out into the city and it was a scene straight from the old Gulf War footage with dozens of burning oil fields off in the desert. Except here, the black plumes of smoke that were seen scattered across the urban sprawl were destroyed police stations, gas stations, and massive truck bombs. The fires would burn all day.

Whatever, this is Iraq, I thought, and went on with my normal routine, which included a run along the perimeter wall of the base. I was a quarter mile away from our compound when the distinct sound of an incoming mortar round exploded. No big deal I thought, we would get two to three-a-day out here on average. They never hit anybody.

Then another. And another. It was a real deafening sound no matter where you were, so it was hard to ascertain how close the impact site was. They kept coming. *Okay this is different,* I said to myself. I ended up taking shelter in a small concrete bunker that fits four to six grown men. I was the only American inside amongst four Iraqi civilian contractors. The mortar rounds kept coming. The indirect mortar attack didn't last more than three minutes. All told, around fifteen rockets and 82mm mortar rounds were fired against us.

I immediately sprinted to the Task Force compound, as our leadership would want to get accountability on all its men. The first person I ran into was SFC "O", the senior Ranger medic in Mosul. "Donov, come with me!" He was carrying his aid bag. We hopped onto our ATV and made a short drive to the 25th ID's headquarters personnel living area, which was literally down the road from our own compound. Doc "O" pulled the ATV up to one of the 'hooches', which is what we called the small white trailer that soldiers lived in. Numerous soldiers were standing outside quiet. A sickening feeling in my stomach began to form at the sight of the soldiers' apparent lack of sense of purpose and lethargic demeanor.

Doc rushed right in through the door but I hesitated. I stood there for a few seconds trying to prepare myself. It didn't work. I walked in anyway. My memory is hazy, but I remember the trailer to be very dark. The mortar round had exploded on the roof and not inside the trailer. We found the soldier inside slumped over on his laptop. I would find out later that he was in the middle of writing an email to his wife.

When the mortar round exploded, a piece of the shell casing broke through the top and entered into the top of his head. He was dead instantly. I resented Doc for bringing me there. What was the point? It was obvious that the initial call confirmed that the soldier was deceased. He could have asked any one of the other soldiers from the man's unit standing outside to help load the body.

We covered the man with his own blanket and lay him in the back of the ATVs small flatbed. He was completely covered aside from the desert combat boots sticking out. His blood slowly trickled down onto the gravel where it formed into a small dark red pool. Doc drove away with the body to the hospital and I made the short walk back to our compound.

It was the first and only time I would see an American soldier who had been killed. It was a horrendous feeling that I can only describe by its similarity to a really bad heartbreak. This was a man I've never seen before and yet here I am ten years later and my heart still hurts for him. I am not a religious man, but I am thankful every single day that I never had to physically witness the death of my Ranger friends who were killed in action over the years. I can't imagine the feeling of hopelessness that would surely ensue.

I later looked him up, Horst Gerhard Moore, a Major with the 25th Infantry Division. His friends and family called him Gary and he left behind a wife and daughter. A second American died in the attack, a master sergeant from the Air Force and another American contractor with Aegis was seriously wounded.

Slowly but surely, over the next few days the small U.S. force began to regain security in parts of the city, which still had no presence of a police force. A small group from our task force was asked to defend a nearby government facility being harassed by insurgent forces. It was either a police station or a Kurdish installation. We took off in a Black Hawk from the FOB and landed on the rooftop of the nearby 12-story Nineveh International Hotel. The flight lasted twenty seconds.

Snipers from both the Army SMU and the Rangers immediately set up shop overlooking the besieged building and began engaging targets on the ground. The fire support specialist and I, as well as a few other Rangers who provided security hung around while the others engaged.

A few days later the Battle of Mosul officially ended, but the city was now completely destabilized. The Iraqi police wouldn't even show back up until December. The mission parameters were now changing for TF North. The Ranger platoon and the Army SMU troop would relocate to FOB Marez, which was an American base about five miles away that was connected to a separate coalition forces airbase. The Command wanted us to have easier access to helicopters because thus far we were rolling out in our Ground Mobility Vehicles (GMV) and Pandur armored personnel carriers.

I remember hoping FOB Marez was as nice and cozy as FOB Freedom was. Then I found out I'm not going with the group. "What? Why?" I asked my team leader. I hated the thought of not being with the unit. "The Special Mission Unit is leaving a liaison team here and they need a RTO. You're it" he replied. It took a few seconds to process until I fully understood how awesome this assignment would be. I replied, "Roger Sarnt!" and went on my merry way.

What's a liaison team you ask? Simple and just like the name states; a small team is responsible for liaising with one unit on behalf of another. That unit would be the 25th Infantry Division that was staying put in FOB Freedom and the other unit is obviously Task Force North that was relocating to FOB Marez. Our mission was to tag along with the 25th on their objectives and supplement their capabilities with on-site interrogations, sensitive site exploitation, and pretty much anything else they might miss. Even the smallest details can sometimes lead to the next high value target. Mosul was now fraught with high-level insurgents who came from Fallujah and the "mop-up" operations had to be done right.

Our little group consisted of Pup the team leader, Trevor, Ivica, Chase, Sam and myself. Aside from Sam and I, all were operators with the SMU. Sam was a longtime operator with a special Army unit that provided intelligence to special operations forces. Ivica, was the oldest operator on his team. He recently celebrated his 42nd birthday and spent a lot of his downtime either running or playing HALO on Xbox. Uniquely enough, he was born in Croatia where for a few years he served in the Yugoslavian military. He moved to the United States in the late 1980s and joined the Army as a medic, later transitioning into the Special Forces. Fast-forward almost sixteen years, and he was now an assistant team leader in the SMU.

Pup, the team leader, whose real name was not actually Pup as that was his nickname, was a veteran of the Ranger Regiment and had been with the special mission unit for quite a while. The rest of the men on Pup's team were semi-new to the unit. Chase was straight out of the Operator Training Course and was on his first deployment with the SMU. We got along very well, as he was also a former communications guy in the Ranger Regiment. For the next month and a half until the end of our rotation, we would live and work together out of the tiny compound that was once the Task Force North headquarters.

The first week or so we were together was pretty slow; the 25th ID didn't have the same operational tempo as us and would plan direct action raids days before they actually happened. The time in between they would go on patrol throughout Mosul in their Stryker convoys. Most of the time we sat around and chatted around the compound or played darts.

I remember our first raid with the 25th ID pretty vividly. We didn't have any vehicles of our own any more as they went with the main force to Marez, so we walked over to the staging area. The Operators were looking all cool with their fancy gear. Many soldiers judge each other based on what they wear and how "cool" they look. They also didn't wear any name insignia, branch insignia, or even rank. So of course here I am trailing behind them on the way to the 25th ID staging area trying to rip the rank off of my collar, as the Regiment had not yet transitioned to sterile uniforms at this time. Chase turned around and caught sight of what I was doing and just laughed, "Too late now!"

Shit, it was. We were already there. I had one insignia off, but the other was dangling on remaining stitches. I don't think anybody noticed my cherry ass. If any of my Ranger NCOs were there, I would have been destroyed for hours and then made fun of for months. You could always tell who the Rangers were at that time. We were the only Army unit who wore a desert camouflage uniform with BDU colored (green) rank and name patches. Sometimes it was hilarious because it was very hard to tell what rank each one of us was unless you were right up close. I can't tell you how many times big Army folks have mistakenly saluted me overseas.

At the staging site, as expected, a lot of the guys were staring at the small group. Hell, most of the time Rangers would get looks from other units questioning whom we were with. Fancy equipment means money, money means importance, and most of the time importance means special operations. So I can't imagine what they must have thought when they saw the Operators roll up with their dual night vision goggles, fancy weapons, hiking boots, and completely sterile uniforms.

My first objective as an RTO with the SMU went down perfectly. And so did all the rest we went on together for the remaining month and a half. I learned a lot from those guys, and a lot about the world they operated in, to include closely held secrets about where they had been and what they had done. It was an opportunity not many of my rank and experience at the time would normally have.

I also received a firsthand glimpse into the world of human intelligence and informant handling. Sam, the intelligence operator, consistently used me as his personal sidekick throughout his duties. We would change into civilian clothes and leave the FOB in his SUV in the middle of the night to drive into Mosul and pick up Iraqi informants who were selling us information. We'd roll right up to the gate guards of the FOB and the only instructions Sam would give them were, "Hey guys, we'll be back in about an hour. Look for this vehicle and don't shoot us up."

He never informed the Task Force headquarters and the rest of the liaison team never knew we were out in the middle of the city picking up informants. Was it reckless? In the eyes of a cherry like myself, probably. But that's what we were taught. In the world that this guy belonged to, conducting counter-intelligence and counter-terrorism operations throughout Iraq, Afghanistan, and other places - it was business as usual. Who was I to argue with somebody who has been doing this for years? Besides, I would sound like a scared little girl had I expressed my doubts. So I rolled with him into the middle of one of the most dangerous cities in Iraq in the back of his Toyota 4Runner, in the middle of the night. Nothing but my M-4 rifle and his Glock sidearm were standing between us and an ambush that would most likely be followed by a beheading on the internet for all the world to see.

This was my first deployment as a Ranger. I realized the world of special operations is precise, complicated, and it'll keep you on your toes. You have no choice but to keep up with the pace. The images I had of massive battles and multi-day engagements did not belong in that world. The men I lived and worked with for such a short period of time made a significant impression on me that lasts to this day and I'm sure until the end of my days.

Eight months later, in August of 2005, I was in Jalalabad, Afghanistan on my second deployment when I noticed a press release on the U.S. Army Special Operations Command website. The headline read, "Two Bragg Soldiers, one Benning Soldier die in Iraq." A sickening feeling formed in my stomach when I saw the pictures of Trevor and Ivica. Their vehicle drove over an improvised explosive device in western Iraq, killing them instantly. A Ranger was also killed and a third Operator succumbed to his wounds a few days later. It was a huge loss to the special operations community. For me, it was difficult to grasp how a cowardly device like an IED could take out such great warriors. Years of dedicated service and grueling training, only to be killed by a scumbag with a cell phone hiding out of sight. It was a hard pill to swallow.

I will always remember trying to converse with Ivica in my native tongue of Bulgarian while he spoke back to me in Croatian, subsequently giving up and telling me, "Man, my Bulgarian is better than yours!" I also remember the many games of darts I played with Trevor, or tirelessly trying to teach him how to use the 117F radio. It's been nine years, and when I look back, these were the individuals who made me want to be a better Ranger. These men are always the first to come to mind. Rest in peace.

-IASSEN DONOV
3/75

WINTER 2004
"FIRST DEPLOYMENT"

Succotash. Again. The waxy lima beans and flavorless corn occupy the upper right corner of my Styrofoam tray. A sort of flank steak with density far in excess of that of the plastic instruments intended to dissect it acts as the main course. I haven't gone back to the salad bar since my senior medic, Sergeant Otic, nearly died from ingesting some of the fecal matter that made its home on the brown iceberg lettuce. It was this or an MRE and I had already gone that route several times this week.

Our dining facility was a dingy white tent that was illuminated by the constant buzzing of generators just outside the front entrance. The large white tent sat in the middle of a small Forward Operating Base (FOB) known as Salerno, just outside of the town of Khost, Afghanistan. It was late 2004 and just a few weeks ago I was at Fort Bragg, North Carolina graduating from the JFK Special Warfare Special Operations Medical Course (SOMC). I had been assigned as a platoon medic to 3rd Platoon, Charlie Company, 3rd Ranger Battalion. Although I had been in the Army for over a year and a half, I was the newest member of the platoon and as a result was dubbed, "The cherry bitch." It was a title that I really didn't mind. I knew that everyone here had carried it at some point and it was only a matter of time before I would be able to pass it on to someone else.

The boys sat around the table and told jokes for several minutes after choking down their dinner. The billowing laugh of First Sergeant Searing was enough to drown out the irritating noise coming from the generators. First Sergeant was nicknamed "The Rhino" and for good reason. The man's arms were bigger around than my legs and he possessed a confidence that was palpable, even amongst other Rangers.

I was still fairly leery of the big man at this point. A group of about a dozen of us recently joined up with the existing elements of 3rd Battalion, which had been in country for several weeks before we had arrived. Many in my group were brand-new privates that had just graduated from RIP. One or two guys had just graduated from Ranger School. Upon our arrival, First Sergeant Searing gathered us into one of the tents to give us a brief introduction to the area. The company commander also introduced himself, gave a short speech and opened the floor for any questions. During the course of his introduction, the CO told us his background including his alma mater, The Citadel.

Despite how intimidated most of the new guys were, things were going well. Until the CO opened the floor for questions, that is. Private Maldo had the burning desire to know some things about the CO's school. I didn't think much of it when he asked, "Sir, is it true that you have to pee in the sink at the Citadel?" With the grace and composure of a veteran Ranger, the CO explained that in many of the dorms the bathrooms were pretty far apart and sometimes you had to improvise. The CO then calmly left us in the care of "The Rhino."

To this day I'm still not sure if he screamed "GET OUT" or "GET DOWN," all I know is that it was nothing but 'assholes and elbows'. The First Sergeant didn't find the inquiry very humorous and he let us know in his own unique way. After a very shitty twenty minutes in that tent we were brought out into the cold night air and made to create a small formation. Our section leaders were brought out and informed about what had just happened. I still had to draw sensitive items such as my night vision device. I was introduced to the taste of Afghan dirt as I low crawled to the tent that acted as our communications room and armory. At this moment I couldn't help but think back to the school house at Fort Bragg where just a couple of weeks ago I was having a barbeque with master sergeants, joking and calling them by their first names. Now I was pulling myself across the ground in a war zone because someone who I had never met just asked a smart-ass question to another guy that I had never met. Welcome to life as a new guy in Ranger Battalion.

I trod lightly in my comments as we left the chow hall under the guidance of our red headlamps. The camp stayed blacked out at night and using white lights had the potential to draw indirect fire so we stumbled around making due with the minimal illumination from those red filtered lights. My home was a bunk bed in the corner of a tent that I share with eight or nine other Rangers. The extent of my possessions fit into two large green duffle bags. Our tent was equipped with a 19" TV that one of the guys had purchased from the bazaar prior to my arrival in country. The squad leader and alpha team leader were both big poker players so the back part of our tent was set up like a miniature casino, which frequently hosted poker nights.

After dinner was down time that was typically spent watching very poor quality movies that were bought at the market for a dollar. More often than not, I would make my way back to the gym for the second or third time of the day following dinner. The gym was the only place that I felt at home during my first deployment. Everywhere else, I was the newest guy in the company, but in that dirt-floored, musky old building, I was one of the strongest guys in our company. The rattling of ancient, rusted iron plates, likely left behind when the Russians were occupying this country, reminded me of the light chatter at the breakfast table of the firehouse, where I used to work before joining the Army. Through each of my deployments, the gym would act as a sanctuary from both the monotony and chaos of war.

There wasn't a great deal of activity in our area at this time. I believe that it was Ramadan and as a result, most of the local terrorists were on vacation. The first mission that I went on was so uneventful that the best part was simply rolling out the gate. It was pitch-black and I found myself sitting in the back of a Humvee with absolutely no armor - the thing didn't even have doors. I had no idea what to expect and beyond that had no clue how to work my NVGs. The last time that I put a round in an M-4 was . . . actually never. We had to qualify with an M16 in basic training a year and a half earlier but I hadn't fired a weapon since. My class was the last RIP class that didn't have a shooting week (December 2003). As I heard some of the other guys yelling in jest at the guy who opened the gate at the FOB, *"I'm scared"*... *"I wanna be a princess"*... *"It's too cold out here!"* I was trying to figure out how to get the bullet from the magazine into the fucking barrel.

The jeep bounced and jarred the bones of its occupants on the two-hour drive to the objective. Green beams projected into every direction from the PEQ-2 infrared lasers mounted on our M-4s as we scanned for potential threats in the distance. We very quietly arrived at the base of a hill. Atop it sat a compound barely visible with the minimal moonlight. In silence, we dismounted and began to pull security in each direction. I was instructed by the platoon sergeant to accompany him. As our element began to make its way up the incline into the darkness, the monocular night vision device attached to my MICH helmet banged against my cheekbone while displaying a very blurry green image. I'd never worn these things before, let alone attempted to walk on uneven terrain with them. There was no depth perception and I stumbled, letting out an audible grunt. "Quiet, Doc!" was about the amount of the consolation I received which came from one of the members of my platoon, who was unidentifiable from the darkness of night.

The walk took about fifteen minutes. I was staged outside the front gate as the assault element breached the door and began to clear the central courtyard. In less than a minute, I was brought into the compound. I looked around to see Rangers moving swiftly and silently from building to building, collecting fighting age males and securing the women and children in a single room. I couldn't help but think of how fucking cool the entire thing was. I finally was able to see exactly what Rangers actually do. Not what I had read in books or heard stories about, but how they actually move with grace and violence, subduing their opponents with a certain violent professionalism.

I was given the task of watching the room of non-combatants after the dust had settled on the initial assault. I had put on several layers of moisture-wicking long underwear in anticipation of the frigid Humvee infil, but the movement to the objective had left me a little warm. The room where I watched over the dozen or so women and children couldn't have been hotter. I removed my helmet and hooded facemask. The older women in the room appeared startled and began chattering among themselves. I asked the interpreter what they were saying. Apparently my blonde hair and face resembled the Russian soldiers that had occupied this region during the 1980s. I found out from the interpreter that the Russians were not very kind to the women when they were here and I saw the look of concern spreading throughout the room. What an absolutely terrifying experience for these little kids! Twenty minutes ago they were sound asleep in their beds and now they have a man in body armor standing over them with a rifle.

I remembered that I had a large bag of candy in my cargo pocket. Every eye in the room was glued attentively to my movement as I reached into my pocket and pulled out the zip lock bag. I kneeled down and offered a piece to the closest child in the room. She was an absolutely adorable little girl who was maybe four or five years old. Her brown hair was matted and wild. Her facial expression was that of great curiosity. In her little nightgown, she hesitantly reached for the brightly wrapped treasure at my fingertips. Like a little mouse that had just secured the cheese from a trap, she retreated back to the safety of the group.

This set off a reaction that one could expect from any group of small children when candy is being dispensed, regardless of the nationality. I instantly became the most popular person in that province. I handed out every one of those sugary treats and couldn't help but think about my young nieces back home. Just as we got the call for exfil, the first brave little girl came back to me and tugged on my pant leg. She handed me a brown necklace that I would later give to my niece, Hailey. It's been over nine years, but to my knowledge, she still has it.

As we made our way out of the compound, I walked through the outdoor kitchen. The walls were stained with soot and it had an almost ancient smell. The burnt iron kettle that was suspended from a hook reminded me of something that would have been used hundreds, if not thousands of years ago. I would come to find out that the majority of the country was caught in some sort of a time warp. Much of the technology and culture had not ever grown beyond biblical times, like a sort of time capsule that allowed us to look into our past.

The drive back to Salerno was just as miserable as the trip to the objective. By the time that we rolled into the security of the gates, I could no longer feel my hands. We did a quick check for sensitive items and set out to dust off our equipment. The thing about Afghanistan is you can try to get clean, but you will always be covered in dirt. Very little of the country is paved and riding in the back of what is essentially a pickup truck will leave every part of you filthy. It was of little concern to me. I hadn't spoken with my family since I had arrived and I knew that there wouldn't be a wait for either of the two working phones that we had for the 75 or so Rangers that were on that outpost. The "MWR" tent was a drafty hut with a shelf in the back with books and items that had been delivered for non-specific soldiers, letters from school kids and drawings, that sort of thing.

There were four desks that had layers of carvings courtesy of the pocketknives carried by each of the Rangers that had sat at that table previously, anxiously awaiting their chance to speak with a loved one. Each one of the four had a phone, but only two of them ever worked.

I dialed the staff duty number and asked to be patched through to my father's home line. The connection was shoddy at best and I wasn't allowed to discuss anything that I was doing or where I was at, but it was a relief to hear my father's voice. He told me that everything was good and that nothing had changed at all. I would later find out that this was not at all true, but his protective instincts didn't want me being distracted by any bad news from back home. The call was short-lived. Someone outside the fence thought that now would be a good time to lob a mortar round at our compound. I'm not sure if the sirens wailed first or the phone cut out. Either way, I'm sure that was the last thing that my pops wanted to hear. I exited the tent to see all of the guys running to the shelter of several concrete bunkers. Many of them had already dressed down for the evening and found themselves in little more than Ranger panties and body armor. The standard operating procedure was to meet in these little makeshift caves until we received an all clear. We sat packed in like sardines for about thirty minutes before being allowed to return to our tents.

The next morning started out just like every other one would for the next few months. With hygiene bag in tow, wearing faded brown undershirts and short black silky shorts, we moved like zombies to the metal box-like latrines. Every step was more painful than the one before. The paper-thin shower shoes were no match for the jagged Afghan rocks. Once inside the humid shower room, we had it down to a precise order of work. *Face shaved. Teeth brushed. Bowels cleared. Move out.* Then the next order of business for me would be to check in with the senior medic at the aid station to see if anyone is there for sick call. PFC "Joe Snuffy" would have a sore knee. "Here's some Motrin" would be the standard response. Then it would be ninety minutes before the dingy white tent opened for breakfast. *I wonder what kind of eggs we will have today, runny or brick hard?* After sick call, I'd be off to the gym again. *What day is it? Chest day, that's what day it is!*

Following breakfast that day, we were informed that we would be going to the range so the new guys could sight in their weapons. Since the last range that I was at was in basic training, I had a preconceived notion on where we would be training today. To my surprise, there was no tower, no pre- dug foxholes, and no gates. It was literally just a desert. We drove out to the desert and set up targets. This reminded me of all of the times that we did this growing up in Arizona. In fact, the terrain was almost identical to where we used to go as kids. The experience was surprisingly laid back. No one was shouting. After sighting in our weapons we worked on line drills where we walked one direction and shot, then the next direction. Walk and shoot, run and shoot, turn and shoot, shoot and shoot. We shot until my finger was blistered. We became familiar with every weapon system that we had, including weapons that were commonly used by our enemies such as the AK-47.

We ate MREs for lunch and shot into the early evening, an event that we would repeat on a weekly basis for the next few months. At night, after dinner, we returned to our tents to enjoy another movie that was clearly pirated. A half dozen of us huddled around that TV, sitting in those foldable camping chairs while sharing the bounty from the care packages that just came in. One particular delivery brought several cases of Girl Scout cookies from the mother of Erik, one of my tent mates. Knowing that he couldn't possibly eat the dozens upon dozens of boxes himself, he shared the contents with his roommates. One particular Sunday, which was for the most part a down day, we decided to have a gangster marathon. We watched all three Godfather films, Goodfellas, and a myriad of other lesser quality movies. I personally took down six full boxes of Thin Mints between lunch and dinner that day. I regret nothing!

The days and nights blurred together in a sort of *Warfighter's Groundhog's Day*. The only moments that we ever spent alone were the three or four minutes secluded in a port-a-potty with a porn magazine illuminated by a red headlamp. It's sick to say, but I still get a little excited when I see red lights. *Wake up. Shave face. Lift weights. Eat breakfast. Shoot. Eat lunch. Practice CQB. Eat dinner. Lift weights. Watch a movie. Take an anti-malaria pill. Go to bed. Repeat.* With any group of highly motivated, barrel-chested freedom fighters, boredom is a very dangerous thing. Idle hands are the devil's playthings as they say, and no one was more familiar than we were.

For most, a birthday is a time of celebration, a time to bring attention to yourself and the things that you have accomplished over the past year. In Ranger Battalion, it is a cause for getting tortured. For that reason, most guys will purposely let the day come and go without mention. Occasionally, you will have a friend that we call a 'Blue Falcon' (BF= Buddy Fucker), that will tell the rest of your platoon that it's your special day. One unfortunate soul thought that he was going to make it through the entire day without incident. We had, however, been plotting his demise for at least a few days. It was right around Christmas time we were watching movies in one of the other squads' tent. We had a brief intermission between films for a quick bathroom break. The birthday boy donned his red headlamp and commenced the 200 or so meter walk to the outhouse.

The six-man element responsible for carrying out the birthday festivities quickly reacted without hesitation. As the target faded into the night, the squad of Rangers affixed their NVGs and removed any colorful clothing, replacing it with an all-black base layer. Mobilizing into blocking positions, we covered any potential means of egress that the enemy personnel may have thought to take. We waited in silence, in the freezing cold dark night for him to reemerge from the row of shitters. Waiting patiently for him to move right in the middle of our formation, we peered through the darkness. He was completely oblivious of our whereabouts. As he drew closer, "CONTACT, CONTACT, CONTACT!" was shouted and one of the privates rushed at him, wrapping him up. Another, and another piled on. He was no match for this type of violence of action. Before he knew what was happening, he was on the ground and being zip tied. He never had a chance. One of the senior privates produced a fresh can of shaving cream and began to go to work on the detainee. Another grabbed a case of bottled water and doused him, drenching him to the bone. The man then was violently dragged to a nearby chain link fence and tied to it. We sang happy birthday as we returned to the warmth of our tent, leaving the drenched Ranger to tolerate the freezing Afghan night. About halfway through the second movie someone remembered that he was still outside. "Oh yeah! Meh . . . we'll get him after this is done."

The way that Thanksgiving came and went was the same as Christmas and New Year's. The days and nights blurred together with the occasional squad-on-squad brawl to break things up. When our rotation ended in early 2005, I had gained the respect of the men around me, but realized that there were hundreds more men in the Battalion that I had yet to meet. I would once again be the new guy; I would have to prove myself to them as well. I would come to find out that this was the nature of life in a Ranger Battalion. There was no place for a guy who would rest on his laurels. If you were a good team leader, you would have to prove yourself as a good squad leader, and then as a platoon sergeant and so on. Battalion is a constant proving ground where you are expected to be at your absolute best on a daily basis. Every day may not be an action packed gunfight the way that it is depicted in movies, but the highest standards are expected to be met on a daily basis, regardless of task. That consistency in expectations is what produces the highest caliber of warrior.

-LEO JENKINS
3/75

Chapter Five

"May God have mercy for my enemies because I won't."

Gᴇᴏʀɢᴇ S. Pᴀᴛᴛᴏɴ Jʀ.

As the Regiment continued to transform to meet current operational needs, the plan to add a support company to each battalion became reality. The "Echo" company would allow the line companies to focus on their primary tasks, while also accommodating the maintenance required of the growing fleet of vehicles each battalion had. The support companies were authorized by the Ranger Force XXI expansion plan that had been in place for a few years at that point. The companies' first volunteers were selected from other units, primarily the 528ᵗʰ Support Battalion out of Fort Bragg. The new volunteers did not go through RIP before assignment, much to the chagrin of the Rangers. The reason for this was because of the date the companies needed to be operational by, which was imposed on Regiment from higher headquarters. Although the E Company volunteers wore a Ranger Scroll and Ranger PT uniform, they were only authorized the maroon beret as opposed to the tan beret the rest of the Rangers wore.

The plan was put into place to get the new companies up to a minimum operating strength first, and then start sending the original volunteers back through RIP. At that point, all new incoming members would go through RIP like any other Ranger volunteer. It did not exactly work out that way, as it became unfeasible to send all the original volunteers back through RIP. In 2006, each battalion held a "mini-RIP" where the E Company support personnel performed all minimum Ranger standards in a one-week course that ended with them being awarded their tan beret, in what many of the line companies dubbed the "Tan Beret Give-Away." Also, during this transition period, support personnel that volunteered for Ranger would be assigned to the Ranger Training Detachment (which ran RIP) with the option to undergo selection or go straight to their battalion. Some volunteers went through RIP; others took the easier route straight to battalion where they did the one-week course to earn their beret. This did not sit well with many, and the support personnel who volunteered for RIP earned the respect of their fellow Rangers while the others were looked down upon.

Despite the rocky transition of adding the support company to each battalion, it was an addition that made the Regiment more lethal and more agile. Rangers no longer had to rely on the availability of outside support, as these skills were now organic to the battalion. The Rangers of Echo Company would go on to not only support the Rangers in the line companies, but also actively participate in missions while deployed. By the end of 2006, all Ranger volunteers regardless of military occupational specialty would have to attend and pass the Ranger Indoctrination Program or the Ranger Orientation Program, making the 75th Ranger Regiment one of the few SOF units to have their support personnel undergo the same selection process as everyone else in the unit.

The look of Rangers again changed as well, with the adoption of the Army Combat Uniform (ACU). This new digital pattern replaced the decades old 'Battle Dress Uniform' (BDU), as well as its desert counterpart. The weapons and equipment of the individual Ranger continued to improve as well, giving each individual the ability to shoot, move and communicate better than ever before.

The war in Iraq was as violent as ever, with the death toll of American service members topping 2,000. Iraqi's had held their first democratic election in over fifty years, and the captured Saddam Hussein went on trial. The men of the 75th Ranger Regiment were hitting their stride in a methodical execution of nightly counter terror operations, providing the muscle needed for the Command's task force to make a deep dent in the ranks of terrorist leadership. The primary focus had shifted to the hunt for the leader of Al Qaida in Iraq, and the hunt was moving at full throttle. Every Ranger in Iraq was busy now, some platoons going on over a hundred missions in one deployment that year.

The war in Afghanistan was not as hectic as Iraq, but Rangers distinguished themselves by leading the rescue effort for Navy SEALs lost on Operation Red Wings. Rangers from 2/75, as well as a platoon from 3/75, spent over a week in the search for Marcus Luttrell as well as his fallen comrades. The terrain was brutal, and the heat was at its height during the summer time operation. The Rangers did not rest until the mission was accomplished though, some going so far as to rehydrate via IVs in order to keep going. All of the bodies were recovered and a small element of 2/75 Rangers found Marcus Luttrell, allowing him to be evacuated safely.

The Regiment fought hard and distinguished itself, further proving they were a force to be reckoned with in the special operations community. The year was unfortunately not without loss though. Private John Henderson, Jr., Private First Class Damian Garza, Corporal Timothy Shea, and Private First Class Dillon Jutras were all Rangers from 3/75, and all made the final sacrifice.

Summer 2005
"MEDCAP"

"I can't believe Marissa would treat Ryan that way, it's just cold blooded."

"It's just not right, especially after all he has done for her!"

"What a bitch . . . Should we watch another episode before mid-rats?"

"Does the Pope shit in the woods?"

We were a few weeks into this deployment and it had already devolved into marathon sessions of the popular television show, *The O.C.* Our platoon hit the ground running when we assisted with the search and rescue operation for the Navy SEALs compromised during Operation Red Wings, but the op tempo had suddenly come to a standstill. The summer of '05 was starting to feel like the winter of '04 when we sat at Forward Operating Base "Salerno"

This time we were stationed at Bagram Airfield acting primarily as a Quick Reaction Force. That sounds really cool, but what it really means is putting all of your kit on and sitting on the airfield for hours while another platoon was hitting an objective. So when the opportunity arose to jock up and walk in the mountains for a day or two, we jumped on it. We had just finished the last season finale of *The O.C.* available in Afghanistan and no one was willing to stoop to watching *Desperate Housewives . . .* yet.

As I entered the room where the mission briefing would be held I saw a very familiar bearded face. "Teddy P?" Oh shit. I had just referred to a master sergeant by his nickname. The last time I saw Teddy, we were students together in the Special Operations Medical Course at Fort Bragg. I had just been made corporal so addressing a master sergeant this way got some very abrasive looks from my superiors. Teddy worked as a medic for a Civil Affairs unit and was putting together a MEDCAP mission (Medical Civil Action Program). The idea was to put a group of Americans into a village of tactical significance and distribute medical supplies and treatment to its inhabitants.

This was a very atypical mission for Rangers to be conducting from my experience, but we really didn't mind. Not just because of the general boredom that we were battling against, but because we viewed ourselves as consummate professionals. We truly didn't see the difference between executing this task and a hostage rescue mission, a search and rescue mission, or a direct action raid. It was our job and it was time to go to work.

We loaded onto two Chinook helicopters piloted by the 160th SOAR. I'm not sure if there is another unit anywhere in the US military that I came to respect more than the Special Operations Aviation Regiment. Each night, men from every unit in the Command put their lives into the hands of those flight crews with absolute faith that they would deliver them into and from harm's way. They are truly the unsung heroes of the US Special Operations community.

Tonight would do little to test their skill. We landed in a rocky riverbed, about five kilometers from the village and stepped from the ramp of the bird with motivation. As the helicopters pulled away, the stark contrast of the incessant violent vibration and dissonance of the dual rotor aircraft juxtaposed with the tranquility of the star filled Afghan night in a way that was nearly maddening. The stars sparkled and shone, like the eyes of the woman that you have been estranged from for far too long upon your return. They greeted us with a shimmer that can only exist in the vast expansiveness of this type of wild.

One-by-one, we stepped off creating a textbook Ranger file. The moon does well to illuminate the outlines of the men in front and behind as we move from the low ground to the security of the terraces ahead. Ahead of me is our Battalion surgeon. Colonel "O" had come to us from another unit in the Command at the time of our deployment. I had spoken with him a few times at the aid station on Bagram but most of the men had not met him. He was an incredibly intelligent man that I found to be highly likable. We also had with us a SEAL corpsman and a few other medics from Regiment, including Sergeant Prokop. Prokop was returning from graduating Ranger school when I first arrived at 3rd Ranger Battalion. He was very accepting of me as a new medic and helped to square me away before I left on my first deployment. A couple of years after I left Battalion, I found out that he was killed in a motor vehicle accident working as a San Diego police officer.

As we moved through the night, I could tell that the surgeon was struggling a little bit. We took a tactical pause and I asked if he was doing all right. I'm not sure if he was accustomed to moving at a Ranger pace over this type of terrain. He made some comment about the weight of his ruck and not realizing that we would be moving this far. I reached for his ruck that was sitting at his side nearly giving myself a hernia as I lifted it. "Jesus, Sir! You win the award for packing the most shit, that's for sure!"

I offered to take his pack for him, an offer that he gladly accepted. All I ever really did during deployments was go to the gym. Since we were sitting in that mission brief during my scheduled PT time, and I wasn't about to miss leg day, I figured it was a win-win situation. Every one of the dozen or so terraces became a weighted muscle up which I found to be a fun little game. It took another hour or so to reach the village. It was still dark and so we had to sit and wait for first light to make contact with the village elder.

My platoon sergeant and I sit back to back against an old tree about 30 meters from one of the small mud houses. I slowly pull apart the Velcro strip keeping my shoulder pocket shut and pull from it a much-needed treat. Most Rangers would have taken the opportunity to pack their lip with chew but I never took to that habit. Instead, I pour the contents of the bright red bag into my hand. *Fuck, I love Skittles*, I thought to myself as I filled my cheek like a chipmunk preparing for winter. The sweat that had accumulated from our infil was creating quite the chill as we sat motionless in the tenebrous evening. This is how these things went. Hurry up and wait.

Immediately prior to this deployment I had to switch platoons. My new platoon sergeant was formerly one of the instructors at RIP. The man was known throughout Battalion for the creative ways that he was able to make men quit the indoctrination course. Naturally, I was a little terrified of him as a result of the torture that he bestowed upon my fellow wannabes and I. For some reason, however, I was curious about the time that he spent as a destroyer of young men's dreams. I begin to inquire about some of the things that happened. I asked about certain guys who were kicked out and others that passed and how those things came to be. When I asked if he ever felt bad about anything that he did during that time he responded, "There was one time in a winter class that had a combination of sleet and snow during our time at Cole Range. I remember there being a giant puddle that the top sheet had frozen over on. We made those guys low crawl back and forth through that ice water all night long."

"Yeah . . .. that was my class, Sergeant." I replied.

"I don't want to talk about this anymore!" He abruptly responded.

As the sun rose, it cast light to the beauty of our surroundings. The modest Afghan homes were dispersed sporadically against the backdrop of the steep mountains. Our Civil Affairs counterparts were making contact with the village elders as we displayed one of the skills that Rangers have become known the world over for: *take a knee, face out, pull security.* The news that there were American doctors in the village handing out medicine had people coming from every direction. This was a very uncomfortable scenario for many of us. We were not accustomed to being in a village during the day. We never did presence patrols, as the Regiment wasn't exactly a 'hearts and minds' kind of unit. The times that we were on target past daybreak, we would do everything that we could to keep any local as far away as possible. We were being forced to adapt to the nature of the mission as fighting age men walked up to us. We were here to create a relationship, not start a fight.

A line started to form outside of one of the larger homes. Within minutes, every man, woman, and child from the entire village stood ready to receive treatment for some type of ailment. When asked, many didn't know how old they were. They would respond with, "Between 20 and 30." That Chinook we came in on was a time machine; it took us back to a biblical age. People that were well into their thirties had never seen a dentist or doctor and it showed. I spent the first couple of hours cleaning out minor wounds, many of which had been festering for some time. Imagine something as simple as stubbing your toe in a grocery store parking lot. We are accustomed to cleaning it, putting some Neosporin on it, bandaging it, and waiting a few days. It seemed like that level of treatment must have been like performing surgery in this village.

At some point during mid-morning things shifted. People from the village started to notice that we were handing out things like Tylenol and Pedia-lite. They stopped being interested in getting treatment and started being concerned with scoring as much free shit as they could get their hands on. When we started to notice that men were getting back in line for another bottle of "Head medicine" or "Belly medicine" we had to tell them no. We had a limited amount of supplies and the bigger guys were using their size to gain a monopoly on them. This is something that we would see when we tossed candy to the local kids from our Humvee while returning from missions. The biggest kids would literally inflict physical violence on the smaller children to get a bottle of water or Tootsie Roll.

When the local men realized that we had caught on to them they too adapted. They began sending in wave after wave of adorable, dirty little kids. I recall one little girl who had a gold flower piercing in her nose. She was maybe five years old but had the courage of a warrior. She would walk right up and tug on the guys pant leg and look up with eyes that had the effect of a microwave on a stick of butter. None among us was a match for that little girl. She got her hands on more Band-Aids and topical antibiotics than aisle nine at Walgreens.

By early afternoon we had run out of supplies and called for a re-supply drop. A pallet of water bottles and MREs dropped from the back of a C-130 exploded about a kilometer outside of the village. We dispatched a squad to recover the contents. We distributed what we could before making our way out of the village. We began moving down the mountain, but with far less weight and a little daylight which made it much more enjoyable than the movement up. Regardless of the benevolent nature of our time in their village, there was still a certain hyper vigilance as we moved toward the extraction point. I, for one, do not like being exposed on uneven terrain during the day. The uneasy feeling that we could take fire at any moment was enough to drown out the expansive beauty of our surroundings.

We were picked up without incident and made another long, cold, cramped, nighttime helicopter ride that would have been the highlight of any young boy's childhood; Most of us just passed out on the frigid metallic floor of that rumbling bird. We landed in Bagram with just enough time to make the last five minutes of "mid-rats." A few of us took the opportunity to load up on individual boxes of cereal and paper containers of goat milk. We had four more episodes of *The O.C.* to get through before the season finale. After our Chinook power nap and fresh stockpile of fruit loops, we were up to the task.

-LEO JENKINS
3/75

Summer 2005
"Barracks Life"

I arrived at 1st Ranger Battalion in February of 2005 while the Battalion was still deployed. I sat on the rear detachment, or Rear-D as it was called, for the better part of two months before everybody came back and I finally met my assigned platoon. At the time, I didn't drink alcohol at all, so I volunteered to be the permanent designated driver for my squad. I didn't really mind because I liked going out with everyone, and it was a way that I could contribute to the squad and start paying my dues. After a few months, I was becoming better at my job and I had seemingly been accepted into my squad. This was due in no small part to my role as a babysitter of full-grown men, so piss-drunk that they could barely speak, who wanted more than anything to urinate in the parking lot or on a brick wall in the middle of Congress Street, in downtown Savannah, Georgia.

During this time we had finally been moved out of the old barracks, which to our knowledge had been condemned some thirty years prior when they were Air Force barracks. As far-fetched as this may seem, you would only need to take one look at them to halfway believe the story. The tiles in the rooms and bathrooms had been ripped up in multiple places, there was mold everywhere, some of the air-conditioning vents were held up by coat hangers, and many of the bunks were held together with 100mph tape. The new barracks were incredibly nice however. They were technically 3rd Infantry Division's barracks, but 3rd ID was deployed so we were allowed to stay in them until ours were renovated. The new rooms were more akin to suites than rooms, which you shared with one other guy. Each guy had his own separate room, and shared a kitchen and a bathroom.

The greatest thing about the new setup was that the rooms were entered from the outside, which eliminated the existence of the hall-way. "The Hallway" was the ultimate symbol of the misery that was the life of a Ranger Private. Each platoon had its own hallway (1st floor: 1st Platoon, 2nd floor: 2nd Platoon, and 3rd floor: 3rd Platoon). The platoon spent most of the duty day spread out among the various rooms doing whatever odd jobs that had come down for us to do. It was great if you had your Tab and needed a job done because it kept all the privates consolidated in one area. As a private, however, it exacerbated your daily misery. You were never allowed to do anything less than sprint through the hallway unless you had your Tab, and God help you if a Tab or team leader ever caught you in the hallway. Such an infraction could lead to you getting smoked for hours as well as roping all of the other privates into getting smoked right alongside you. Rarely did anyone ever get smoked alone. No dirges were ever sung by Ranger privates mourning the day the hallway was eliminated.

On one particular Friday evening in the new barracks, we had a long weekend and I was actually planning on spending a quiet night alone in my room. Shortly after I had already gone to bed, I heard a knock on my door. It was my roommate (who I had, and still do have a tremendous amount of respect for), so I opened it to see what he wanted. He was drunk and proceeded to give me his version of the familiar "you're a good dude" speech. Like I said before, I have a tremendous amount of respect for this guy and so I was actually quite glad to hear that particular speech albeit in slurred form. After a while, he left and went into his own room and I went back to bed. I was then woken once again by a knock on my door. This knock was preceded by the voice of another guy in my squad yelling "Farnum! Wake up! Come give me a hug!" I rose from my place of rest, slightly irritated at this point, and begrudgingly opened the door. I delivered the hug that he had previously requested and sat down as he delivered *his* version of the "you're a good dude" speech. Once again flattered but at this point very tired, I listened to the whole thing and then walked him out after he was finished. "Let's try this again," I thought as I climbed back into bed.

What I didn't know at the time was that my night was far from over. A short while later after I had fallen back to sleep I once again heard a knock at my door. This time, fully irritated, I jump up and flung open my door to see who the hell was waking me up this time. To my immediate surprise I see a staff sergeant in full duty uniform whom I didn't know. Standing there in nothing but my Ranger winter PT bottoms and not really knowing what to think, I very quickly snapped to a groggy version of parade rest. He was holding onto a guy I recognized as a drunkenly slouched senior private from my platoon. For the sake of this story, and in order to protect the guilty we'll call him Forde.

The Staff Sergeant then asked me, "Do you know this guy?"

"Roger, Sergeant," I replied, "he's in my platoon."

He then proceeded to tell me that Forde was picked up by the Military Police at the gate and dropped off at Staff Duty. I was then told that I needed to watch him and make sure that he didn't leave.

After the Staff Duty NCO left, Forde went over to my fridge opened it up and yelled, "Farnum, where's the booze?!"

I told him, "There is no booze, and quite frankly, I think you've had enough."

He then opened up the freezer and yelled, "Where are the Hot Pockets?! Farnum, you're a single man, where are the Hot Pockets?!"

Slightly amused by this, I explained that I didn't have any Hot Pockets.

He then turned to me, "Let's go fight somebody!"

"Yeah, let's not" I replied.

I then just dragged one hand down the side of my face, rolled my eyes, and sighed. This was going to be a long night.

Then a thought occurred to me. My stepdad drank heavily when I was growing up and would pass out as soon as he sat down to watch a movie.

"Hey, I have an idea," I said. "Let's watch a movie!"

I went over to my TV and started rummaging through my stack of movies. It was a really old, really small TV with a built in VHS player that I had scrounged up somewhere, and I had a stack of VHS tapes that I had acquired through the same process. I grabbed "The Fifth Element" and threw it in. I sat him down in one of my chairs in front of the TV and waited. It wasn't more than fifteen minutes before he passed out. I was relieved and felt a slight sense of accomplishment but was still very aggravated and tired. He then leaned over, crawled onto the floor, and passed out again. I turned off the TV and crawled back into bed after making sure that all the doors were locked.

A few hours later, although it didn't seem like that long at the time, I woke up to the sound of my bedroom door opening. My first thought was, "Oh God, he's escaping!"

I jumped up and rushed to the front door to try and catch him only to find that the front door was still closed and locked. I then heard him behind me in the bathroom pissing. My initial relief was cut short as I heard him hit and miss, hit and miss, hit and miss. My only thought at this point was how I was going to have to scrub that entire bathroom in the morning. Fan-damn-tastic!

Forde then walked out of the bathroom back toward my room and me. The entire front of his pants were soaked with piss. I backed up to allow him to go back into my room, trying to not let him touch me. He walked into my room, dropped trou, and laid down in the middle of the floor, bare ass in the air. I grabbed a bed sheet and covered him up with it. Furious, I crawled back into bed.

About 9:30 the next morning, I heard him rummaging through my stuff. He nudged me and said, "Farnum, I can't find my ID. Have you seen my ID?" I hadn't seen his ID nor was I in the mood to help him find it. "I'm just gonna walk home." He lived off post and I was so enraged about the whole night that I didn't care. "Whatever . . . fine . . . go . . . just go." He left and I went back to sleep.

I woke up a few hours later and decided to start cleaning up my room before I started on the bathroom. We just had a layout so my room was wrecked from me digging through all of my bags trying to find pieces of equipment that nobody ever used but we were responsible for keeping track of anyway. Clothes were strewn all over and I just started throwing clothes into my laundry bag. I then realized that all of my stuff was wet. I took a whiff of what was in my hand and knew immediately why everything was wet. Ol' dude pissed all over all of my stuff!

Gagging, I continued to throw all of my piss soaked clothes into my laundry bag until I came across a pair of jeans that I didn't recognize. I reached into one of the pockets and pulled out Forde's military ID and driver's license. This guy, who was easily two sizes bigger than I was, somehow squeezed his happy ass into my jeans, and walked out! Needless to say I was livid, and stayed that way for most of that weekend.

I didn't hear from him until a couple of days later. He called me because he needed his military ID to get back onto post before we had to be at work. He then said something along the lines of, "Hey, man. I'm pretty sure I may have pissed all over your stuff."

"Yeah dude, ya did."

"Yeah, I figured I'd give you a couple of days before I called to let you cool off."

By this point he was right, and I had cooled off. We met at a bar that was close to his house where I gave him back his IDs and he gave me back my pants.

-RICHARD FARNUM
1/75

THE RANGER MEDIC

One of the cornerstones of Ranger effectiveness is the medical training each individual Ranger receives. Not only is the platoon medic a graduate of the prestigious Special Operations Combat Medical Course, but it is not uncommon to see Specialists and Sergeants that are Nationally Registered Emergency Medical Technicians. At the lowest level, all Rangers are annually certified in Ranger First Responder (RFR) training. Not only has this emphasis on medical proficiency saved numerous Ranger' lives on the field of battle, but it has saved the lives of civilian non-combatants and enemy fighters alike.

The Ranger combat life saver training had existed since the early 1990's as a modified version of the Army's program. The course taught at 1/75 during the 1992-95 time frame was essentially the Ranger version of the old Basic Trauma Life Support curriculum along with several Expert Field Medical Badge-like tasks such as the litter course and manual carries. The Army-wide requirement was one Combat Life Saver qualified soldier per squad, but the Rangers had already instituted one EMT-B per squad in the late 1980s. The Regiment therefore modified the Combat Life Saver requirement to one for every fire team, doubling the Army minimum requirement. Additionally, the Ranger Combat Life Saver certification was a critical requirement for several support personnel such as cooks, finance, chaplains, and radiomen as they were key members of the casualty control points.

In September 1997, the Regimental commander, then-Colonel Stanley McChrystal, directed that all Rangers were to be Combat Life Saver qualified regardless of rank or position. This was a key part of the "Big-Four" that (then) Colonel McChrystal and Command Sergeant Major Mike Hall instituted. Each individual battalion continued to run and modify versions of the Ranger Combat Life Saver program for a couple of years. In conjunction with the focus on medical training was the integration of Tactical Combat Casualty Care (TCCC), which had been introduced by Captain Frank Butler. By late 1998, 3rd Ranger Battalion had modified their version of Combat Life Saver into a TCCC course. The other battalion's then integrated portions of TCCC into their existing programs as well. Because it was so drastically different from the Army Combat Life Saver program, it took on the present name of Ranger First Responder (coined by 3/75 in 1998). By March of 2000, the Regimental Commander directed the Regiment to do a complete analysis of Combat Life Saver and RFR to determine the best training path forward. The decision was made by the summer of 2000, with the Regimental Commander directing that RFR would be the course taught to all Rangers using the 3/75 version, known as RFR 1.0. In October of 2000, RFR was integrated into the Ranger Indoctrination Program curriculum for every incoming enlisted Ranger. By the summer of 2001, RFR had become a relatively common training practice conducted by Ranger platoons prior to assumption, and sometimes during, their ready alert status.

In July of 2003, as real-life combat operations had become the norm, the Regimental Commander directed that every single Ranger in a rifle platoon would receive annual RFR training. This was to ensure it was a platoon-based and focused requirement and to alleviate the lack of compliance caused by staff and support personnel. It was during this time period that the Regiment, in keeping with Abrams Charter, began exporting versions of RFR to other units. The earliest to adopt the RFR program of instruction was the 10th Mountain Division, 101st Airborne Division (renaming it Eagle First Responder) and the 82nd Airborne Division. The Regiment and subordinate battalions sent Ranger medics to assist those units in standing up their programs.

In October of 2003, Major Jeff Cain (former 1/75 Battalion surgeon) was assigned to the U.S. Army Medical Department Center and School and began pushing that they adopt RFR. By late 2004, they had completely revised the Army Combat Lifesaver course to reflect RFR 1.0 and the tenets of TCCC Army-wide. After this, Army Combat Life Saver and RFR began a relative parallel growth and change as each adopted updates to TCCC principles. Generally, RFR stayed about a year ahead as it was easier for a single unit to implement changes to the course and the Rangers had taken on roles in the Committee on Tactical Combat Casualty Care formerly established in 2002 with then.

Coupled with RFR training was the development of the Ranger Bleeder Control Kit. Similar to CLS then RFR training, each of the battalions had their own variants of first aid kits in the late 1990's. As the concepts of TCCC became more engrained in the training programs, various versions of tourniquets became a predominant component. The early common tourniquet was a pre-made cravat and wooden dowel concept based on the traditional improvised stick & rag tourniquet. Along with those involved with TCCC development, several tourniquet concepts were explored. The initial Ranger tourniquet immediately following 9/11 was the Ranger Ratchet Tourniquet, which was very similar to the ratchets Rangers used for lashing vehicles. This was the primary tourniquet until around 2003-2004. By 2005, the Ranger Regiment had fully adopted the early versions of the CAT tourniquet. The bleeder kit evolved over the same time frame as the Regiments medical staff explored the best trauma dressings. Alongside the Army's adaptation of RFR, there was a parallel adaptation of the Ranger Bleeder Control Kit as the Army Individual First Aid Kit (IFAK).

Armed with RFR training and an advanced IFAK on every Ranger, even the lowest common denominators in a Ranger platoon were very capable, medically speaking. Often times, it is this non-medic Ranger who is the first to respond to the wounded – sometimes even applying self-aid if the situation arises. A great example of this is Medal of Honor recipient Sergeant First Class Leroy Petry, who hails from the 2nd Ranger Battalion. During the mission that he eventually received the Medal of Honor for, he picked up a live grenade that had landed next to him in order to throw it back at the enemy. The grenade exploded, resulting in his hand being completely severed at the wrist. Instead of drawing other Rangers out of the fight to take care of him, he did as he was trained and performed self-aid by putting on his own tourniquet and stopping the bleeding so that he could get back into the fight.

The next level of care comes from the platoon medic, who is typically a sergeant who actually holds the health care specialist military occupational specialty. After completion of the eighteen week advanced individual training (where the medic leaves as a nationally registered EMT-Basic) that all Army medics go through, the Ranger medic will also have attended advanced follow on training. The 75th Ranger Regiment's six-month pre-SOCM (Special Operations Combat Medic) course will come first, with the prospective Ranger medic attending college classes as well as receiving on the job training. They then move on to Fort Bragg to attend the Joint Special Operations Medical Training Center's prestigious SOCM course, which is nine months in duration. This is where they train alongside their peers from other SOF units such as Navy SEALs and Army Special Forces. They graduate SOCM as a US SOCOM certified Advanced Tactical Practitioner; this includes certifications such as NREMT-Paramedic, Advanced Cardiac Life Support, Basic Life Support, Pre-Hospital Trauma Life Support, and Pediatric Education for Pre-Hospital Professionals.

The education a Ranger medic receives before he even steps foot into one of the battalions, mixed with the experience they gain as a member of the nations primary special operations direct action force, makes them some of the most capable and professional trauma practitioners in the world. It's all well and good to tout certifications and special training, but proof of their proficiency is "in the pudding," so to speak.

From October 1st, 2001 to March 31st, 2010, the 75th Ranger Regiment suffered 419 casualties, which include 32 deaths. Based on the data collected in the Ranger Pre-Hospital Trauma Registry (PHTR), the Joint Trauma Registry maintained by the Joint Trauma System (JTS) and autopsies performed by the AFIP, none of the Rangers who were killed in action died from injuries that could have been prevented in the tactical pre-hospital environment. This was proof that the RFR training every Ranger received, as well as the advanced medical skills every Ranger Medic possessed had kept the preventable combat death number at zero for the 75th Ranger Regiment. All current data since the end of the study indicates that this number has not changed, representing a remarkable accomplishment. Over the course of a decade of sustained combat, the 75th Ranger Regiment is the only unit in the armed forces, SOF or conventional, that can claim zero preventable deaths in combat.

September 2005
"Tal Afar"

The speed at which the plane descended onto the airfield in Mosul was evidence of the increased threat level. The C-17 went into a complete nosedive, circled the airfield twice, and then made a hard landing on a short runway. The ramp of the aircraft lowered with an incredible amount of force. Air Force loadmasters screamed in on their forklifts to unload pallets loaded with all of the gear we would need for the 3½ month rotation. Once on the ground, it started to sink in . . .some of us might get killed on this deployment. Fuck it. My will was squared away, and my father had a power of attorney to pay my bills while I was away. I could focus on the task at hand.

In the spring and summer months of 2005, Mosul had suffered over three hundred attacks on coalition forces a month. This did not include the random slaughter of civilians and Iraqi forces that also happened on a daily basis in and around the city. IED attacks, mortar attacks, small unit attacks, and sniper attacks; suicide bombings were a normal, everyday occurrence. Al Qaeda in Iraq had a penchant for executing and beheading civilians to enforce their rule. Our platoon had been going after kidnapping and death squads all summer. The death squads would execute innocent men, women, and children, and were not afraid to use children as human shields as well. The enemy defended their territory to the death, and was armed with machineguns, car bombs, explosive vests, grenades, and AK-47 rifles. Al Qaeda fighters do not negotiate or surrender. The territory they chose to die for was not an open field, or a piece of rocky, mountainous terrain. We fought our enemy in rooms, on streets, and in small alleys. Our enemy was not swayed by our element of surprise, extreme firepower, or technology. Al Qaeda in

Iraq's best-trained and most lethal fighters had traveled thousands of miles to get their jihad on in order to try and kill our fellow soldiers, as well as innocent people.

Our platoon took contact nearly everywhere we went. Anytime that we ventured out into Mosul or the surrounding area, somebody was always trying to kill us. Insurgents had attacked the airfield on an almost nightly basis. By the time our two platoons of Rangers left after the short 3 ½ month rotation, the amount of attacks on coalition forces went from three hundred a month down to three. The night of September 4th, 2005 was just one out of 110 days and nights of constant close combat.

Tal Afar, Iraq is a small city located between Mosul and the border of Syria. In late October of 2004, the media announced that the Battle for Fallujah was about to take place. Rather than face a large force of battle hardened Marines, a large percentage of the hardened foreign fighters and their leadership fled to Tal Afar turning it into an Al Qaeda strong hold. Military intelligence estimated Tal Afar held hundreds, if not thousands, of the most dangerous terrorists in the world. Tal Afar was so dangerous that even the conventional units surrounding the city would rarely venture into it. They were quick to learn that Al Qaeda controlled that city.

On the night of September 4th, 2005, my platoon was tasked with striking three separate houses located within Tal Afar. The mission had actually been in the works for a couple of days. There was a large military offensive planned for the town in the near future. This mission was an extremely dangerous one, as we were being told to enter a city not even the Army or Marines would enter without tanks. All of our missions to that point were equally as dangerous. To us Rangers, it was another night to hunt the enemy, and we welcomed the chance to get into a fight. In the middle of the afternoon we met in the briefing room to go over the details and finalize the assault plan. We were to capture or kill the Al Qaeda Emir of Tal Afar, his spiritual leader, and anyone else we could capture alive.

If you were on our radar, it could go a couple of ways. You could either surrender to the main assault element after they blew apart your front door, or you could die trying to fight back. It does no good to kill someone you need to talk to, but if we saw something in someone's hands that could kill one of our friends, or us, we usually ended that person's life without hesitation. It wasn't always that dramatic though, sometimes we were able to silently enter a house and blind fold and flex-cuff the potential combatants before they even knew we were there.

When I went into a house with an assault force full of Rangers, I was immediately filled with a confidence that I doubt anyone except from our community could ever understand. We were the best, surrounded by the best. We had the best snipers, equipment, training, leadership, and tactics, shit . . . we had the best everything. On paper, we were the best platoon in the Regiment and we knew it.

We had a certain level of violence of action, which we brought onto target with us each night. The night of September 4th, 2005, was no different. As our country reeled from the devastation of Hurricane Katrina a week earlier, a small group of Rangers were about to venture through the darkness, into a fortified city controlled by hundreds of dangerous men. We were about to unleash a little bit of devastation of our own. Our country half a world away, and some of our families were affected by the hurricane, but those thoughts were put on hold. We had work to do.

Before loading up on the Stryker vehicle, I found the bronze cross that my mom gave me a couple of days before I deployed to Mosul. I had made it for her in my high school art class. I knelt down by the back of the open ramp, rubbed the cross, and sent her good thoughts. I took a knee with some Ranger buddies and said a prayer before we got switched on for the evening. After our prayers, a Ranger buddy came up to me and asked, "Will you go to war with me brother?!" I answered him with a bump from the Kevlar knuckles on my Oakley gloves. The ride was smooth en route to our objectives.

I had no idea at that time, riding inside that Stryker that within a couple of hours, this vehicle would soon be practically empty.

The first target building was located on the outskirts of the city. Before we could even set up the breach of the objective, the sniper element attached to our platoon saw weapons in the hands of two fighters on the roof top. They fired immediately and dropped the threats. The sound from their .308 caliber weapons was loud as hell. I wondered if those shots had woken up insurgents in the area or at the next target building only several hundred meters away. Everything seemed quiet though.

The silence ended with a hasty breach of the front door. The lead assault team used a short-barreled shotgun to defeat the locking mechanism, followed by a swift kick to the door. The first man rode the door in and a whole team followed. My team then flowed in after and began clearing the house, while establishing a strongpoint at the bottom of the staircase inside. My team then flowed up the stairs to complete our team's task of securing the second floor and the rooftop. I went up a small staircase, which was lined with sacks of grain and other crap that only hajj would put on a staircase. My team leader stood to the left on the side of the door to the roof. I stood offset to the right of it. You can get shot through a door if you stand in front of it. The barrel of my M-4 was pointed directly at it. If some insurgent were stupid enough to peek their head out, then they would eat my bullets.

I waited for a squeeze, or a simple touch from the Ranger buddy I knew was behind me. When I felt what I needed, I nodded with my barrel letting JD know that I was set. He gave me a silent countdown, and then opened the door. I flowed out to the roof like I had thousands of other times in training and in combat. The Ranger, who was grasping my shoulder upon exit, cleared the roof while I located the insurgents the snipers had killed. I immediately kicked their weapons out of reach, and visually checked their hands for detonators from a short distance. Once I was confident they were dead and would not blow up, I moved in and searched the bodies. One insurgent had a suicide vest on, wore a chest rack, and had an AK-47. The other dude had a rack and a Dragunov sniper rifle, and was armed with grenades, one being held firmly in his dead hand.

The thought of entering that house and being the first to go up the stairs against two armed men like this, immediately made me grateful that we had the best snipers in the world. The snipers that were attached to both platoons ended up wreaking their own havoc that deployment, and were just as deadly - saving us some work.

I myself was tasked with conducting a detailed search of the house called sensitive site exploitation. It's similar to a small-scale crime scene effort that should be done and completed in less than ten minutes. Sometimes, you have to do this while under fire, or even while the entire house is engulfed in flames. This process provides valuable information that is used to prosecute those we detained or lead us to the next high value target. Important people above my pay grade took this information and made important decisions. It had to be accurate and detailed. Ten minutes after breach, I completed my assigned tasks, and after the leadership gained accountability of all friendlies, we loaded up and moved out to the next target building. *Well, that went way too easy*, I thought to myself.

The second target building was about 800 meters away. It was snuggly nestled smack dab in the middle of the city. This was where the high value targets we were going after were supposedly resting their pretty little heads. Riding in the back of the Stryker, I made a hasty check of my equipment, and rechecked the status of my night vision. I was good to go. I made sure my tac-light and laser were on. My team leader put his thumb up. This was his way of asking, "Hey asshole, you got your shit ready?" I squeezed his thumb. That provided him with confirmation through both touch and sight. It was me saying, "Roger, Sergeant . . . up, up."

We had to get off our Stryker as fast as possible at this next target. The word coming through the radio was, "Four personnel on the rooftop, sleeping . . . over" Once we start movement to the objective, security had to be locked on again.

Due to the narrow streets and alleyways of Tal Afar, we had to infil almost two hundred meters away from the target building. We were told to ride with our troop hatches down in Tal Afar because an officer from a regular Army unit had been shot in the throat the previous night by a sniper. This goes to show the level of skill the enemy we were facing possessed. For a sniper to make that shot on a moving target is downright impressive. We usually rode around Mosul with our hatches open because we were always getting shot at by insurgents on the way to and from missions. Plus, with such a large vehicle, it helped to have extra eyes to negotiate the power lines and obstacles that were in our way every time we went out.

I glanced down at the forearm pad on my arm to see the description and identifying marks of our target. The picture we had of him was that of a black silhouette. A majority of the time we had no picture to go off of, just a silhouette. The paper described the HVT's scars, what weapons he was known to carry, what he liked to wear. It detailed whether or not he was known to wear a suicide vest, and also questions to ask him should you find him. The forearm pad also contained a small map of the surrounding buildings. My team leader gave me the 30-second hand signal. I acknowledged him. 30 seconds out from any house that is possibly defended by armed terrorists is always a little nerve-wracking. You just have to settle your mind, breathe, focus on the task at hand, and remember everyone comes home no matter what. In order to do that, I would cheat a little.

Seconds count in a gunfight. It is usually who is faster that will dictate who will win. The victor lives, the one who loses is buried six feet under. I was taught the importance of shaving seconds off. My weapon was on semi-auto immediately upon exiting the vehicle. My index finger was my only safety. This wasn't the standard operating procedure, but in this environment, I felt that I needed to take any advantage available. Other equipment that I had with me was turned on, checked and ready to go. Pouches were unbuttoned in case I had to do a tactical reload. Since we didn't have side arms yet at this point, we practiced reloading and failure drills thousands of times until we could do it within split seconds, in the dark. Some of us could reload faster than someone transitioning to a secondary firearm. I knew where every amount of ordinance was on my teammates back or on their kit in case I had to get to it.

The amount of training, skill, planning, and knowledge that goes into a single hit is just plain surgical, and precise. Fuck, sometimes it is just inspiring to know you are among the best, with the best officers and non-commissioned officers in the world.

The ramp dropped. We exited in a matter of seconds and grabbed our ladders from the back of our Stryker. We waited for the lead element to begin their order of movement, and then we headed out. Hunting once again.

We immediately began to scan every door and crouch under every window. Security en route to the second house was shit tight. We did not talk, but rather used hand signals. We knew who everyone was by the way they walked. We had been doing this for years with each other. We didn't have to talk. We used rates of fire to talk to each other. If somebody's rate of fire increased you knew that you were either covered and could bound forward or break contact. We talked with our weapons, and gave commands with our lasers. We kept radio traffic to a minimum. We did not want to alert anyone to a small force of deadly Americans that were now creeping through a city controlled by Al Qaeda in Iraq.

The alley that we walked through was only a few feet across and uneven. It was probably hundreds of years old. A feeling of uneasiness gripped me like a vice. I felt squeezed in this fatal funnel, alert to possible threats from rooftops, upper windows, and doors. Even with so much going on in my head, over the radio, everything remained silent. All you could hear was the occasional silent whisper of someone talking to an overhead asset, and the sound of gravel and pebbles crunching underneath our Merrill boots.

The uneven, cobblestoned alley played hell on my ankle. I had endured a class 3-ankle sprain on my first deployment to Southwest Asia and I kept going on missions instead of letting it heal. Needless to say, it always rolled, so I had to wear mountain boots and an ankle brace to give it enough stability while we conducted missions. We sprinted, ran, and walked with over 65lbs or more of body armor and equipment for our job, and I had a constant fear of it rolling, thus becoming a burden to my comrades. If it did happen, I was just going to have to eat the pain, and focus on the task at hand.

We crept through the narrow alley, the only light in that dark space came from our "green eyes" which was the light emitted by our night vision devices. There was little to no illumination that night, which we would find out in the next couple of minutes, would work to our advantage.

As we set up for the assault, I would not say that we became complacent by any means. Yes, we had done this hundreds of times. Rangers understand that complacency kills. On the way up to the objective we received word from an asset that there were multiple personnel on the roof, armed, and one was moving. Okay, the bad guys were awake. My level of alertness went up as I expected to be ambushed in the alley. I started to look for doors I could kick down so the assault force could flow into them and take cover. Mentally, I was prepared to kill anything that was in my way.

Everything was quiet. The night was hot. My team leader turned his head and whispered softly, "JT, snipers set." This let me know that our main assault team started their task. As they were setting up the breach, an asset we had requested to come on station after the building was secure buzzed the target building without warning. Come to find out, it was not our asset at all, but a Kiowa scout helicopter tasked to the regular Army unit, which surrounded the city. The element of surprise was gone. Whoever was trying to go back to sleep was now wide-awake. Without any warning, a head peeked out the front door. With the breach compromised, the assault team instinctively entered the house.

At the time, I was in the trail assault element taking a knee around the corner. I heard somebody from the lead assault team yell, "BREACH COMPROMISED!" So, I waited for the slightest movement to be made by my fellow teammates. A few seconds passed, which seemed to last forever. No one panicked. We waited for our brothers to do their job.

BOOM!.................BOOM! Two loud explosions were followed by screams. Blood curdling screams. Panic gripped all of us. This was not one guy screaming. Holy shit, multiple guys were hurt or worse. Everything we had trained for was now a reality.

Surprise gripped most of us. Fear gripped a few. The severity of the situation we were now faced with crept over all of us as cries of, "Oh my GOD!" along with moans, and cries for help from numerous close friends filled the alley. Up to that point a large majority of us had never even fired our weapons in combat. That was about to soon change. As the cries for a medic rang out by our fallen brothers, I sprinted past other Rangers to gain entry to the house while instantly making peace with the fact that I might get killed in the act. As the first one in, I could barely fit through the front door with all of my gear. I forced myself in, and instantly I was hit with a sight. In that small hallway, we had suffered five serious casualties. Wounded Rangers were gripping at their legs. Some were screaming, and writhing in pain. Others were just crying for help. The smell of blood, flesh, and gunpowder mixed together in such a small space filled my nostrils, and is something I will never forget.

I glanced into the four small rooms as I flowed past them to establish security in the courtyard. I moved past my wounded comrades and made my way to the corner of the hallway to pull security. I automatically knew that I had 30 Rangers right behind me. As I arrived at the corner of the hallway where it opened up into the small courtyard, I saw my dear friend Joe lying on his back and reaching out towards his legs. I thought his legs had been blown off, so I mentally prepared myself for what I was going to have to deal with. As I knelt down next to Joe, I noticed another seriously wounded Ranger with my peripheral vision within feet of us. Another really good friend of mine, JB, slid in on his kneepads and immediately began work, conducting RFR. Training immediately kicked in for all of us. This was a moment that would come to test all of us as men.

When Rangers are in a house or conducting operations where bullets and shrapnel are flying all around us, it is important to be fully aware of your surroundings at all times. Friendlies were flowing past me into the courtyard while firing their weapons in order to establish a hard point on the rooftop to provide security for us as we tended to the wounded. I was going to work on Joe regardless, even if it meant being shot in the back. I knew where my comrades were and I was confident they were taking care of business. I trusted my life to these men. I could rest easy knowing there were Rangers in the same house as me.

Joe was a Ranger buddy whose girlfriend was friends with mine. We regularly hung out back home. We were all friends but some more so than others. This was one of my dear friends lying on his back. Joe was one of the strongest and most mentally tough people I have ever met. To see this man on his back screaming in agony was something training could never prepare you for. Trying to hold down a 230 pound man who had just been blown up is something that training does not prepare you for either. Luckily, my body and mind were working in tandem together, like a machine from the dozens of times I practiced this under fire during training. I thought to myself, "don't panic, and conduct a head to toe assessment" while making sure to talk to Joe. I wanted to reassure him that he was okay; I was there now, and for him to keep his spirits up.

He made reference to his girlfriend Michelle. "Tell Michelle that I love her," he strained to say.

"Fuck you, Joe, you tell her yourself," I replied. "You're okay, bro," I said trying desperately to reassure him. I knew with his screams that he had an open airway and it did not sound labored. As I conducted my head to toe assessment I scraped his back with my Oakley gloves, looking for blood and holes that I could attend to. I then heard a distinct metal sound close behind me.

Tink . . . tink . . . tink . . . .

I glanced over to my friend JB and we both looked down at our ankles. There was a blue grenade. I jumped on Joe to shield him from the potential blast, and JB did the same to his patient.

When you are waiting on a grenade at your ankles to go off, the seconds you count while anticipating such an explosion last forever. I waited for a few more seconds, and realized it was a dud. I looked over to JB and all he could do was just shake his head. It was as if he couldn't believe what we had just been through during those short 7-10 seconds either. We went back to work as gunfire screamed from every direction. There was a large fight going on in the house and yet, we remained unscathed.

I continued my head to toe where I had left off and started to take off Joe's heavy equipment. I placed his MICH helmet to the side and undid the straps to his body armor. I lifted the front of the plate carrier over his head, trying to be careful I didn't hit him in the head with the heavy plates. Blood was coming out of his ears, nose and mouth. I undid the buttons of his field top in order to get him some fresh air. I put his rifle over the back of my ankle just as if I was in an RFR training lane. I fetched my Gerber knife out and with three swift cuts I opened up his tan shirt as well as each pant leg, careful not to cut him.

Blood squirted all over my face. It got in my mouth, up my nose, and in my eyes a bit. It was all over my clothes and my gloves making them extremely slippery. I reached for his tourniquet, which he secured with retaining bands, so it could easily be ripped away for a situation just like the one we were in now.

His life was spilling out over this dirty floor, and I had to stop it. I noticed he was peppered with small holes and the majority of his injuries were to the lower half of both legs. He had one of the new CAT tourniquets, a plastic one, which had a plastic handle so you could turn it to tighten the tourniquet around the wounded appendage. The CAT was also made of super sticky Velcro and trying to get the Velcro unstuck, and fit it around Joe's massive tree trunk thighs proved to be an issue. He was still spurting blood. With each heartbeat, his blood gushed from his main wound.

I finally got the Velcro unstuck and threw the tourniquet around his leg. I tried to get enough of a grip on the plastic turn handle, but to be honest, with bloody gloves it is really hard to do. I couldn't get a firm enough hold of it. It slipped. "Fuck this shit," I said out loud, frustrated that they gave us these stupid CAT tourniquets in the first place. I carried an extra ratchet tourniquet on my kit, so I ripped it from its retaining bands and slipped it easily over his leg. I pulled the strap as tight as I could, cranked on the lever, and his blood loss stopped instantly. I took some of his blood and with my finger, made a "T" on his forehead. This let the medics know that he had a tourniquet on. I made sure to work smooth and fast, fighting the urge to panic. I was not dead . . . yet. Although it seemed like an eternity, the time that had elapsed from the compromised breach to this point was less than a minute and half.

BOOM! A large explosion threw me off balance, and I landed on Joe's bad leg. He immediately passed out from the pain. I made a fist and with my knuckles did a sternum rub to his chest to try and bring him back to consciousness, but to no avail. I tried slapping him as hard as I fucking could, also to no avail. This was my dear friend. I did not want to hurt him further since I had just been the cause of him losing consciousness, but I had no choice. I was thinking to myself how much of an asshole I was for causing him that much pain. I checked his pulse and breathing, and everything seemed fine.

We had two medics with us as well as the battalion physician's assistant, but they were busy working on other wounded Rangers. Help was coming. Joe was still unconscious, and he felt cold and clammy. He looked pale white so I began to start to treat him for shock. As I was doing this, my team leader JD made his way over to my location. He was an EMT-Paramedic, so he tapped my shoulder and said he was taking over to give Joe a much-needed IV, and to bandage his wounds. Joe was in excellent hands now, so I linked up with my squad leader and my other teammate, to go room to room looking for threats to eliminate.

I heard yelling and screaming coming from the rooms, hallways, and rooftop. To the left of me was a small hallway that led down stairs to a room. A fellow Ranger was being engaged with grenades and small arms fire. Come to find out later, the insurgents were rolling grenades into the room from a small shaft in the wall, which was located in an adjacent house. On the roof, Rangers were engaged by small arms fire as well. You could hear the enemy on the roof top yelling in Arabic, throwing frags down on those of us located in the courtyard and open hallway. This house needed to get cleared STAT!

The three of us started to clear the right side of the courtyard. The first room we cleared was a small bathroom, so it just took us a quick glance to see that there were no bad guys to shoot and could move on to the next room. We made our way underneath the staircase that led to the rooftop. We had Rangers on the roof playing tennis with bullets, engaging enemy directly over our heads on the opposite roof. My team flowed into another short room, cleared it, and then we headed to the last room on the right. We cleared that room, and as the last man coming out of the room, I instantly picked up rear security on the roof and across the courtyard. As I scanned for threats, I immediately stopped where I was in the middle of the courtyard, frozen with fear. I was staring at a window where 3 enemy fighters had just set up a PKM machine gun less than five meters away from me. They didn't fire.

Holy shit, I thought. *I'm not dead yet.*

I started to come back from my split second daydream and yelled that I had a threat in front of me. "Sergeant! Machine gun, 12 o'clock!" I waited an eternity for fellow Rangers to start firing with me. I was met with an eerie silence. The insurgents still did not fire at me. Holy fuck, I can see them but they can't see me because it is so dark. They were scanning for targets to fire at but with so much going on I figured they did not want to reveal their presence either. I thought about all the Rangers in the fatal funnel behind me working on wounded comrades. I felt utterly helpless and alone in that courtyard, staring at that machine gun, even though so many bad ass Rangers surrounded me.

One of the fighters locked and loaded the machine gun. I had to think of something soon or I was going to probably end up getting shot to death and being riddled with 7.62mm machine gun rounds. I was starting to hate this fucking house. I decided that since I had friendlies to my six o'clock, I was going to blind the enemy with the tac-light on my weapon. A split second earlier, the thought about taking cover and throwing a grenade in their window did cross my mind. If I ended up missing the window the chance that the grenade could blow up my friends or me was a distinct possibility.

The light from the end of my weapon blinded the shit out of them. They covered their eyes, so I ran to the room I had just cleared seconds before with my team in order to take cover before I started to engage them. Getting into a shootout with a machinegun position only feet away from me with no cover seemed kind of foolish at the time. There was a window directly across from theirs. We had to be no more than 10-15 meters away from each other. I broke the glass to the window so they would lock on my direction, and not aim at my friends. I knelt down, and right then was where I became a believer in God. I thanked him for a wonderful life, for wonderful parents who had adopted me and gave me a chance to become something great. I asked him to protect them and my girlfriend at the time. I then asked him to guide my shots. I said a quick amen and pressed the button on the pistol grip of my M-4 that turned my infrared laser on. I took a deep breath, relaxed, and pointed my weapon at the machine gunners throat. For once in the last couple of minutes, there seemed to be utter silence. I noticed that the firing and explosions had stopped. The IR laser was locked on my target and I pulled the trigger. I fired and my shot found its mark hitting the gunner in the throat. His head lurched back and his friend to his right jumped on the gun and started firing.

Bullets were flying at me and in the direction of the Rangers on the staircase, on the roof, and the wounded in the hallway. The other insurgent started to throw frags at my window, so I just took a knee and ate it. The explosions and flying glass was deafening. My ears have been ringing every day since that night. A grenade rolled in thru the door to the room I was in and all I could do was chuckle and say "4," marking how many times I had almost been killed in the last three minutes. It didn't go off. I decided I was going to wait for a lull in firing, and then pop up and kill them.

Waiting for a machine gun to go through two hundred rounds of ammo while glass, grenades, and mayhem are exploding around you is nothing short of surreal. Finally, the lull I waited for came and I went to the door. I switched firing hands to my left hand so that I could remain behind cover. The two insurgents ran for a piece of wall that they tried to use to climb up to the roof where their friends had been shooting at us from. I unloaded a full magazine at them, wounding both of them. After my magazine ran dry I dropped the mag and reloaded a fresh one. Our snipers who were set up on the roof of a nearby building finished them off with headshots. As I was posted in the door way I started to take more fire from the rooftop. Fuck, how many terrorists were there?

I looked to my left expecting to have friendlies cover me, but there were none to be seen. They had taken cover in the four small rooms where the bullets and grenades would not be able to reach them. Some sought cover outside the house. I was still by myself, nearest to the enemy. I looked again to my left as bullets whizzed by my head. "5," I thought to myself. Just then the Sergeant Major and a dog handler shooting his 9mm pistol covered me while I ran to the front door out of the house. I wanted to make it to the safety of the armored Stryker vehicles, all of which ended up getting stuck in the narrow alley coming to our aid. They had to listen to everything transpire on the radio while their brothers were getting shot at and blown up. The Stryker crews also took a tremendous amount of fire trying to get to those of us that were inside that house.

I made it outside. I noticed that my squad leader was directing the Strykers so we could evacuate the wounded, and exfil the fuck out of there and just call in airstrikes. I checked the Strykers for my assault team since we had been separated since the beginning of the engagement. My squad leader was directing vehicles. My team leader was wounded as well, but still rendering aid, so I had two out of three. Where the fuck was my other teammate? I rechecked all the vehicles, which to my astonishment held more wounded than we had initially taken to begin with. I went to the front door to the house where my Ranger buddy, Steve, was taking a tactical pause. I was scared shitless to go back in to that house.

I explained to him how I could not find my teammate and how scared I was to go back in there. He responded with, "We have to. Follow me!" So, I followed him back in.

We ended up finding my other teammate. He was making his way up the stairs when the machine gun started firing, shooting him in the back. The bullet went through his back and out his chest, missing his heart by millimeters. He was now our most critical casualty and we had to get him airlifted immediately or he would die. The thought that I had just gotten my friend shot and he may now die was something I was going to have to think about later. How he was still alive is testimony to the courage and skill displayed by the best medics in the world, and to God watching over us that night.

There were weapons strewn about, left on the ground by wounded Rangers. Sensitive items needed to be policed up so they did not fall into the hands of the enemy. There were live grenades and demo charges that if kicked or stepped on could make our night even worse than it was already. Without having to be told, training kicked back in. My platoon Sergeant, though wounded himself, was busy as hell doing other things. I started to drop red chemlights to mark the unexploded grenades that had their pins pulled. Thank God they were old Russian relics. Under sporadic fire, I made a couple of trips back and forth to vehicles to drop the sensitive items off. I made my way back into the house, and then fell in behind the battalion PA. I noticed an insurgent that had made his way from a hidden tunnel lift his weapon to the back of the PA's head. As soon as I saw the weapon lift, I instantly turned, fired, and kept firing until there was nothing left of his face. I then turned around and headed back out of the house.

I remained outside, and pulled local security making sure the city did not come down on top of us. I witnessed our platoon leader carrying one of our seriously wounded squad leaders on his back, out of the house to a waiting Stryker. Our Medical vehicle was filled to capacity, so we had to put the wounded on other vehicles. The Rangers who had initially cleared the roof actually ended up capturing the HVTs we were going after in the first place. After we loaded the last of the wounded and detainees, those of us that were basically not shot or blown up loaded up on the last two vehicles. Three of my squad were wounded, one critically, clinging to life. One assault team had all their Rangers seriously wounded in the initial ambush. My adrenaline was still kicking even sitting with one other in the back of our Stryker. The severity of what we had just been through started to sink in. We made sure to check each other for wounds since our adrenaline was kicking into overdrive. We were fine except I had a hole in my sleeve and a long burn mark like someone had burned my arm with a metal rod. I had been grazed but I was no worse than some of my friends.

We moved the critically wounded Ranger to an awaiting helicopter that evacuated him to the nearest combat support hospital. We then took the other seriously wounded casualties to the hospital on the airfield of Mosul.

Like I said at the beginning, this was just one night out of many where we faced death in the face. We went on a rampage after that night. We ran hard, and we fought even harder. The remarkable thing about Rangers is we were able to fill our vacant slots with Rangers from another company, guys we had never worked with before, yet we did not skip a beat. We performed exceptionally well and made lasting friendships with these Rangers from C Company. Privates and gunners from our Stryker crews were now in the assault teams, and I was made an un-tabbed fire team leader in combat, which was unheard of in Battalion. It was an honor, not to have merely served, but to have served with these remarkable heroes.

As we flew back to Fort Benning at the conclusion of our deployment, half of us expected to get killed upon landing. We thought it would be a fitting way for the deployment to end. Two days before we landed at Benning, our sister platoon from A Company, 1st Platoon, was supposed to go home in two days as well when they suffered casualties of their own. A grenade fell through the hatch of one of their Strykers, with grievous results. Such is life as a Ranger; such is war. TSAF!

-JT
Dedicated to my son and the men of A Co. 3/75
3/75

Winter 2005
"The Phantom Shitter"

As many a Ranger story begins, so does this one, no shit, there I was . . . . However, only half of this statement would be accurate for this particular story. There was shit, and to be more specific, a shit . . . . Now before I get into the dirty details of this little deployment drama, let me explain something that I feel has gone missing from the public eye concerning Rangers. We are obsessed with poop, and sadly, I don't even think most of us realize it. I guess I first realized it when I would head back to my hometown to hang out with old college buddies. Things I did in my new life in Battalion, to them, were considered . . . how should I put it? *Off.* Things such as pooping with the door open while still engaging in conversation, asking them to come look at my greater bowel accomplishments, and simply just talking about the Lincoln log I had left behind that day in such detail that a police sketch artist could draw it with his eyes closed.

With that said, pooping is a big part of Ranger life. I don't think I can exactly say why, but my guess is that from infancy in the Army, you learn that everyone poops, there's never enough toilets, and the ones that are usually provided are a lot different than the ones you've experienced your whole previous life. Also, remember growing up? If you had a brother, remember how it was sharing a toilet/bathroom with him? Now multiply that by 40 at a minimum! So long story short, if you were poop shy, you'd better get over it quickly and cope. Just like Rangers cope with day-long smoke sessions, jumping out of airplanes with 250 extra pounds strapped to them, ridiculously long ruck marches, and of course the ever elusive enemy trying to take your life . . . we laugh about it.

Through the course of my military training, all the way up to getting into Battalion and going through Ranger School, I've experienced a wide variety of pooping styles. There is the E-tool seat poop, the sitting-on-a-downed-branch (or log) poop (hands down the best, if available, for outdoor drops), and the big-open-room-with-nothing-but-toilets-and-grunting-men-after-downing-blueberry-pancakes poop. I would be remiss to forget the buddy-assist poop where there is nothing to sit or balance on, and your legs are so smoked you can hardly squat, so your buddy kindly holds your hand to support your squat and whispers words of encouragement as you try to push out the two MRE's you ate for breakfast while getting your feet inspected by the Doc. Last, but certainly not least, the landmine poop. I'm sure you can tell from the name, but it is when you're a complete dick and no longer give a fuck so you quickly evade the eye of the Drill Sergeant or R.I., slip off into the night, deploy your landmine and sneak back inside the wire before anyone knows you were missing.

So now that I've scraped the surface of inserting SEAL Team 6, here's my tale. It's my epic poop story, the one that will stick with me for the rest of my life. To those of us in A-3-3 during that cold, late fall/early winter in Jalalabad (J-Bad), Afghanistan we refer to it as, "The Phantom Shitter." Now, there are many phantom shitter stories out there, but this one is mine. It was a day just like any other day, hotdogs and hamburgers for lunch, check all of the vehicles, some classes by the team leaders, a little P.T., all in all, a good day to be a Private in 1st Ranger Battalion. And then it happened. "Everyone get the FUCK in the bathroom!"

To fill you in real quick, we were staying at the airport in J-Bad, down the end of the runway all by ourselves in what used to be an Afghan police station. It was one building divided into two parts, one side the living quarters, the other the showers and toilets. The bathroom was pretty big, big enough to hold the whole platoon in the shower section. Now this bathroom was unique as the toilets were only for "Number two," if you had to piss, you went around back of the building and aimed your .50 cal. into the PVC pipes sticking out of the ground at angles. But inside, when you did discharge your submarine, you wiped and then threw the paper into the trashcan next to each station as opposed to flushing it.

With that said, all the privates rapidly scramble like cockroaches when a light is flicked on, into the bathroom as the tabbed Spec-4's, team leaders and squad leaders moseyed on in behind them as per Ranger standard operating procedure. However, on this specific occasion they were in for a surprise, this wasn't just going to be a fun time for the privates, everyone was invited to this party - group punishment! We all stood at the position of attention in the shower section and as a group we were addressed with, "Who did it?" from the platoon sergeant. I guess the puzzled look on everyone's face, except for one of course, led him to elaborate. "Which one of you fucks left that gigantic defecation in stall three?" As everyone started to think this is a joke and crack smiles, the whole platoon is dropped.

Now to the average civilian reading this, it may seem like an everyday occurrence, but let me tell you, when you are getting smoked . . . right alongside your leadership . . . it is a bad day. Nothing good can come of it, they get mad that they are getting smoked and guess who they take it out on . . . yep you guessed it, sticking with the theme of this story, shit rolls downhill. So there we are, all in the front-leaning rest, cranking out four-count pushups, mountain climbers, flutter kicks, and whatever other sadistic methods to get one to talk they could conjure up. The whole time everyone must still be thinking the situation is kind of comical and will be over momentarily, no way the whole platoon is getting smoked over someone's larger than life stool sample. We were wrong.

After a while, and still no confession to be had, we were put to parade rest and one by one, escorted back to stall three by a team leader, while the platoon leader and platoon sergeant stand by the door, order you to step into the stall, stand at parade rest, examine the excrement, and then state if it was yours or not, to which I myself replied, "Negative, Sergeant!" One specific platoon member worthy of mention during this process was our platoon's smallest guy. He is escorted back there for his personal viewing, and you could hear the platoon leader and platoon sergeant order him to look at it. After a few seconds they ask him if it was his, to which his response echoed throughout the entire bathroom in his strong Mississippian accent, "Sarn't, that turds bigger den me!" That brought upon one of the quietest laughs I've ever heard.

After everyone, staff sergeant and below, had filed through and took a good look at this feat of human achievement, the smoking continued. I wish I could tell you for how long, but anyone who has endured a solid smoker knows that just like Happy Gilmore, you go to your happy place, fake motivation, and try not to be the first one to give out. After a good amount of time, certain individuals start to laugh and enjoy the suck as they say, while others get pissed, and I'm talking fucking pissed. Yelling at others to confess while swearing profanities randomly. The most common phrases often yelled are, "Come on guys," or the ever so popular, "What the fuck!"

I guess it finally became clear to the leadership that no one was going to confess to that brown, protein packed monster, so with threats of breaking gravel into smaller pieces for the rest of the deployment, we were dismissed. The next day I believe we all pulled nails and screws out of beat up pieces of lumber left behind, and maybe caught some residual smokings throughout the day. For the most part, the phantom shitter escaped unscathed and was never to be heard from again.

Unfortunately this is the end of my story. There is no closure to be found here and one is left to his or her own imagination of what man could be capable of this level of "violence of action." Two things always left me curious about this case, one being the obvious "who done it?" I always thought that during someone's going away speech, in front of our company formation, their last line would go something like, "and for all those in A-3-3 in J-Bad . . . it was me, I'm out!" But it never happened, at least not during my time. The other thing you may ask yourself, which I ponder in my bed late at night on those cold nights . . . who, and furthermore how, did they get that turd to flush? Clearly someone had to remove it, chop it up, or perhaps as an old squad leader of mine used to say, "Just blow it in place!" The one thing that I do take from this story and my career of pooping while living the Battalion lifestyle is this: in the final stanza of the Ranger Creed, when they mention Intestinal Fortitude, I always took it to mean guts, courage, and heroism. After J-Bad, I realized it also just literally means, *intestinal* fortitude, and by God that Ranger had it! RLTW!

-J
1/75

Chapter Six

"The art of war is simple enough.
Find out where your enemy is. Get at him as soon as you can.
Strike him as hard as you can, and keep moving on."

ULYSSES GRANT

2006 brought about a major change to the structure of the Regiment, with the addition of a battalion for the first time since 1984. The Regimental Special Troops Battalion was provisionally activated on July 17th, 2006 and would be officially activated on October 16th, 2007 in response to the rapidly changing nature of Ranger operations. The RSTB consists of four companies with four different missions; enabling the Regiment and other special operations forces with increased flexibility and capability.

The Ranger Reconnaissance Company (RRC), formerly known as the Ranger Reconnaissance Detachment (RRD), is a Special Mission Unit (SMU) with its own selection and training course. It is considered the premiere special operations reconnaissance asset to both the Regiment and other special operations units. Their known missions include finding the enemy, penetrating enemy networks and safe havens, and facilitating the defeat and destruction of the enemy.

The Ranger Communications Company (RCC) specializes in command and control, as well as communications in support of the Regiment and other special operations forces. They are experts in both conventional and special forms of communication, staying proficient in all equipment used in the operating environment.

The Ranger Military Intelligence Company (RMIC) conducts human intelligence, signal intelligence, imagery intelligence, and all source analysis operations in support of the Regiment and other special operations units. RMIC Rangers are experts at their craft, attending premier intelligence training courses that set them apart from their peers. Many become proficient in foreign languages, and are among the most deployed Rangers in the Regiment.

The Ranger Selection and Training Company (RS&TC), formerly known as the Ranger Training Detachment (RTD) and Ranger Operations Company (ROC), is considered the "Gateway into the Regiment." The RS&TC conducts the Ranger Assessment and Selection Program (RASP) 1 and 2. Formerly known as the Ranger Indoctrination Program (RIP) and the Ranger Orientation Program (ROP), RASP 1 and 2 are the selection courses that all prospective Rangers must attend and graduate from in order to gain assignment to the 75th Ranger Regiment. The RS&TC also conducts the Small Unit Ranger Tactics (SURT), and the Pre-Special Operations Combat Medical Course (PSOCM).

The Regiment also ditched the traditional black cotton t-shirt and short "Ranger panties" for the more modest yet upgraded black physical fitness uniform in use today, but not without protest from the lower ranks. Ranger panties didn't leave much to the imagination, but were extremely comfortable and didn't retain odor like the new shorts did. Although not authorized as an official uniform anymore, Rangers still sport them to this day both on the beach and in the gym.

The violence in Iraq continued, and the country remained the focus of the 75th Ranger Regiment in 2006. Gains were being made though. The number one target in the war on terror, Abu Musab Al Zarqawi was killed in an airstrike on his position, and recovered by special operations soldiers after a nearly two-year manhunt by the Task Force. Saddam Hussein was finally put to death, hanged by his countrymen after being tried in an Iraqi court. Changes also came to the wars leadership, with Donald Rumsfeld, the Secretary of Defense, resigning his position. The death toll continued to rise, reaching the sobering mark of 3,000 American service members killed in action. Among the fallen in 2006, were Staff Sergeant Ricardo Barraza and Sergeant Dale Brehm, both from the 2nd Ranger Battalion.

By this point in the war, Rangers were a cornerstone of the national counter-terror strategy. They were working primarily as individual platoons, conducting missions autonomously on targets all over Iraq and Afghanistan. The way Rangers fought had been in transformation over the past few years, but in 2006 the Regiment had hit its stride and was completely comfortable with their newfound role. They were taking it to the enemy every single night, arriving at the cutting edge of battle in helicopters, Strykers, and even special warfare boats.

The Regiment had perfected the small unit raid and was using it on an industrial scale. In August of 2004, the Command's Task Force that the Rangers were operating under conducted eighteen raids. By August of 2006, they were averaging over 300 a month! This was primarily due to the fact that Task Force commanders were no longer using Rangers as security for special mission units; they had discovered that they were just as effective in counter terror operations as the SMU's they had previously supported. This allowed commanders to use fewer men on more targets, which worked perfectly in concert with the Task Force's newly developed targeting methodology – Find, Fix, Finish, Exploit, Analyze, Disseminate or simply referred to as F3EAD (pronounced "feed"). Gone were the days of planning for an objective days in advance, Rangers and their Task Force brethren were now receiving missions so rapidly that the 'Time Sensitive Target', or TST, became the norm. On TST's, the platoon would execute a shortened version of mission planning, sometimes launching within minutes while receiving the details on the way to the objective. This strategy worked with frightening results, with some Ranger platoons dismantling entire enemy networks within a single three-month deployment.

June 2006
"Breaching in Iraq"

In the beginning of my time in 3/75, I was a machine gunner, and I was not a fan. By my second deployment they had moved me over to be a squad breacher. I excelled at this because I understood the operation of doors, gates, and the construction of buildings and weak points due to working with my father since I was a small boy. My dad taught me all of the ins and outs of construction, to include framing, foundations, electrical, plumbing, and fine carpentry. So getting into a house or building silently was easy for me, especially in Iraq. Most of our target buildings had fortified doors because the occupants inside were up to no good. They were still no match for a 22-year-old Ranger, who grew up installing all types of doors and learning the fine art of construction since the age of nine. I could easily and immediately identify a door then assess the quickest way to breach it.

I also learned how to build my own charges and demolitions. We were taught at our internal breachers course on how to make various explosives and charges that would blow through steel gates, doors, walls, or even implode buildings. All of this came naturally to me. My main method of breaching was with the shotgun. Everybody knew I was the go-to guy when it came to breaching. When we hit targets, I was almost always the number one man to enter a compound or move to the building. The teams would flow right in after I breached the door or gate. I then moved behind them, opening any doors or removing any debris that blocked their path.

Earlier in this current deployment to Iraq, I was assigned directly to a Special Mission Unit as a gunner for one of their vehicles. Running multiple missions day and night, it was the best experience and group of guys I ever worked with in my life. Eventually I was needed back and was re-assigned to my team. We moved from one city to another, and we were the first SOF direct action unit to stand up one city, in particular. Within the Task Force as a whole, our area of operations was the entire northeast region of Iraq.

At the time, I remember some of the other units in the Task Force were pissed off because it was an active area, full of work to be done. We were on call 24/7 with a high value target capture/kill hit list that was long enough to keep us busy for a while, not including the other insurgents that surrounded them. We had our own portion of the airfield, and the 160th SOAR directly supported us, as always. They had no other task but to fly us to and from our objectives, as well as providing close air support on missions. We only had connex boxes with no power to use as a ready room, which meant our kit and equipment was always blazing hot by the time we had to launch for a mission. We had the support guys on our SOF compound start construction immediately for a ready room, as well as overhead cover for our Stryker's. They built what is now called, The Sergeant James Regan Ready Room.

One mission I remember, the platoon sergeant called me over the radio to come breach a steel door the others could not get into. I gained entry into that door in about five seconds. Unfortunately, I had shrapnel from the door and ricochet from the shotgun covering my arm. Later that night I had doc pull all of the shotgun pellets out of my arms along with some metal splinters. To be honest, I was used to it and the adrenaline ensured that I felt nothing. On mission, I wanted my brothers to have the best chance to overwhelm the enemy with violence of action. With that in mind, I may or may not have put some extra C2 Data Sheet and detonation cord in some of my charges to give my brothers the upper hand when entering a building.

Eventually, I was questioned on my charge building techniques. This came after the ground turned to Jell-O as the mud flap charge I built blew straight into the target house, giving my team an alternate, unplanned entrance into the target building. My squad didn't even have to use a door or secondary charge. The original plan was to blow the main gate, then have me run up and then breach the door to the target building, allowing our guys to flow in. Well, I didn't have to do that on that mission. The charge had blown a hole straight through the gate and into the house, shattering every window in the house in the process. This was a three-story building that was about 4,500 square feet. Maybe next time they won't put their front gate so close to their house.

Our SOF compound was a base inside of a base, which was guarded by regular Army soldiers. I felt so bad for those guys. We were walking around in sterile Ranger panties and T-Shirts while they were guarding our compound dressed in full kit, in blistering heat that reached 130 degrees during the day at times. Needless to say, those guys always had a smile on their face when we walked by or acknowledged them. I had respect for those guys because everybody has a job to do in the military. I was just happy I busted my ass in the beginning of my military career so that I didn't have to endure such duties.

My squad was hanging out in our room, playing Halo, and a few guys were in the gym. It was about midnight, Zulu time, when our pagers went off for the code that we will be going on a mission. We gathered everybody up and ran to the ready room (connex box at the time), donned our kit, and linked up at the airfield. Once there, we assigned chalks/birds and loaded up, taking off within minutes of receiving the notification on our pagers. It was a capture/kill mission, with an offset infil, which meant we were to land about seven kilometers away and hump it in. Which sucked, a lot. There were no other special orders, other than we were going after this guy and to collect intelligence on the target . . . the usual. We had other special attachments from a government agency with us as well, to help with interrogations and such.

Honestly this was just another day on deployment for us. There was no better way to get to work than sitting in the door of an MH-60, or a Little Bird with feet dangling and the wind crushing you in the face while hoping a bird wouldn't crash into your face. That was pretty much our biggest concern after seeing what a bird could do to the windshield of a helicopter.

It was about a thirty-minute flight. We received our 10 minute warning, 5 minute warning, and then finally our thirty second warning. The birds flared, and landed right through a brown out from the rotor wash kicking up dust, dirt, and rock. Landing was unusual due to the time sensitive targets we were conducting at the time. We usually fast roped onto almost every target, due to operating within cities and urban environments. I didn't mind landing at all after the night prior though . . . .

My team was supposed to help provide security for our snipers, roping directly on to the target building. I was the first off the bird to rope onto this rooftop to clear and secure it for the snipers. Under NVG's, the rooftop looked clear. Not so much, the rooftop was littered with electrical wires that the pilots, nor we could see at the time. Unaware, we gave the little bird pilots, thumbs up, and threw the ropes. The rooftop was only about twelve feet away, so I didn't even bother putting my feet on the rope. I slid down, legs out ready to absorb the impact of the landing until one of those thin wires I could not see came between my legs and right into my man junk. Needless to say, it sucked. I dangled there, bouncing up and down and hanging onto the fast rope. I eventually continued my decent after getting myself clear of the power line. I signaled to the pilot to move the birds a couple feet left after I hit the rooftop, so my other buddy didn't have to endure the awesome experience of getting your nuts crushed. Suffice it to say, I was more than happy to not be fast roping tonight.

Once we landed, we moved across the open farmland, shit ditches, and suburban mud villages with small amounts of electricity illuminating the small suburban mud towns. In some places it looked like you went back in time. We finally reached the main street and moved down it for about four kilometers, with dogs barking at us and people looking out their windows to see what all the commotion was about. We moved in the shadows, and we all had NVG's, so I wondered what the people on the inside of those buildings could actually see. During our entire movement, you would see IR laser pointing at any possible threats and illuminating rooms inside the buildings we passed. Our security was up the entire time and there was no time to think about how much the movement sucked. We finally came to a trail on a palm grove that would lead up the hill to our target building.

When we were close enough, each squad would move to their designated side of the building, usually forming an L-shape so all four sides of the building were covered in case of squirters. Our rules of engagement at the time were if you feel threatened, or they have a gun, you were clear to engage. If they run from the target building, we were clear to engage. When we reached the objective, we were still about 100 meters from the actual structure, so my squad moved on line in an open farm field. There was an extra building that was separate from the target building that was not on our imagery. So, two other guys and I went to go check it out. I moved through a thin woodline about five meters thick, which led into a drainage ditch about four feet deep filled with water, and about four feet in width. I found a good place, and jumped across. I was already tired of having my feet soaking wet and muddy and they had just dried out.

After we all crossed, we moved up the side of the target building slowly and quietly, using hand and arm signals to let each other know of our movement. We could hear voices and people walking around inside. I came to the corner of the target building, checking out the building that was not on our imagery. I "pied off" the corner in order to gain a better look at what we were dealing with. As I cleared the corner, my buddy behind me threw me to the left. I heard his suppressed M-4 discharge two rounds and looked to my right and front just in time to see the two rounds impact on an insurgent's forehead while his AK-47 was still pointed at me. The insurgent had come down a set of stairs from the unknown building and was about to take me out. This all happened in a matter of split seconds, but time seemed to slow down at this point. My buddy just saved my life . . . .

This was just the beginning. We had stumbled onto a hornet's nest of Al Qaida fighters that were living there with women and children. As soon as my buddy took those shots, a barrage of AK-47, machine gun fire, and hand grenades rained down on us, and the rest of our squad in the open field. With our IR lasers illuminating the targets above, all three of us returned fire and immediately dropped several fighters on the rooftop. It was a very target rich environment. We had to maneuver through gunfire and hand grenades to the open field about 50 meters to the right of our squad's position to obtain a better angle on the insurgents.

Once there, I repositioned myself again for a better angle on the rooftop. I saw the rest of my squad in the prone, becoming one with the earth and unable to move, returning fire when possible. I maneuvered myself to where I had the best vantage point and started eliminating targets. Very quickly they honed in on my location, and at this point I had nowhere to go. I was so close that if I had dropped into the prone I would actually make a larger target for them to shoot at. If I stood up and ran, it would be the same result. I put as much accurate M-4 fire down as possible. I was there long enough to remember that I could easily get shot right now, and honestly I do not know how I was not hit. These thoughts were actually going through my mind at the time, while continuing the firefight. God must have been with me that day, because at this point, I was less than fifty meters from the building in the wide open. No cover or concealment, just dirt on the flat farmland.

My squad eventually maneuvered out of harm's way, and I did as well. I moved back when I heard the AC-130 gun ship firing danger close, which gave me the chance to move about 75 meters to the right where the other three guys were in a mud cow pasture that was filled with all kinds of farm animals. Once we were clear of the target area, we were about 100 meters from the building we were receiving contact from. The AC-130 rained down ordnance, turning the ground into Jell-O. I had never felt anything like it. Honestly, I do not know how the mud cow pasture did not collapse on top of us. Minutes later, all rounds were expended.

I linked back up with my squad, and I would be the first to move across the target. My squad followed me as I moved to the ruins of the target building; all buildings were on fire and that dump truck was everywhere. Once I hit that woodline, I saw one of the men I shot. Littered with bullet holes, he fell off the rooftop and into the drainage ditch along with an unwounded five-year-old boy under his arm. Miraculously, the boy was still alive and was with his father. I guess the boy was knocked out from the over pressure because he looked dead as well, lying in a stream of red blood.

I continued to press on to the objective when I came along the same wall where my buddy saved my life. My foot and leg became stuck in something heavy and I could not get it off. It was like my foot was stuck in mud. My buddy behind me and I quickly hit our tac lights and it was the torso of a person. It was un-identifiable; it had no head, arms, or legs - or clothes for that matter. It didn't have any skin on it. I had put my foot right into the torso's intestines and my foot was caught up in the rib cage. Once free, I cleared across the objective and we detained several women, which were about all that was left. The men on the rooftops were turned to piles of mush; there were just random body parts and hair in piles on the rooftops.

Objective secure. We gathered whatever intelligence we could find, and called in a regular Army unit to clean up the mess. We gave them credit for the entire mission; we were able to cross off one of our top ten HVT's that night, along with some other big ones. We never publicly received credit for the success for our missions. If it were a big time HVT, we would typically give the credit to whatever Army or Marine infantry unit covered that area. When the Army unit arrived, I remember the commander of their unit rolling up and saying, "Holy shit! You guys blew the shit out of this place, are you ok!?" I just stared at him with a fat dip of Grizzly in my mouth and said, "Yup."

It turned out that the guy who had eight bullet holes in his body lying face down in that drainage ditch was still alive. Everyone said to me, "why the hell didn't you put two in his head?" In accordance with the Geneva Convention, we are trained that the first man who clears the across a body can ensure they are dead with a double-tap, but once you pass them you can no longer shoot them. So, he was now our problem. We left the mess to the regular Army to take care of, and we exfilled out. We ended up guarding his fat, shot-up body for a week until he died . . . learned my lesson.

For my actions on that mission I received an Army Commendation Medal for Valor for saving the lives of my squad members. Honestly, I did what any other Ranger would have done if they had been in my same situation. I saw my brothers pinned down, and just lit those insurgents up as fast and accurately as possible without thinking about my own safety. As any Ranger will tell you, I was just doing my job.

-Dan
3/75

June 2006
"The Task Force"

It was June 2006 and I was assigned to the Command's task force in central Iraq. This time period was undoubtedly the worst and most dangerous time of the seven-year war. Service members from all of the coalition countries were being slaughtered by hundreds of IEDs as the Sunni/Shiite civil war was in full swing. The man responsible was the leader, or "emir" of Al-Qaeda in Iraq and from 2004 to 2006 he was a higher priority target for the U.S. intelligence community than Usama Bin Laden himself.

This was my third deployment with 3rd Ranger Battalion, with one previous to Afghanistan in 2005 and my first to Mosul, Iraq in late 2004. Here they had me serving in two roles: as the Ground Force Commander's radio operator as well as 2nd Platoon, Charlie Company's radio operator. Although they may seem pretty inter-changeable, this now meant that instead of being responsible for all communications between the ground commander and the op-erations center while on an objective, I was also responsible for all radio systems internal to the platoon, to include five Stryker vehi-cles. The previous platoon radio operator was fired, and being a se-nior communications guy in 2006, I was somehow stuck with this stressful assignment - which I excelled at in spades, I might add.

Our first month of the deployment we were based out of Bagh-dad's Green Zone, within an area specifically called the mission stag-ing site, or simply the "MSS." Alpha Company's 2nd Platoon was the night platoon and Charlie Company's 2nd Platoon (2C) was the day platoon. The operational tempo was so busy that we would hit two targets a day sometimes! It was an awesome tempo for the individual platoons. But for me, being a part of the GFC's team meant that I would have to go on every single objective both day and night. Later, 2C was moved to Balad Air Base in order to conduct direct action missions against targets in nearby Baqubah. The command element, which included myself, SSG Ball the fire support NCO, and the commander, would stay with them for the rest of the deployment.

Operating in Baqubah was much different than operating in the Baghdad area. We engaged in firefights on what seemed like 75% of the objectives (opposed to roughly 25% in Baghdad) and because of the long distance from Balad to Baqubah we hit most of our targets via helicopter insertion from the 160th SOAR. If we didn't have the birds at our disposal, we'd have to slug around for more than an hour inside our cramped and uncomfortable Stryker vehicles to the objective. We were just the guys on the ground; we had no idea the dynamics of the area and why Baqubah was such a hornet's nest. If memory serves me right, our platoon was the primary Task Force assault package for that city. We definitely had enough work to keep us busy.

Although I conducted numerous combat missions in my past two deployments, this 2006 deployment is where I actually felt like an operational Ranger. By the end of the three month period we must have undertaken anywhere between 60 and 70 direct action missions, almost half of which were by air assault. There is no greater feeling than riding in a Black Hawk in the middle of the night with your legs dangling off the side. Our element, the command & control (C2) team always had our own bird to ride in and we rarely packed in like sardines as the rest of the platoon always did. These rides almost always included the two-man sniper team, the commander, the fire support NCO, and myself. Everybody was able to be on the door with the exception of the commander who was always on the inside plugged into the radio getting the up-to-date intelligence from the surveillance platforms flying over the objective. Out of the many missions we went on, one in particular I will carry with me for the rest of my days.

It was either late May or very early June when coalition forces captured a key associate of the number one terrorist leader in Iraq, who at the time was ranked higher than Bin Laden himself. After days of interrogation, the individual gave up the location to seventeen known safe houses in the Baqubah area where the terrorist leader could possibly be located. We immediately put all of our assets on these locations. It was important to monitor the situation and plan ahead accordingly. U.S. forces had let this target slip through their fingers before, and we weren't going to let it happen again.

Sometime during the day on the seventh of June, one of our ISR assets spotted what was undoubtedly the target at one of the newly revealed locations. The Task Force commander at that time, Lieutenant Colonel Tom Di Tomasso (now retired), immediately began initial planning to launch a strike package. If the name sounds familiar, it's because he was one of the Ranger platoon leaders on the ground in Mogadishu in 1993, where he was awarded the Silver Star and Purple Heart for his actions. He was also included in Ridley Scott's movie *Black Hawk Down*. At this time, Di Tomasso was serving as the Deputy Commander of an Army Special Mission Unit.

The SMU Operators with a handful of Rangers from the 3rd Ranger Battalion boarded 160th Black Hawks in order to assault the safe house. As he pored over the images of the target building, Di Tomasso realized that the best way to get guys on the ground was in a clearing a short distance from the location. Fearing that his men would be compromised well before they touched down, Di Tomasso relayed his hesitations to his boss, General Stanley McChrystal. Fearing that the target could slip out once the helicopters began their approach, he recommended an air strike against the target. McChrystal ended up agreeing and at 6:12 pm local time, an F-16 fighter jet dropped two

500-pound bombs on the compound. The pilot, who was already operating in the area, had no idea who the target was, or his importance for that matter. The Task Force team and a small contingent of Rangers from our platoon (2nd Platoon, Charlie Company) arrived on the scene shortly after and recovered the dying high value target from the Iraqi police who were in the process of loading him up in an ambulance. Shortly after the team recovered the wounded terrorist he succumbed to his injuries and passed away.

Rangers along with most special operations forces are nocturnal creatures. We slept during the day and operated at night. So at around 6:12 pm, most of the platoon including myself was ether still fast asleep or getting ready for the "work day" as the summer sunsets came at around 8:00 in the evening. We didn't know or realize that a small team from our platoon was currently helping recover the body of the most wanted terrorist on America's radar.

Then something big came up. We were told to get our gear and vehicles ready for numerous direct action raids. It was probably 8:00 pm and none of us knew the target had been killed. The Task Force was given the locations of seventeen safe houses. The high value target was killed in one of them. That meant there were 16 other Al-Qaeda safe houses in Baqubah just waiting to be hit. The intelligence in each location would be invaluable and would set Al-Qaeda in Iraq back drastically.

Objective Avalanche was the name of the operation. "Avalanche I" was the air strike against the high value target, and Task Force commanders wanted the rest to be assaulted simultaneously. The Task Force strike package consisted of both 1st and 2nd Platoon (my platoon) Charlie Company 3/75, a Special Forces CIF team, a British SAS assault team, and two troops from the Army SMU. 2nd Platoon had two objectives to hit and were officially named Avalanche 15 and the follow-on as Avalanche 15A. Unfortunately we had to drive, as the Army SMU had first dibs on the 160th birds.

We thought we were going to get into some real shit that night! Lay the hate on some terrorist bad guys and make off with their computers! I don't remember exactly, but I think the first objectives that were hit by the assault forces were either a dry hole or peaceful arrests - ours included. The most eventful thing to happen on our first objective happened while I was taking a knee on the backside of the building. I was looking up at the second story and noticed there was a door there. It didn't lead to anything though. Not a balcony, not a walkway - nothing. It was literally a door on the side of a two-story building. It was very baffling. Well, the darndest thing happened next. I saw shadows moving around on the other side, which I assumed was the platoon clearing the house. I clearly remember thinking to myself, "Shit I hope nobody opens it up and runs right through!"

I was pretty close in my foretelling. The Ranger on the other side pulled out his breaching shotgun and fired off a round right into the lock. I wasn't more than fifteen feet away when I took the hundreds of incoming wooden shards to the face. There was no real damage to me as I was being a good Ranger and wearing my eye protection! But that could have turned out much worse for me.

At this time most of us thought we were on a mission to find the high value target the whole task force was focused on. We still didn't know he was killed just a few hours earlier. I'm sure the recovery team had to take the body back to Balad so the forensics people could officially identify it.

As we wrapped up our first objective, I received a call on the satellite radio from who I assumed was LTC Di Tomasso relaying that the target was killed. I passed the word to the commander and he passed it down to the platoon leader. Shortly thereafter all of us had heard the news. We were ecstatic to say the least, assuming he was killed on one of the other objectives, preferably not by 1st Platoon, and definitely not by the SF guys! We loaded back onto the Strykers and made our way to the second objective, Avalanche 15A. We better get into some shit this time I thought.

Wrong.

We hit the building, found some guy and his family. "This is lame," I remember thinking while providing security from an adjacent rooftop. The sniper next to me expressed a similar sentiment. Looking back in hindsight, I guess it makes sense that these safe houses weren't teeming with armed bad guys. Not much of safe house if you stick out like a sore thumb because of "military aged males" coming in and out.

We were about four or five hours into the night. After five hours of continuously looking through your night vision goggles, it starts to play tricks on you. For some it would really mess up their depth perception or would render their non-night vision eye (we were still using the PVS-14 monocles in 2006) completely useless. For me, it just made me incredibly sleepy. The elation of the targets death had worn off, most of us wanted to leave these uneventful objectives and return to Balad.

That's when the call came over the radio, "Hey guys, get ready to load up. We're going on a follow-on objective."

"Fuck!" Two, and soon to be three lame-ass objectives was just too much for one night. Apparently the man they found claimed that his brother is the owner of the home we just raided, and he will gladly take us to him. *What a shithead of a brother*, I remember thinking. So we loaded up in our Strykers once again. I think it was probably around 5:00 am at this point and the sunrise was only an hour away. The drive didn't take longer than ten minutes; we ended up parking our vehicles under a highway overpass. Iraq had a strict curfew at night so no civilian vehicles were on the roads.

We split the platoon down the middle; one half would stay and man the vehicles, the rest of us would walk a half-mile to the brother's location. Since I was the guy who listened in on the SATCOM channel, I already knew that the rest of the assault forces were back home either sleeping or wrapping up their after-action reports. There was no chatter from the operations center on the channel other than with our element.

Roughly eighteen of us went on foot to the new objective. Was it Avalanche 15A1 or 15AB? I don't know, I don't remember, and frankly I didn't care. We left the vehicles behind because they were too loud and could easily give us away. We crept on foot to what appeared to be a rather large construction zone for office buildings. "What the hell is this place?" I thought. It looked nothing like a neighborhood. It was literally just a complex of large unfinished office buildings. Yet another dead end I assumed.

That's about the time all hell broke loose. We immediately began to take automatic fire from what seemed like three different directions. That first 20-30 seconds of contact was the most intense enemy incoming fire I had ever received. I'm assuming that applied to some of the other guys as well. We took cover behind a small wall that might have been the foundation for a future building and began returning fire. I don't think anybody could really see where the incoming rounds were coming from. It literally seemed and sounded like a dozen guys were engaging us.

The first thing I noticed was the giant halogen light attached to the top floor of an unfinished eight-story building. It was shining directly above us and nobody seemed to notice. One of the snipers was next to me, so I pointed up and said, "You should take that out." He agreed, and without saying a word raised his rifle. One missed shot. A second missed shot. And finally a third missed shot before I brought my own M-4 up and caught sight of the light through my ACOG. One shot was all it took . . . giving me the bragging rights. We were now engulfed in complete darkness and there was no way the bad guys could see us, although the relentless fire never ceased or lulled.

At this point, we were about a minute into the engagement. On this very rare occasion, we actually did not have any air support from either the 160th's attack helicopters or even the AC-130 gunships. We did on the initial two raids but all the birds went home after our second objective. Rangers slowly began to accurately identify where the insurgents were holed up and returned precise rifle fire in their direction. Under night vision we could see their muzzle flashes magnified no matter the distance. There was no point in keeping the Strykers away at this point; everybody in a two-mile radius knew we were there. So we called them in for support; more specifically we wanted their .50 caliber machine guns equipped with thermal scopes. They arrived with guns blazing.

What a sweet sound it was, assuming you weren't standing too close. They were engaging enemy targets as they found them but we continued to receive not sporadic but intense small arms fire from multiple directions. Some guy, who we thought was fucking over his brother, legitimately led us right into an ambush. *You've got balls, sir. I hope you're enjoying Guantanamo.*

We began to move away from our positions towards a small cluster of buildings where we believed the closest insurgents were holed up. We definitely didn't own the battle space at this point. As we moved through the rubble, I heard the distinct call "Frag out!" come from one of the platoon's squad leaders. I took a knee beside the wall I was hugging and didn't move. It's best to not run around when a grenade has been released, especially if you didn't know its intended destination.

The explosive blast was on the other side of the wall that our element was taking a knee beside. It didn't knock the wall down nor did I feel any overpressure. My Sordins, our electronic ear protection and communications headset, completely shut off. I thought they broke! Being a radio operator, my communications equipment ran through my headset. If I can't use my headset, then I can't use my radios, which would render me completely worthless. In today's day and age in combat, having communications up was paramount. Then I remembered how they were designed. It was a rare occurrence that only happens when the decibel level is so high that the headset will automatically shut off in order to save the user's hearing. They were designed to soften or completely cancel high decibel levels (as in this case) but to amplify lower levels such as having a conversation.

We went through the opening in the wall and into the adjacent area. Two Iraqis lay dead from the explosion, one younger and one older - much older. I couldn't believe how close they were to us. We weren't more than twenty meters from the spot where we first took contact.

Our small ground element comprised of two squads, which is not exactly the most ideal maneuvering element, began to gain momentum as they cleared building after building. The Strykers were engaging targets from a good distance away and the enemy fire began to subside. Daylight was creeping over the horizon as the summer sky began to show the first signs of purple haze. I took a position on a rooftop with the ground force commander. Nearby, our fire support NCO had no fire support to call in so he just engaged targets as he saw them. It was only about thirty minutes after we first took contact, but we were no longer receiving enemy fire. Either we killed them all (very doubtful), or they buggered out once the Strykers unleashed the .50 caliber machine guns.

Daylight was now in full swing. Curious Iraqis living in the nearby areas were trying to get close enough to see what had happened. Air support also came in the form of two Apache gunships. But this mini-battle was already over. We were still grateful for them showing up. No idea what unit they were with, but they stayed with us over the area until we exfilled.

Some of the squads who went out to search the buildings where there were confirmed insurgent sightings reported back massive amounts of blood and spent ammunition with no bodies. In another building they came across a dead insurgent rolled inside a rug. Whoever was trying to recover the body must have left in a real hurry as Rangers were closing in. The .50 cal gunners reported killing 6-8 insurgents, the squad leader's grenade took out two, and then there were the unconfirmed number of bad guys killed by our small arms fire. If somebody would have told me for certain that a minimum of a dozen Iraqis engaged us I would have replied with, "That's it?"

The platoon sergeant, a veteran of most likely all of 3rd Ranger Battalion's deployments since 9/11 expressed to us that it was, "the most intense firefight I've ever been in." A squad leader would later express his disbelief that not a single Ranger took so much as a single scratch. That was indeed unbelievable. We loaded into our Stryker's and were ordered back to the MSS in Baghdad, rather than back to Balad. After what we went through, I figured I could get away with a quick nap during the 45-minute drive back.

"Donov - wake the fuck up!" the Major barked at me not more than thirty seconds later.

"Goddamnit . . . ."

When we arrived at the MSS, our humble abode from the previous month, our platoon was ordered to a small airfield where the 160th birds were kept. What looked like the entire SMU squadron was formed up (sort of) next to a small element of 160th personnel. We formed up (not sort of) next to them. The SAS and Special Forces elements must have gone their separate ways. Even our sister platoon must have made its way back to Tikrit.

Lieutenant Colonel Di Tomasso stood in front of the gaggle, what we called a, "sort of formation." I don't remember his speech word for word, but it definitely went something along the lines of, "We killed him, but don't think this is over. There is still a lot of work to be done. Bin Laden is still out there, Zawahiri is still out there, and al-Qaeda in Iraq is far from beaten. Our job is unfinished and we are going to keep getting after it here, in Afghanistan, and in Africa. But for today, great job!"

Hey, I want to go to Africa too, I remember thinking wishfully. I felt proud to be part of this operation and to stand in front of this warrior who commanded these titans among men. Although the glory went to the pilot of the F-16 jet who was on a routine mission, we all still felt a large sense of pride and accomplishment because at the end of the day, it was the efforts of the Task Force's relentless raids against Al-Qaeda that led us to the number one most high valued target in the world.

-Iassen Donov
3/75

JULY 2006
"SKITTLES"

While in the military, many orders are yelled at you. The lower the rank you hold, the more you are yelled at. Being yelled at in that environment doesn't necessarily mean you did something wrong, it may mean what is being said is a matter of life and death, literally. Many of these yelling orders came during training exercises being held within the safety of a US military base. All these orders were very specific and simple such as, "GET OUT OF THE FUCKING DOOR WAY!" or "HURRY THE FUCK UP!" There was one particular order that always made me internally laugh because of the irony. When my superiors would yell, "BE FUCKING TACTICAL!" my subconscious would always respond to that remark with a very snobbish, "Well him screaming for us to be tactical isn't very tactical at all." With all joking aside, that order was burned into my mind as the difference between life and death. That order would echo whenever I would put on my equipment. I knew I personally could be tactical and move about with stealth that would make a ninja proud. Yet, the equipment I carried had to be controlled in order to remain tactical.

In Tim O'Brian's book, *The Things They Carried*, O'Brian writes, "There was at least the single abiding certainty that they would never be at a loss for things to carry." Timmy is basically stating that no matter the conflict or time in history, soldiers will be forever loaded down with the burden of heavy equipment and emotional baggage. I was no exception to this single abiding certainty. Putting on my mission equipment, or "Kitting up," as we referred to it, was a lengthy process. I would start with my body armor and everything on it; seven full magazines of 5.56 ammo (210 rounds), two concussion grenades, two fragmentation grenades, one smoke grenade, an exploitation kit, an explosive breaching kit, a detainee kit, a bleeder kit, one tourniquet, fast rope gloves, compass, knife, watch, headlamp, strobe, team radio, eye protection, eight anti-structure rockets, and water. Once I was kitted up, I could don my helmet, put gloves on, and sling my rifle.

Now that I was fully kitted up, I would find a quiet room and jump up and down frantically. Any piece of equipment that would make a noise or shake loose, I would have to figure out how to silence it and tighten it down. I would then stand in front of a mirror and pace back and forth whilst looking in the mirror for anything that would shine back off my kit. Anything shiny would have to be subdued. Once I was satisfied with my adjustments, I would store my kit away with such a caring manner you would think I was placing an infant to bed. This manner of care was because I was told that my equipment could save my life as easily as take it, especially if I wasn't tactical.

My first year in the Army was all training time with the intent of preparing for war. We would wake up every day before the sun came up and start our morning exercises. The physical training would begin with a five to ten mile run to warm up. Once the team was nice and exhausted the real pain began. We would do strength/team building exercises where we would have to rely on our teammates to complete the drill. We would all be smoked to the point of muscle failure yet we'd all get through it together. The physical pain was so brutal our bodies would tremble as our minds tried to make sense of it all. Each day was a slightly different exercise in physical fitness, yet each day we pushed through it. Whenever any team member would cry out in agony, the squad leader would remind us to "suffer in silence." This was the squad leader's way of saying, "SHUT THE FUCK UP AND BE FUCKING TACTICAL!"

To suffer in silence is not just reserved for morning PT alone, yet is instilled in every aspect of special operations training. While conducting airborne operations, strict noise discipline was enforced.

Although every time I jumped out of an airplane I wanted to scream in fear, I had to find a way to make that leap in silence. During hand-to-hand fighting I wanted to yelp in pain when I got my eye gouged, but instead I had to ignore the pain and fight back. Whether its pain, excitement, or fear we learned to ignore our natural responses in life by staying silent and being tactical.

In the summer of 2006, our platoon was in the fields of Afghanistan conducting a raid on an enemy training camp. The raid did not go as planned, partly because we underestimated the number of enemy combatants we assumed would be in our area of operation. Within the first hour on the ground we realized we were heavily out-numbered and out-gunned. An extraction was called in to retrieve us from the battlefield. Once the aircraft was loaded with approximately half the platoon it slowly took off to return to a forward oper-ating base. Suddenly the training camp we thought we had subdued came back to life. A barrage of small arms and machine gun fire came roaring in the direction of the helicopter. As the aircraft rotat-ed in a clockwork motion, two rocket propelled grenades slammed into the fuel ballast, which forced the helicopter to crash land. As I watched this from my fighting position only 200 meters away, I thought, "How many of my friends just died?"

There was no time for emotion, no time to think about the blood of my comrades, it was time to suffer in silence, remain tactical, and secure the crash site.

In the book, *The Things They Carried,* O'Brien writes, "Made stu-pid promises to themselves and to God and to their mothers and fathers, hoping not to die." In this statement O'Brien is referring to the general consensus that when facing the dire end, all soldiers make deals with their creator in hopes to survive. There is an old Army saying similar to this one, "There are no atheists in foxholes." He also mentions that this act is "stupid." While this may seem as an insult to religious folks, I agree, that this act is somewhat stupid. I never put much thought into how I would act once facing the end.

I guess, I just assumed if it were to happen in combat it would be a quick, painless bullet to the face and if I were wounded bad enough, Doc would give me morphine and I would just fade away. Either way, I never envisioned myself as the type of man pissing his pants and praying for someone to save him. It's just not the way I act. At least that's not the way I hoped I would act.

The platoon set up a 360-degree perimeter around the dead helicopter. The firefight ended as abruptly as it had begun. An eerie calm settled as the stalks of corn swayed back and forth with the breeze. In the distance, I could hear the sounds of cattle grazing and livestock clucking away. The sun was slowly rising across the valley as the morning prayer songs played on loud speakers. We were all down in the prone position paired up with another operator in the muddy cornfield. I was lucky to be paired up with my friend Ron, a sniper from Philadelphia. The platoon radios were all communicating with the tactical operations headquarters trying to figure out a way to get us off this mountain. Ron and I made small talk while the command staff played on their radios. The sun was now fully up and we knew we were in trouble; we never work in the light, the darkness has always been our advantage. I suddenly heard someone breaking brush towards my right, it was the Air Force Combat Controller (CCT) and he was very excited. He squatted down between Ron and I and said, "Dig in, it's coming in danger close." And with that, he hopped up and was off to the next fighting position to tell the morbid news.

It turned out while my bosses were screwing around on their radios, and I was admiring the scenery, we were about to be overrun, big time. We would find out later that the morning prayer was actually a reinforcement call to the surrounding villages. Within a couple of hours, over 300 enemy fighters surrounded the thirty of us. The CCT had to call in 500-pound bombs to be strategically dropped outside our perimeter. Because the enemy was closing in fast, he had to call the bombs to be dropped at "danger close," meaning there was a very good chance of us getting hit.

My friend Ron and I accepted the fact that this may be the day we die. I reached into my pocket and pulled out a pack of Skittles I'd been saving for the flight back to base. I had prepped the Skittles the night before by opening the pack, releasing all the air, rerolling it and tightening it together with tape. I did this because I knew the enemy could hear the Skittles moving in my pocket and I had to remain tactical. I opened up the candy snack pack between the two of us and placed it on the muddy ground. I presented it as if it was our last meal. We took our time savoring each little Skittle, appreciating this token of normalcy in the midst of a hellacious war. I thought of my family; the pride in my father's eyes, my mother hugging him, my sisters all smiling with their hair flowing in the wind and finally my nephew and his laugh that always said, "You're funny, Uncle Billy!"

When the bombs hit the ground, the entire world shook. The explosion was so loud it just turned to white noise. The corn above us leaned back against the concussion. Trees shattered and turned to splinters. Shrapnel was flying over my head splitting the foliage with ease. And just like that . . . it was over.

-VILHELM RED
1/75

JULY 2006
"SKITTLES: A SNIPER'S PERSPECTIVE"

This was the beginning of our deployment for yet another rotation in the continuous circle that all the Ranger Battalions lived in and accepted as the new norm. We were planning on grabbing an HVT in the Helmand Province, one of the most heavily reinforced and openly anti-American territories in Afghanistan. At this point in time, all of Helmand was a stronghold for Al Qaeda. The area in its entirety, is mainly flat with large amounts of crop fields comprised of poppy and marijuana, which was a large cash crop used to make additional money for Afghanistan's growing radical Islamic forces.

It was pitch black and I opened my eyes to the screaming of, "one minute!" Funny, I thought we had a few more. The last time I closed my eyes after looking at the light board, it had said *ten minutes out, enemy on target* with the addition of a smiley face drawn on it. A light board is just a piece of Plexiglas with illumination tape stuck to it so you can write on it with a china marker and every one can see what it says in the dark. I felt the bird start to pitch, the rotors becoming louder as the engines fight the air while lowering us into the blackness of the Helmand. My heart rate increased as I felt the humidity and smelled the dank air. We were about to land so I prepared to explosively exit and encounter anything that may be waiting for us. Everyone moved up on a knee while trying to stay upright, fighting the aircrafts violent motions. We reached for our safety lines while also checking each other and ourselves; a good pat on the back or thumbs up is sufficient.

Everyone was prepared to unhook from the floor links, so I reached up and pulled down my PVS-15 dual night vision goggles, and re-entered the familiar green world of war. I quickly dialed in the focus as a final check and went through my PCIs (Pre-Combat Inspections) once more. I patted down my kit and pounded a bottle of water, a sequence I've done so many times before. I immediately pulled back the charging handle on my rifle, just far enough to glance down and see that a shiny new round is in my SR-25's chamber.

As the bird flared, I tried to maintain my balance and prepare to run out the back of a complete fatal funnel. No imagery ever tells you the condition of the LZ; you may step onto solid ground or mud. I felt the bump from the landing gear hitting the ground and begin to make a speedy exit from one of the loudest aerial platforms in the world. Yup, fucking mud, and mud for a speedy exit is not ideal for the 40-plus Ranger assaulters that all weigh in the ballpark of 250 pounds or more, depending on his job, weapon system, and what the target load out required is in addition to the standard basic load.

As I ran out the back of the aircraft and onto the muddy ground moving as fast and quietly as possible in the black of night, my head was on a swivel looking and taking in everything I could. *Where will I move if I take contact right now?* The same thing we've rehearsed and been told time and time again, but these are very real thoughts and there is not always ideal cover. On some occasions you do the actions almost subconsciously, in addition to all the other things going on around you. I saw my friend Austin pause quickly and reach down towards his foot. He had lost a shoe running through the muddy field, had to pick it up, and quickly stuff it somewhere in order to keep moving to the release point. Not an ideal event, but funny nonetheless.

We moved out of the field and down to a low-lying area. We did a quick route recon and decided we were going to use a creek that smelled like complete and total shit, but it was the best way to get where we had to go as well as provide some cover if we took contact. Off in the distance, I could hear the sounds of breaching charges and 'bangers' (flash-bangs) going off as well as gunfire as the main assault force breached and cleared their target compound.

For this target, I was a sniper team leader attached to Reconnaissance Team Two that was led by Tim, their team leader. We were to observe and isolate the lower eastern part of the objective, consisting of a few fields and some smaller structures, which Wade and I had cleared prior to setting in to our positions. They were small and seemed to be a place to store the harvested poppy and marijuana as they were piled high full of crops. As we walked out of the structure, we heard the familiar sound of gunfire and looked up to see tracers streak through the night sky. The radio sprang to life, relaying that another element was in contact, so we moved back into the ditches we were lying in previously.

Now back in our defensive positions, I was lying there and jumping back and forth between the radio channels we were operating on, as well as listening to all the events happening on target. After a short period of time, which in reality was about an hour or so, I heard the call to prepare for exfil. Time is a thing that flies when you are moving around, adrenaline pumping, and is often based on when you hit the ground as well as how long you have until the sun breaks. It was a very real thought to have due to the area of operation for that night's events. We were in the absolute most hostile area within the Helmand Province, the Sangin Valley, an Al-Qaeda haven where they operated openly and freely during this time period.

A few moments later, one of the blocking positions reported more contact and began to engage. It's times like this where I'd instantly react and get the job done, regardless of all the other things happening around me, to include gunfire, explosions, incoming aircraft, and having to be somewhere on time. We took a smoother route back to the original insertion point as we had found another irrigation ditch. It was a slightly drier one, to the left of the fields, and to the front of a small bridge leading over the nasty creek we originally used for cover and concealment en route to our over-watch position.

Still moving, I saw the first bird come in to extract the first element. As the MH-47 made its approach, the insurgents within the area who had been hidden, waiting for us to begin our extraction, opened up with a large simultaneous ambush. A fury of fire erupted everywhere; insurgents began engaging with everything they could bring to bear, including RPGs and a variety of belt-fed, automatic weapons. As the Chinook lifted back off into the night, it attracted fire but hauled ass away, unscathed. At this point, I was still following my teammates up to the bridge that was no more than a few logs. Almost all of the team crossed the bridge when all hell broke loose again.

The next bird came in to extract the main assault force (1B), and right after they began to power up in order to take off again, gunfire erupted from outlying positions in the field and from the rooftops in other compounds around the area. The assault force rushed into the vulnerable aircraft, which had just become a large bullet magnet, but I was distracted with jumping back down into the creek. I quickly rested my SR-25 on the bridge and began to engage targets, yelling, "contact on my laser!" while firing into a burst of enemy muzzle flashes across one of the fields we had just crossed.

To my right, Danny, a Mk-46 gunner for our team along with Wade began to immediately suppress the small woodline about 200 meters away where I was marking the contact. I was firing at the same time, and the most amazing thing was that there was no lull in the return fire. However, by this point, all other parts of our element were also rapidly engaging the initial area of contact.

I saw Wade drop or crouch back into the ditch, now filled with Rangers firing and communicating, as I was changing a mag. Almost immediately he and I were back up and re-engaging like we had rehearsed this a thousand times. We were all suppressing the area where we were taking fire from, and it would stop briefly, then continue to start firing again a few moments later. They must have had their "dead gunner" drills down; this happened about three times, and the amount of gunfire we were raining down on them was extraordinary.

As all of this was going on, one of our "goose" teams maneuvered to the right of us and prepared to fire their Carl Gustav 84MM

Recoilless Rifle. They hit them twice, once is usually good but twice is awesome, and they didn't hesitate for a second. They loaded up another HEDP (High Explosive Dual Purpose) round with an air-burst option for delivering an explosion directly above an enemy position. They set it to airburst and prepared to engage the bastards still shooting at not only us, but also the bird lifting off behind us. It was so loud, Dan was yelling "Fire!" we were yelling "Fire!" and then it went BOOM! . . . Someone behind me screamed to reload and re-engage, but the goose team was already rocking through the reload as if no one had said anything. They beautifully performed the ever-important crew drill, and just like that another round was loosed in the direction of our enemy. They prepared to send some more death down on the enemy and I could somewhat make out a muffled "back-blast area clear" call followed by another thunderous boom out of the tube.

We had now been in contact for a good couple minutes, and again there is no real concept of time, as all this seems to run together as the events play out. We didn't hear anything from that woodline anymore, hopefully because we killed every last one of those savages. But as all this was going down, the now fully loaded Chinook with 1st Platoon, B Company was being shot to shit as they lifted off. We found out a very short time later that they had sustained enough critical damage to the aircraft and had no choice but to put her down. The pilot did the best thing possible and stayed close to the target, staying near all the other Ranger elements still on the ground. This allowed us to rapidly move to support the downed bird and her passengers.

All of this was happening as we were rapidly losing the cover of darkness. We often talk of how we own the night, but we can also own the day, although these are not the ideal set of conditions to do so. As professionals, we always try to stack the deck in our favor. The force on the ground was more than a formidable opposition to any enemy. If they couldn't get another bird in, there was rumor of a possible contingency to take down a compound and fight through the day until the next period of darkness for a new extraction.

The beauty about the Ranger Regiment is shit will go wrong, but we are the best at adapting to shit going wrong. It's why we are so good at what we do in combat. We have leadership who will assess the situation, set the right conditions, and execute from the hip. They will then act without hesitation and succeed, because the men you work with to your left and right expect what you say will work and that your plan will not fail them.

At this point, contact had gone from continuous to reduced and sporadic. Somewhere along the line, we had our AC-130 go "Winchester" - meaning the platform was completely out of ammo. To put into perspective the level of contact and number of enemy in the area, this ended up happening twice during the mission. We were now configured in a hasty defensive position consisting of Battalion Reconnaissance Teams Two and Three, a 60mm mortar team, and a Gustav team. We were all generally in the same area, near the creek with a small wall running along the upper area of the creek we'd been fighting from, somewhat close to where we first got inserted into this pit. I was now looking through a crack in that wall. As I was sitting there, I was re-configuring my kit with one hand, moving mags around, double checking all my shit, readjusting pretty much everything, and eating some wet Skittles out of my pocket.

I had opened up and duct taped the Skittles bag shut prior to the mission for an easy snack, so I could open and close them easier. Unless of course, they got soaked during some unforeseeable circumstance like jumping into a creek to avoid gunfire, I probably should have contracted some fucked up disease from eating them. I probably also should not have shared them with the other guys, but if one of your brothers asks for some Skittles, you give him some. I was later given a healthy dose of Cipro from John, our team Doc. It's the little things that are a bizarre comfort. I remember drinking some water out of my Nalgene bottle, waiting for the next step to happen. I was soaked and covered in mud, but it is what it is. I saw other guys doing their own checks. As one watched for the enemy, another reset his kit and prepared once again for the task at hand. We were far from done tonight and a new magazine is a must, never go into another gunfight without putting a fresh magazine in your weapon. It is a sin not to, and thirty is always better than, "I think I've got twenty-five."

I was set with my new position, staring through a crack in a wall about big enough for my barrel and a decent sight picture into the field we just received contact from, taking in everything I could with my scope. We had a very diverse set of weapon systems gathered, and we all came to be sitting along this wall after what had just happened, in one of the absolute worst places in Afghanistan. It was a force to be reckoned with if the enemy decided to start some new shit. *Bring it.*

Radio chatter was going crazy, the main reason being we had just been informed that the bird went down a short distance from our current position due to an RPG and heavy gunfire. The first call over the radio was a bunch of casualties, and my heart sank. Then a few very long minutes later, we received another net call stating no casualties with the exception of the platoon leader, who had a superficial gunshot wound.

After receiving the news of the bird going down with everyone surviving, I felt relieved. Having grown up in B Co., I knew pretty much everyone, to include many outstanding Rangers. I remember Mike, the other recce team leader, saying we were the closest element and that we were moving to the crash site. As we all moved to the site, moving along small foot trails that wound along the irrigation ditches, I could hear gunshots: some close, some further away. The AC-130 arrived back on station and quickly became very busy. We were in a target rich environment, and that AC-130 is the Ranger equivalent to an invisible angel of death. I could hear the faint sound of it up in the sky doing a racetrack around our position, raining hell down on any enemy personnel stupid enough to be out in the open.

A few hundred meters later and we arrive at the crash site. The Chinook was in the middle of a bunch of poppy fields with ditches running around the whole area like a grid. We moved over and got into the ditches in order to strengthen the hasty perimeter that had been already set by the platoon and the crew from the downed bird. After we settled into our new positions, our visibility was blocked due to the high poppy crops and sun that was slowly coming up. We were in one of the wildest places in the country and without the cover of night, we became quite exposed.

The enemy was starting to mass in the outlying areas. The AC-130 began to engage again, with quick and deadly force. In a few instances our forward observer, Mike, would come by jumping into our ditch letting us know to stay low as he was calling in danger close fire missions on our side of the perimeter. It echoed through our headsets, which meant you better have your head down when rounds start raining down, shaking the ground. You kind of had to smile a bit when looking at the big picture from what and where we were at by this point. The next stage of the plan that would be coming shortly combined the craziest and fastest exfil I've ever had the privilege to be a part of.

The plan to get us out had finally come to fruition. We had our Chinooks back on station and they were doing mini-gun runs on all the outlying tree lines that were around the poppy fields, irrigation ditches, and the walled compounds. They were again receiving fire from enemy positions and there were additional hostile forces gathering in the outer areas. They were now another addition to our close air support and it was very welcomed. Leaving this shit hole without (in most everyone's case) being shot down was now quickly becoming a reality.

So the quick version of the plan was that the AC-130 was going to provide additional fires as the exfil birds came in one after another to pick us up. Groups of the assault force would rush into the aircraft and off they would go. Sounds simple, but the coordination between air and ground assets had to go smoothly, or smooth enough. The other things that had to happen for this to work would include all Rangers on the ground moving up in our ditches. Even up on a high knee, the crops were still too high for us to see and if you were too high above them, you exposed yourself. That could be a fatal mistake, but the goal was to lay down heavy suppressive fire in every direction so the teams running to the aircraft had a wall of lead going down range, keeping all the enemy down long enough for the bird to get back off the deck and into the air, three different times.

As the first bird came in, everyone moved up on a knee and began laying down the most ferocious volume of fire possible. As all this happened I remember thinking, "We are no-shit laying down suppressive fire just to exfil, are we in fucking 'Nam?" As I was firing out of this ditch with everyone else, the amount of gunfire was indescribable. It was a wall of hot lead, and all the different sounds of weapons going off to include the additional assets on station above us firing made the feeling of the ground shaking. The amount of destruction that was going down range in every direction was mind blowing. The pounding and the ground shaking from the explosions was one of the most unbelievable experiences I've ever been a part of. Just like that, the first chalk ran and loaded the bird. As they tore out of the HLZ, rocks and dirt blasted us from behind which was pretty standard from any bird coming in.

Time came for the next group to get out, and this all happened in rapid succession to reduce the chance of the enemy hitting another aircraft or a Ranger running towards the bird. I will also add they landed, literally, as close to us as they could, which was the beauty of the 160th SOAR - they are the best in the world and I've seen them do unreal acts on so many targets with their aircraft. They are like the Jedi of rotary wing, they will get it done - *Night Stalkers Don't Quit!*

So with the second lift up and away, we were next. We received the quick warning that we are going next and just like that, we heard the loud whomp, whomp, whomp sound of the rotors as the bird

came in fast and flared behind us. Half of us were still pulling security and firing in conjunction with the air assets still on station.

I was up and running behind Ben, who was our platoon Sergeant for the recce section at the time. As we ran, I had the stupidest
thought I may have ever had. I was smiling and in my head saying, *Get
to da choppa!* I was literally grinning ear-to-ear as I ran through the
hot exhaust from the engines, hauling ass up the ramp and through
the bird to the front near the cockpit where the two forward gunners
were. I glanced out the window briefly, as one of the crew was down
on his mini-gun surveying the area for any threat within reaching
distance of his gun. I leaned up against the airframe and grabbed my
safety line, pulling it out, and looking for a quick hook-up so that as
soon as the last few Rangers boarded I could snap in.

Again, I began going through my kit, magazines first, from right to
left. The ones on the right were expended as I change mags from right
to left. So I move towards the left side of my kit and also my non-firing
side, being a righty, I pulled the mag from my SR-25 and put in a fresh
one. My mag count was down to a little more than three 20 round
mags left out of seven. As an assault sniper, you don't carry a huge
amount of ammo, because you never anticipate an engagement that
you will expend that amount of ammo. This was based solely on the
targets we usually encountered, and 140 rounds is (for most cases)
enough - but sometimes you have these unforeseen days.

The bonus of a 7.62 weapon system is if you absolutely have to,
you can use machine gun ammo. It is a last resort scenario though,
as you are now taking ammo from a dominating weapon system
meant for suppressive fire, and one of the most casualty producing
systems we carry at the platoon level. Not to mention, it is horrible for a match grade sniper barrel. As I was checking my gear, I
looked over at Major Hammer and just smiled and nodded. I looked
down the airframe as guys are running in and being counted on by
the crew chief and another Ranger leader, and I see Sergeant Major
Harlem run on and immediately man the empty M-240 on the right

side of the aircraft where the crew chief, who was outside, would normally be. Seeing actions like this made me so proud of the men and the organization that I was a part of.

As the last man ran aboard, I reached down to snap in, and just like that I was pressed to the floor, ramp coming up as we gained altitude. The mini gun next to me opened up as we proceeded to leave the beautiful shithole that is the Sangin Valley as fast as I've ever been removed from a target. I have never been in an exfil where the bird lifted off with that kind of mind-blowing force. The Chinook is the fastest helicopter in the Army and when they open her up, it is awesome.

We flew back to Kandahar and to the giant tent we were all temporarily living in for the current target set. It was a total shit hole with bunk beds and a hundred or more guys from our Task Force living on top of each other. The ride back was the same as any other; guys were doing the usual things like slamming some water and leaning on each other to take a nap. There was the occasional loud laugh over the constant loud whir of the engines, followed by a knuckle bump or pat on the back. Everyone was covered in mud and sweat, the usual stink of tearing it up all night as if the madness earlier was just another day. *But the thing is . . . it was.* You never knew what you would encounter on a target, or how it would ultimately play out. We were extremely lucky to have no casualties other than the platoon leader being grazed by a round when they were being shot down. That in and of itself is mind blowing; you don't get many divine intervention cards, if any.

On our way back from the target, the downed Chinook was being destroyed by an AC-130 dropping a couple 105 rounds into it. The bird was beyond any means of recovery and was destroyed so that the savages couldn't remove anything from it. Looking back on the whole thing, I am amazed at how seamlessly the transition from another day and another target can go through so many different phases successfully. The reason for this is the rapid adaptability of the Rangers and their leadership to make decisions, act on them, and overcome everything that confronts them. With those same basic principles being applied to everything, success is the usual outcome. That is why the 75th Ranger Regiment is the best in the world.

-R.J.S.
1/75

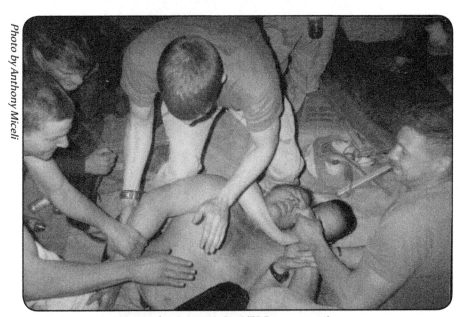

Marc Anderson, an A Co. 1/75 Ranger, receives
his birthday "pink belly" in Afghanistan, 2002.

An A Co. 1/75 Ranger scans for targets on Takur Ghar in 2002.

A Ranger clearing a building during
the initial stages of the Iraq invasion in 2003.

2/75 Rangers on a combat mission through the Kantiwa Valley in Afghanistan,
November 2003.

1-B 3/75 Rangers on H-1 Airfield in Iraq, 2003.

A 3/75 Ranger is "balled up" on his birthday in Afghanistan, 2004.

3/75 Rangers on a mission in Afghanistan, 2004.

Two 3/75 snipers before
a training mission in 2005.

A 3/75 sniper preparing to take off on an MH-6 "Little Bird" in support of a successful HVT raid in Afghanistan, 2005.

1/75 Rangers pose for a group photo in Afghanistan, 2005.

1/75 Rangers on a reconnaissance mission in Afghanistan, 2005.

3/75 Rangers call for fire on enemy positions in Afghanistan, 2006.

A 1/75 sniper scans for targets on a mission in Afghanistan, 2006.

Rangers from 3/75 stand in front of the
new James Regan Ready Room in Iraq, 2007.

Jason Dahlke on a reconnaissance patrol
in the mountains of Afghanistan in 2008.

C Co. 1/75 Rangers after a combat mission in Iraq, 2008.

A Ranger from C Co. 3/75 scans for enemy insurgents during a combat operation in Helmand Province, Afghanistan, July 2009.

A squad of Rangers from 2-C, 1/75 in Afghanistan, 2009.

A Ranger scans for targets while on a mission in Afghanistan, 2010.

Kevin Pape's squad from 3-C, 1/75
before a combat mission in Afghanistan, 2010.

A 1/75 Ranger dog handler with his multi-purpose canine after a mission in Afghanistan, 2011.

A Ranger from 3/75 on patrol in Afghanistan, 2011.

Chapter Seven

*"It is foolish and wrong to mourn the men who died.
Rather, we should thank God that such men lived."*

<small>George S. Patton Jr.</small>

I have always been patriotic. I was raised to respect the flag, respect your elders, and to love your country. Growing up, I never felt a chill crawl up my back when I heard the national anthem though. I did not used to stop mid-stride to stare at a flag waving on a pole. I did not tear up when I watched the 4th of July fireworks go off while *God Bless America* played on the radio. All that changed in a C-17 on the return from my second deployment.

We had woken from an Ambien induced slumber and were on the final approach into Savannah, Georgia. We were returning on the night of the 4th of July . . . just in time to miss all the festivities. Everyone was excited to be back home after a long trip to Afghanistan though. As we started to circle Savannah, someone pointed out that you could see fireworks going off below us through the small porthole on the door of the aircraft. A few of us took turns looking down there; much to the dismay of the crew who wanted us to stay seated and buckled. After we returned to our seats, and as we were about ninety seconds out, Staff Sergeant "Joe" started belting out the *Star Spangled Banner*. What ensued was moving to say the least. Every barrel chested freedom fighter on that aircraft started singing it with him. I don't know if words can accurately describe the sights and sounds of sixty of the most lethal men on earth singing their country's anthem at the same time. No concert, no musician, no performance will ever compare to the camaraderie and national pride that filled the inside of that aircraft. As we sang our hearts out, I looked at all the black and white infrared flags attached to our shoulders and thought to myself, *there is no place on earth I would rather be than on this aircraft, with this group of men, and this flag on my shoulder.*

Patriotism can't be taught. Patriotism can't be forced down your throat as something you "should" feel as an American. I firmly believe that it is learned, maybe even needs to be *experienced.* That night I learned what patriotism truly felt like. That night I was a "born again American." I didn't care if we missed the Independence Day festivities, the last few minutes of that flight was a better celebration of America than any cook out or day at the beach. It was like the first time you realized you loved the girl you were dating. I fell in love with America, and remain deeply in love with her to this day. There is no amount of politics, economic woe or reality TV shows that will ever make me fall out of love.

In 2007, the Regiment continued to be fully engaged in operations in both Iraq and Afghanistan. This year was the most costly up to this point in the war for the 75th Ranger Regiment. Sergeant James Regan, Private First Class Kristofer Thomas, Private First Class Ryan Garbs, Corporal Jason Kessler, Specialist George Libby, Corporal Benjamin Dillon, and Sergeant Steven Ganczewski all made the ultimate sacrifice.

FEBRUARY 2007
"JIMMY"

Prior to my Iraq deployment, Sergeant Regan was my team leader in Weapons Squad. I met Corporal Regan during my first deployment to Afghanistan; he came over right after he graduated from Ranger School. He was very smart, older and mature. I would talk with him about college and what I should do with my career and so on. He was a no-nonsense team leader. He would help me with anything I needed. When you're a new private, you spend about the first six months proving yourself. Well, I was only in 3/75 for three months prior to deployment, so yeah, I was still proving myself. Corporal Regan proved to be different, though. He mentored and taught, instead of other methods of correction typically utilized on new guys.

I went through two more training cycles/deployments with Corporal-turned-Sergeant Regan before this trip to Iraq. We came to know each other very well. Everybody was close in our platoon. At the time, I was still a breacher and team leader for my squad. This was my third deployment to Iraq and we had returned to where we had stayed before. By this time everything was complete, we had a ready room as well as an overhang for our Strykers. It was a drastic improvement since our last rotation only months prior. This deployment was a mix of HAF's (Helicopter Assault Force) and GAF's (Ground Assault Force) missions.

Early on in the deployment, we were out on a mission during the middle of the night. We were on a GAF and I was sitting in the rear left position of the Stryker closest to the ramp that mechanically lowered. En route to the target, our Stryker was hit by an IED. I remember a bright flash and that was it, as I was knocked unconscious from the over pressure. I came to with everyone in the Stryker yelling my name and hitting me while the Doc was doing blood sweeps. I told them to get off of me and that I was fine. I was definitely out if it, and it definitely sucked. Well, that specific seat must have been special because nobody else in that Stryker was affected by the over pressure except me. Knocked me out cold.

Several missions later, the code for a GAF came across our pagers for a capture/kill mission in a very shitty area. We did our mission planning as usual, and loaded up in the Strykers. My squad was the number two Stryker in the order of movement as we departed for the long ride to the objective. We were sitting in the back of the cramped, dark Stryker for a couple hours falling in and out of sleep with nothing to do but stare at each other, drink Rip-Its, or spit dip. Out of nowhere, we heard a large explosion. My first thought was, *Holy shit, we just hit an IED!* Our Stryker was not the target however. It had hit the third vehicle back. But it was so big; the explosion felt like it was on top of us.

The radio chatter began, confirming that it was the third Stryker. The Stryker was disabled from the blast, so we moved it out of the blast area as quickly as possible. We had to empty out of our Stryker to begin loading it with the other squad, which included the platoon sergeant and a medic. They were all ok, just dizzy and shaken up from the large IED. The only person that was not removed was Sergeant Regan. He was still in the Stryker. Sergeant Regan was sitting in the exact same spot I was when I was the only one affected by a blast just missions prior.

I grabbed the hooligan tool off the back of one of my other team mates who was carrying it, as some of the breaching equipment was spread amongst the lower ranking guys. While running behind the Stryker that was struck by the IED, we were all frantically trying to pry open the damaged back ramp. The medic was still inside the Stryker doing whatever he could to stop the bleeding and tend to other injuries Jimmy sustained in the blast. Finally, they told another medic and me to jump on top of the Stryker. We were to pull

Regan through the top hatch of the Stryker, then get the stretcher set up as we called in a MEDEVAC. I was so pissed off. I hopped on top of that Stryker as soon as I heard that was the plan, while the medic took off his belt and wrapped it around Regan. He handed me one end of the belt and the other medic the opposite end. We pulled him up like it was nothing. My adrenaline was pumping and I was pissed off.

Somehow I ended up with both sides of the belt, and pulled him through the top hatch and into my lap on top of the Stryker. The Stryker was now being towed towards the MEDEVAC HLZ. The other members of my squad were busy preparing the litter for Regan to move onto for transportation to the bird once we hit the HLZ. We would then be able to move him from the top of the Stryker down to them, and they would carry him over to be evacuated.

I sat with Regan on my lap while they were doing this, as he lay there going in and out of consciousness. I was giving him sternum rubs to try and keep his attention, calling his name, "Jimmy" as we all referred to him, and telling him he was going to be ok while urging him to talk to me. I continued to monitor his vital signs and breathing, which were not good at all. Once we arrived at the MEDEVAC HLZ site, we loaded Sergeant Regan onto the litter. I remember handing him down to my guys, and seeing them running off into the brown-out that the Blackhawk made from the rotor wash, and Jimmy disappearing into the dust. I didn't know it at the time, but that was the last time I would see Sergeant James J. Regan.

We continued our mission. Unfortunately, we were en route to the target building so the mission continued as usual while dragging that downed Stryker with us. We were so pissed off that we vowed to shoot every person on that target. In the end, we are not merciless killers no matter how good the vengeance would have felt. We hit our target silently, meeting no resistance that night. We captured who and what we were looking for and began our exfil with a handful of detainees. We received updates during the mission of

Regan's status, reporting that he was doing well and was going to make it, but he was still in critical condition.

When we arrived back at the SOF compound, the chaplain was there to tell us he passed. We all mourned as if losing a brother, or any other close family member. I was still covered in his blood, which I did not want to wash off. I don't know why, I guess I felt like it was a part of him or something. I can't explain it. The new ready room we had built was re-named the "Sergeant James J. Regan Ready Room" that day.

Sergeant Regan was killed in action on February 9th, 2007 and I remember that day like it was yesterday, it will be forever burned into my mind. I can never do anything else but serve my country for the rest of my life. I crushed through my bachelor's degree in just two years and seven months, thinking of Jimmy when he attended Duke University. He was my role model and motivation to get my degree fast, along with other things I have done in my life, which he had already done in his. I continue to do so today. Every day, other men fall protecting our country. What makes me better than them? Nothing. I regret leaving the Ranger Regiment, but continue to serve our country in the private sector as well as being a sniper in the Army National Guard, and an instructor for the US Air Force. My heart truly lies in the pursuit of closing with and destroying the enemies of our nation. Since my six-month window closed to return to the Ranger Regiment many years ago, I seek to get back in the fight any way possible. To fight with brothers who are like-minded, ridding this world of terrorism. I am currently writing this from Afghanistan, working in the private sector.

-DAN
3/75

EARLY 2007
"OF MOTTOES AND MEN"

I never was a Ranger, and frankly, I never wanted to be. That's probably fortunate for me, because I'm not sure I would have made the cut.

After completing a branch detail to the Infantry with the 101st Airborne Division and transitioning to Military Intelligence, I served in the 2nd Infantry Division in the Republic of Korea. It seems silly now, but pre-9/11, Korea is where you went if you wanted to do something "hard" OCONUS. I got my first company-level command in Korea, and after two years my wife and I returned CONUS for the MI Officers Advanced Course. While in the Advanced Course, my branch manager paid our class a visit. She had a list of available duty positions, but there was only one I wanted: the 5th Special Forces Group in Fort Campbell, Kentucky. She had a requirement for my grade and specialty, and just like that I was on orders. It was that easy.

The ease of getting into an SF Group as an enabler was, as I found out, a major issue. At the time, and as far as I know continuing to this day, Special Forces was the only ARSOF unit that was willing to take pot-luck when it came to enablers. All enabler assignments to Group were "needs of the Army," a soldier could go to 10th Special Forces Group just as easily as he could go to 10th Mountain. The major problem with this was, of course, quality control. "Need of the Army" attitude towards enabler functions meant that some good and some not-so-good enablers made it into support positions in Group. Overtime, the screw-ups of the poor enablers overshadowed the accomplishments of the good ones, and enablers as a whole were often mistrusted or unempowered. 5th Group was great to me personally but I didn't think I could reach full potential in an organization in which the enablers as a group were not the professional equivalent of the operators we supported.

So, after commanding the Group Military Intelligence Detachment and the Group Support Company, I transferred "across the airfield" to 2nd Battalion, 160th Special Operations Aviation Regiment. In the time that I was a Night Stalker, I frequently deployed to Afghanistan in support of a joint SOF task force, where I served as the J2 for the SOF aviation element. It was there that I first worked closely with the Rangers. I remember one particular mission involving our unit in which a Chinook got shot down during an objective. Despite the massive damage to the aircraft, the pilot was able to safely (but somewhat roughly) put it down in a field. People said it was a miracle that no Rangers or 160th members got killed, and maybe it was. But I kind of think that it was more due to the design of the aircraft and the skill of the pilots than anything else. I remember watching the Predator feed as the Task Force destroyed the damaged bird. That was a whole lot of money and capability up in smoke, but it had to be done to prevent the aircraft and its sensitive equipment from falling into the hands of the enemy. But it was still a good day because everyone came home off of that objective. "Humans are more important than hardware."

Prior to my time in the 160th, my only experience with the Rangers was in the form of a previous battalion commander who had been an officer in a Ranger unit, and a battalion XO who, before becoming an officer, had done some of his enlisted time in the Regiment. To say that I found both of these men unimpressive would be an understatement. Fortunately for me, I had several opportunities to work closely with the Ranger Regiment and find out that there was probably a reason those two clowns I had to work with earlier in my career were no longer in the Ranger Regiment.

It takes a special kind of man to be a Ranger. Even from the outside looking in, it's clear that being a Ranger is nothing short of a way of life. One can go to a three-month school to earn a Tab that says Ranger, but to "be" a Ranger; it takes a commitment to a punishing Spartan lifestyle of training, hardship, and deprivation as well as near-constant combat deployments.

For me, the type of person who thrives in the Ranger Regiment was exemplified by a photo that hung in the entryway of the Task Force headquarters building in Afghanistan known as the Joint Operations Center (JOC), or the "plywood palace." There were several pictures placed conspicuously on the walls of the JOC. One of the most motivating to me was that of a man hurtling headfirst down from a New York skyscraper towards certain death; one of the Twin Towers' 9/11 fallers. *This is why we are here*, I'd think to myself whenever I walked past.

But there was another very powerful photo on that same wall. This particular one featured a young man sitting upright in a hospital bed, right hand raised at a 90-degree angle, an oxygen mask attached to his face and tubes running from his chest. Flanking him on either side are two equally grim-looking young men dressed in fatigues and holding a US flag pulled tightly between them behind the wounded man's hospital bed. Although there is no caption, it is clear what is happening: a re-enlistment.

The men in the picture look like young men. Because the operators in all of the other direct-action task forces are all MUCH older, there is nothing these three men can be other than Rangers. Seeing that picture gave me chills; despite being severely wounded in combat, this young man was signing up for more. He wasn't lying in that bed feeling sorry for himself, he simply "Rangered up" for more opportunities to combat America's enemies alongside his Ranger brothers. *This is the kind of people I'm working with*, I remember thinking about this photo.

Since our unit supported all of the various "customers" in the national SOF task force, I was able to work with just about all of the US SOF units that have direct action as a specified mission. I quickly learned that each unit has its own specific culture and unique way of doing business. I also learned that I liked working with Rangers the best.

The Rangers' mission planning was what really stood out to me. They would plan meticulously, execute aggressively, and conduct ruthless after action reviews (AARs). Excruciating attention to detail was in their organizational DNA. Working with the Rangers in Afghanistan, it was clear that the Regiment had progressed far past its legacy role of pulling security for other units and was fully capable of conducting a wide range of special operations missions and even commanding a subordinate task force on its own.

I did several short deployments as a Night Stalker, and was able to develop a good working relationship with several Rangers who were on similar short deployment cycles.

My role in the mission planning process was limited; the Rangers had their own planners and their own intelligence officers, and they were quite good. Nonetheless, every morning I accompanied the 160th senior pilots and planners over to the Ranger headquarters area, located on the backside of the plywood palace that housed the Task Force, and sat in on the morning brief. At this brief, the pilots and Rangers discussed the upcoming night's mission. At this point in the war, even relatively complex missions were routine, and although planning was thorough, it was not onerous or time-consuming due to the number of times the pilots and Rangers had worked together in the past, and the standard operating procedures (SOPs) that the two units developed between them.

Particularly sensitive or complicated missions necessitated additional planning meetings. I attended these briefings as often as I could, and helped out where and when I was able, which was not often. But I had good interpersonal skills, and I was a pretty good intel officer, so I made some good connections within the Regiment.

The 160th pilots sometimes invited me to go along on missions with them. I usually turned these offers down, because it was hard for me to do my job in support of the mission if I was actually on the mission. Even though I was a prior infantryman and figured I could probably handle myself even if the worst happened, being a relatively inexperienced outsider meant that I would most likely only end up being in the way if things went sideways. But I realized that if I turned down missions long enough people would start to think I was scared and would reflect poorly on the S2 section, so I went on one or two per rotation.

Most of the few missions I went on were completely uneventful, but I do remember one trip to Jalalabad, or "J-bad" as we called it. Our pilots were flying in support of a Ranger HVT mission, and the plan was to travel in either three or four MH-47s full of Rangers from Bagram to Jalalabad, land and refuel, and wait for the trigger to conduct the mission. This was a pretty cut-and-dry operation, something the Rangers and 160th pilots did almost every night.

I was along solely as an observer; I rode in the "jump seat" immediately behind the two pilots. This gave me a literal front-seat view of the operation, and because I had a headset, I could hear the radio chatter as well. I'm a big guy, even bigger all geared up for a mission, and the jump seat was relatively small. I shifted my feet to get into a more comfortable position and accidently jarred loose the co-pilot's radio cable. He noticed and got it fixed right away so it wasn't a big deal, but I was more than a little embarrassed.

Before we left on the mission, my battalion commander made it clear to me that I was to get off the helo at J-bad, and the strike package would pick me up when they returned from the mission. That was what I planned on doing anyway; I had a good friend who was doing deep-cover HUMINT work out of J-bad and he had already agreed to host me for the evening while the op went down. The flight out to J-bad was uneventful; the only action was the crew chiefs conducting the usual test firing of the machine guns shortly after takeoff.

When we landed at J-bad, the first thing I noticed was the terrain. It was dark, of course, but through my NODs I could see that the

FOB where we just landed was set in a bowl, with high ground on pretty much all four sides, and a small village just outside the wire. It looked like this base was practically BEGGING to be over-run. Appearances can be deceiving, however, and when I linked up with my HUMINT friend he outlined the base's impressive defense system. He also explained that while there was in fact high ground around the base, much of it was a lot farther away than it looked through NODs. Apparently the local tribes were friendly too, so they rarely got more than the occasional indirect fire round shot their way.

Our mission got postponed while we were on our way to J-bad, so I was able to get caught up with my friend at length over some cold soda and Pop Tarts in their unit's break area. The Rangers we flew in with linked up with the operational unit there at J-bad and continued mission prep. We had a "no later than" time to execute the mission, and if the hit didn't go down at that point, we were going to load back up and return to Bagram. About 15 minutes or so before the NLT time, I said goodbye to my friend and went back out to the landing zone. It was still dark, of course, but I could see well enough to find my way back through the airfield and to the helo I rode in on. On the way, however, a large laser dot suddenly appeared on the chest plate of my body armor. Thanks to all the dust in the air I could tell that it was coming from one of the helicopters and I wasn't being targeted by a sniper in the village or surrounding hills. I flipped down my NODs and immediately found the culprit, one of my pilot buddies sitting in the cockpit of one of the MH-47s. With my NODs on I could see him holding a ground laser designator and pointing at me. He probably thought I was going to freak out seeing that big green dot on my chest, and I probably would have had it been coming from anywhere other than one of the aircraft. I made a gesture in his direction that let him know I was on to his antics, and the laser switched off. I couldn't see facial expressions at this distance but I knew the pilot in question well and knew he'd be smiling.

I was smiling too as I boarded the aircraft I rode to J-bad in and prepared to return to Bagram. After checking in with the pilots and the crew chief, who informed me that the mission was cancelled and we would soon return to Bagram, I went back into the cargo area of the aircraft, took off my helmet, and using my assault pack as a pillow, fell fast asleep. A short time later, I heard the MH-47's rotors start spinning and I groggily put my helmet on and secured my assault pack for the ride home. I was about to make my way back to the jump seat when a large group of Rangers hustled into the back of the helo. They moved with a sense of purpose that people simply didn't have when they were mounting up for a ride home. These guys had the switched-on look of men about to "land on the X." Uh oh.

The ramp began to close and the Rangers clipped in their safety lines as I began to think about how I was going to explain to my battalion commander how I ended up going on this op, after he specifically instructed me not to. I decided there was nothing to be done now, so I sat back down on the floor and clipped in too. One Ranger, probably an NCO, went from soldier to soldier doing pre-flight PMIs. When he got to me, we looked at each other through NODs, and I gave him a thumbs up. He looked at me without reacting and went on to the next guy. I'm sure he was thinking something along the lines of *who the hell is this guy?*

They had a dog along for this mission. The dogs were always muzzled while they were on the helos. I asked a crew chief about this once; he explained, "Oh yeah, they have GOT to be muzzled. Sometimes they get so scared or amped up, especially coming back from an op, that they'll put a bite on anyone who happens to be around. A detainee, a member of the strike force, a crew chief, yeah, they need those muzzles." I thought that was odd given the way I usually saw the dogs back on the FOB, they always seemed so calm.

The noise from the rotating twin blades reached a pitch that indicated takeoff was imminent. I watched enough Predator feeds to know what happened immediately after landing. I decided that once the ramp went down I'd run out with the Rangers and after establishing 360 degree security, I'd attach myself to the nearest tabbed Spec-4 until the platoon sergeant or platoon leader decided what to do with me on the mission. I'd be the best ammo bearer or litter carrier I could be tonight, I resolved. It didn't occur to me until after my sleep induced grogginess wore off that I could just stay on the helo and fly out with the crew after the insertion.

It turned out to be moot anyway, as the helos all suddenly powered back down. Whatever order had sent the Ranger strike force running out to the helos was now countermanded and the mission was cancelled yet again. I don't remember who we were after on that mission but he must have been someone important, because we spent the whole night at J-bad, waiting to have enough intel to go get him. We were there so long that we ended up flying back in full daylight. This was a very rare thing for our Task Force, which operated almost exclusively in total darkness, where our comparative advantage was at its best. Flying home in daylight made the pucker factor a little higher, but it gave me the opportunity to see Afghanistan in the daytime, something I had only done once or twice before.

This part of Afghanistan was absolutely beautiful. We flew through low-laying valleys full of water and green trees, past fields filled with crops, and over clusters of children and farmers who waved at us as we passed. We had an uneventful flight back to Bagram, and I think everyone was glad to be back on base and to catch some sleep after a mostly-uneventful but nonetheless long and tiring night.

Someone once said that war is long periods of boredom punctuated by sheer terror. I think that description is accurate. Many missions were cancelled, or were "dry holes" that resulted in no shots being fired. That's one of the reasons I kind of laugh when I hear videogame producers talking about wanting to make their games "more realistic." If you want to make a war game more realistic, have the character spend three or four hours in full kit, sitting on the tarmac in almost total darkness, waiting for an op that may not even happen because it got weathered out, the intel trigger wasn't met, or your higher headquarters called it off for some inexplicable reason and you never even find out why. THAT would be a realistic video game.

As a staff officer, and as just a guy who is always curious about what was going on, I went to the morning ops briefings in the Ranger briefing area and sat with the pilots from my battalion.

At this point I had been promoted to major and was sometimes the senior Night Stalker present at these briefings, with most of the pilots being either senior captains or chief warrant officers. While I was technically the highest-ranking unit member present, I was a non-pilot staff officer, and wasn't in charge of anything past my own PowerPoint slides. Nonetheless, because of my gold oak leaf and the fact that they had seen me around so much over the last couple of deployments, some of the Ranger officers referred their questions to me. Towards the end of my time with the 160th, after several deployments to Afghanistan working with the Rangers, our pilots briefed the acting Ranger commander, whose "day job" was the operations officer for one of the Ranger battalions. One time when we were briefing this particular operations officer, he made a perplexed look on his face and looked back over his shoulder in my direction. When the pilots briefed the Ranger task force commander, who was usually a lieutenant colonel, they would start off their spiel with "NSDQ, sir," which was an abbreviation of our unit motto and this particular officer didn't know what that meant. Stopping the briefing, he asked,

"Hey, what does 'NSDQ' stand for again?"

"Night Stalkers Don't Quit," I informed him.

"Well that's . . ." he started and then paused, struggling to find the right word. Ending his sentence with the word he felt was most appropriate (although disparaging to the unit), he turned back around and the briefing continued. I took his words in the spirit in which I thought he meant them—good-natured ribbing between men who knew each other well—but I wasn't sure how the pilots would feel. Unlike my service in 5th Group, which was (and is) a "needs of the Army" assignment for enablers, I had to make it through assessment to get selected as a Night Stalker, and had to graduate from Green Platoon like the pilots. I was a Night Stalker through and through; our motto, our creed, and our unit were and still are very important to me. But I think there is often just a different level of esprit that operational types in SOF units possess that support guys like myself simply don't. I glanced down at the pilots to check their reaction, and while one of the flight leads caught my glance and rolled his eyes in a way that I knew meant "Freakin' Rangers," none of them seemed particularly put out. But I noticed that some of the older Ranger NCOs sitting in the front of the briefing area looking at us, with their faces positively aghast.

I didn't give the operation officers comments or the expression on the Ranger NCOs' faces another thought until the end of the briefing, when it was traditional for everyone to rise and salute the commander. Since this was the Ranger headquarters, we always refrained from sounding off with our unit motto and merely saluted silently. But this time, a loud cry of "Night Stalkers Don't Quit!" competed with the usual thunderous "Rangers Lead the Way." The interesting thing was, our motto didn't come from our pilots, it came from that handful of Ranger NCOs.

As we prepared to leave, some of the Ranger NCOs approached our group of Night Stalkers. "Hey sir, we apologize for what he said," one began, "We remember what the 160th did for us in Somalia, we have nothing but respect for you guys."

I explained that it wasn't a big deal to us. "It's cool, we know he didn't mean anything by it." But it was a big deal to the Rangers, and the NCOs still looked dubious. One of them said, "Yeah, well, if someone said something like that about our motto . . . ." He didn't finish his sentence; he didn't need to.

Note to self: never insult the Rangers' motto.

What the operations officer said wasn't a big deal to us. He meant it as a joke; the people it was directed towards took it as a joke. We didn't think it was funny, but at the same time it wasn't going to fundamentally affect the nature of the relationship between the two units. In fact, if anything, my opinion of the Rangers only increased after this experience, seeing in the reactions of the Ranger NCOs, the respect true warriors show each other.

I'm not a pilot, and I think I was still in high school during the Blackhawk Down incident in Somalia. But to those Rangers, it didn't matter; I represented something bigger, a concept much larger than myself. To them I was a Night Stalker, a representative of something that they respected. I left that briefing room feeling pretty good.

-CHARLES FAINT
LIEUTENANT COLONEL, MILITARY INTELLIGENCE

Summer 2007
"Stars"

It was the summer of 2007, a warm dark night. The stars were countless on nights like this. No light from the city to drown out their
majesty. What a beautiful and hypnotizing sight. I forgot everything
that was going on around me. When I looked up, all my cares melted
away. Even the noises of the diesel engines were overwhelmed by
their glory. As I stared up at them I thanked God for their beauty
and I prayed that, like the stars, my men and I would live through
the night.

"One minute," came the cry over the radio; after a short prayer,
I turned my gaze from heaven and looked into the eyes of the men
who placed their very lives into my hands. Six men who were willing
to go, without question, anywhere I tell them because they trust me.
We had trained hard together, and they had given me everything I
had asked for. In return, I had done everything in my power to keep
them alive. I would lay my life down for every one of them, and I
knew that they felt the same towards me.

"Thirty seconds, get ready," said the vehicle commander. "No
movement on target." I looked at the guys that are about to charge
into a night of unknowns, fully confident that everything will fall
into place. They looked at me waiting for silent commands. I cut the
lights. Eyes that had showed compassion and love now show no
emotion, no remorse, and no fear. All six pairs of evil green eyes are
looking at me, and waiting for me to join them. A chill runs up and
down my body as I think about the fear these men have bestowed
on those we have hunted in the past. I reached up and flipped down
my night vision goggles from atop my head and the night gave way
to a clear picture in green and black. No more darkness. I am one of

them. In our element we were unstoppable. We owned the night, and the darkness could not hide our prey.

It is said that the time for something to go wrong is on the way to the target. The ramp dropped and we rushed out of the back of the metal beast, weapons pointing in all directions looking for the slightest movement. As I watched my men establish a foothold on the street, I knew that at the slightest sound, all weapons would fixate on that position, ready and eager to fire. However, not a trigger would be pulled unless an enemy hostile was identified.

I pointed them to the target building, and the only sound was that of the vehicles. The vehicle commanders had their heavy machine guns pointing at the target house to cover us as we moved. I looked up at the commander as we silently edged towards the two-story building.

"Door closed," the commander said, "shifting to the roof."

At once, all the heavy guns moved rapidly towards the roof of the building. If somebody tried to ambush us from the roof, the guns would open up and turn the roof into Swiss cheese, and the ambushers would become the ambushed.

As the guns moved I sent my demolition team, the Alpha Team leader and his rifleman, to the front door. A two-man team well versed in opening doors meant to keep us out. They ran but made no noise, even with all of their heavy equipment. As they approached the door, the Alpha Team rifleman stayed focused on the door. If it opened he would lead the charge into the building. The Alpha Team leader pulled out an explosive charge and prepared it while simultaneously running forward. He placed it between the doorknob and the door jam, right over the locking mechanism.

The team leader and the rifleman began to back away from the door. They moved to a corner of the building just three feet away, and crouched into a small ball. The team leader held the ignition system in his hand.

"Charge set," my Alpha Team leader said.

Not knowing what lay in wait for us behind the door, I commanded, "Burn it" into the radio.

"Burning," he replied.

Sliding his finger into the pull ring of the ignition system, he pushed the pin in, turned it a quarter turn, and pulled.

The night was no longer silent as the sound of shredding timber filled the night. Windows shattered and pieces of glass fell to the ground. The walls around me shook. Where a door once stood, only smoke remained. Like water bursting forth from a dam, men flowed into the unknown.

I was fifth into the building. I heard the sounds of gunfire. Bang, bang, bang, bang, bang, bang! My team had thrown a diversionary grenade, commonly called a 'banger', into the room. It is what we do to scare the enemy and keep them off balance. The sound is so real, but often it is mistaken for gunfire.

As I entered into the room I looked straight across a vast space to an entrance leading to a hallway. Pieces of brick and mortar flew off the wall. Flashes of light came from around the hallway corner. I looked for a target across the way but was blinded by the wall.

"Contact front," I called over the radio. "Alpha left, Bravo right," I yelled over the ear piercing gunfire.

I moved to a staircase to my right, coming into position to begin the assault. As I looked to my left I saw my Alpha Team rifleman, a man that I had trained and had come to know over the last two years, bent over at the stomach and dropping to the ground. My mind raced with the worst thoughts. *He has been hit, abdominal wound, he won't make it.*

"Weapon down!" the unwounded rifleman yelled, while transitioning to his sidearm.

As I came to the staircase I still could not see down the hallway. With no idea how long the hallway was, I chose to use a diversionary grenade. As I pulled it out of my kit, concrete started to fly all around me. The staircase, inches off my right side, had become the impact zone for an enemy who was firing sporadically, pulling the trigger but not aiming at anyone. I did not think twice about the rounds grazing my head, my men were depending on me and I needed to act.

I looked across the way at the rifleman, whose weapon went down, now holding a 9mm handgun. I stared at him in the eyes. He had a wife back home; she had no clue that I was sending her husband, of two years, into a hallway and possibly to his death. He knew this and nodded his head at me signaling that he was ready, willing, and eager to go. I tossed the grenade down the hallway. Bang, bang, bang! I headed into the room on my right with my Bravo Team, while my Alpha Team proceeded down the hallway.

"Clear!" yelled my Bravo Team leader before I even got to the door.

Bang, bang, bang, bang! Rapid gunfire broke out behind me. I turned around and did not see anyone. The hallway opened to the right. Bravo Team and I moved rapidly down the hallway, rifles raised, unsure of the status of Alpha Team. As we approached the corner to the right, I heard more sporadic gunfire and the sound of a door opening. I flowed around the corner not knowing what to expect. There was an open door to my front, leading outside, and a body, lying still on the ground.

The walls were riddled with holes. The white tile that lined the floor was now covered in blood. Eyes once filled with life and courage were now empty. There was no movement. I looked at the shell of where there was once a man. I walked up to the body, with no emotion.

"One enemy KIA," I reported over the radio.

"Is it him?" my commander called back.

"Roger, it's him."

"All clear out here," my Alpha Team Leader said, bringing his team in from outside.

I looked up at the stars on the way back to base. The sky was beautiful and peaceful, with no violence in the heavens that night. I thought about what happened, as I lost myself in the splendor of the stars. I said a prayer, and thanked God for once again delivering the enemy to us, and every one of us home. There was something about the stars that gave me peace. Their warmth melts everything away.

-TIM TRASK
1/75

Chapter Eight

*"Let your plans be dark and impenetrable as night,
and when you move, fall like a thunderbolt."*

SUN TZU *"THE ART OF WAR"*

2008 was a year of transition for the war in Iraq. On November 17th, the Iraqi Parliament ratified the Status of Forces Agreement (SOFA), which was an agreement between Iraq and the United States that fundamentally changed the relationship between the two countries. President Bush and Prime Minister Maliki signed the agreement on December 14th, 2008 with an effective date of January 1st, 2009. The SOFA dictated that military commanders would continue to move U.S. combat forces out of major populated areas, with all of them being out by June 30, 2009. The agreement also stipulated that all U.S. forces would withdraw from Iraq by December 31, 2011. The United States would, however, continue to fight Al Qaeda and other terrorist organizations in Iraq as needed.

The 75th Ranger Regiment also modified its structure with the addition of a fourth rifle company to each of the three line battalions, which was in concert with the expansion of all Army special operation units. The addition of "Delta Company" brought an additional 118 Rangers to each battalion, which then underwent a lengthy training and validation process that was much more rigorous than the typical Ranger training cycle. Each of the three rifle battalions took experienced Ranger NCOs from the original three line companies to form the core of the new leadership, which were then augmented with brand new Rangers to train for the upcoming combat deployment.

The addition of the extra rifle company completed what was a four year Regimental transformation. The 75th Ranger Regiment was now fully staffed and trained for what would be very challenging years ahead. The Regiment was unfortunately not without loss in 2008; Sergeant First Class David McDowell, Specialist Christopher Gathercole, Specialist Thomas Duncan III, and Sergeant William Rudd all made the ultimate sacrifice.

NOVEMBER 2008
"IRAQ"

If there were anything I remembered from my first deployment to Iraq in 2008, it would be the buildings we scaled. It didn't matter if they were two, three or four stories high; we were getting to the top of that building. The majority of the time the ladder never reached the roof. So we would have to climb to the very top of the ladder, lean up against the wall and then reach up to grab a buddy's hand. In my case, I had to jump up to grab his hand, ensure that I had a strong grip, and pull myself up. I had to do this with all of my equipment, which would increase my weight to roughly 240 pounds. We would even lay the ladder down as a bridge between buildings and cross from rooftop to rooftop. There were instances where there were no ladders, so we would just jump to the next roof. I remember looking down from four stories high atop a building and thinking to myself, *this sucks*; yet I still loved my profession. What other job in the world allows me to visit another country, climb on top of buildings, and kill or capture the worst kind of men?

One of the other things about Iraq that lingers with me was clearing rooms and buildings. By the end of this deployment I was a close quarters combat expert. There was one particular mission I remember well. Our platoon was sent to hit a huge mansion that was home to a high level Al-Qaeda accountant. The plan was for two squads to breach and clear it; 1st Squad had the first floor and 2nd Squad (my squad) had the second floor. The remaining squad, 3rd, climbed buildings to pull over watch for us. As soon as the last rays of sunset were gone and the shivering cold weather of Iraq in November kicked in, my platoon stepped in to the Strykers, and rolled out toward the target building. Sitting in the Stryker, our squad leader would brief us again on the mission, ensuring we knew every detail that was important for the night. Not a second after he was done briefing us, my team leader would also verify that I knew every step that was going to happen. I would respond back by telling him every detail of the mission in a practice known as "back briefing."

Our squad leader then said, "5k away." I racked a round in my rifle, turned on my NODs, and then waited in silence for the Stryker to stop. As soon as we were two kilometers away, the Stryker came to a halt and dropped ramp. Like a hive of killer bees, we moved out expediently toward our objective. Moving out toward the objective you would think the people of Iraq would hear the millions of street dogs barking and howling at us, but not once did any of the local inhabitants check outside. Upon reaching the target building, 3rd Squad began to climb on the roofs and pull security on the target building as well as the surrounding buildings. We then were told to be ready to climb up over the wall too. Sergeant Pape said, "I'm pretty sure we can get that gate open," so our squad leader said to give it a shot. My buddy gave him a tool to pry open the gate, and ever so quietly the gate slowly moved opened. Sergeant Pape looked at me and said quietly "I don't feel like climbing fucking buildings today," I responded, "I feel the same way."

Once the gate was open, I could see a huge mansion with a giant courtyard that had a swimming pool, which was the first time I had seen a pool in Iraq. Not long after the gate was open, 1st Squad showed up and moved toward the breach point to inspect the door. Before taking out the explosives, they checked to ensure that the door was not locked, no need to use explosive if you can perform a silent breach. With luck the door was unlocked. Over the radio, "Door is unlocked, 1st Squad preparing to breach," was heard by everyone.

1st Squad stacked up on the door and slowly opened the door into the unknown mansion. As soon as they moved in, their flashlights lit up the first room. My squad went in next, looking for the stairs to the second floor. As we entered the room, guys from 1st Squad were already detaining two male suspects. We flowed through the room into the main part of the building, where the stairs were easy to find. Like wolves, we moved quickly, looking for prey to attack. One Ranger is dangerous, but if there is a pack of them, you best start running. Once we cleared the stairs to the second floor, Alpha Team moved toward one end of the hallway, and Bravo Team (the team I was in) moved toward the other end. We came upon a room, and I entered it while simultaneously raising my weapon. We moved swiftly, clearing the room with our flashlights . . . only to find it completely empty.

We then moved toward an open door that led to a second room. Flowing through the room I realized we were so quiet yet moving so fast, it seemed like something that you only see in the movies. But there I was, doing it, and it was very real. As we moved through the second room there was nothing but emptiness. We cleared toward the closet, it was just full of expensive-looking clothing; before we moved out, something caught my eye. I looked at the bed and told my team leader, "There looks like there is something underneath the blanket." I moved to the opposite end of the bed and with my left (non-shooting) hand I removed the blanket violently, revealing a shocked, frightened couple looking into the barrel of my M-4/M-203 combination. I quickly brought my left index finger to my mouth and whispered, "SHHH." Nodding their heads, they did not move and remained quiet. My team leader told me to watch them as he helped everyone else clear the building. "Roger, Sergeant," I said, and moved toward the male suspect, taking him off the bed and zip-tying him. I quietly said in Arabic, "Don't move, or else I'll shoot," with an alarmed face he responded in English, "I won't move a muscle."

The mission was a huge success. We caught the accountant, found an excessive amount of money, some weapons, and information leading to other Al-Qaeda members. Once again we caused another huge dent in the Al-Qaeda network. I recall not long after this mission our hulking, super powerful yet very intelligent Weapons Squad leader approached me. He asked me, "Norcross! Do you plan on scalping anyone on this deployment?" Half-joking and half-serious I responded, "I plan on doing that, Sergeant." With a huge smile on his face he said, "Well when you do, make sure I'm there. I want to learn the proper way on how to scalp someone." I laughed and said, "You can count on me."

I don't think he knew at the time that I was being honest. Before I left home, I had a ceremony performed on me called the 'Protection Way.' During the ceremony, the medicine man told me to bring back the scalp of the enemy, so that when I'm finally out of the Army, another ceremony can be conducted for me with the scalp of the enemy, as is tradition. I come from a long line of warriors that dates back to when Spain controlled Arizona and New Mexico. Since then my family has served in every conflict America has been in. I'm glad to say that I fought with a group of warriors of this caliber. It was a fulfilling experience to be a part of history and to have served with 75th Ranger Regiment. I never scalped anyone, of course, but I will never forget those times, especially the friends I made, nor will I forget our fallen comrades. One for the Airborne Ranger in the Sky!

-Leopold
1/75

NOVEMBER 2008
"AL QAIM"

We were about halfway through our deployment to Balad, Iraq and many changes were in the works during this trip. The Status of Forces Agreement (SOFA) had been signed and would be taking effect at the beginning of the new year, as well as a presidential election had just recently wrapped up. The military's focus had begun to shift from Iraq to Afghanistan, leaving fewer Rangers to take on the workload that still existed in Iraq. This had our platoon gainfully employed, flying all over the country on a nightly basis.

It was the night of November the 28th, and it was beginning to look like we would have a night off. Usually, if we didn't have a mission by about seven in the evening, chances were we wouldn't be going out at all that period of darkness. That night was a little different though, as the number one high value target in Iraq at the time came up on our radar. He was the leader of the Islamic State of Iraq (ISI), which was an Al-Qaeda front organization. This was one bad dude, and the intelligence that set this mission in motion was reporting that he and many other HVTs would be having a meeting at a wealthy Iraqi's house in Al-Qaim, Iraq just outside of the Syrian border.

Since this mission came down so late in the evening, a lot more effort had to go into the planning process, especially since the target was a three-hour flight away. The decision was made that our platoon would be flying out in three MH-60 Blackhawk helicopters, and since we wouldn't have time to walk in, we would be landing right on the 'X'. The target building was rather large, so one squad would land to the front of the building just outside the courtyard walls, one squad (primary assault) would land right on the roof of the building, and the squad I was with would be landing to the rear of the building. This was a pretty big fish, and he reportedly always traveled with a well-armed security detail. The word was put out to expect a gunfight.

It was almost December, and as we stood on the flight line in Balad it became very clear to all of us that it would be a chilly ride out there. The birds started to spin up, and before long we were boarding the black special operations helicopters for the long journey west. Generally, the helicopters we ride to work on have the doors removed so that we can get off the bird faster, and also so we can fit more people in by having guys riding with their legs dangling out. In the wintertime it is too cold to fly without doors on though, but unfortunately for us the helicopter crews had not put them back on yet. This made for possibly one of the most miserable flights of my life. We had a three-hour flight ahead of us, and because of my position in the aircraft, I had the cold wind blowing directly into me the whole time. My hands were numb, my face was numb, I couldn't move my legs, and I had snot frozen all over the right side of my face. I must have looked like a mess!

By the time we reached the refueling point that was the last (and only) stop on the way to the target building, I absolutely hated my life. Despite the miserable flight, I was still excited to be on this mission though, excited that we were going after public enemy number one in Iraq. This mission was the Ranger bread and butter – land on a high value targets house in the middle of the night to capture or, if he so chooses, kill him. Nowhere else in the military will you simultaneously love and hate your job as much as you do on any given day in a Ranger battalion.

After the brief stop to top off the gas tank, we were back in the air with just a short trip to the target building. I had checked and re-checked everything I was carrying, making sure I was ready for what would inevitably be a shootout when we landed. Before I knew it, the 'sixty seconds' call came, and we had the lights of Al-Qaim flashing by below us. My adrenaline began to pump ferociously and

I prematurely located and grabbed onto the D-ring on the end of my safety line, which kept me safely inside the helicopter until I was ready to de-plane the aircraft. You don't want to be frantically trying to un-hook when the bird is landing on the 'X' like we were tonight.

My right hand on the pistol grip of my rifle and my left on the D-ring, the thirty-second call rang out. *Here we go*, I thought to myself, teeth beginning to grind together in anticipation. The bird began to flare and descend, and the brown out from the rotor wash that ensued was one of the worst I had ever seen. Suddenly and without warning, the helicopter jerked violently back up in the air just before landing. Fuck, I thought to myself, we must be taking fire! Maybe an RPG was shot at us? We were warned to expect them during the mission briefing. Shit just got real; *please Lord, just let us get off this bird so we can fight!*

Just as soon as we jerked back up in the air, we were coming down again what would be a block further away from the target building. I still had my left hand on the D-ring, and as I felt the helicopter jolt from landing, I pressed the gate of the D-ring open, releasing it from the floor and quickly shoved it in my left pocket while simultaneously jumping off the aircraft. Without missing a beat, we were in a full sprint towards the target building trying to cover the extra block we gained as fast as possible. I still didn't know what caused our sudden relocation, and was surprised that we weren't already in contact. As we were running, I could see the squad on main assault was already on the roof and their helicopter was taking back off. We made it to the courtyard wall that surrounded the target building, with the squad spreading out to take up positions conducive to pulling security for the squad on the front of the building, who were moving to conduct a call out.

I hadn't heard any gunfire, and as I looked around I noticed low hanging electrical wires all around the area our helicopter was originally supposed to land. Maybe that was why the pilots decided to suddenly reposition? No matter now, we were here. It couldn't have been much longer before the call out was complete and the 'building secure' call came over the radio. One of my jobs within the platoon was to help conduct sensitive site exploitation (SSE), specifically focusing on anything electronic, so I moved to the main entrance and entered the target building ready to do my job.

The house was impressive in both size and design; you could definitely tell that it was no normal citizen who lived here. I had a fear that our guy wasn't here based on the lack of a fire fight, and my suspicions were confirmed after all the detainees were searched and the radio call came that he had left the target building at some point during our three hour flight out. After my portion of the SSE was completed, I went down to the prayer room to take over watching the women and children that were in there. That's when I became both pissed off and intrigued.

Generally, when you land on top of someone's roof in the middle of the night and ran sack their house, they aren't too pleased with you. That wasn't the case with the residents of this Iraqi mansion though. As I silently stood watch over the assortment of females which consisted of small children, teenage girls, and adults, they were giggling and in a generally good mood. I told them to 'shut up' in Arabic and one of the teenage girls had the gall to respond, in perfect English mind you, with "Do you know who my father is? You will not be here long." To say that I was shocked would be an understatement. My first thought, which I kept to myself, was *do you know who the fuck we are?*

I quickly dissolved my feeling of surprise and realized the fact that they spoke English and had an ego. This created a prime opportunity for me to exploit them for any intelligence on the whereabouts of our target and his men. Excited at the possibility of contributing to the mission, my demeanor switched to the smiling, cheerful South Dakotan who just happened to have found himself in their house tonight. I began to make small talk, asking them how old they were, if they went to school, and how long have they been speaking English. They started chatting as if I was their long lost friend, asking me if I had ever been to New York and what were cowboys like in real life? Before long I transitioned into asking them about their guests earlier in the night. This is when one of the adult females jumped into the conversation, rather defensively but still cheerful, and said, "My husband had guests but they were not here long." I asked her who they were and what they talked about while they were visiting. She replied, explaining that when they are over the women are not allowed in the room because they were discussing "men's business."

I prodded a bit more, finding out that whatever it was that they were discussing, the people doing the talking were important and did not come around often. Well, I am no detective but that seemed to me to indicate that the guy we were looking for was in fact here just hours before. Maybe him and his entourage were still nearby? Because of how late in the night the mission took place, the sun was now cresting over the Iraq horizon. The call was made that we were going to set up shop inside the target building for the day to action possible follow on targets.

A squad was sent in the early morning to go hit a much smaller house containing a person of interest about a block away, with a few of us providing over watch from the roof of the mansion. I remember manning one of our platoon snipers' rifle on the roof, rotating the crosshairs of the scope through every male that was walking in the area, just wishing for one of them to produce a weapon and give me a reason to squeeze the trigger. Kind of sadistic in retrospect, but it was a product of the mindset required in a war zone. The daylight raid went off without a hitch, and a few males who were of interest to us were brought back over to the mansion. While the platoon leadership started to figure out possible courses of action in light of the new detainees, the rest of us set up a rotation for security and rest.

We weren't prepared to stay very long on this target, and by noon most of us were hungry and running low on water. We had already made a courtesy call to the battle space owner (BSO), a US Marine unit, before we departed Balad to let them know we were doing a hit in their back yard. We ended up having one of their command-ers come over early in the morning to aid in talking to the detainees since he already knew most of them from the Iraqi version of a town hall meeting that he routinely conducted. Our platoon sergeant talked to him about our food/water situation and the Marine made a call back to their FOB to run some MREs and water over. Man, it was nice to see them roll up! The food and water was sorely needed by the time they arrived in the late afternoon, and I thought to myself that the Marines were now even in my book, as a few encounters with them earlier in the deployment were not as pleasant.

Now, remember that the women that resided in the mansion were perfectly comfortable with us being there, and had even made tea for us at one point during the day. Because of their ego about their wealth and family prominence in western Iraq, they didn't ac-tually think we would take anyone. Well, after we finally arranged transportation to come pick us up (the 160th SOAR birds that dropped us off were no longer available), we had to round up and zip tie the two guys we were taking with us for further questioning. The women absolutely lost their shit. They were screaming, yelling and just generally pissed off that we had the audacity (in their eyes) to take the men back with us. I personally found this very satisfying.

We moved out to an open field across the street to await the Ma-rine helicopters that agreed to extract us. This was my third deploy-ment to Iraq, and I had never seen an actual camel before. Well, this mission finally allowed me to check that box, as there was a herd of them just off of our designated HLZ. Finally, the Marine CH-53 "Sea Stallions" flew in and made a few racetracks before coming down to land. Ready to get the hell out of that town, we sprinted aboard and immediately sat down, exhausted but relieved to be on our way out. Once we were in flight, a rather funny situation arose between one of our snipers and the Marine crew chief.

The chief wanted all rifles pointed down, with muzzles resting on the vibrating deck of the aircraft. Well, that was easy enough for the rest of us, as the optics on our rifles were rather durable. The sniper in question was not about to do that though, and potentially mess up the 'zero' on his precision rifle, or damage the suppressor on it. If you can think of what it's like when a parent is cruising down the interstate while a child in the back seat is misbehaving, this situation was very similar. I couldn't quite hear everything, but it basically amounted to, "You better knock it off! Don't make me pull this helicopter over!" The matter was not helped given the fact our sniper had a very smug *fuck you* grin on his face while declining to follow the instructions given. Before the situation got out of hand, one of the squad leaders stood up and calmly explained to the Marine why the sniper had to keep his rifle pointed up, and reassured him that everything would be fine. Needless to say, I don't think that Marine crew chief was sad to see us get off his bird!

We ended up taking a short flight back to Al-Asad air base where we switched over to a C-130 for a ride to BIAP and eventually back to Balad. This, I thought to myself, was much more comfortable than the ride out here last night! Within minutes the entire platoon was passed out asleep for the duration of the flight back.

We didn't get the bad guy that night, but he could only run for so long. I was proud to find out that the information I gained during my SSE lead our sister platoon to spin up for a follow on target, which lead to the capture of our targets' close associate. It was a win for the good guys.

Staff Sergeant Anthony "Cookie" Davis was killed in action in Iraq during that deployment. It was in the following training cycle that we held the memorial service, the first for many of us, as 1/75 had not had a Ranger killed in action since March 4th, 2002. The battalion Command Sergeant Major bellowed out SSG Davis's name during the "final roll call" and as I stood among that formation of Rangers, it was all we could do to keep our composure. Hearing another man call out the name of the fallen, as if they were still standing in our ranks . . . is one of the most soul stirring things you can experience. We are brought up as young boys being told, 'men don't cry', and the tempered steel that is a Ranger is as stone faced as they come- even in the direst of situations. But standing in that formation you could hear the sniffles . . . the emotion in the air was as palpable as the Georgia humidity. We recited the Ranger Creed soon after, and prior to that day, I had never heard the Creed recited like that. It was the same words we had all recited hundreds of times before, but the feelings that accompanied them were much different this time.

That day I came face to face with a set of emotions I had not yet experienced. I looked at the family sitting in the front row of the crowd, mourning their fallen Ranger. I couldn't help but picture my own parents, or my fiancé sitting there. Realizing your own mortality at such a young age is a very powerful experience. Combat doesn't necessarily make you think about it, as you are very much in the moment as it is happening. It's not until later when you feel the tidal wave of a thousand men's hearts breaking in one formation . . . mortality becomes very real. We do, in fact, die. We don't live forever. When we go, people will mourn. Our loved ones will feel immense hurt on our behalf. In a Rangers line of work, that may happen sooner rather than later. 'Sacrifice' is not just a word to be used flippantly. Facing those feelings, accepting those feelings, and deciding how you want to live your life in light of that information is very powerful indeed. It ages you beyond your years. I have attended many memorial services since then, but that first one will stay with me forever; it will impact who I am as a man, a husband, a father, and a human for the remainder of my days.

-MARTY
1/75

"A RANGER WIFE'S PERSPECTIVE"

I will never forget overhearing a young wife tell my friend that her husband was amongst those killed during a mass casualty incident that happened to my husband's unit. This newlywed's life had just been turned upside down. She was experiencing every wife's worst nightmare. We had just been notified a few hours before but it hadn't fully sunk in. We weren't told the names of the fallen at the time of the notification so we were always left oblivious, but to put a face to the notification makes your stomach sink. It is too close to home. You always know that it is a possibility, yet it doesn't ease the pain.

We were reminded of the possibility of loss every year when we filled out the pre-deployment information. We almost became numb to the fact that we were pre-planning our husband's funerals when we were going through the motions. Then it happens and you are thankful you did write those plans down. I went home that night and bawled my eyes out. I felt relieved that it wasn't my husband yet guilty at the same time. I woke up the next morning and all I wanted to do was talk to my husband. I wanted to hear his voice and know that he was ok. That was not an option and I decided I would not be able to go to work today. I was liable to hit the next person who told me a "four month deployment wasn't bad at all." I needed to be with people who could empathize with the situation.

My phone already had a few messages from other wives formulating a plan to meet that day. We gathered at the house of one of my friends and drank coffee trying not to replay what we had all just learned. Soon, more wives started to show up all bringing food and wine. We needed this. We needed to be together. We did what we do best, we supported each other. We spent the day laughing, crying, and consuming a few beverages. We were working through the emotions the best way we knew how. Sometimes the room fell silent, and that was ok too, as we knew that we were all reflecting and digesting the horrible event.

The next few weeks seemed like a blur. We spent the time caring for each other, aiding the families of the fallen and trying to keep a positive attitude knowing that we were only half way through the deployment. During this time I relied heavily on my fellow Ranger wives. They understood me in a way that my friends and family could not understand.

Homecoming finally came, but it was bittersweet. It was the first time they had been home for Christmas in three years. I remember hugging my husband so tight, my stomach filled with the usual butterflies, and then remembering that not everyone was coming home. Usually we spend the first night alone but this homecoming was different. Some Rangers were hosting a welcome home party and my husband was insistent on going. I didn't argue either because I knew it was important for them to be together and blow off some steam from the difficult deployment.

After all the Rangers were home from leave they had the memorial for the fallen. My husband had spent hours the previous day shining his boots and ensuring his Class A uniform was perfect out of respect for those no longer with us. The ceremony was perfect. My favorite memory from the ceremony was when the Rangers all rose and shouted the Ranger Creed. My heart filled with pride and I realized that these deaths were not in vain but for their brothers to their right and left. Any one of these great men would have been willing to make the ultimate sacrifice. I was amongst so many great warriors and heroes. Never did the Ranger Creed give me so much peace as it did that day.

TSAF, RLTW!

–Hillary
3/75 Ranger Wife

Chapter Nine

*"Lest I keep my complacent way I must remember somewhere out
there a person died for me today. As long as there must be war,
I ask and I must answer - was I worth dying for?"*

ELEANOR ROOSEVELT

T
he SOFA agreement took effect on January 1st, 2009 and fundamentally changed the way that Rangers conducted operations in Iraq. It was now mandatory to get permission from an Iraqi judge to hit a target, which severely slowed the pace of operations. This marked the beginning of the end of the war in Iraq, as well as the beginning of the transition to Afghanistan being the main effort. General McChrystal took over as commander of all operations in Afghanistan, which brought about changes to the way the counter-insurgency effort was approached as well as the rules of engagement used in combat operations.

The Rangers saw changes to their uniforms and equipment come once again. They continued to wear the ACU uniform for formations and any time they were in public, but for training and deployments they adopted the Crye Precision Multi-Cam camouflage pattern, which was a significant improvement welcomed by all. The new uniform boasted built in knee and elbow pads as well as specially designed field tops for the summer months. Rangers also expanded the selection of boots they wore to include a variety of civilian hiking boots, wearing whatever worked best for the individual Ranger and the environment they would be operating in. Rangers tested the new

FN Special Operations Combat Assault Rifle (SCAR) suite of weapons, with C Co. 1/75 being the first of any unit to deploy to combat and kill the enemy with them. The individual Ranger was now better equipped than at any other point in the unit's history; every Ranger had his own customized rifle, his own sidearm, his own radio to communicate with, and the best night vision devices available. This allowed the highly trained Rangers to maximize their already elite level of shooting, moving, and communicating on the field of battle.

Rangers had embarked on over 8,000 operations up to this point in the war, were operating in the most austere environments in the world, and going places in Afghanistan that had never seen American boots on the ground. Regimental Reconnaissance Company (RRC) Team One conducted another combat military free-fall parachute jump, this time with a tandem passenger in Afghanistan on July 11th, 2009 in order to emplace tactical equipment. The Haqqani Network became a principle focus of Ranger operations, along with Taliban leadership and the Al Qaida operatives that were still in the country. Combat operations did not leave the Regiment unscathed; Staff Sergeant Anthony Davis, Corporal Ryan McGhee, Corporal Benjamin Kopp, Private First Class Eric Hario, Staff Sergeant Jason Dahlke, and Sergeant Roberto Sanchez all made the ultimate sacrifice. For 1st Ranger Battalion, SSG Davis was the first Ranger to be killed in action in almost seven years as well as being the only 1/75 Ranger killed in Iraq.

JULY 2009
"ON KILLING"

His mouth was open, lazily. Eyes wide and bloodshot, brown, and sunken deep from exhaustion or stress, or both. His hair was long, black, matted down with sand and dirt. The night had taken a toll on him. His skin was dark brown, youthful. A razor had never touched his face, yet he had no facial hair. He wore what resembled black pajamas, dirty as his hair and face were. He was crouched under a tree branch. He held his AK-47 down by his knees as he crouched, his dirty hands loosely grasping the fore grip and pistol grip. It was pointed towards the ground and away from us. He was unprepared, and more than likely poorly trained, if he was ever trained at all.

We made eye contact and he didn't move. He just stared, mouth open and eyes wide. As if in awe, as if the shock of the situation alone had paralyzed him. At the moment that he crouched under the tree branch to look up at us, I was pointing downhill in his direction, telling my team leader I'd heard something. A brief moment passed, it seemed, where nothing changed. He remained crouched, I remained pointing, and we did not break eye contact. I was shocked that someone, anyone, could get so close to us. On top of that he was armed, he was one of the men we were sent to this innominate valley to hunt this morning. He was outgunned and exposed. He knew it, his body language showed. In this moment that we shared frozen still, I could have understood him if he chose to speak. But he didn't choose to speak, he didn't choose to run, and he didn't choose to fight. He just stared at me staring at him, pointing.

Maybe several seconds passed like this, or perhaps none at all. I drew my left hand back to the fore grip of my rifle while pulling my butt stock into my right shoulder by the pistol grip. With my thumb

I flicked my safety selector switch from safe to semi-automatic. He remained frozen. I squeezed my trigger. The crack of a round leaving my barrel was answered by a puff of dust off of his black shirt. The red reticle of my optic blurred as I loosed thirteen more rounds through him. He remained still. The red overt laser from my team leader's weapon bounced on the man's chest as he acquired and engaged with an equal amount of gunfire. We broke trigger rapidly, if wildly, until at last the man fell to the ground, rolling unceremoniously behind a bush.

Cameron sat upon the wreckage of a log hut amidst the wreckage of a camp no one had ever heard of and no one would ever hear of again. On a map of Afghanistan, I couldn't have pinpointed our location within hundreds of miles without luck. They hadn't named the camp, as far as we knew. It didn't matter much being that it was all broken logs and holes now, and you don't give names to broken logs and holes.

I took a seat beside him and watched as an Apache attack helicopter circled above like a caffeinated bird dog. Cameron leaned and spat, watching it thicken in the sand. In the movies they'd have us smoking cigarettes, helmets undone and cocked sideways whilst surveying the burning ruins of a terrorist camp. We just sat there though, thinking and saying nothing. Nothing burned. Just splintered logs and holes.

I held a rifle in each hand propped on their butt stocks. One was mine, the other belonged to a guy who was sprawled out a football field away, one arm underneath his body, another reaching towards nothing. Broken ribs protruded through his stomach and shirt. His face was flattened and distorted from the concussion of a hand grenade. When the last machine gun burst ripped through him, he bounced and we all thought . . . *huh?*

Turning my attention to the latter I inspected the old wood and the rusted metal of the fore grip. Dark red blood clung to it and I wiped it on my pant leg. The wood had a shine to it now and I looked away, happy with that. I turned my attention back to the helicopter and waited.

"What happened?" Cameron asked.

I told him about the young man and how he found us and how he froze. There wasn't much to it. Certainly no heroism or gallantry, and if there was it was on the end of the one who sought us out in the first place. And now he lay in mud made of sand and his own blood. It told not like a war story but as an explanation as to how I came into the ownership of a Chinese-made rifle.

We sat again in silence save for the chopping of rotors overhead. I thought of the man I shot and how long he would lie there, how his friends would carry him out. I imagined him slipping from their hands onto a hastily made litter, blood on their hands and the litter, and the brown mess he left. What they would do, if anything, about his broken ribs and the holes in his gut? Where would they take him and how would they talk as they did?

"How far was he?" Cameron broke the silence and my train of thought.

"Fifteen meters."

"Damn," he leaned again and spat quietly, aiming for the brown spatter his last had left. "That's a good kill, brother."

The families of twenty young men would soon be burying their sons and brothers. They would comfort each other with the promise that our actions would not go unpunished, as news station tickers read US troops kill twenty in overnight raid.

-BRYAN
3/75

2009
"THE SWAN SONG"

In the summer of 2009, I was once again in Afghanistan, and once again working with Rangers. This deployment was my fourth to Afghanistan and seventh overall. Although I hadn't been back for a while, there was still a familiar feel to the Task Force compound. The beat-up plywood B-huts were the same, the noise and the smell were the same, and of course the operational tempo was still sky-high. There were a few new photos on the wall of the JOC, and while there were a lot of new faces on the compound the mission and the enemy hadn't changed much.

There had, however, been some major cultural and organizational shifts in the Task Force since the last time I spent time in "The 'Stan." For one thing, I immediately noticed that the Regiment had evolved enormously since the last time I was here. Having transitioned out of the "outer cordon and airfield seizure" box that people kept trying to put them back into earlier in the GWOT, the Rangers were now responsible for the Task Force's "main effort" theater of operations. This was a huge increase in responsibility that reflected the Regiment's new role and the trust that the Task Force had in the Regiment's abilities.

My own responsibilities in support of the Task Force had increased as well. During this deployment, which was my last combat tour in support of what was now known as OCO, or "Overseas Contingency Operations," I oversaw the exploitation side of the Task Force's overall intelligence effort. In this capacity, I had duties and responsibilities greatly in excess of anything I had experienced before. It was by far the best assignment of my career.

Something else that had changed since the GWOT started was the way the Task Force prosecuted targets. One of the unique things about the way we did business by this point was the focus on the "F3EA" targeting concept. The acronym stood for Find, Fix, Finish, Exploit, and Analyze. This later became F3EAD (pronounced "feed"), with the D for "Disseminate." F3EA/F3EAD was a very intel-centric targeting model, chiefly used for man hunting but transferable to other kinetic and non-kinetic operations. Focusing on F3EAD created a culture throughout the Task Force in which speed, trust, accuracy, and teamwork were key components. The "network to defeat a network" aspect of F3EAD helped foster true fusion between operations and intelligence functions, which enabled the Task Force to create an operational tempo that worked faster than the enemy could react. It took a while for F3EAD to catch on within the Task Force, but long before I arrived back in Afghanistan in 2009, the concept had made believers of us all.

On my last deployment, the Ranger Task Force commander had something very close to a photographic memory. He regularly recalled specific details about operations or enemy personalities that were first discussed weeks or even months previously. While this was a great quality to have in a commander, many staff officers found it utterly terrifying. This was because the commander had such keen attention to detail, everyone had to step up their game. "Good enough" wasn't sufficient anymore; everything had to be completely right. More than once I saw a staff officer or junior commander get flamed for lack of attention to detail. Consequently, we all had to keep up with not only what was happening now, but also what had happened in the past. This, of course, helped us better predict what was going to happen in the future, which was much more important.

As an intelligence officer, I noticed and appreciated that the very first thing that this particular commander had all of the subordinate task forces talk about at the Overall Evening Briefings was exploitation, specifically what information was acquired, and how was that going to drive future targets. Exploitation is, of course, mainly an intelligence function, and sometimes a gap can develop between the operations and intelligence sides of an organization. But because intel was important to the Task Force commander, it was of utmost importance to all of the Ranger leaders. In fact, the way this particular commander ran the Ranger Regiment was a textbook case of how the operations / intelligence relationship is supposed to work: operations direct intel, and intel drives operations. As a major contributor to the exploitation effort, I greatly appreciated his emphasis on exploitation functions.

The best part was, it worked. The commander, his operational planners, and his highly competent J2 oversaw a Task Force enabling effort that hummed along, with intelligence leads that drove operations literally every night, and sometimes multiple times in the same period of darkness. Exploitation became such a key component of the Task Force operations that it was emphasized as the most important aspect of the entire F3EAD process, and exploitation operations were cited as the "center of gravity" in support of the Task Force mission.

Part of exploitation intelligence or what became known as "EX-INT" included the handling of captured personnel. Several years prior to this deployment, this particular commander had been wounded badly in Iraq by an insurgent who had been released just days before. So he always took a personal interest in ensuring that the right detainees went to the "big house" and the detainees who weren't a threat got released. Sometimes there was disagreement over releases, and the commander once loudly and enthusiastically informed me that I was becoming a "Taliban enabler" and the Task Force lawyer a "Taliban facilitator" for pushing for the rapid release of detainees with no intelligence value. He meant it as a joke, of course; in the end the commander always sided with our recommendations, and we were able to provide the legal justification to put the worst of the unlawful enemy combatants into long-term lockup while returning the others to their homes as soon as possible, with a little money in their pockets for their troubles.

During this deployment, I ran the Task Force's intelligence exploitation facility and we never knew what might come in through the doors of our facility. Whether it was people or "stuff," it was enough to ensure there was never a dull moment. Due to the sensitivity of exploitation operations, I was given complete latitude with regard to hiring and firing. Military or civilian, permanent party or augmentee, I could turn down anyone I didn't find suitable, and could shit-can anyone that I felt wasn't making the grade. We were even permitted to have our own internal screening and training process. One day a new arrival reported to the facility. This arrival was expected, because an element in Iraq had shut down and the excess personnel were flowing in to augment Afghanistan. As was usual practice, my NCOIC brought the new arrival up to my office for an initial interview. What was unusual was that my senior analyst, a civilian who was prior-service Navy, followed the new arrival into the office that my NCOIC and I shared. Not only that, but he brought some of the other analysts in with him.

The reason this was unusual was because our senior analyst, a man I admired enormously and who was absolutely critical to the facility's success, usually couldn't be bothered with "officer business" and normally didn't concern himself too much with the initial arrival of new officers, especially very junior officers like the spanking-new O1 that was now standing at parade rest in my office. Why were he and a handful of the more senior folks in the facility standing there with those grins on their faces? Then it hit me. The new arrival, an augmentee, was wearing a "Secret Squirrel" patch.

I don't mean a patch from a classified unit. I mean a circle patch with a squirrel in the middle, above which rested a "SECRET" tab. Now in our Task Force, virtually no one wore unit patches of any type. This was definitely the case with enablers that didn't leave the FOB, especially ones who were augmentees. No one in my facility, and as far as I can recall, no one who worked on the Task Force's main base area wore any type of patch on the sleeves of our ACUs other than a US flag. But here was this female Navy ensign, who thought it would be OK to wear an unauthorized and, quite frankly, stupid patch all the way from Iraq to my office in Afghanistan, calling all kinds of unnecessary attention to herself and our Task Force. That's why everyone was there in my office—they saw the new arrival and her unauthorized patch, and having worked with me for a while knew that I was pretty hard on people who made poor decisions, especially officers. They were there to watch the fireworks.

But my anger at the new arrival immediately subsided. Yes, I was mad at her because she was wearing a stupid, attention-grabbing patch as a member of a Task Force that valued secrecy and discretion, especially since as a fellow intel officer, she was a member of a career field in which credibility is everything. What I was really mad about was that she came all the way from Iraq to my office in Afghanistan, and no other officer or NCO jacked her up and told her to get her stuff straight. To me, that was a MUCH bigger problem. I excused everyone except the ensign and my NCOIC from the office. My senior analyst and his entourage slunk away, disappointed they weren't going to get to see what they thought was going to be an epic ass chewing. But there was no ass chewing, not this time. I simply explained to the ensign that she could go ahead and take that patch off, as in right freakin' now, because she wasn't going to need it while she was part of the Task Force, and then I sent her on her way. We ended up deciding she wasn't suitable to work in the facility, and a couple of days later when I informed her we were sending her to work elsewhere on the compound, I explained to her why her first impression on her new boss (me) went so horribly wrong. She ended up doing her time in the Task Force in a different support role, and I heard she ultimately ended up working out OK. But she missed the opportunity to work in the most dynamic, challenging, and satisfying intel function in the entire Task Force because of a dumb "hey, look at me!" move.

Most of the people who worked for me were augmentees. My XO was a tall Marine Major who chain-smoked, which was an uncommon habit for officers. He worked out extremely well and we remained friends after the deployment. There was another Marine officer who worked for me, a young captain, who had been some kind of mixed martial arts expert in the Corps. He was quite boisterous and popular within the facility, and it was not uncommon from time to time to hear shouting and loud laughing coming from the office he shared with three or four other people. One day, the plywood wall that separated my office from his started to shake slightly and I heard the guys next door talking loudly. I had my headphones on and was trying to watch a VTC, and I was greatly annoyed with what I thought was another impromptu MMA match in the office next door. It went on so long that I was on the verge of getting up to go yell at them to knock it off when the XO walked by and gave me a thumbs up, saying, "Dude! Earthquake!" That's when I realized that it wasn't just the one wall shaking, it was the whole facility. I laughed out loud as I experienced my first-ever earthquake.

A young Army First Lieutenant worked in the same office as the Marine captain. One day, I got an email from her, in which she expressed her undying love for me and suggested we run away together to some far-off tropical paradise. Or something. I don't remember exactly what it said because I stopped reading it after the first paragraph. Since I knew that her shift had ended and she had departed the facility about a half hour before the email was delivered, she couldn't have sent that message. And since I had been in the unit for three years at that point, I knew immediately what happened: she had committed the cardinal sin of not locking her computer when she was away from her desk.

Leaving one's computer unlocked is a minor security violation, because it potentially allows unauthorized people to access your system. So, to help people be more security conscious, it was traditional that whenever an unsecure computer was discovered, an email went out from the offender's account. The content and the recipient of the email varied, but it was always something that would be sure to embarrass the person who owned the account.

In order to reinforce the teaching point, I replied to the message with, "1LT XXXX, report to my office first thing in the morning to explain this." I was at my desk when the lieutenant arrived and checked her email messages. Because I replied to the email that "she" sent the night before, she was able to read the content of the original message. A short time later, she burst into my office, totally aghast. "Sir! I didn't send that message! I don't know what happened, but it wasn't me!" she began. I cut her off, "So, you're saying you don't want to run off with me?" "Um . . . no?" she replied, unsure how she should answer something like that. At that point I let her off the hook and told her what happened. Enormously relieved, she burst out laughing. After I dismissed her, I heard her yelling good-naturedly at her office mates for setting her up for failure like that. But I bet she never left her computer unsecured again.

It wasn't all fun and games; we all worked our butts off at the facility. 16+ hour days were the norm, with no days off. But it was good work, meaningful work, and no one complained. Our Task Force frequently captured hard drives, cell phones, and other electronic devices. Sometimes those devices held material that we could use to produce intelligence to support F3EAD, but more often than not, those devices contained things that were . . . less useful. I'd say about 2/3 of the digital media we captured contained pirated movies, propaganda videos . . . and porn. Lots of porn. The sheer volume and the types of pornography that were in the possession of the supposedly "pure" jihadists exposed one of the fundamental hypocrisies of their ideology: while they were supposedly fighting in part to preserve the honor of women and to resist Western decadence and corruption, they were quite happy to load themselves up with Western pornography. All of the jihadists had porn. EVERYONE. It was so widespread that when several years later I heard on the news that a treasure trove of digital media had been seized on the Bin Laden raid, I remarked to my wife, "I guarantee that at least half of that is porn." It turned out I was right.

While the porn exposed our enemies' ideological hypocrisy, the propaganda videos revealed their true nature. Some of the propaganda included video footage of jihadists carrying out attacks against Coalition forces, but since most of these kinds of attacks tended not to end well for the insurgents, there weren't a whole lot of these videos. But there were a lot of videos that featured beheadings. I guess it was a lot easier for the Taliban and foreign fighters to cut the head off a guy who had his hands tied behind his back than it was to win a firefight against ISAF forces. I think as Americans, we have a hard time understanding that there really are genuinely evil people out there in the world, people who wouldn't hesitate to saw the head off a guy while he was still alive and struggling, and not only do it in front of his wife and kids but would film it so the rest of the world can see it, too. Those kinds of people can't be reasoned with; there is no bargaining with them, there is no room for negotiation. Those kinds of people only understand violence, and the only way to protect the rest of the world from them is to either kill them or lock them away forever in a place where they can't hurt anyone else ever again.

After we got done exploiting captured enemy materiel, the usual practice was to take it to the engineers on base and have it all burned or blown up. I stopped this process and we began sending things that were useful back to the US to be used in training, and I modified our briefing room to display weapons and other items that were unique or interesting. I happened to be walking by the materiel exploitation area of my facility when I heard some of my guys talking some Rangers about a peculiar device that they had found on the objective of the mission they just conducted. It was clearly a piece of military equipment, but it was unlike anything we had seen before. "What is that?" I asked. "We don't know sir, we were hoping you could tell us!" a Ranger replied. My guys took a look at it but couldn't immediately determine what it was. When they were done I handled it too. Three things immediately jumped out at me: whatever this thing was, it was broken; the writing on the device, whatever it was, was Cyrillic, which meant it was Russian; and . . . it had the radiation warning symbol. "Um . . . since none of us know what this thing is, and it's some kind of broken Russian radioactive device, maybe we should take this to a safe place OUTSIDE the facility until we figure it out?"

I didn't think that the device . . . whatever it was . . . was much of a threat; at least I hoped it wasn't. But given that we didn't know what it was, and it was broken and had some kind of radiation in it, I thought it was prudent to have the device . . . whatever it was . . . removed from the facility until we could figure out what it was. In the morning we had some of our tech experts take a look at it, and after some research they determined it was some type of Russian artillery sight or compass (I don't remember exactly), and the radiation warning was due to the tritium to make part of it glow in the dark. So, good news! We weren't all going to get cancer. But that started a new informal from us: "if it's radioactive, and you don't know what it is, blow it in place on the objective, please don't bring it back to the facility." We offered it back to the Rangers after we established it wasn't a threat, but they told us to keep it and we put it in the display case that our facility NCO cut into the big table in our conference room and covered with a sheet of Plexiglas.

We kept captured weapons on the wall as well. One of the most noticeable was a Russian-made AK-47. While AK-47s are quite common in Afghanistan, this one was unusual due to its age and its unusual décor. Its last owner, a member of the Afghan Taliban who perished during the mission in which it was captured, had decorated the weapon extensively. He began by laying down a base of aluminum foil against the wooden stock, and then wrapped all of wood, and the metal barrel, with narrow but fairly thick translucent orange plastic tape. Under the tape on the pistol grip and butt stock, he had included color pictures that looked like they were cut out of newspapers. I assumed they were pictures of parents and either a wife or girlfriend, but we had no way of knowing. I did know that having one's weapon covered with aluminum foil and hunter-orange tape wasn't very "tactical," and given that the tape on the barrel hadn't melted, it seemed unlikely that the most recent owner hadn't fired his weapon much, if at all. I wondered if his main goal was to go down fighting the infidels; if so, the Rangers obliged him. I asked the Seabees to cut the receiver and fill the barrel with lead in order to de-militarize (de-mil) the weapon, and we put it on the wall of our conference room. It was usually the first thing that people noticed and commented on when they came into the room for briefings.

The Rangers also captured a guy who had in his possession a cleverly modified Pakistani starter pistol that had its barrel block removed and home-made lead bullets added to the starter blanks, thus making it into a crude gun. The barrel was smoothbore and the bullets probably wouldn't travel very far, but it seemed like it would still function. It looked like it was modified from starter pistol to actual pistol rather easily, and I remember wondering if this type of pistol was specifically made to allow it to be modified in this manner. We had numerous other weapons on the wall as well, but the one that I remember most was a PKM machinegun. It was unique because it had a 7.62 bullet hole in the feed tray cover from the firefight in which Rangers killed the guy firing it and captured the weapon. And it was important because it was captured during what was arguably the most significant mission the Rangers carried out during my last deployment.

The Rangers conducted hundreds of operations during my time in Afghanistan, and I have forgotten the names and the details of most of them. One mission stands out though. While most of the Ranger missions I observed or supported were raids, this objective was more like a deliberate attack. From what I recall about the mission there was a terrorist training camp, complete with reinforced fighting positions and logistical support, in the mountains of the restive "P2K" (Paktika, Paktia, and Khowst provinces) region of Afghanistan. After a great deal of planning and shaping operations, the area was pounded by air support and artillery, and the Rangers went in, delivered to the cutting edge of battle by my old unit, the 160th SOAR.

I watched the fight from my usual position inside the JOC. It is almost surreal to watch a real-time battle unfold over a video feed. There is action; movement, flashes of light, a white flicker on the screen when a large explosion happens. But there is no sound, at least not from the video. Radios crackle, there are loud announcements, but there are no sounds of gunfire or explosions inside the JOC. It makes the battle seem less . . . real for those watching. But it is VERY real for the men in the fight. There is also a great sense, at least for me, of utter powerlessness. We could all see what was happening, but we were powerless to directly influence the fight. This was especially true of enablers like me, who don't have a role in coordinating and supporting the immediate fight.

Although the mission was a success, the Task Force ultimately lost two Rangers killed and others badly wounded. A couple of days after the battle, we had a Task Force remembrance ceremony. In most units, people who felt like they had more important things to do blew off many "mandatory" events. Remembrance ceremonies weren't mandatory; they didn't need to be. During a remembrance ceremony, EVERYONE turned out. The JOC emptied, people interrupted their sleep cycles, and planning and operations were temporarily put on hold. Only the people who absolutely could not be excused from duty (guards, radio operators, the extremely ill, etc.) remained at their posts. The remembrance ceremonies were extremely moving emotionally. They usually involved a motivating speech by the commander of the Task Force, and a eulogy from a friend of the deceased. At the end, the Rangers, in unison, recited the Ranger Creed and we were dismissed to continue the mission. There were a lot of moist eyes in the ranks after the ceremony was over, and it wasn't because of the dust. America lost two Rangers on that objective: SSG Dahlke who was KIA and PFC Hario, who made it off the battlefield but later died of complications from his injuries. I don't know where that objective fell in the order of major battles for the Regiment, but to me it was definitely the most memorable battle that occurred while I was in Afghanistan.

In terms of deployments, the one in 2009 was my swan song. It was the best, and last, of my seven tours in Iraq and Afghanistan, and I'm glad it was with the Rangers. The Ranger Regiment has come a long way in just the short period of time that I was affiliated with Special Operations, and the Regiment has clearly come into its own and has adapted well to the changing SOF environment. I look forward to seeing the Regiment continue to shape its role in the defense of our nation, and hope to one day have the chance to support the Rangers again.

-CHARLIE FAINT
LIEUTENANT COLONEL, MILITARY INTELLIGENCE

August 2009
"A Fight in the Mountains"

The Global War on Terror (GWOT) had been going on for over eight years at this point. In the early years, we had a small presence in Afghanistan while in conflict, mainly, with Iraq. The draw down and retrograde of Iraq had allowed us to push hard in Afghanistan. In August of 2009, the men of Alpha Company, 1st Battalion 75th Ranger Regiment received the news they would be surging ahead of the other companies for the upcoming deployment. I personally didn't know what to think, and had no idea what was to come. The time had come, and just like any deployment, we headed off to do our pre-deployment tasks as we had done many times before. We received our shots, filled out our family separation forms, ate our last meal in the States, and boarded the flight just like any other rotation. This rotation would however prove to be different than any deployment I had ever been on. I have stories that will forever live with me both good and bad, but here is how that rotation started . . . .

We arrived in Salerno to be greeted by our brothers in 3/75, which we would be supporting. The camp we lived on was already packed and they had set up two additional Alaskan Structure tents for living, and three for our ready rooms. The two living tents housed the entire company to include our enablers. Without a doubt, it gave a new meaning to 'nut to butt' as our cots were side-by-side with barely enough space to stand up between them to walk out of the tent. Our briefing room for targeting and daily instruction was crammed and poorly put together. Nothing was favorable, and to be honest, it was so horrible all we could do is laugh about it at the time. It didn't stop the mission though, and we continued to have our morning updates, which consisted of a lot of talk and no action. Countless times we were told "today or tomorrow" we would execute one of the targets we were looking at. The only thing that seemed certain was we would eventually be assaulting a training camp in the Paktika Province. Days passed, and a few targets were executed, but we still hadn't hit this training camp and moral was dwindling every day.

Prior to one of the most mentally challenging days of my life, we had built a pretty detailed plan to action this training camp that we had been talking about for weeks. It was about nine or ten kilometers up in the Sreh Petaw Sar Mountains in the East Paktika Province. History shows this area as one of the most dominating terrains through stories that dated back to Alexander the Great, who, due to the rugged and extreme terrain, failed at conquering what is now modern day Afghanistan. Every piece of imagery we viewed was a nightmare and as soon as a new set of eyes saw it, they too sighed. We had been watching the area for weeks at this point and had confirmed our High Value Target (HVT) was there.

We all heard rumors of what was there and at the time, I was only a Sergeant so it was all above me. But we had gone over tons of imagery of the area we planned to assault that showed enemy fighting positions. We watched aerial video footage of the training camp where we saw fighting aged males learning how to move in tactical formations, shoot guns, and so forth. We received briefing upon briefing of what was up there, which was sometimes described as many as 350-400 terrorists. These men had come from Uzbekistan and other areas to the north to fight us. They set up training camps in the mountains because they didn't think they would be bothered, which gave the command an idea to use a kinetic strike on the training camp prior to our infiltration. Sure, we have all heard of dropping a few bombs to soften the objective, but this was a request of over a hundred thousand pounds of explosive ordinance prior to our infiltration. A request this large had to be approved by the President, himself.

Time passed and finally on August 29th, 2009 the warning order dropped and the request for a kinetic strike on the objective would be executed! Key players went into the Tactical Operations Center (TOC) and the rest of us sat outside to get back briefs from our immediate leadership. After the brief was done, my sniper team leader came out and briefed me on the final details. At 1845 hours, Zulu time, the pre-assault fires would have the green light, allowing myself and others to watch it in the TOC as it went down. It was something I had never seen before and watching it on a television, I'm sure, did it no justice. The fires included High Mobility Army Rocket Systems (HIMARS) from Bagram Airfield and Salerno, as well as F-15s, A-10s, B-1 Bombers, and a variety of other assets supporting the mission prior to our infil.

Shortly after it started we suited up and made our way to the flight line where we boarded three helicopters. We planned our infil for as soon as it was confirmed that there had been no movement on the objective for thirty minutes, and once 2nd Platoon was on the ground, the ships would return and pick up 3rd Platoon and infil them to support us.

As we approached our designated helicopter landing zones (HLZ), we took contact to which the helicopter crews responded with a volley of mini-gun and M-240B machine gun fire while rotating to land so we could put troops on the ground. Because of the instant contact, the third ship was unable to land and flew away while the initial two ships landed and dropped their ramps. I came off running with the rest of the guys while looking north in the direction of the other bird. They had instantly taken contact as their bird was landing and as we came off ours; I wasn't sure what was specifically going on, as the radio net was pretty heavy with traffic.

We had essentially landed right into an L-shaped ambush as we came off the birds. We returned fire with good fields of fire based off their forward line trace as we assaulted through the enemy. The only thing I could see at this point was tracers and strobes as I scanned my sectors looking for enemy personnel. After a short while the gunfire subsided and a cease-fire from our end of the HLZ was called.

I cannot account for what exactly happened on the other bird but one of the men monitoring the radio, Mack, stated:

> *"While I monitored, I could hear that 2A was taking contact from enemy forces. I briefly struck my commander on the shoulder and brought his head close to me so I could inform him that 2A was taking contact and that they had two enemy killed in action (EKIA) and that we have one friendly wounded in action (FWIA) with a gunshot wound (GSW) to the neck. I will never forget the look he gave me. He immediately got on his MBITR radio to inform 3A leadership about what was going down on the HLZ. The commander had also been talking to the pilots on his headset to confirm what I had told him. As he was confirming, I heard the RTO on the ground report to the TOC that the friendly casualty was unconscious and stable."*

We had heard the call for a medic over the radio and that someone was hurt but had no idea who it was at this point, and you have a feeling inside of you that's hard to describe. You're angry but sad and curious; you sit there looking to your left and right into the blindness of the night or the greenness from your NODs without a clue who might have been hurt. The mission must continue though, and so we coordinated over our radios for the other element to consolidate on us with the casualty.

At this point, the group with our friendly wounded in action (FWIA) had begun to move towards the location in which my group was. During their movement, the third bird that originally could not land was brought in to infil the remaining troops and MEDEVAC our wounded. They landed and the ramp dropped followed by a bunch of hard charging barrel-chested freedom fighters without a worry in their mind ready to bring pain to those who hurt our own. Our FWIA and the medic treating him were then loaded on the same aircraft as calls were being made about two enemies on the southern ridgeline. An AC-130 engaged both, resulting in two enemy killed in action (EKIA).

At 2226 Zulu, the ground force commander reported that there were seven confirmed EKIA in a wadi in the vicinity of HLZ Loyd along with one friendly killed in action (FKIA). I would later find out that one of the new Rangers, PFC Eric Hario, was instantly killed as he was running off the bird. This objective was his very first mission.

At this point, we had been receiving reports of five enemy personnel maneuvering on us to the northwest of the objective so the ground force commander gave his approval to the JTAC to do a call for fire mission. The assets in the sky eliminated the threat resulting in five more enemies killed in action. Shortly after, our assets and ground forces spotted one enemy to the west, and my sniper partner and myself stepped up and began to engage him. We both shot a few rounds and connected. They called in gun runs from an A-10 to confirm he was dead.

We had been on the HLZ for almost two hours at this point, in what seemed like constant contact. The ground force began clearing through the southern portion of the HLZ, when a moment in which I'll never forget happened. We were walking through the wadi and I was with the 2nd or 3rd Squad in the order of movement. I stood about 10-15 feet to the back and left of the man to my right. It was pitch black, and at the time, I didn't know or care who I was next to. Slowly taking one step after the other, over difficult terrain with tons of boulders and broken mountain everywhere, we continued to clear through checking our every step and assuring we had eliminated the entire threat. Then out of nowhere, a burst of enemy rounds came our way. Instantly someone dropped while the remaining Rangers returned fire.

The aggression and rate of fire was insane, rounds were flying and ricocheting in every direction. It seemed as if the rifleman went through an entire magazine and the SAW gunner, an entire drum. As they suppressed the enemy, I arrived at the wounded's side and began to try and elicit a response out of him. I received nothing, and soon had another Ranger buddy next to me to help rip off his body armor to examine him for wounds. I remember reaching down by his

Kevlar helmet into a pool of blood thinking he had been shot in the head, but couldn't find an entry or exit point. While we searched, our surgeon on the ground had reached us. We did what we could to help, and then let the surgeon try whatever he could, although it seemed as if nothing could be done. This happened in a matter of seconds, but it's an event that would change so many lives forever. This objective would be the last mission that Staff Sergeant Jason Dahlke would go on in his long and distinguished Ranger career.

We finally finished clearing through and called in for the 2nd Strike Force, which was 3rd Platoon. They infilled and we loaded our second 'Angel' of the night (friendly killed in action) on the bird and it left with our brother in arms at 2340 Zulu. We had now been on the HLZ for almost three hours and had not even begun our journey up the mountain to the main part of the training camp. The terrain was so difficult to maneuver they brought in AH-64 Apache gunships to blow up the side of the mountain enough for us to actually climb it. After multiple runs we finally began our journey to the top. Enemy chatter confirmed they were consolidating and calling for reinforcements that the gunships intercepted and killed.

This movement to the target would prove to be the most miserable and physically exhausting walk I'd ever done in my life. As we climbed up the mountain, which was more like a crawl, we took contact yet again. One of the squad leaders near me engaged an enemy hiding in a bush with a suicide vest, and when shooting him, the vest partially detonated. My comrade was about ten meters from the insurgent when a huge ball of flame erupted. I remember a couple of others helping me pull him out of the fireball. I thought his legs were gone. While we pulled him out, it was clear that shrapnel had gone in many different directions. However, we quickly realized the wounded warrior thankfully had both his legs regardless of the countless pieces of shrapnel in them. Our medics and other first responders were already treating someone else for a sucking chest wound about 150 feet further up the mountain. A military working dog also had his nose partially blown off and they were both deemed urgent casualties.

At this point, it was obviously a serious moment but as I looked to my left I saw a practically half naked man. He was half naked because they were looking for other wounds, but regardless, I found it funny he was wearing nothing but his underwear in the middle of an all-out battle. Being 9000 feet up in the air after countless firefights, the last thing you expect is someone being treated in his whitey-tighties. Simultaneously they were passing his dog off to us below, I remember a couple of others and I trying to clean off the dog's nose but he was too amped up. We couldn't really treat him and continued to pass him down to the men below us.

The moment that was once comical turned serious as I remember looking to my right to where my Ranger buddy stood. This man had been really close to one of the men we had just lost, close like family. He looked at me, and I at him... I saw the dirt and sweat streaks on his face and he said some of the simplest words, yet held some of the deepest emotion I had ever seen from him. He said, "When is enough, enough?" and at that moment I replied back with, "No fucking shit . . . ." It's hard to truly describe or make someone who wasn't there understand what myself and the guys around me began to feel. We had finally realized that two of our friends were killed and knew who they were.

We were now passing down a guy with a sucking chest wound and his dog with half his nose blown off to our brothers below. Just at our feet we had another brother with shrapnel in his legs and tiny blood spots all over his pants. The look on everyone's face was the same. We all had been covered in dirt and blood, with sweat streaks or tears (whatever you had the balls to admit at the time) down our face. We were broken off from climbing hundreds of feet in elevation over very little distance. We hadn't even hit our halfway point, and who knows what else was to come our way, as constant enemy chatter mentioned the enemy consolidating and preparing to attack us again.

The truth is, we all had negative thoughts and our spirits were broken, and these were the strongest and most emotionally cut off people I'd ever known. After 3rd Platoon finished packaging the urgent casualties, they moved them to the HLZ where we originally landed to conduct the CASEVAC.

3rd Platoon had just finished doing post-assault operations and exploiting the HLZ while the CASEVAC element put our wounded dog handler and his dog on the bird. At this point, one of the assets observed scattered enemy personnel in the vicinity of a few tents/buildings about 500-800 meters away from us to the northeast. We called for fire, resulting in multiple JDAMs being dropped on the structures. Shortly after this, our CASEVAC element linked back up with us. The commander on the ground reported their findings, which consisted of multiple AK-47s, fragmentation grenades, ammunition and chest racks. He then ordered the guys of 3rd Platoon to blow the items in place with our own demolitions. Shortly after that and prior to continuing up the mountain, we had to hold still because an asset in the air was dropping more bombs on three different locations, which had enemy movement.

We dug deep physically and emotionally just to keep moving up this mountain and as we were about 3/4 of the way to the top, we found a place to take a rest. It was big enough to make a patrol base and we half-assed it for sure. Thankfully, we had Apache gunships covering our movement the entire time, because at this point, we all just flopped down on the ground. I remember walking through the middle of our group with my head down, morale at an all-time low. I was working my way through the patrol base to get to the highest point I could with my sniper partner, and as we made it to the highest point in the patrol base, we heard random shouting from across the valley that was dividing the next mountain range and us. At this moment everything changed, the mentality and the physical exhaustion seemed to subside for now and it was because I, as well as others, have considered this to be one of the greatest shots ever made in Ranger Battalion.

The enemy had to be a good 700-900 meters away, and out of nowhere my sniper partner who was standing upright took one shot that dings this guy right in the neck. I only know this because I saw it through my 18-powered scope. The guy dropped instantly and his enemy "friends" had to try to recover his body at the crest of the mountain. I'm not sure why it happened (partner's gun may have malfunctioned or I just decided to do it), but I began to engage the enemy using my partners shoulder as my bipod. At this same time, two Mk-48 machine guns began to "speak," a term used to describe one gun shooting a burst and then being answered by the other gun shooting a burst, going back and forth until they finished firing. I'm not sure if we hit anyone else but no one crested that hill again and shortly after, our assets dropped Hellfires on the bodies lying at the top of the mountain. I think this moment kind of helped motivate everyone, because nothing negative happened to us, and we eliminated the enemy. That shot is something that is still talked about today by the Rangers who were out on that objective.

After things settled down, we prepared to continue movement on to the last section of our objective. The mission had now gone into the day by many hours at this point, and we continued to climb the mountain. Finally the assault force reached the summit and cleared through the objective. As we moved through to the end of the training camp, we secured multiple anti-aircraft weapons, bunkers, tents and other tactical equipment from the enemy. By now, the sun was beginning to set and we had finally reached the end of our mission. Our commander reported multiple enemies killed in action, machine guns, AK-47s, ten or more chest racks, and various other items, which we could link to our intended high value target.

The enemy camp represented the highest point that I had ever been, in a terrain I had never seen before. We could see all around us in all directions as we sat there in a patrol base while the sun set. We looked to our left and our right, spread out pretty good but close enough to chat with a friend or two. We talked amongst each other about what had happened, and what we missed back home, we laughed and then had silence for those we lost. The feeling was surreal and something different, only the men that walked those mountains, or lost brothers will ever understand. Time passed and the sun set, and shortly after, the Night Stalkers came to in and took us home to where we would reflect on the mission and everything that had happened for next months and years to come.

On the 29th of August 2009, Alpha Company 1/75 and attachments lost two amazing men. This story is dedicated to them and their brothers that embarked on that mission. I gained friends and family that night and they will live on with me forever.

Staff Sergeant Jason Sean Dahlke, 29, was born Nov. 8, 1979, in Tampa, Florida. Jason was on his sixth deployment in support of the War on Terror, with three previous deployments to Iraq and two deployments to Afghanistan.

Jason enlisted in the U.S. Army from his hometown of Jacksonville, Florida in May 2004. He completed Infantry One Station Unit Training at Fort Benning, Georgia before moving on to and graduating from the Basic Airborne Course. He then continued on to the Ranger Indoctrination Program, which he successfully graduated from in December 2004. He was then assigned to Company A, 1st Battalion, 75th Ranger Regiment on June 1, 2005. He served there as a rifleman, grenadier, machine gunner, fire team leader, section leader and squad leader. He also served in the battalion recce platoon for one deployment as an advisor to local national forces. Jason returned to A Company as a squad leader in February 2009 and served in that position until his death.

He was the recipient of numerous awards and decorations to include the Ranger Tab, the Purple Heart, two Army Commendation

Medals, Army Achievement Medal, Army Good Conduct Medal, National Defense Service Medal, Afghanistan Campaign Medal, Iraq Campaign Medal, Global War on Terrorism Service Medal, Army Service Ribbon, Overseas Service Ribbon, Combat Infantryman Badge, Expert Infantryman Badge and the Parachutist Badge. He was posthumously awarded the Bronze Star Medal, his second Purple Heart and the Meritorious Service Medal.

Private First Class Eric W. Hario, 19, was an infantryman assigned to 1st Battalion, 75th Ranger Regiment at Hunter Army Airfield, Georgia. He was born December 9th, 1989, in Monroe, Michigan. Hario was wounded by enemy fire while conducting combat operations on August 29th, 2009. He was medically evacuated to a combat support hospital where he died. He was on his first deployment in support of the War on Terror.

After graduating from Monroe High School where he lettered in football and wrestling, Eric enlisted in the U.S. Army in June 2008. He completed Infantry One Station Unit Training at Fort Benning, Georgia. After also graduating from the Basic Airborne Course, he was assigned to the Ranger Indoctrination Program, which he also successfully graduated. He was assigned to Company A, 1st Battalion, 75th Ranger Regiment in January 2009 where he served as a grenadier.

His awards and decorations include the National Defense Service Medal, Global War on Terrorism Service Medal, Army Service Ribbon and the Parachutist Badge. He was posthumously awarded the Bronze Star Medal and Purple Heart.

- BORGE
1/75

FALL 2009
"DRINKING FROM THE FIRE HOSE"

I vividly remember the day that I passed RASP (Ranger Assessment and Selection Program), then called ROP (Ranger Orientation Program), and donned my tan beret – easily the proudest moment of my life. I couldn't have been more excited to begin my new job, and I felt especially thankful for all of the people who had helped me achieve my ultimate goal as a young Army officer. I'm not sure about other branches of the Army, but for an infantry officer, being a Ranger is the most fast-paced, aggressive and competitive job you can have in the Army – and it was my turn to begin.

After I finally signed in to my battalion, the first person I met was a major on battalion staff, who (unfortunately) was known throughout the Ranger Regiment for crushing junior officers' souls and basically being a total asshole. His first words to me were something along the lines of, "Get the fuck in my office and shut up. I want you to know that whatever you have accomplished prior to today doesn't mean shit. You've got a chest full of medals and one deployment under your belt, but what have you done for the Ranger Regiment? . . . You haven't done shit, and I want you to remember that. An E-4 with a Ranger Tab and a couple of deployments has earned more respect than you."

Leaving his office that day I wondered, "What the hell have I gotten myself into?" It took me about a year before I realized that he was sincerely doing me a favor by knocking my ego down a few (or more) notches, and humbling me, because the responsibility placed upon a Ranger platoon leader is something that truly can't be explained in a chapter or two.

Fortunately – or perhaps, unfortunately – one of the first major exercises that I completed with the battalion was an airfield seizure.

Without dragging out the details of what an airfield seizure consists of, needless to say . . . I was terrified. Standing in front of an entire task force while briefing your small part of the plan is nerve racking in and of itself, not to mention the glare of hundreds of eyes of the whole (more experienced) task force staring down and judging you. Leading up to the first rock drill (the detailed dress rehearsal of how the mission will go down), my first and major concern was to understand the multi-level, multi-mission exercise and try to not get fired for incompetency. Luckily for me, the whole training event went smoothly and I made it through relatively unscathed. That is, if you don't count getting dragged across the tarmac and acquiring a serious bit of road rash.

The airfield seizure exercise – as intimidating as it was - was my first true experience of what makes the Ranger Regiment special – the world class NCOs at every level within the Regiment. I came to the Regiment from an exceptional conventional infantry unit, and I felt that I had been exposed to top notch NCOs. But truly, nothing could prepare me for the quality of NCO that I was able to work with in my platoon in Ranger Regiment. Being dropped into a platoon was truly the "eye-opening shock of my life." I only had about thirty seconds to transition with the platoon leader I was replacing, which didn't quite set me up for success. Luckily, I had a highly proficient platoon sergeant with more than ten deployments under his belt, and my company had some of the most experienced platoon leaders in the battalion.

Being a Ranger platoon leader is a completely different experience than being a conventional rifle platoon leader. Unlike a conventional rifle platoon leader where the PL maneuvers the squad and leads the platoon during combat, the responsibilities of a Ranger PL are much different. As a Ranger platoon leader, I was responsible for designing from scratch and planning my own training events (under the guidance of my commander), determining and requesting all the resources my platoon would need, working through the massive bureaucracy within range control, and executing the training.

Even the responsibilities "on target" for a Ranger PL are massively different than what you would do as a conventional PL, because the model of the "fighting platoon sergeant" was born, adopted, practiced, and entrenched throughout the Regiment. The platoon sergeant, with his years of experience, moves squads, fire teams, and Rangers around on target, while the platoon leader deals with the "up and out fight" controlling assets, passing information to the Ground force commander or Task Force commander at the JOC (joint operations center). The PL is responsible for thinking of the 'next step in the plan' while the platoon sergeant "fights the fight."

On my first real combat mission as a Ranger PL, I took almost no leadership role. Rather, I sat back and tried to figure out what I could to do help, passed up information to the commander, and basically just tried to stay out of the way. When my platoon arrived back at the FOB, my platoon sergeant gave me a hug and said, "Thank God I finally have a good platoon leader." I wasn't quite sure of what to make of that until I walked into the JOC, and my company commander looked at me and said, "Well, don't worry. I'm glad you popped your cherry on an easy mission, but get ready to drink from the fucking fire hose because this shit is about to get real."

That first deployment with the Ranger Regiment would change my life and my leadership. I couldn't have been more proud to serve with the modern day Spartans of combat – the strongest, hardest, most courageous men that I have ever met – the Rangers and Ranger NCO's of the 75th Ranger Regiment.

-GARRISON EAST
3/75

Chapter Ten

"I offer neither pay, nor quarters, nor food;
I offer only hunger, thirst, forced marches, battles and death.
Let him who loves his country with his heart,
and not merely with his lips, follow me."

GIUSEPPE GARIBALDI

A major change to the way Rangers were selected for service in the Regiment took place in 2010 with the transition from the four-week Ranger Indoctrination Program (RIP) and three-week Ranger Orientation Program, to the eight-week Ranger Assessment and Selection Program (RASP) and three-week RASP 2. Rangers would now arrive at their battalions with more training and would be better prepared to immediately start conducting combat operations. The first RASP 1 class, 03-10, began on January 11th with 155 volunteers who were culled from hundreds of volunteers in the pre-RASP screening process. They graduated on March 5th with 56 Rangers.

The commander of all operations in Afghanistan, General Stanley McChrystal, resigned his position in June after politically embarrassing remarks that his aides made were printed in a *Rolling Stone* Magazine article. He was replaced with General Petraeus, who was widely respected for his counter insurgency strategy in Iraq. The strategy that had been outlined the year prior for Afghanistan did not change however, and those on the ground continued to fight in an increasingly violent environment.

The year 2010 proved to be the most costly in the 75ᵗʰ Ranger Regiments history. Sixteen Rangers gave their life in some of the fiercest combat operations that had been seen in the 21ˢᵗ Century. Rangers were taking on the hardest missions in the worst terrain in any conditions. The Regiment had become accustomed to short duration direct action raids that were almost always completed in one period of darkness in Iraq. The majority of those raids would not see even a single shot fired. In Afghanistan, not only were they conducting direct action raids, but they were also conducting movement to contact in enemy safe havens, often staying out for days at a time. The Regiment's flexibility as a special operations unit was put to the test, and the individual Rangers were being pushed to their physical and mental limits.

The fallen Rangers include:

Sergeant Joel Clarkson
Corporal Michael Jankiewicz
Staff Sergeant James Patton
Sergeant Jason Santora
Sergeant Ronald Kubik
Captain Kyle Comfort
Sergeant Jonathan Peney
Specialist Joseph Dimock II
Sergeant Justin Allen
Sergeant Anibal Santiago
Specialist Bradley Rappuhn
Sergeant Andrew Nicol
Specialist Christopher Wright
Sergeant Martin Lugo
Sergeant First Class Lance Vogeler
Staff Sergeant Kevin Pape

APRIL 2010
"MY CIB, RITE OF PASSAGE"

That night was a very interesting night. Once again, we went after another Taliban commander. From the "eyes above," it looked like there was something huge going on. Large caches of weapons were being transported and there were a lot of people on target. It was determined that this type of activity can only be Taliban. Once we arrived on target, we cleared the first compound. No one was there. There were about ten rooms that were all empty, and I started to realize that they knew we were coming. The squad leaders and team leaders both received word that enemy fighters were watching us and to be careful. As we cleared the next compound, we found people and started to collect intelligence. After all of that was done, the sun was up and we began to prepare for exfil.

The thing about conducting an exfil during the day is that the enemy could now see where we were. In fact, on our way out, we heard a gunshot from one of our snipers. He came on the radio and told everyone that he shot a man who was using a radio to call for reinforcements. We then cleared the body after ensuring he was dead, and then we searched him. The rest of us were behind a wall pulling security for the group. We then started to see people moving around from a distance. We continued to move to the landing zone so our helicopters could pick us up. We heard and saw the helicopters come closer and closer when all of a sudden more shots were being fired.

At that point we were in a firefight with helicopters about to land. The guns on the Chinooks began to rain down on the enemy. Without hesitation we quickly ran up onto the bird. One of our guys was coming up off a knee, and saw an enemy fighter only twenty meters from him. He opened fired, hitting him in the chest. Once we were all back on the bird, the guns opened up again killing whatever was in sight. Upon return to the FOB, we all talked about it and waited for the other platoon, who was still taking contact. It was an intense night, but thankfully all of us made it out alive.

-DAVID BOUCHARD
3/75

2010
"Dogs"

1st Ranger Battalion started its Multi-Purpose Canine (MPC) Program in the spring/summer of 2007 with just four original handlers. The program expanded to twelve handlers and twelve dogs in 2009 so that every line platoon would have a dog team designated to them.

I myself made my way to the canine section in February 2009 after passing a three-day selection process conducted by the senior handlers, trainer, and the kennel master. I had re-enlisted back in 2007 during a deployment in the hopes of making my way to the K9 Program. I spent much of my childhood in the Midwest on a farm, and had always taken a liking to being around working dogs so it just seemed natural that I ended up in the K9 Program. I served three deployments to Afghanistan as a MPC handler. Out of my ten total combat rotations while in the Regiment, those are by far some of my most memorable. There are no words to describe the bond between handler and dog, and seeing firsthand the morale boost that a dog brings to the team was amazing to witness.

Once the Ranger platoon learns to trust you and sees firsthand what you and your dog are capable of "bringing to the fight," it becomes that much easier to work together. These dogs are worth their weight in gold on the battlefield when utilized correctly and to their full potential. It is without a doubt, a very gratifying position because you truly get out of it what you put into it as a dog handler.

On any given night on deployment, I was utilized by the platoon during many different aspects from route clearance, interior/exterior detection of explosives on target, and the most exciting of all, chasing squirters who were running from the target. Obviously that's the most exciting, but it's only a small portion of what the K9 team brings to the table every night. You learn to be ready on the fly because nothing ever really goes as planned, but you always resort back to the basics and provide the team with the best K9 asset that you can while learning from your experiences. The more missions you go on with your dog, the better your team becomes.

My longest deployment was the spring/summer/fall of 2010 in Kandahar, Afghanistan. My assigned platoon was one of the ones that surged a month or so before the rest of the battalion, and we were to become what was known as "Team Merrill" that spring. Our mission set included conducting stay over day missions and clearing NAIs throughout Afghanistan. Now, as a dog handler, this brought up some concerns that were later laid to rest in my own mind. Taking a dog out all night on target, and then throughout the day in 100-degree heat was not something we had done before. Anyone who has been around our Belgian Malinois and Dutch Shepherds will tell you that these dogs will go until they drop dead, they love to work that much! So it was that much more of a responsibility on me, as a handler, to monitor my K9. Dogs can't talk to you like another Ranger can, to tell you he's hurt or tired. You just had to know and monitor your dog while trusting your instincts. I am truly grateful that I never had any issues and I'll go ahead and say it – 'My' Belgian Malinois was a freaking stud!

That summer would also turn out to be one of the worst for 1st Ranger Battalion, as we lost six Rangers that deployment, and one EOD augmentee lost his legs. I can remember clear as day after one ROD in early June 2010; we were standing on the airfield just off the tail of the CH-47. We had just returned back from a more than 36-hour mission as the guys walked by me. Almost all of them patted my dog on the head or pet him with watering eyes because we all knew we had lost a brother that day, Doc Peney, and another was severely wounded. I do not know what in my mind told me to do it, but I just did it and I saw firsthand the morale and comfort that a dog could bring to a team at a time like that. For lack of a better term, it was *amazing* to witness and it felt good at that moment to be able to do that for my brothers.

Being deployed in Kandahar and living right next to the airfield also allowed me the opportunity to go out with other Ranger platoons throughout Afghanistan so I stayed busy that summer as a dog handler. As an attachment, you never turn down a mission, even if it's with another platoon. It was a fulfilling deployment as a dog handler because I was able to utilize and experience every aspect of being a dog handler. As I said before though, it was a deployment full of hardship and loss, but we all pulled through and stuck together like any Ranger Battalion does. I will always look back on my time in Battalion with a smile because of the bonds made, the brotherhood shared, and the life experiences I gained. As another Ranger buddy once said, "I am proud to look back and say I was blessed to WALK AMONG GIANTS!" I still to this day resort back to some of the basic K9 handler skills I learned at the very beginning and use them in my private sector job as a K9 Handler today – it just stays with you.

I think 1/75 has done an outstanding job with its K9 Program, we have one of the best trainers out there and he has molded a lot of guys into great handlers and produced some outstanding MPC Teams for 1/75. The assistant trainer, being one of the original four handlers at 1/75, is also worth his weight in gold for his vast knowledge of the MPC's and the ins and outs of being on target. I don't know what the future holds with the wars dwindling down, but I truly hope that Battalion does not view the working dog program as something they can do without, these dogs have proven their worth over the last decade of war. Sooner or later, even if the wars completely trickle off, they're going to be needed again somewhere, and it would be a damn shame to start all over again after all that has been gained.

-LYNE
MPC ROBBIE & MPC LUCKY
1/75

Summer 2010
"Team Merrill"

The 1st Ranger Battalion finished off another deployment in December of 2009. Everyone was happy to be home and heading to see their family for Christmas. After we returned, D Company received a new first sergeant from the 3rd Ranger Battalion. During the formation when he was introduced, our company commander also gave us a very motivational speech: "Men, you have been selected to deploy early. Your performance over the last two deployments has set the standard. We will deploy early to Afghanistan and swing the fucking mallet!"

After the CO's speech, I thought about the upcoming deployment a lot. Mostly because in my last two deployments, I didn't fire a single shot in combat. *Maybe this year was going to be different?* Probably not, since I was a "goose" gunner. Goose gunners hardly ever see any action. Nonetheless, we trained for this deployment and we trained hard, going all over the country to prepare for the rigors ahead.

Before long, it was time to get ready to leave. We packed up and headed out, going through the motions like any other deployment. Once we landed in Bagram, we set up where all Rangers do inside the SOF compound. In those little, reddish-looking wooden huts - you know, the ones that have the shitty mattresses? Not a cozy place at all. We grabbed our gear from the pallets and bedded down.

I woke up and went to the bathroom. It was early, as the sun wasn't up yet, but it was probably around 5:30 am on the 19th of May. As I was making my way back to my room, I heard gunfire. I turned to look behind me and saw what looked to be tracer rounds down by one of the towers. I was very confused by this, as it was almost unheard of for Bagram, the largest base in Afghanistan, to be attacked. Still, I got a strange feeling from it.

I went back to the room and I told the men in the hut, "I think we might be under attack," but no one cared. As for me, I was concerned so I headed back outside because I wanted to be aware of what was happening. I looked at the guard tower thirty feet directly in front of our hut and saw the guards watching everything that was going down at the next closest tower, which was probably 400 meters from us. I thought to myself, *Man those guys should be watching their sector.* Not even a minute after I thought that, three RPG rounds flew overhead, barely missing their tower. I ran back inside and yelled to the men, "WE ARE UNDER ATTTACK!"

Like everyone else, I was in my PT uniform consisting of short black shorts and a tan t-shirt. I began strapping up my body armor, my helmet and grabbed my M-4. I took off running towards the tower and I saw Sergeant B. running up the stairs. As I headed towards the tower, my thought was, 'Damn, he got ready fast!' Sergeant B. took the corner. As soon as I arrived at the top of the stairs he screamed, "RPG!" I saw it go sailing by us and then exploding in midair. Fired up, we started scanning over the wall looking for the men who are trying to kill us. The sun was coming up so our NODs were useless. The vegetation was so thick that we couldn't see anything below us. We had no clue where it was coming from. Other Rangers quickly met up with us on the tower. We had it locked down. Rangers were spread out all over the wall, guns facing out into the vegetation, just hoping to see someone to shoot. I remember the tower guard saying, "Here, I'll get out of you guys' way. I'm sure you have more experience."

A half hour passed by. We hadn't received any more small arms fire or seen any more RPGs flying by. Maybe they'd moved on. Then about seven minutes later and Apache gunships were laying waste everywhere. At one point, I counted seven helicopters. There were also two AC-130 gunships in the air as well. Whoever these guys were, they just woke up a damn hornet's nest.

After a half hour or so we heard an explosion. Come to find out, some Regular Army Second Lieutenant had thought it would be a good idea to chase after one of the enemy fighters through a minefield. The mine took off his foot and wounded his battle buddy. A Ranger medic took off to go rescue them not knowing he, too, entered a minefield. Someone yelled at him to *STOP* and he luckily did. After they alerted him to the dangers around him, he slowly retraced his footsteps and safely made it out. As for the fighter, he didn't make it that far and ended up stepping on a mine as well. He, however, did not survive.

I remember our first sergeant coming up and yelling at us that we didn't have our eye protection on. It pissed a lot of us off because we got up that damn tower within minutes. He came strolling in after we got it locked down and started bitching at us about eye-pro. In the heat of the moment, we grabbed everything we needed at that very moment. Body armor, helmet, and gun. We couldn't care less about digging through our rucks looking for eye pro at that point in time. The hours to follow were boring. Basically we were just waiting for the all clear so we could go back to our daily lives.

After the "ALL CLEAR" was announced, a brand-new Ranger went to the phones and started talking about what just happened. He was RFS'd right then and there. There are some things you just don't speak about over the phones. This attack ended up making national news back home. I'm sure it definitely scared our loved ones, knowing that we just left and this went down. A picture in the Stars and Stripes later showed one of the fighters with an RPG on his back tangled up in the concertina wire. He didn't make it very far before he was shot and killed.

We were less than 24 hours of being in Afghanistan and we already saw some shit go down. I guess this was a sign of how this deployment was going to go for the Rangers of Delta Company, 1/75.

KANDAHAR, AFGHANISTAN.
MAY 20TH, 2010

We arrived in Kandahar and there was no time to sit down or relax. We geared up right away and got to work. We loaded our magazines and dressed our helmets in camouflage. Intelligence reported that around 450 Taliban fighters had taken control in and around Kandahar City. They were ambushing vehicles and setting up IEDs everywhere. Their safe haven was in the Zari Panjway District, dubbed "the IED capital of the world." The plan was for the 101st Airborne Division to move in to clear Kandahar. But before that was to happen, Airborne Rangers from the 3rd and 1st Ranger Battalions were there to "soften" it up for them.

After spending the last five months with our new first sergeant, we had developed a strong bond with him. We had respect for him and we accepted that messed up beret of his. He told us in the brief once, "Wherever we go, we WILL take the hard road." And that is exactly what we did.

Seventeen hours after arriving in Kandahar, we loaded up on the birds and began going to work. We were told that the helicopters were being shot at almost every time on infil, and we should expect the same. We should also expect a firefight as we exit the birds. To be honest, it sounded like a suicide mission.

Coming in, we didn't take any fire. We unloaded the bird as quickly as possible, expecting a firefight. The bird departed. Everyone was scanning the area. Nothing. Not a damn thing out there but the silence of the night. We began to move out. We moved in a single file line for most the time. We were definitely taking the hard road alright, by walking up and down the damn grape orchard mounds. We were not used to walking in this kind of terrain. Everyone was falling and disappearing into the five-foot ruts in the field. Rangers were laughing at each other.

We reached the target building, set up, and cleared it. It was an empty, run down building. It didn't look like anyone has lived there for quite some time. I thought to myself, 'Was this really what we all came out here for? What a waste.' Then we moved to exfil. On the way out to the LZ, we received reports of seven fighters moving towards us. Then it was five, then three, then down to two. The company commander and a few others headed over to apprehend them. They captured the two insurgents, discovering they were from Pakistan. They both had their shirts off trying to hide in a field. I will try not to judge them and what they were doing out there. At least they still had their pants on.

We set up for exfil and waited for the birds. As the birds were about 2-3 miles away, we could see them taking fire. Tracers flew through the air along with an RPG. Amazingly, the birds were untouched. They landed, and we ran like hell to load up and get out safely.

Strangely enough, when we returned to base, all the talk is about everyone falling, not about the birds taking fire as they came in. Either way, it was always a good day when all the boys returned to base safe and sound.

KANDAHAR
MAY 22ND, 2010

I woke up a little after the sun set. We were sharing a temporary building with the regular Army. We had upstairs, and they had downstairs. I laid there in bed thinking, *I should get up*, but everyone was still sleeping. As I lay there, a voice came over the loud speaker. I thought to myself, *No, our luck could not be this bad. This base is not under attack.* I can't tell you if it was ten seconds or ten minutes after that thought when an explosion rocked our building from just outside. I jumped to my window to see what had happened. I saw two U.S. Soldiers walking around outside. It looked like someone was lying down but I could not tell because of the dust.

Everyone was now awake. Our guys turned on the lights and I couldn't see shit because of the glare. All of a sudden a regular Army soldier ran into our bay asking for a medic. I yelled, "PENEY!" because he was the first one dressed. Doc Peney ran outside to tend to the wounded. He found a man whose ass was blown and who also had a broken femur. This was the second time I witnessed Doc Peney spring into action and save a life. The first was in 2008 when an Afghan boy was shot in the chest.

Anyway, talk about being in both the wrong and right place for that guy. Why? They said he was just outside smoking a cigarette when the rocket came in and landed next to him. Lucky for him, Rangers have the best-trained medics in the military. They got him inside and went straight to work on him, ending up saving his life.

Reports started coming in, "Enemy fighters have breached the compound." Everyone was ordered to stay inside. Rangers took to the roof. I knew enough about our boys that I did not need to head up there. Everyone was going to be up there looking for a kill. As for me, I headed downstairs looking for a job. Rangers had one exit secure. The other exit was not, so I placed myself there.

I looked out the doors as people were running and trying to take shelter. I told the people who are near to come inside the building. When I checked my six, I saw the most fucked up thing. In the middle of the hallway, a soldier was laying in the prone position with a M-249 machine gun aimed straight at me. I walked over to him and politely said, "Come with me." He got up and walked to the door. He was a short, stout, nerdy guy who probably didn't hit the gym too often. I told him, "I want you to face that way, and I am going to face this way. We will pull cross coverage since we can see more this way." He replied, "OK." I explained to him why I wanted him here with me at the door, "If you decide to open that M-249, I am going to have a really bad day along with the people directly in front of us in the other building. From where you were laying, you can't see if someone squats down and gets on the other side of the door. If they throw in a grenade through the window, we are screwed. We have to be able to see and eliminate the threat before it has a chance to get that far." I asked him what he does for the Army. He said he is a mechanic. I guess that explained it.

Another soldier walked up to us, and I let him know that we had this side covered. It was dark, and when he finally reached us, I saw his rank was Captain. He then asked me what unit I was with. I said what I am supposed to say, "I'm with Task Force Blah Blah Blah." He said, "Never heard of them." Well, no shit. We don't tell people who we are for a reason. He then walked away. Some guys from my brothers' platoon showed up to relieve me. I headed upstairs and looked outside. Helicopters started shooting. I saw rockets flying through the air. I couldn't tell if it was enemy or friendly firing that was going on out there, but it was a wild sight.

It didn't last long. I looked at the ground where the rocket hit. There was a one square foot crater in the ground along with medical supplies and blood. A few hours went by, and the voice came over the loud speaker, "All Clear."

Kandahar
May 25th – 26th, 2010

We received word that we would be going on Operation Akita Push, and it would be a Remain Over Day (ROD). Our task was to clear named areas of interest (NAI) and move to a pre-planned compound. We would then set up a secure 360-degree perimeter before daylight, and fight the Taliban from that position all day.

When darkness fell, we were to move to exfil. It was now time to *swing the fucking mallet.*

To me, this was our Alamo. We were heading to set up in the Taliban's backyard and let them bring the fight to us. This kind of operation was new for me. I was used to night raids where we were on the offense, not the defense. I had no clue what to expect since this was my first time outside the wire in broad daylight. I also remember hearing a sergeant say, "Bradley, I hope you are good under pressure, 'cuz if you have to fire that thing, all eyes will be on you." I replied back, "Yeah Sarge, no pressure at all now that you say it like that." He chuckled as he walked away.

We flew out and cleared the NAI. We found weapons and IEDs that were still in the making. Our EOD guy blew them up in place. We headed to our Alamo and quickly set up our perimeter. With the explosion from destroying the weapons, the Taliban definitely knew Americans were still in the area.

Morning came and we continued to wait for the Taliban to come out and play. They did not disappoint us. They started taking shots at us with small arms fire. They were in small numbers, maybe one to five fighters at a time. The Taliban tried to set up a mortar position but they were too slow. Our mortar team shot a mortar round that landed on them first. They did it with the first shot as well. When the mortar sergeant called back to adjust fire, the reply back was, "No man, you're good. Pink mist." Later, we intercepted a message saying, "They killed the commander!"

Since I was a Carl Gustav gunner, I pretty much had nowhere to set up without having someone or something in my back blast area. So I moved from 2nd Platoon's area of operation and into 3rd Platoon's. It was a cozy spot with a mud wall with a tree over me providing me with shade. I couldn't complain. I pulled out my range finders and started writing down the distances to places where the enemy could hide. There wasn't much out there though, just a huge open field with two grape huts and a dirt field. Where the field ended was a massive woodline, but it was over 400 meters away though.

More small arms fire came our way from the east. I heard our Mk-48s open up. I was pumped. Then three RPGs flew overhead. All of a sudden, we were taking machine gun fire from our side. Nobody knew from where though. We all had our heads down while quickly peeking over to try and see where it's coming from.

It lasted minutes. I pulled my range finders out to see if I could spot them. I was scanning the woodline when I saw something. It was a smoke signature! Those bastards fired so damn much that they just ratted themselves out! For as long as I live, I will never forget that moment. I was excited, and I said, "First Sergeant! I've found them." His reply back is simple, "Well, get the goose." I felt dumb from the way he said it. It's not like I can just take a shot with an M-4 or something. Everyone has to know this thing is about to go boom.

This is it; don't fuck up, I said to myself. I found the range to the smoke signature. 418 meters. I grabbed the HE round from my assistant gunner. I set the round to 400 meters. I set the range drum. I wanted to make sure this round explodes in their faces and not behind them. They were never going to see this coming! I handed the round back to my AG. He loaded it up. Everyone cleared the back blast area. I took aim at the top of the smoke signature. It was roughly around five feet tall. I yelled, "GOOSE GOING HOT!" Everyone repeated it. I squeezed the trigger, *KA-BOOM!* The round ignited and I was hit with the overpressure. It sent a shock wave through my body. Dust and rocks got kicked up all over the people around me. I watch the round as it screamed toward its target. As soon as it reached the smoke, it exploded. Direct hit.

First Sergeant said, "Great shot!" My little brother's platoon sergeant said, "That landed right where it needed to be!" I quickly unloaded the round and prepped another round. After that shot, everything went quiet. We picked up their radio frequency and listened in on their chatter. "Akmed! Come in Akmed. Akmed, Come in!" But Akmed did not answer.

A few minutes later, our ground commander called in the birds to see if they could confirm any EKIA. The pilots responded back with three confirmed EKIA. They then bombarded the woodline with rockets and machine gun fire. By then, I'm pretty sure Akmed's friends knew he didn't make it.

That shot right there was D Company, 1/75's first time firing "The Goose" in Afghanistan since it was stood up in 2008. The company commander said to me, "Keep that round casing. We are gonna put it in our trophy case." So I did what he said, and kept it.

It was quiet for about an hour, before they came back to fight. They were shooting at us from somewhere close. Someone said, "They are in the grape hut!" I went to grab an HEDP round. Then I heard, "NOT YOU BRADLEY! Get 3rd Platoon's goose gunner over here. You've already had your shot!" That was 3rd Platoon's platoon sergeant shutting me down so his guy could shoot. I understood we weren't able to use this weapon system very often.

The only problem I had with it was the other goose gunner was located on the other side of the compound. It made more sense for me to take the shot and end the engagement immediately. But I was not in command and had nothing to say other than, "Roger, Sergeant." Instead, we waited for the other gun team to get over to my position.

Finally, they arrived out of breath. I sat there and watched them. They must have sprinted to us because they were breathing hard. They looked nervous. They were loaded up and ready to fire. He took aim. He yelled out, "GOOSE GOING HOT!" Everyone repeated it. *KA-BOOM!* The round came screaming out of the barrel and jetted through the air and landed about a hundred meters over and to the right of the target. The platoon sergeant screamed in anger, "LOAD ANOTHER ONE!" They did, and fired again. This time the round landed short. The platoon sergeant was highly pissed off and said they were done shooting. Now I understood why that platoon sergeant did that: to give his guy a chance to shoot. 'To share the love' so to speak. I had no problem with it at all.

We picked up more of their radio chatter. The guy in the grape hut was still alive. His buddy called to him and said, "DON'T MOVE! The Americans have set up IEDs all around you!" Hearing that made the day so much better and those missed shots well worth it. We were all laughing. It was a great idea though. Maybe we should set up IEDs? Fight fire with fire.

The day wore on. It was 107 degrees outside and we were out of water now. The people who have water were sharing with others. A small resupply came in, but it didn't last long. Guys were receiving entire IV bags from the medics just to stay hydrated.

A little later the sun started setting. The snipers came off the roof. They were up there all fucking day! Their faces were burnt from the sun. One of the staff sergeants looked like hell. I remember Doc saying, "I have one more IV bag left, who wants it?" Nobody said anything. I still had water, but I wasn't going to pass it up. I said, "I'll take it." Then I saw the look on that sniper's face. It wasn't a look of sadness or anything. It was a look that told me he needs that IV bag way more than I do. I said, "Never mind, give it to him. He needs it more than I do." He opened it up and downed it right there. Like I said, I was in the shade most of the day. He was on the roof with none. When you are out there and it is just the men, you have to take care of the pride to make sure we all come home. Out there, you are family. Brothers.

It was now dark. We continued to wait to make sure we were able to move out safely to the HLZ. We started moving. It was a long walk, and I was trailing the AG of one of the machine gun teams. I knew who it was. It was a private, a short guy from Tennessee. For being as small as he was, about 5'3", he was a guy who sure could run fast.

I saw him stumbling. He kept on doing that, "bend over with a ruck sack" technique to keep the weight off his back. If you ever had a heavy ruck on your back, you know what I'm talking about. He was sucking. We were walking next to a grape field ditch that was full of water, and he fell in. He climbed his way out. We stopped. I walked up to him and ask him if he had any water. He said no so I gave him mine.

Every time we stopped, I headed back to him to give him more water. He was sucking, like I had never seen a Ranger suck in combat before. I took his ruck that was filled with belt fed ammo of 7.62 rounds for the Mk-48. To be honest, it did not feel that heavy to me. But when a man is dehydrated that bad, his own body weight is heavy enough.

We continued walking. All of a sudden, I saw him fall into the ditch again. He was waist deep. When I got to him, he saw me. He took a deep breath and blew it out while dropping his head down. He wanted to give up on life. I extended my hand to him.

He gladly took it and we continued moving. He was falling behind now. I grabbed his body armor and started guiding him forward. I felt him trying to give up. I started yelling in his ear, "Ranger, we are almost there, you better Ranger Up!" We finally got to the LZ. Everyone was on a knee. A half hour went by. Another fifteen minutes passed. Rangers were starting to sit down now. I did as well. The cool night air felt good on my sweaty skin and soaked shirt. I was tired. My eyes were getting heavy. I fell asleep.

I woke up to a captain in my face telling me that the birds are coming in and to get on a knee. I must have been snoring? I can only wonder how many others fell asleep. We hadn't slept in over thirty-six hours! The birds came in. We ran on, snapped in, and took off. We got back and continued to stay awake until our weapons were clean. We then took showers. A fresh cool shower to wash all that sweat off felt so good. Afterwards, we went to bed. I can't tell you how long everyone slept for, but it was between twelve and sixteen hours. It was well-deserved sleep; I did know that.

KANDAHAR
MAY 31ST – JUNE 1ST, 2010

Before long, we were off to conduct Operation Doberman in the Zari Panjway District. This time we would be conducting a movement to contact. 2nd and 3rd Platoon of D Company along with one other platoon full of Afghan troops fighting alongside their Special Forces advisors were to take control of three pre-planned compounds. The compounds are located 500 to 1000 meters apart from one another. 2nd Platoon would be located furthest South, 3rd Platoon furthest to the north, and the ODA and their Afghan fighters in the middle. Each platoon was to establish a 360-degree perimeter before daylight.

Our last mission out of Kandahar Airfield would be another ROD. This is the second one we conducted as Team Merrill in four days. These RODs are no joke. After the last one, it took days to reenergize our bodies. We prepared for this mission by loading up extra ammo and water for a resupply just in case we needed it. We learned from what happened last time and did not want to go through that again.

After the mission brief, we geared up and got ready for the manifest call. Each Ranger sounded off with, "Here, Sergeant!" after hearing their name. They then loaded up onto the bus and waited. Once every name on the manifest was called, the busses headed to the airfield and dropped us off at the MH-47 Chinooks.

Our platoon sergeant and our medic walked between our two single file lines to get a correct head count. After that, we loaded up onto the helicopters, sat down, snapped in, and waited to take off. Once the birds were in the air, everything became more serious. We were heading into the unknown, a dangerous place.

The Chinooks landed us in a dusty field. The back ramp dropped and Rangers exited the bird to pull security. The birds took off and we began to move out towards our designated compound. With multiple helicopters moving in and out, the Taliban fighters knew that Americans were playing in their backyard again.

We quickly walked to the compound, which was occupied by a family. We told them they had to leave, go somewhere safe from here, and not to return until tomorrow. We paid them some money and they are happy to leave. I was sure that this family would spread the news that American forces kicked them out of their home. This will then lead the Taliban fighters to our exact location. That is fine. We did not come here to hide.

We started setting up our stronghold. My fighting position was set up at the southern end of the compound in order to provide effective fires to the south and west. I was sitting between a short building, which I could see around, and a longer building that provided cover at my back. The buildings were probably ten feet apart from each other. At the end of the short building there was a large mound of dirt. It did not provide enough cover as it was, so I walked into one of the rooms where they were keeping the animal feed and started using multiple bags of feed for additional protection. They were large and extremely heavy; we found some logs and sticks to use with them as well.

It was now morning and still quiet. Nothing was happening. I could feel the heat coming on. It was going to be another hot day with temperatures over 100 degrees. I decided to start building some type of shade. I used my poncho liner and some bungee cords. I saw my squad leader sitting in the sun without shade. He was located just behind us, against the wall on the short building. He arrived a few days later than the rest of the company because he just became a father and stayed back for the birth of his daughter. This was his first ROD of this deployment. I figured I would build him some shade, too, as he pulled security.

As I was building his shade, we intercepted more chatter from the Taliban. "Drink your morning tea and then we will fight," a Taliban commander said. I was not sure how long it takes to drink tea, set into a fighting position, and then kick off the fight. It couldn't be that much time so I tried to hurry and finish building my squad leader's shade. The grape hut had a bunch of half foot wide by two feet tall holes running all through its walls. A friend of mine who was located inside of it asked me to grab the sticks from under their feet so they weren't tripping over them. They also gave me a poncho to help out my squad leader and I gladly started gathering up the sticks from inside the grape hut.

I returned to grab two more sticks to run through the eyeholes of the poncho liner and then my squad leaders shade would be complete. As soon as I walked into the grape hut, the fight kicked off. Bullets were flying through the holes and into the grape hut, impacting all around us. I threw my body on the ground to avoid being hit and looked around. Everyone else was lying on the ground. The men who are on the ladders inside the grape hut looking out of the higher holes were ducking behind the walls for cover. I heard RPGs screaming overhead. So many bullets were coming in! I had never seen or experienced rounds impacting this close to me before. It was scary close. One of our senior medics was hit. A bullet scraped along his back shoulder, but it was only a flesh wound. He continued to shoot and fight on to the Ranger objective.

My squad leader ran inside the grape hut and said, "Let's use the goose!" I was all for it. We ran back to our fighting position, and my AG loaded up a round. I was going to fire an HE round over a wall where we believed the enemy fighting position was. I took a knee and aimed. In my mind I was thinking, *I am going to be shot.* I pulled the trigger. *KA-BOOM!* The round flew out of the barrel and exploded where it was supposed to; the shooting stopped.

We brought in the Apaches to see if they could locate these fuckers and kill them because we couldn't see them. But the enemy was smart. The pilots informed us, "They have set their weapons down and are now walking with small children." They knew that we WOULD NOT engage them as long as there are children by their sides. They were free to move and roam wherever they pleased. The air support was now useless and the only way to kill them was for our air support to move out and be ready to fight again.

The birds left and the fighting soon continued. It was an enemy sniper this time. He had 3rd Squad, who was on a rooftop, pinned down. My squad leader informed us that we had taken casualties. I did not ask whom. He informed me that we were to pick up and reposition on the east wall to locate and kill the enemy sniper with the goose. So, we grabbed our gear and moved out.

When we arrived at the wall, it was easily eight feet high and Rangers had dug out portholes throughout it. Our snipers were there trying to locate the enemy sniper. They believed he was positioned behind a wall. My job was to fire an HE round directly over that wall and kill him.

There was a four-foot wall to my left. I climbed onto it. On the other side of the wall I was standing on, there was a twenty-foot deep cliff that led into a large well. My first fear was falling over the wall and into the well, which was full of water. With all the gear I had on, I would not be able to swim. I would immediately sink and once I dropped off my gear, I would not be able to climb out. I would have to wait to be rescued. The only option I had was to not fall. My squad leader grabbed on to my belt and ensured that he had me. I then peaked over the eight-foot wall and let our snipers walk me on to the target.

The wall the snipers were talking about looked to be a piece of an old building. There was a blue door in the center of it with no roof or other sidewalls connected to it. It was just a single wall that was once a part of a home. But the only thing homely about the wall now was a random chair sitting on the concrete pad. They believed he was behind that wall.

I pulled out my range finders, peaked over the wall, and saw the target was roughly 150 meters from us. My squad leader set the round at 150 meters. He and my AG loaded up the goose and handed it to me. I peaked over the wall again and was fearful that the sniper was going to shoot me in the face after already exposing myself once. Nonetheless, this was my job and what I must do. I took my time to place the round where it needed to go. A wasted shot meant I would have to pop my head over this wall again, and that was a risk I don't want to take.

KA-BOOM! The round jetted out of the barrel and went screaming through the air. The snipers were watching the round as well. They said, "Perfect shot dude!" The shooting stopped again. We learned that the Taliban does not like the destructive sound the goose makes when it goes hot. They stopped shooting after every time we used it. I would like to think it is because I was killing those bastards off, but the truth is it was probably just confusing to them. They had no idea what the hell was being shot at them. The 84MM recoilless rifle is the loudest weapon system that I have ever worked with. I called it "My boom-stick" for a reason.

Since the shooting stopped we had a resupply coming in hot. It is a Black Hawk helicopter. He was coming in fast and landed in the wrong damn spot, completely out in the open. Our leadership informed him he landed too far out and that kicking the ammo and water into that area was going to endanger men's lives; he would have to move in closer to us.

I saw the pilot pick up his bird, fly towards one of our buildings, and then hit the "air brakes" before spinning his tail-end around 180-degrees and setting it down beautifully. He did almost of this all while flying sideways. It was one of the most Hollywood things that I've ever witnessed. It was fucking awesome and I wish I had a video of it. I'm pretty sure even in making a movie, they would not be able to perform what this pilot had pulled off. It was the sickest thing I've ever witnessed. They kicked out the ammo and water, and then quickly got the hell out of there. Our job was done here as well so we headed back and reestablished our fighting position.

Once back at our fighting position, my squad leader explained the situation. Two of our Rangers were hurt pretty damn bad. They needed to be medically evacuated right away or we were going to lose them. The plan was, when the birds came in to get them out, the entire 360-degree perimeter would start shooting for thirty seconds so the birds did not get shot down. During the kick off time, I would use my M-4 and lay down suppressive fire along with the rest of the platoon.

The birds were coming in. "It's go time." I started shooting at a building, aiming at the door way and the windows. The birds came in and landed safely. When they got ready to fly out, we were going to start shooting again to keep the enemies' heads down. The wounded quickly got loaded up and we got the call to start shooting again. The birds safely flew out, we could only hope they made it out soon enough.

The Apaches were still hanging around from when the resupply came in. The Taliban stood down and were probably not going to fight until they left. I asked my squad leader, "Who were the wounded Rangers?" He said, Kapp and Peney. It felt strange because just the other day Kapp and I were walking to chow, talking about our dreams. Kapp says, "I'm always a badass in my dreams. I'm killing mother fuckers." I told a different story. "Not me," I say, "I am always getting shot in mine." I guess I will never forget that conversation.

Since we were not in any contact, this was our time to refit and eat. I grabbed my four extra goose rounds and a couple of extra magazines that came in with the resupply. After that I headed into a small room about twenty-five feet away from my position. We were taking turns eating our MREs. The Apaches then pulled off station.

I was sitting in the room preparing to eat my MRE when my squad leader came in and said, "Hey, the Taliban say they're going to start fighting us again in fifteen minutes." I looked at my watch and said, "Roger that." I continued eating while keeping track of that fifteen-minute window.

Eleven minutes passed and I figured it was time to head back out there to get our man-dance on with these bastards. At the time, it never dawned on me how smart these fuckers were. They must have remembered where I shot my first goose round from, so they set a machine gun aimed at my fighting position.

As I was walking back between the two buildings, I passed the short building where my squad leader was sitting. He was sitting out of the Taliban's view from the south side. As I passed him, I walked into my position and quickly lay in the prone. Immediately after laying down, machine gun fire started impacting the wall directly behind my AG and me. The rounds were flying within inches of us. The bullets passed making a sound like someone was flicking a piece of paper. It had that cracking sound to it.

I could only imagine what it was like for that bastard who was behind the machine gun shooting at us. Did he see me walk into view, jump, become excited, and then quickly tried to kill me? Or was he looking somewhere else and flinched when he looked back to his target area, seeing me walking and then laying down, fully realizing that he just fucked up and missed his chance? I will never know. The only thing he and I both know is that he had a chance and blew it.

As we were still lying there under fire, something bounced off my foot. It must have been a ricochet from one of the rounds hitting the wall. I looked over at my AG, his face was buried in the dirt, and his eyes are continuously flinching as if someone was throwing a punch at him. There was so much gunfire. We were pinned down and we could not move. The only thing I can think of was, "Will somebody please shoot this fucker and get him off of us?!"

The shooting stopped and my squad leader said, "God damn Bradley! They wanted you bad!" I replied back with, "Yeah, no shit Sergeant!" Our platoon leader ran over and said they were firing from over another wall. I was to fire that goose over that wall and kill those bastards. After what they just put us through, I had no problem doing so! Payback is a son of a bitch!

I checked the range, and my AG set the distance and loaded up another HE round. I was hoping that these bastards were in the middle of reloading their machine gun because I was about to expose myself. It was a pretty damn ballsy move, but you have to take those kinds of risks to ensure the platoon's safety. These men needed to be killed.

I took a knee and fired the round to the south. "KA-BOOM!" The PL said, "Nice shot Bradley." He then left our position to check out the rest of the platoon. That man was a hell of a leader and I'd follow him into harm's way any day.

The shooting stopped again and the Apaches returned. The Taliban were still walking with children. It was depressing to hear that because we know we could not kill them. They were now moving to our east side, which made sense. They hit us from the west first and then the south. I guessed we could expect to take fire from the east next.

Our squad leader, my assistant gunner, and I moved inside the short grape hut since we were exposed out in the open. 1st Squad was also located inside and we took turns pulling security with them. We did our best to keep a sharp lookout, but there were so many places the enemy could hide. Vegetation was everywhere and they could easily have been low crawling through it.

The Apaches pulled off station and the fighting began again. They were shooting small arms fire and RPGs at the platoon and we believed it is coming from a building 250 meters directly in front of our fighting position to the east. I heard the machine gunners returning fire with the Mk-48 from the long building next door.

Our PL ran into our grape hut and was trying to see exactly where they were shooting from. I was posted up on the south-side wall looking out one of the 1x2 foot holes providing security. I didn't see a God damn thing. Matter of fact, I never even saw a single damn Taliban fighter that day. I felt as if I was fighting a ghost.

Our PL yelled over, "Bradley, get the goose. We are going to shoot that damn building where they are engaging us from."

"Yes sir!" I replied. I grabbed the HEPD round and loaded it into the goose. I knew this was going to be a ballsy move. 3rd Squad and the neighboring machine gun team were going to lay down suppressive fire while we ran outside to take a shot at those bastards.

My squad leader and PL were going to escort me as we ran up near our old fighting position. We counted to three, our suppressive fire opened up, and we took off running between the two buildings straight east. In my mind, I was worried (to be honest I was scared) but I did not show it to anyone. I was just hoping that the enemy put their heads down during that small window while we were exposed. We could have easily made ourselves targets of opportunity.

We made it to the edge of the short wall. We did not pass it because that is where a machine gun had us pinned down earlier. My squad leader and PL positioned themselves directly on my left and right out of the back blast area. 200 meters in front, a wall covered the first floor of the building, making the second story the only place to hit.

I aimed into the doorway on the second floor and pull the trigger. *KA-BOOM!* The round looked like it was on target and going to hit as it screamed through the air. It missed the building by three feet and landed directly behind it. I could see the smoke rise up over the wall, from the right side of the building. I grabbed another round and loaded it up to reengage. Before I pulled the trigger my PL says, "Stand down Bradley! The Apaches are coming in." I did so and we ran back into the building.

I took that miss to heart. I was angry and mad at myself. I felt as if I let everyone down. The men were shocked to hear that I missed. They were not angry with me though. At least we were no longer being shot at. We stayed on watch for hours. There was no sign of the enemy and all was quiet out there. While pulling security in this grape hut, we talked to each other about dumb shit to pass the time. We told jokes, talked about girls, and talked about food we are missing from home. We tried to make the best of it because it was very boring just standing there. However, we knew it only takes a second to become very dangerous so everyone was on guard, staying alert.

We heard gunfire again, but this time it was further away from us. It is the platoon that was located between us and 3rd Platoon who was now in contact. I hoped they fought them off better than we did and killed them all! It was getting late in the day now and the sun would be setting soon. We ended up catching some chatter from the Taliban, "When the helicopters come in, we will charge them and shoot them down." I'd say it is a good plan, but how the hell do they know where the birds are going to land? Not even I know that yet.

The exfil plan made its way down to us from higher; they wanted us to jog 870 meters west to the LZ. As soon as those words were said, everyone immediately started bitching. "We do not know if those fuckers planted IEDs out there!" one Ranger said. "Exactly. What happens if someone steps on it or they have set up an ambush? Then we are really screwed" another Ranger said. The "what ifs," continued to bounce from one Ranger to another. Nonetheless, we started planning for this jog to the LZ. At one point, I was going to carry a ladder, the goose, my M-4, and one of the goose round containers from the resupply. I just did not have enough hands and hated this idea as much as everyone else. It was all bullshit. We knew that we already had a 360-degree perimeter set up and plenty of room for the birds to fly in and get us out. Why couldn't they not just land in here? That is what we all wanted to happen.

It was dark, the bitching stopped, and it was now quiet. I believed it was quiet because the many thoughts that were running through everyone's heads about the exfil plan. An 870-meter jog?! Do they even know how far that is? One Ranger said, "I'm going to sprint." That isn't a sprint, it's a Goddamn marathon when you are loaded down with this much weight and in the hills of Afghanistan.

An hour later, we were told the birds were going to land inside the compound and we would not have to make a dash to the LZ. The men were excited, happy, and motivated. Most of all, we all wanted to get out of this hellhole we had been fighting in all day. One good thing, there was illumination from the moon. It was completely dark.

We received the call to pull off the perimeter and stage up. Two birds were coming in, one at a time. I would be flying out on the 2nd MH-47 that lands. The first landed, and it felt like it was sitting there forever. I was thinking, "Hurry the hell up!" They finally left and did not get fired upon. The second MH-47 made its way in. It landed safely and we all made a mad dash for the ramp. We sat wherever we could and snapped in our safety lanyards. We had the correct headcount and we too flew out of there without being fired upon.

We made it back to Kandahar and unloaded the birds. Everyone cleared their weapon and the company commander arrived with the buses. Before he let anyone on the buses he pulled us all into a circle so we could hear him. He then said with the most serious face, "Men, I regret to inform you, Peney did not make it."

It was the worst news that D Company 1/75 has ever heard since standing up in 2008. Rangers' heads drop along with their hearts. The emptiness that just filled us was painfully bitter. It hurt like hell for many because Peney wasn't just a Ranger medic; he was a friend and a brother. For a few, Peney was their best friend. He looked after and gave a damn about the men in his platoon. He cared about his job and always tried to do it right.

Our company commander updated us about Kapp as well, "He is in stable condition. We will head out, drop our gear, and go see him. He can hear you, but he can't respond back to you." Everyone loaded up the buses and it was a long silent drive back.

We arrived at the hospital and the doctor explained to us what our company commander has already told us. We headed into Kapp's room one by one. Rangers walked by his side to tell them who they are and to get well soon. I walked to his bedside and said, "Hey Kapp, its Bradley." When I said that, he waved his hand and motioned his head as to say, "What's up?" I wished him well and walked away. Rangers were now grouping in the hallway after they wished him well. I looked and I see Kapp's barracks roommate walking out. His eyes were filled with tears and wiped them away as they rolled down his cheeks. It is a very emotional time for 2nd Platoon.

We all left the hospital and headed back to our building. We cleaned up and went to bed. The next day, we were going to wake up so we could head to the airfield and see Peney off. It was not going to be easy saying good-bye to him, especially for the men who knew him best. Morning came and we were patiently waiting in formation at the airfield for Peney's body to arrive. A Stryker slowly moved down the airfield and then came to a stop. Rangers moved to the back of it and waited. When the ramp opened, there was a coffin with an American flag draped over it. Rangers slowly and respectfully removed the casket and carried it to the C-17. Rangers were given the order to "Present, Arms" and we held the salute until Peney's body was loaded onto the aircraft. Jon Peney was heading home and now we had to find a way to brush off the pain and continue to fight for the rest of this 6-month deployment.

A couple days passed and we held a memorial ceremony for Peney. The entire Task Force stood quietly in formation. The men who knew Jon the most were the ones who did the talking about him. One-by-one, those men gave great speeches about what kind of man he was. As they spoke about him, their voices would begin to break. They tried to fight through the tears and pain. It was an awful feeling knowing there wasn't a damn thing we could do to bring him back.

The ceremony was just about over and people formed into a single file line that snaked around the dirt driveway. Then a song started playing over the speakers. It was "Amazing Grace." That was when my emotions began to break. I did my best not to cry and show emotions, but they finally got the best of me. The line moved very slowly as one person at a time knelt down to pay his respect. A good hour passed, and finally the last person said his good-bye. It was the right way to say farewell to a fallen comrade. We then regrouped and

2nd Platoon formed a half moon around Jon's photo and took one last photo with him.

The men who worked with Jon Peney will always remember this: he was selfless. He just graduated Ranger School and married days before deployment. He had the option to stay back home, take some well-deserved rest, and spend some time with his new wife. After all, he earned that time off after spending months in Ranger School away from civilization and his loved ones.

Jon wasn't that kind of man though. He was the kind of man that was not going to let his brother's head down range without him. I don't believe he had a selfish bone in his body. The world became a little darker after losing a man like that. R.I.P. Brother.

JUNE 6TH, 2010

We were heading to Orgun-E also known as OE. We had all our bags packed and loaded on a C-130. It was packed tight, so there was not much room to move and we all knew that this was not going to be a comfortable flight. Then again, Rangers never go through anything that is comfortable.

We landed in Salerno and unloaded all of our gear. Everyone seemed happy just to be off that cramped ass bird. Men started checking to make sure they had all their sensitive items. We finished checking and then flew out on CH-47s the rest of the way to OE. The ride was a little more comfortable, but not by much. My legs fell asleep from being stuck in between the break in the seats. I remember thinking to myself, 'Damn, I hate this.'

We finally landed and again, we unloaded our gear and re-checked to make sure we had our sensitive items. We carried as much of our gear as possible. The rest went onto a tiny flatbed truck. We followed the truck and it parked near our rooms for the short stay.

Again, everyone unloaded the equipment, and gave an "UP" on their sensitive items. It was late, or I should say, early. The sun was about to come up. Everyone had picked their beds and made their "whack shack." We all racked out shortly after.

In the middle of the day, a loud explosion woke me up. My heart was pounding out of my chest. I looked around and no one was doing anything except for sleeping. So I laid there with my eyes open wondering if we were going through this experience again as we did in BAF and KAF. Are we under attack again?

I continued to hear rockets flying over our heads and exploding. They were so damn loud! I did not know what to do. My heart continued to race. I could not sleep like that and I became angry because I had no clue where they are coming from. I wished I could just run outside and kill the men who were launching rockets at us.

I grabbed my gun, helmet, and body armor. I headed outside and there was no one out there. I stepped into the shelter right outside the door. I sat there for five minutes and realized no one else is going to come. In my mind, I wondered how the hell are guys our sleeping through this? I got up and returned to my room and felt stupid for even going out there.

I was back in bed and rockets continued to fly over. I could not sleep so I told myself, "Fuck it. If you die, you die. It is my time. Nothing I can do about it." Slowly my heart beat stopped pounding and I fell asleep.

We woke up and everyone went off to get chow. As we were walking I asked, "Did anyone else react to that incoming fire?" One guy said, "Fuck no, I slept right through that shit." I couldn't believe it. I told them what I did and they laughed. I joined in laughing after I told them how dumb I felt. It was kind of funny.

Someone said, "Did you hear about our 'terp?" Most of us said, "No?" We were then told that a Ranger noticed on each of the attacks, our interpreter was nowhere to be found. Then he would appear as if nothing happened. It started to make sense. How else could we come under attack within twenty-four hours of every base we flew to? When he was brought to our leadership and they asked to see his cell phone, every contact in his phone was deleted. Needless to say, whether the 'terp had something to do with it or not, we couldn't trust him and he was then off to Bagram.

We entered the chow hall, grabbed our food, and sat down. The entire chow hall was decked out in college flags. I saw one that was from my hometown, "University of Toledo." I was filled with pride and said out loud, "Hell yeah! That's my home town!" as I pointed to the flag.

A soldier walked up to me and said, "Hey man do you remember me?" I looked at him and look back at my Ranger buddies. They had blank stares but were curious to find out where this conversation was heading. He continued to speak, "I'm friends with your little brother Kyle. We went to high school together and you were a wrestling coach. Is Kyle here?"

I replied back to him, "No man, Kyle got busted up pretty bad on a 4-wheeler. He was in the hospital for a couple days. He should be coming over here sometime in July, though." I could tell it saddened him a little. He would have definitely rather seen Kyle than me. At least with my little brother there, they would have had something to talk about.

He continued to speak, "Funny we are both here on this small ass base together." I say, "Yeah, how about those rocket attacks earlier today?" He says, "Yeah, those were cool. We actually got to fire and defend the base." I asked him what he did and he says he was in artillery. We then told each other to take care and parted ways.

As we walked back to our compound, Rangers kept passing by and saying, "We are having a meeting, everyone needs to go into the TOC." So we listened and immediately headed there. As we walked in, both 2nd and 3rd Platoon were in there. It was packed. All the leadership was there. First Sergeant and the company commander stood in front looking back at everyone.

Our CO began to speak, "Men, the reason why I have gathered us here is because it has been brought to my attention that some men in the company are trying to get out of their platoons. Well, men, that is not going to happen. I know the loss of Peney has made you realize that we are not Superman, no one is. Still, nothing has changed. We came here to do a job and we are going to swing the fucking mallet. We are the tip of the spear. You need to get your minds right."

This meeting was a rude awakening. I did not know men wanted to leave because they were scared to go outside the wire. I can understand that they were scared; you have to be crazy not to feel something in combat. You have no clue if you are going to come home or not. A little thing called *courage* makes you keep moving forward *and complete the mission, though I be the lone survivor.* Not to mention, your brothers out there depend on you. *You go, we go!* was my mind set.

First Sergeant began to talk and his words were straight to the point, "Men, you are the best trained soldiers in the world. You are stronger and faster. You have nothing to be afraid of. I can't even believe we are having this talk. If you honestly don't want to be here then pack your damn bags and we will send you home."

There was only silence after they were done talking. They dismissed us and sent us to have a meeting with our own platoons. Our platoon headed into the gym and our platoon sergeant began to speak. "Well, I guess we need to talk about this and get this all out of our systems. Anyone want to go first?"

I did not have anything to say so I did not raise my hand. No one else did either. He said, "Alright, I'll go first." I don't remember everything he said, but what I do remember is him talking about Peney. "I was on the bird with Peney looking into his eyes when we lost him. I can still see the dust settling down on his eyes..." I was pretty much quiet the whole time. Only a few people spoke and our meeting is over.

As we all walked back to our rooms. I heard some of the 3rd Platoon guys complaining about the first meeting. Maybe they were the ones who talked about wanting out? Doesn't matter, I knew I was staying. I worked with those guys for three years; I am not giving up on them.

As I was walking back to my room, I remembered a day when we were stateside cleaning our weapons in the company area. I walked over to my little brother's cage and talked with him. 3rd Platoon was close. They all called each other by their first names. I remember Kyle asking why my platoon doesn't and I think my reply back disturbed him. "I keep it professional. And to be honest, I don't want to get to close to anyone because if we do lose someone, I'm not going home all fucked up over it." I told everyone that before I left for the Army, "I am going to come back home the same guy that left." Kyle said, "That's fucked up, bro." He is right, it is fucked up, but I have made myself mentally ready, something every soldier should do. Prepare yourself to see some shit and do some shit that nobody back home will understand.

Another mission brief had just taken place. We were to conduct another ROD. 3rd Platoon was going to infil first and start heading out to the target compound to get their man-dance on. There were supposed to be seventeen enemy fighters staying in this compound. The guy they are going after is a guy we already captured back in 2008 when we were stationed in Salerno. I remember one of the squad leaders saying, "Man, we should have just killed that fucker then." Just goes to show you, once a shit-head, always a shit-head.

2nd Platoon was to climb a mountain and secure the top. 3rd Platoon would then meet up on the closest mountaintop next to us. We were to wait for the enemy to come out and fight. We got ready, loaded up on the birds, and infilled into a riverbed. It was completely dark out. There was no illumination and we tried not to trip over the massive rocks. We started moving out and were walking slowly. Even with our NODs, it was still dark. We began climbing up a small mountain first to get to our mountain, which was three mountains over. This was going to take a while . . . .

About an hour or so later, the Apaches moved in to cover 3rd Platoon. They opened up and started firing. We were getting a great show. We were at about the same elevation as the Apaches. I didn't even know 3rd Platoon was in contact until I heard it, *THE GOOSE!* A massive explosion echoed through the mountain range. A few minutes later, the goose created another explosion. The Apaches continued to light up the target compound and we continued to climb the damn mountain.

We were so far away from 3rd Platoon, that the only noises that we heard from them were the two goose rounds and the Apaches. I did not even know they used grenades, a LAW, and their Mk-48s. Those sounds died off before it even made it to us. They engaged the fighters and had killed the seventeen insurgents. I was later told that their bodies were shredded up so bad that the Afghans they were working with started puking as they were lining the bodies up in rows. Two Rangers took rocks to the face from an RPG round the enemy had fired. They stayed in the fight though, nothing too serious.

3rd Platoon found RPGs, AK-47s, grenades, chest racks, ammunition, and IED materials. These were some very bad guys. The good news is we will never have to go after that shit-head or his friends again.

2nd Platoon kept climbing and we were finally coming down the backside of the first mountain. My AG was struggling trying to keep up. I kept looking back at him and trying to maintain my eye on the man I'm following.

Along the way, I took his rifle and our platoon sergeant carried his round ruck so he could keep up. I was mad that he was unable to perform his job and that others had to pick up his slack.

The terrain was dangerous to move on. Rocks and cliffs surrounded us. I lost sight of my squad leader and started to head up the mountain. I then saw a laser signaling to where they were and started moving back down to them. As I did, I saw my squad leader walking over to me. He saw something that I didn't, a four-foot drop off.

I stepped over the dark edge and he stopped me from falling and completely eating shit. I thanked him for saving me. I waited for my AG to catch up and made sure he was aware of the small cliff as well. We stopped to take a small break and let everyone catch up. They gave my AG his round ruck and weapon back.

We were climbing up the second mountain and it ran right into the third so it would be a straight shot. We would not be coming down the backside of the second mountain. We began to move out.

We kept moving higher and higher. There was a cliff to the right of us and we were walking on a very narrow path. Up ahead, there was a downward-slanted rock ledge that led to a massive drop. This was scary and dangerous, as Rangers had died in similar situations in years past. I stepped onto the rock ledge and began to make my way across. It was slippery and I fell. I started sliding down towards the cliff on my stomach. I was reaching and kicking trying to stop myself from going over the edge but I was loaded down with so much damn weight I couldn't stop. I was in a panic then all of a sudden I stopped sliding as if an invisible hand had caught me from behind. Relieved, I slowly crawled back up the rock and to the other side. I believe someone was looking out for me that night.

I waited for my AG and helped him across by stepping out on the ledge and putting my hand out for him to grab so he didn't make the same mistake I just made. Falling off a cliff was not the way for a Ranger to go out.

We reached the third mountain and were closing in on the top. The Afghans turned it into a competition between them. They started racing each other to get to the top first. As they passed by me, I did not follow because when the fighting starts, that is where I want to expend my energy, not racing up a mountain.

About ten minutes later, they reached the top and I saw something that I have never seen an Afghan do. They were coming back down the mountain to grab rucksacks from the Americans. I know they do not have to help anyone of us, but it was a very friendly gesture.

Multiple times they ran up and down the mountain to grab rucks from the men who were struggling. One of them runs down to me and he says, "RPG? RPG?" while holding out his hand, asking if he could take the goose from me. Well, you know me; I wasn't going to let someone carry my weight, especially a foreign troop. I was going to show them I'm just as tough.

I pointed down to my AG who was about twenty meters from me. My AG said that he couldn't go any further because he has cramps in his legs. The Afghan soldier gladly runs down the mountain to get his round ruck. I told my AG, "MOVE YOUR ASS TO THE TOP NOW! You are carrying nothing." He tried to argue with me and said he couldn't. I got mad again and climbed the last twenty meters without him. Finally he got off his ass and made it to the top.

It took us five hours to climb up that beast of a mountain. The view up there was the most beautiful sight I have ever seen in my life. We were able to see seven mountaintops away from us. It was an amazing sight and I wished I had had a camera with me.

We began to make sand bags and fortify our fighting positions. 3rd Platoon was making their way up their mountain. The sun was starting to come up so they set up their 360-degree perimeter on the much shorter first mountain we climbed earlier.

We were scanning, looking for enemy. The only thing we could see from this high up was a small village 1,400 meters below us. Those people are waking up and know we are on top of the mountain. They gathered around and sit and watch us.

The closet mountaintop to us was 400 meters away, the rest were over a 1,000 meters. Nobody was going to fuck with us. We had too much standoff. And I was sure that no crazy ass fighter was going to attempt to run up this mountain to fight us. It was looking like we climbed up this bitch just for the view.

As we scanned the area, we found what looked to be a cave entrance. A dirt trail ran straight to it. Talks ran through the platoon about a team heading down there to check it out. Instead, I received the call to take a shot at it and close it up with a goose round. The range was 322 meters down and away from my position. I took aim on it and fired. The round impacted the mountain three feet too high above the entrance. I asked for another shot on it but quickly get denied to do so. "We need to conserve the rounds in case we need them later." the PL said, I completely agreed with him. I'd rather shoot back at men who are shooting at us rather than shoot at rocks.

It was around 6:00 pm local time and we were able to see a storm brewing up in the distance. It continued to move closer and closer. We could see the falling rain, the flashes of lightning, and hear the rumble of thunder. We got the call to pack up and started moving down the mountain.

As we were cautiously heading down the mountain, a couple of Rangers sprained their ankles. They pushed through the pain and continued to move. It started to sprinkle and darkness fell upon us. It started to get cold but we were warm because we were sweating. We got soaking wet as it started to rain harder. Our NODs were not working due to the weather. Some were not turning on, but I was lucky, because even though mine kept fogging up, they were working.

We arrived at the bottom of the mountain near the riverbed. Our platoon sat down and began waiting for it to get late so we could move out to our next target, which was only a kilometer away. As I was sitting there, my body started to cool off. The wet shirt and cold air began to make me shiver. I remembered I packed a rain top. I pulled it out of my ruck, removed my body armor, pulled off the wet shirt and put on the dry top. I then put on my body armor and sat there in comfort. A Ranger sitting next to me says, "Damn, I should have brought one." One thing you need to know is how your body operates. Mine works well in the heat but not so much in the cold.

After being up for twenty-four hours, we were put on a rest plan. Most of the guys go to sleep. When I was woken up, I was told we were going to be moving out in ten minutes and to wake up anyone who is still sleeping. Everyone else was already awake. I changed back into my soaking wet top to keep at least one dry shirt. I was now cold and miserable again. We began to move out, and as my body temperature started to rise, my shirt began to dry out.

As we were moving out at a fast pace, my AG began to fall out again. He was tired and kept tripping and falling over the rocks. He fell off a one-foot drop. He hit the ground and his weapon went flying into the darkness. He screamed in pain, and I yelled, "SHUT THE HELL UP!" He said he hurt his ankle. I asked him where his weapon went. He had no clue. Well, it had to be around there somewhere so I started looking. I had no sympathy for him. Other guys were still walking after they sprained their ankles coming off the mountain.

Our platoon halted and a medic and our first sergeant came running back to his aid. The medic gives him a "lollipop," which was actually powerful medicine to dull the pain. As I was looking for his M-4, First Sergeant asked me what I was doing. I told him and he started yelling at my AG for not having his weapon slung. This AG is just as bad if not worse than my last AG. Now I was stuck with a guy who couldn't carry his own damn weight.

I found his weapon and brought it back to him. I grabbed his round ruck and started to carry it. He stood up and we started to move out again. I continued to keep an eye on him. Every time I looked back, I was getting more pissed off. He was walking fine while I was sitting there sucking. The anger helped push me though.

My AG knew I was pissed off. He kept asking for his round ruck back. I was too pissed off so I ignored him and kept walking. I kept going and he kept asking. Soon I was smoked from humping that weight and trying to keep up with the fast pace. I finally broke and gave it back to him.

We then took a knee and he came up to me, asking for water. I asked him, "WHERE DID ALL YOURS GO!?" he said, "I drank it all." I got mad at him again for not conserving it. I knew he was a bigger guy, but if he needed a lot of water to run on, he should have packed more water bottles with him than just a Camelbak. Now I was stuck giving him mine. I was frustrated with this guy. Never in my life had I ever been so angry with another Ranger. Finally, we picked up and continued moving out.

As we were walking, I saw the machine gunner's AG falling out. He, too, was out of water and said his muscles were cramping up. So I grabbed his assault pack, gave him and my AG more water, and kept moving. I carried it until my muscles were smoked. I gave it back to him and he carried it a short way. The medic and our first sergeant came back to check on my AG. I told them about both AGs being out of water and smoked. The medic gave them a water bottle. First Sergeant told me to sit right there and watch over those two while the rest of the platoon cleared the NAI. Our forward observer walked up to us and passed over another water bottle and the two of us continued to babysit those men.

Our platoon cleared the NAI. They found RPGs, mortar rounds, AK-47s, grenades, and IED-making material. We set up and prepared to exfil. The plan was to blow up the weapons cache with a laser guided missile from Bagram. It did not do enough damage so they dropped two 500-pound bombs on it, as well.

When we arrived back at OE, First Sergeant came up to speak with me. "Your AG is fired!" I told him, "Thank You!" It was not that he was a bad guy. It was that he was out there putting the platoon members' lives in danger by not being able to do his job. We were only as strong as our weakest link. The good thing about being in Regiment is that you have to prove yourself every single day. Just because you made it there doesn't mean you get to kick your feet up and relax. If you can't perform, you are sent packing. My new AG, though, was a tough, scrappy kid from Boston who had arrived at the 1st Ranger Battalion just three weeks before deployment. This kid had a heart of a lion and I looked forward to working with him.

A squad leader felt my pain and came up to talk with me. "How do you keep getting stuck with these crappy privates?" he asked. I told him, "I don't know, probably because nobody else wants them.

But I have 'Boston' now. He's gonna do just fine." We packed all our bags and headed back to Kandahar.

We arrived back at Kandahar from OE. We were not staying in the same building because other soldiers had moved into it while we were gone. So instead, we were staying in a huge circus tent with the heat hitting over a 100 degrees every day. We slept during the day when it was the hottest. Some of us laid in bed sweating because the two AC vents that ran across the tent did not blow cold air far enough to reach us. We were miserable to say the least.

A machine gun team leader came up with a great idea. He used empty water bottles to connect a tube running from his bed to one of the hundreds of holes in the AC vent. Everyone else then did the same thing and soon there was a spider web of water bottles running to each Ranger's bunk. The cool air was no longer wasted and it was easier to fall asleep.

We had another mission. This one was going to consist of us staying out for 48 hours (June 24-26). Thinking the RODs before were hard, well, this one was going to make those ones look easy. Forty-eight plus hours is a long time to stay awake. We were going to set up in an area where U.S. forces hadn't been yet. Like the times before, we were to set up and wait for the Taliban to come for us. These "Alamos" are crazy, I thought, but then again, someone has to get out there and kill these fuckers. Time to be brave, Ranger up, and get our man-dance on with those wannabe warriors.

We were at the airfield waiting to board when a team leader walked up to me. He said, "Hey Bradley, do you have a grenade on you?" I said "No" so he handed me one. Now I feel like a real badass. I have my M-4 rifle, 9mm pistol, the M-3 Carl Gustav, a SOG knife, and now a grenade. We loaded the birds and flew out.

We infilled, cleared an NAI, and took over a compound that could house 2nd and 3rd Platoon. We paid the family that lived there and told them the same thing as the other families – don't come back until tomorrow. They left and we started setting up our fighting positions.

It was still dark and we hastily worked before the sun came up.

We were blowing portholes into the walls with demo. In order to connect the compound next door, we had to take down a wall by hand. The PL wanted to make sure we were able to get a litter through in case any men were hit. My AG and I looked for tools. We found a pickaxe and started tearing down the wall using that. We took turns until the job was done. My AG and I found a good fighting position mixed in with 1st Squad. It was going to be another hot day of 120 degrees so we started trying to make shade. I ran around with my AG finding all the distances to the buildings, the walls, and anywhere else the enemy would try to fight us from, and wrote the ranges down on a piece of paper.

We picked up chatter from the Taliban. They said something about attacking us but they are going to wait for the "big one." They came back to say, "The Big One's trigger does not work." Rangers laughed and made fun of them saying things like, "You should've checked your shit," "Watch out for incoming arrows next," and "They might throw rocks at us." It didn't matter what they use against us. Our plan was that when they started firing at us, we'd shoot back at them with the goose. I liked the idea. Let's shut them the hell up.

A few minutes passed by and they started shooting. Bullets were flying over our heads and hitting the outside of our walls. We believed they were shooting from the right side of the building that was 100 meters away from us. I told my AG, "Load up an HPDP round. We are going to blow that building up."

The Ranger who called me into the hut to remove sticks on a previous objective shot off a high explosive 40mm grenade round as we were moving up to the wall. I heard it explode and his squad leader exclaimed, "Holy Shit! I think that was an arm!"

3rd Squad continued to fight back as I lined up this shot. I remembered that these rounds shoot high so I aimed lower to ensure this round was not being wasted. It was my only HPDP round. *KA-BOOM!*

The round jetted out of the goose and impacted the building with a massive explosion. We waited for the dust to settle to see the damage. One-third of the building was destroyed. The fire from the northeast building stopped. We called in the birds to see if they could tell us if we have any EKIAs out there. They came back to tell us there are, "three confirmed EKIAs." The kills were split up between the three of us but who really knows how they died without examining the bodies. Maybe everyone else killed them, and I killed none. That will be something God and I discuss the day we meet. But at the time, it was all about killing these men off and trying to keep each other alive. As long as they were dying, that is all that mattered to us in those moments. We are keeping each other safe no matter who was getting the kills.

More fighting broke out and this time they hit us from the southwest portion of the compound, which was 3rd Platoon's side. 3rd Platoon fended them off and held their side of the compound. After that engagement, we picked up more chatter. They planned to hold off the fighting and collect their dead. For an hour or more, there hadn't been any shooting. It was midday and other Rangers were baking in the heat. When I got relieved from pulling security, I did my best to build them some shade.

I had just cut down a small tree with small leaves that would provide some good shade when an RPG and machine gun fire started coming in. I low sprinted back to the wall where my goose was. This time, we moved to a different fighting position so as to not shoot the goose from the same spot.

We believed they were now shooting from the left side of the building. My AG set the round for ninety meters so it could burst in the air. We were going to send hundreds of ball bearings their way. I took aim and squeezed the trigger. *KA-BOOM!* The round exploded where it was meant to. The fighting continued so I was told to shoot the building. The only bad news was I only had two HE rounds left. These rounds were not made to destroy buildings. My AG loaded up another round and this time the HE round impacted the building.

The round caused very little damage. Our mortars were doing their best to drop rounds on it as well.

Our PL ran over to our position and yelled out, "Hey, we have enemy fighters low crawling up to our positions from the other side this wall (the east wall). Who has grenades?" Remembering I received one from a team leader out on the airfield, I quickly said, "I DO, SIR!" Three other Rangers ran up to the wall and pulled out their grenades. The PL said, "On the count of three, pull the pins and throw your grenades over the wall." He counted to three and we all pulled and threw. We continued to fight. The Apaches then came in and cleaned up anything we missed.

All was quiet and had been for the last few hours. We figured that they must be out collecting their dead again. Only a few people were on guard pulling security. Others were sleeping and trying to rest up for the walk tonight and the fight for tomorrow. My squad leader was on the wall, and was replaced by another Ranger. We were taking 45-minute shifts. I was to replace that Ranger.

Five minutes before my shift, I started getting my gear on to pull security. It looked as if we were going to be just waiting for darkness to fall so we could move out. All of a sudden, an RPG flew in and it hit one of the walls. It hit somewhere to the left of us. Again, we returned fire.

Over the radio, I heard, "Fire the goose!" I dropped my M-4 and grab the goose. We set another HE round to impact the right side of the building. I went to set the range drum and it was locked up. It would not budge. I told my squad leader, "My weapon system is down!" I pulled out a rag and a bottle of CLP. I squirted it on the range drum and turned the knob. It was turning and I pulled a rag out of my pocket and wipe off the mud that was oozing out of the cracks.

Every time I shot a goose round, a massive cloud of dust surrounded me. Those small pieces of dirt and dust locked up the range drum. That was the first time I had ever experienced that (I share this information with you in case any future Rangers encounter this problem. Make sure you have a rag and CLP with you!)

About a minute later, I reported back and told my SL, "The goose is back up!" He pushed to the side and I moved into his place and fired another goose round. It was another direct hit on the building and the Taliban stopped firing. The Apaches arrived and stayed until it was dark.

After the last engagement was over, a private I worked with for the last two deployments walked over to us. He was trembling and nervous as fuck. He said with a shaky voice, "Does anyone have a cigarette?" We all said, "No" and ask him why. He explained to us what happened, "That RPG blasted through the building and stuck in the fucking wall. It didn't explode though; it's still in the wall. There were three of us in there."

He told us that a civilian who was working with us took some small shrapnel to the head. His injuries were not life threatening. They bandaged him up and he stayed out there with us like a soldier.

It was scary thinking about it, if that RPG would have exploded inside that room with them in it, we would have lost them more than likely. War is such a strange damn thing. You just never know when your time is going to come. A man can only have so much luck before it runs out.

We stayed for a few hours after dark, broke down, and moved out. 3rd Platoon was heading to clear an NAI. They were to then link up with 2nd Platoon, who was to move out to the pre-planned compound and start setting up the platoons' strong hold. The ground was flat and hard from being so damn dry. We were able to move fast because of this. It was still hot outside and I was sweating like I had been all damn day.

We arrived at the compound we planned to take over. I set in next to a wall that overlooked a field and a road. It was quiet outside, except for the barking dogs and the women and children who were now screaming and crying. Many times I have heard these sounds. I know it sucks for these families who are trapped in the middle of war. It is not their fault that the Taliban has brought us to their country. We can only hope that when this is all said and done, we leave this country a better place than how we found it.

3rd Platoon cleared their NAI. They found a ton of IED-making material. They were about a mile from us and began heading our way. Soon they were far enough away and a 500-pound bomb was dropped on the building. I saw the explosion through my NODs. A huge flash lit up the sky and a second after that, I heard the boom sound it made. Another was dropped to ensure the material no longer existed.

Everyone outside pulling security was told to come inside now because the compound had been cleared. My AG and I looked for the best possible spot that would allow us to engage the enemy at the furthest range on 2nd Platoon's portion of the compound. There was a dried up ditch that ran north and south. We decided to post up there and face to the east where many civilian tents were sitting. We were expecting the Taliban to run off those villagers and fight us from there. The people who lived in them looked to be sheep and goat herders. Everything else around 2nd Platoon's area of operation was dried up fields of dirt with woodlines that were far away.

As we were setting up, our PL and our interpreter talked to the man who owned the compound. The owner was mad, but we were explaining to him that he needs to take his family far away from here because the Taliban are going to come. He understood and he shook our PL's hand and bowed. We gave him money like we have done with the other families, and they moved away from the danger that was sure to come.

The night passed uneventfully and it was quiet all day, but we were just baking in the heat. We watched the Afghans walk from their tents to a well to pump water. We then picked up some chatter from the Taliban saying, "Yes, we know where they are, but we do not have a problem with them." Hearing this made us laugh.

Almost an hour passed and still no attack from the Taliban. It was probably 2:00 pm local time. We were all relaxed except the ones pulling security. Some of us had our kits and helmets off as we sat there trying to beat the heat. I saw a dog breaking away from the tents. He was sniffing towards the ground and was heading straight for us. I thought to myself, "Wow, this dog doesn't even see us. I wonder how close he gets before he shits himself when he finds us here." All of a sudden I saw the dog flinch from fear and about fall on his belly. I looked left to see and hear an RPG screaming by from 3rd Platoon's area of operation. Following that was machine gun fire. I hit the deck, and low crawled about ten feet to my helmet and body armor and threw it all on in a hurry.

I was ready to fight, but the Taliban did not attack us from our side. I was hoping to get the call to move to 3rd Platoon's location, but the call never came. They had it under control and it was very boring as we stood our ground. We were not in the fight but we had to keep the 360-degree perimeter. Our mortars were dropping rounds and then got shut down.

An A-10 Warthog sings a song of beauty. It was music to our ears as it fired upon the enemy. It came in so fast. Those Taliban fighters were killed without even knowing what the hell just hit them. That awesome machine is so quiet, so fast and so deadly. I never even heard it coming in until it fired that cannon and already flew by.

We picked up more chatter and a Taliban commander saying, "Good job, that was a good attack. Come to my position so I can get a count of who is still alive." It wasn't long after that and the A-10 came back. The pilot smoked four of them that were in a truck with RPGs. The last chatter we pick up was, "It is getting late, and we are done for the day."

As we waited for darkness to set in, I could only hope that it comes fast. I continued killing all the damn ants I saw around me. I must have killed over 200 of the little bastards throughout the day. Hours passed and finally it was time to move to exfil and head back to base.

We got back to KAF and took showers and started cleaning the dirt from our weapons that was caused from the "brown out" when the CH-47s came in to take us out. After finishing up, I stayed up and write down everything I experienced in the last 48 hours. I did this after every mission because I wanted to remember what we did before it becomes nothing but a blur in our minds. These stories of what we did will one day be lost to the pages of time. Time eats away everything and I wish my Grandpa had left something behind like this back from when he fought in WWII. It would have been an honor to read.

The next day came and I must have slept for twenty-four hours. I was not sure what was going to come of the day so I stayed up for a few more hours. Everyone was sleeping so I went back to bed to catch up on as much sleep as I could as well.

Two days after conducting the mission, we had a meeting. We received an update to the 48 hour mission we conducted. On a Taliban website they posted, "We have killed a bunch of US forces last night in our battle. We have also shot down one of their helicopters." Rangers started laughing and booing the news update because it was not true. No Rangers were killed in those firefights and no helicopters were shot down. To be exact, during that two-day span, we had a confirmed twenty-one enemies killed in action. That means between 3rd Battalion and 1st Battalion, in a little over three weeks since our arrival, 120 Taliban fighters were killed. From the 450 they started with, only 330 remain.

As dangerous as it was being out there, we were up for the challenge of taking away the battlefield from the Taliban. The "Deployment of Alamos" was working and getting it done faster than we expected. We love you America. Your boys are working hard for you! Rangers Lead The Way!

-COLBY BRADLEY
1/75

AUGUST 2010
"IN THE WATER"

As long as I have been in Ranger Battalion, there have been certain things pounded into me. First, in your Battalion, everyone hates Alpha Company. Second, everyone hates 3rd Battalion. Finally, the Army Special Mission Unit is way better than the Navy Special Mission Unit. For me, this was the truth for a long time, as my platoon had only worked with the Army SMU and the "Vanilla" Naval Special Warfare teams (Non-SMU), which were much different than their 'Big Brothers'. My point of view changed on this deployment to Afghanistan, though. I was among a few Rangers who deployed with the Navy SMU and my experiences differed a lot from what most others had told me about working with them.

It was 2010 and we were assigned to integrate with the Naval Special Warfare SMU in Logar Province. To say we were expecting the worst is an understatement. Most of the plane ride over (when we were awake) was filled with bitching about how bad it might be. Once we arrived and did the normal relief in place with our sister Battalion, we started to meet the Team guys we would be working with. During the first part of the deployment, it was like any other two different units coming to know each other. Imagine it like a special operations version of a middle school dance. We played *Call of Duty* in our hooch and they played in their hooch.

Things started to change after about two weeks in as we had been on a dozen or so missions together at this point. During one particular mission, as we were on our approach to the objective, a decent sized stream lay in our way. You would think, SEALs . . . water . . . just walk into the steam and keep going right? Wrong on so many levels. I learned that night that no one likes to get wet. Even a SEAL, who has been to BUD/S and swam in everything from a submarine's torpedo tube, to a whale's vagina, and everything in between. Everyone hates to get wet. So what do I do? Well, I had seen the movie *Navy SEALs* with Charlie Sheen about ten times, so I walk through the waist deep water. Most people would just say, "fuck it" at this point, and just follow that person through the water. Not the SEALs. No, they decided that they think there is a bridge about 1.2 kilometers away that looks good.

So my squad and I were sitting on the other side of this river waiting on the team guys to go find this bridge. I was not even mad about getting wet or waiting for them. I was mad because my Lifesaver candies were wet with this nasty ass water that I was just in. Once the mission was over, and we were waiting on the helicopters to come and pick us up, we started to make fun of the SEALs around us for not going in the water. I don't know how, but to this day I am convinced that me walking in some water is what broke the ice between us. The next briefing, we came with a rope bridge made of tampons for the team guys and everyone had a good laugh about that. No, I don't remember how we found the tampons, but like with anything in Battalion, shit just appears when you ask for it.

Most of the time we went out on missions, it was just 12 -14 of us split into two teams to augment the team guys with whatever they needed. It was a symbiotic relationship with our two units working fully integrated with each other. During this time, I could feel a shift in attitude as we started to trust each other more and become a team. What transpired next was something that would cement our bond forever, as we still talk to each other about it to this day.

We had been receiving more and more intelligence about a group of Taliban setting up ambushes on Route One near our FOB. One night we had some great intelligence and some assets overhead that spotted one of these groups setting up for an ambush later in the night. We did a quick brief and everyone loaded up on the buses. All of the leadership went back to the JOC to watch the assets fire on them.

After the first missile hit, we were on the buses and in the air, no more than two minutes later. The objective was only seven kilometers away, so the ride was short and you could feel the energy in the bird.

As the bird landed and we exited the aircraft, we took fire from the woodline. We were glad and had expected this. I told our Mk-46 gunner to place 10 – 12 round bursts into each muzzle flash until his 200-round drum ran dry. This would allow the SEALs time to get out of the wide open farm land that we had landed on and move behind a building for cover. They would then be able to start clearing the ditch that was now a trench for the enemy fighters. Everything was going almost to plan with the exception of a few tweaks here and there until we were just inside of 35 meters away from the enemy. Now, for people that don't know, that places you inside hand grenade range. That is when it becomes more of a fight of will than of who has the better gear.

On our last bound forward, the far left side was about to move when they took fire from a PKM machine gun. Right after we started taking fire, I could see the tracers chewing up the ground and the Rangers on the end of our line. I could hear Doc yell "Ranger down!" while sprinting over to the left side of the line. Right as that was going on, the SEALs were also leading a charge into the trench, taking an overwhelming amount of fire directed at the first guy into the trench. I could hear on the radio as I was moving to cover our Ranger that a SEAL was also down and others were hit. I placed the Mk-46 gunner and a Ranger team leader next to me to create a wall so that Doc and another squad leader could pull the wounded Ranger behind cover to start working on him.

As I looked over my shoulder at Doc and the squad leader calling in the CASEVAC, I could see just behind them was a small six-inch berm in an otherwise wide-open field. This at least gave the casualty some cover, even if we had to work in the open to save him. I yelled at Doc to move him and told the team leader next to me to help treat him since he was an EMT. During this time I checked the Mk-46 gunner to see if he had been hit and he checked me. All we found was a small through and through gunshot on the outside of his arm. As I was checking him, the Mk-46 decided this would be a great time to try and fit two rounds into the barrel at the same time. So while the gunner was trying to fix his gun in record time, this forced me to fire at an almost cyclic rate to keep the rate of fire up.

Once the Mk-46 was back up I could see they had packaged the wounded Ranger up for the bird that was coming in as CASEVAC. During this time I also saw that some team guys had made the long IMT to us in the middle of the field and were coming in line with the Mk-46 gunner and me. *Quick back-story about the movie Navy SEALs again: Remember when you see them take fire from the enemy and they peel off, turning to run by the next guy, hitting him on the shoulder, until they've all repeated through to the last man and are out of contact?* Yeah, that is 100% what happened when the team guys came on line with us after the CASEVAC birds took back off. To say that I was surprised is a total understatement, I don't even know if it registered what was happening until I was being slapped and saw a guy running behind me. I won't lie, I had a huge smile on my face when my brain clicked on to what was going on and I realized what I was about to do.

As I fired two more rounds, I turned off to my right and then ran to my left and broke contact, hitting the guy who was about two arms lengths away from me. As I approached the end of the line, I went back down to a low knee and could not help but again be disappointed. As usual, the movies made it look way cooler then it was. We did this until we had put about 75 meters between the ditch and us. We then made our way into the other ditch on the opposite side of the field, and once everyone was in the ditch we called for fire on the other side of the field with AC-130s. We then moved to the exfil site about 800 meters away.

On the ride back to the FOB, I checked on the Mk-46 gunner and prepared him to move to the hospital once we touched down. He would later be awarded the Distinguished Service Cross, which is second only to the Medal of Honor, for his actions on the objective that night. As we left the bird, we walked up to the receiving medics and they checked us for wounds that we could not find. It was at this time I asked about my friend we had to CASEVAC off the battlefield. I already knew in my head that he most likely was already gone after I saw him while they were moving him to cover, but one always keeps hope that your best friends will be ok. I ran in to my platoon sergeant and he told me what I had expected; he did not make it. It was like a shot to the face, it was all I could do to get in a truck and ride back to the compound. Once I made it into the gate my body went on autopilot with placing my kit away and restocking my ammunition in my used magazines.

I don't remember when exactly the other guys came back, but I remember seeing our fallen Ranger's best friend. They were as close to brothers as you could become without being related. He asked for an update on how everyone was doing, as he still had not heard the news. I could feel my eyes over flowing with tears as I told him he was gone. At first he didn't believe me, but I think the look on my face said it all. He broke down in a bunker maybe twenty feet from where I delivered the news to him.

The next few days were a blur of helping prepare my friend for his Angel Flight amidst uncontrolled emotions that came and went. I could not even play *Call of Duty* for a long time, as it was the last game we all played together right before the mission. We had paused the game so we could all continue together when we returned. When people would just say his name, all that emotion would come out and consume me.

After I returned from the ceremony at the airfield to send our friend and the SEAL who had also been killed to be with their families again, it was a changed environment with the team guys. It was a very emotional time for everyone at the camp as we dealt with what we could, and placed it on the back burner when missions came and went. This also led to what I think was the greatest mixing of the two forces as we were now a part of them, more or less. I learned more about their unit than I had ever known, and my respect grew for them every day I was there. Now just to clear things up, we had a sister platoon who had a total opposite experience with them at the same time. It was hard for them to wrap their heads around how much they treated us as equals as it flew in the face of most Rangers' experiences.

At the end of our deployment, it was crazy for me to think of my first experience with an SMU back in 2004, just pulling security and being a top gunner for them. I was now clearing buildings right alongside them, and helping them plan missions as an integral part of their team. It is a testament to how far Rangers have come and it makes me smile every day. At the same time, a steep cost has been paid for us to be where we are today - a reminder that I carry not just on my wrist but in my soul every day. It took me over two years to come to terms with watching my friend die in front of me, but I am grateful for all the help everyone gave me along the way.

–Martin
1/75

September 2010
"Lost in the Sauce"

This story takes place in Panjway District, Kandahar Province, some-time during early September 2010. I don't remember the objective name, and I couldn't show anyone the place on a map, but I can remember the details of the night as clear as I did the day after they happened. At the time of this mission I was a nineteen-year-old private first class, and I was a rifleman in a line squad.

On this night, our mission was to conduct NAI clearance and then set up a ROD site in conjunction with our sister platoon. Second platoon (my platoon) would infil about an hour ahead of first platoon, and we would attempt to clear one or two NAIs before linking up at the potential ROD site with first platoon. So, basically, my platoon would clear a couple of houses where intelligence had reported possible enemies. First platoon would take over a house, and together we would fortify the position where we would remain until nightfall, and then exfil back to our FOB. The entire purpose of our ROD sites was to attract enemy activity so we could engage them. We were being used as a "shaping" force, so that the regular Army units could move in to the area after we left, benefiting from our effects on the Taliban fighters in the area. This was as much as I understood about the types of missions we were conducting at the time.

To provide some perspective for this story, I have to explain my level of awareness at this point in my career. By now, the reader should have a basic understanding of how information is disseminated in the Army. It trickles from the top down, and the lowest tier of dissemination happens at the team leader level. All of our team leaders carried radios, to receive information from the squad leaders, who took orders from the platoon leader or platoon sergeant, who had their information and orders from the company commander, and so on and so forth. As a rifleman, all of my information was received from my team leader, Specialist Rose.

This was only my third mission ever, and all I knew at this point was the golden rules of being a private: go where your team leader goes, shoot what your team leader shoots, and take responsibility for your actions. Or something like that. I've forgotten most of the things I used to know as a private, but those are pretty much the basics. You follow your team leader, and watch his back. The team leader is always focused on his objective, which in our case was climbing. Our squad would get to the compound just ahead of the main assault squad, climb on the walls, and try to get an idea of what was going on inside the compound so the assault squad wasn't going in blind. I would carry a litter and medical equipment, just in case we took casualties, and I also carried the ladder for my team leader (because privates carry the heavy shit). I would usually never climb; instead I set the ladder up, sat at the bottom, and simply held the ladder just in case it fell. It was a pretty lame job, but such is the life of a private. I would also provide extra security to our rear, since my team leader would be totally focused inward on the objective compound.

So, in summary, being a private means that when on a mission, you aren't part of the information flow going through the command nets. You only knew what your team leader had time to tell you, so situations had a tendency to be even more confusing for new Privates, who are generally "lost in the sauce" when the shit hits the fan.

It was still pretty warm in Southern Afghanistan in September, and our infil flight was fairly short and comfortable. We used two MH-47 "Chinook" helicopters to infil our entire platoon. I sat packed on the floor of the bird with all the other Privates. About five minutes into the flight the door gunners did their test fires. First the mini-guns tested their weapons. *BRMMMMMMMMMMMMMMPH! BRMMMMMMMMMMMPH!* Their extreme rates of fire made them not even sound like guns, but some sort of power tool. The M-240Bs went next. *DAT-DAT-DAT-DAT-DAT! DAT-DAT-DAT-DAT-DAT-DAT!* The slower, staccato bursts of the M-240Bs were very distinct. The sulfuric smell of gunpowder hovered around the interior of the bird, before being eventually swept away by the wind flowing in the open gunner windows and out of the back ramp hatch. The barrel from one of the SAW gunners sitting in the chairs above me dug into my ankle. I kept my composure until he shifted his weight onto his gun, digging the barrel deeper into my ankle. I swatted his barrel off my leg and pulled my leg up against my chest. Something like this would happen every five or ten minutes, and I'd shift my body weight or bend my legs. Usually if the flight was longer than forty-five minutes, you couldn't feel your legs by the time you arrived at your destination. I leaned against the heavy litterbag strapped to my back. I kept one hand on my ladder tucked under everyone's feet, constantly reminding myself not to forget it.

Finally, after what seemed like ages but was probably only twenty minutes, "TEN MINUTES!" Everyone echoed the command and held up all ten fingers, signaling that we were ten minutes from infil. I remained sitting, and flipped down my single tube PVS-14 night vision goggles. Almost everyone else in the platoon had dual tube night vision goggles, except for me. Life sucks. My PVS-14s powered on, projecting a green image onto my right eye. I left the 14s on, but tilted my helmet up a bit to give my eye a rest before it was staring at a green light all night.

"SIX MINUTES!" That was the cue to get moving. On the six-minute call, everyone on the floor heaved themselves up to a knee somehow. I struggled to get up, and grabbed the hands of whoever was sitting on each side of me in the seats, and they pulled me up to my knee. I bent over, putting one hand on the floor to take some strain from my knee, which ached from all of the weight pushing it into the hard floor, even with kneepads on. I checked my safety lanyard, which was hooked into the floor, just to make sure I knew where to unhook it from when the time came. I tilted my helmet down, and made sure my 14s were focused for viewing further out. This made everyone in the bird look blurry, but distinguishable.

While looking out the small window, I could clearly see the terrain below us. It looked like an alien planet. Mud houses, farm fields, and orchards seemed to be randomly placed all about. Fires burned in the distance here and there. I felt the butterflies in my stomach. It was almost the same feeling you get before a wrestling match or a race, except the fear was amplified. You were scared to make a mistake. If you fucked up, you might get someone killed, but more than likely, you'll just get put on your team leader's shit list, which nobody likes to be on as a private. Then there's the looming question of what the night will bring. Are we going to take contact on infil? Will it be a quiet night? Am I going to step on a pressure plate? There were a million variables that went through my mind on infil, and I didn't start functioning until I actually stepped foot on the ground. On the bird, I had the luxury of second-guessing and pondering. Once I left that ramp, I had to simplify my thoughts, and just do my job. I waited for the one-minute call.

BRMMMMMMMPH! BRMMMMMMMPH! BRMMMMMMMPH! My body jumped, like when someone pops around a corner and says, "BOO!" *BRMMMMMMPH! BRMMMMMMMMMMMMMMMPH!* The left side mini-gun started up, and it wasn't a test fire this time. *BRMMMMMPH! DAT-DAT-DAT-DAT-DAT!!!* The M-240B joined in, both guns trying to defend us from what I would later learn was machine gun and RPG fire. One of the most helpless feelings in the world is taking fire while in a helicopter, because all you can do is sit there and hope to God that the bad guy doesn't get a lucky shot and down your bird. "ONE MINUTE!" The call came, and everyone postured themselves to be ready to get up and run off the ramp. We could feel and hear the rotor blades cutting through the air as the bird dropped. The engines and rotors on a helicopter are loud, and it's almost impossible to have a conversation on a helicopter. It's not like the movies. Finally, the bird sets down, but rougher than usual. The gunners have stopped firing by now. I stand up, and I wait for the crowd of Rangers in front of me to run off the bird.

It isn't even five seconds into it when a large flash whites out everyone's NODs. I haven't even stepped off the bird yet, but I don't think anything of the flash, which sounded like a gunshot. I would later learn that, by some dumb Taliban luck, we had landed with our ramp right on a trip wire "Ponzi" grenade, and the first man off tripped the grenade. Somehow when the device detonated, it only sprayed the right side of the bird with shrapnel, and a piece traveled up between one of the pilots' legs, but no one was wounded. We all got off the bird, and set up a messy half-moon shape. It looked like a Fourth of July celebration and laser light show were both going on at the same time. Off to our right, there were rapid-fire explosions going off, compliments of an AC-130 Specter gunship's 40mm cannon. The explosions were only maybe 100 meters from us. There were infrared lasers and infrared spotlights everywhere. The FOs were marking our positions with powerful lasers, all types of aircraft were pointing with their lasers down onto enemies that we couldn't see while Little Birds and the AC-130 were raining hell from above.

We all just kind of sat there. Instead of storming the building, like it goes down in the movies, everyone seemed to be pretty bewildered by the situation. You never want to commit to a situation that you don't understand, and our leadership took some time to get their bearings. I had absolutely no clue what was going on. How many Taliban there were or where they were - nothing. I finally found my team leader, Rose, and asked him what was going on. "Specter is engaging squirters, we're getting ready to climb on the target compound. Just stand by." He held his hand up for a second like he was listening to a voice mail, and received some new information from his radio. "Ok, let's move." We start moving out in a spaced out single file line, a common formation used in Panjway to battle the threat of pressure plates. Theoretically, as long as you walk where the guy in front of you walked, and nothing blows up, you'll be safe.

I was walking with the ladder behind Rose, and our medic, Douglas, was walking behind me. We were Alpha Team, so we are leading out. Bravo Team was trailing just behind us, led by Sergeant Lee. Our squad leader, Sergeant Dale worked his way to the front and started walking in front of my team leader. We moved along the right side of the compound, walking under low hanging trees that skirted the outer wall. I held the ladder in my left hand, and suit case-style carried my gun in my right hand. While it's arguable that carrying your gun like a suitcase is a shit-bag maneuver, I always thought it was stupid to have my gun hanging around my neck and banging into my ladder making noise.

We walked under low hanging trees for maybe thirty meters, when suddenly an infrared spotlight shined down onto a low wall, no more than ten meters in front of us. The spotlight lit up the whole area we were in, and flashed repeatedly, indicating suspicious activity. We all froze to take a knee, and Rose and Dale brought their guns up, scanning with their own IR lights. They scanned for a minute, maybe, and couldn't see anything. I would later learn that there were six enemy fighters with weapons hiding behind the wall, which would later be seen on footage from the ISR platforms flying overhead. Whether they became scared, or didn't know we were there, I'll never know. The situation wasn't as tense for me as it probably was for Rose and Dale, because I was lost in the sauce and didn't even know what a flashing infrared spotlight meant. I just knew it wasn't good. I thought we might be lost or something. Dale and Rose started doubling back, and we just slowly crept back out the way we came, and then made our way to our originally intended climb spot.

I set the tall ladder up against the wall, which had a ditch running alongside it, and then an orchard surrounded the entire compound. My team leader and squad leader climbed up, and then one of our snipers followed them up. The roof they were on had a sort of wavy structure, so that they could sit in between each hump in the roof as cover. By this time, the Specter gunship had started firing again, shooting powerful 105mm artillery rounds, which rocked the earth when they exploded. I sat down at the bottom of the ladder, and I heard yelling and screaming going on in the compound. I had to make myself useful somehow. Fuck it. I climbed up the ladder, and rolled onto the roof and sat there on a knee for a second, not sitting in the low part of the roof, but silhouetting myself against the night sky, a classic mistake.

Sergeant Dale turned around, "Get off the fucking roof!" Clearly I wasn't that useful. I lowered myself from the roof onto the ladder, and as soon as I did a burst of rounds flew over my head and also impacted the roof where I had been sitting. *CRACK-CRACK-CRACK-CRACK-CRACK* One thing that's always been curious to me is how you almost never hear the gun, but only the supersonic *CRACK!* of the bullet as it passes near you. I was off that ladder quicker than ever before. I got on my stomach and crawled into the ditch, not sure how to feel about my recent luck. Doc Douglas was laying on my right side, and our platoon FO, Sergeant Wayans, was on my left. I heard Wayans calling in Little Birds to suppress the enemy fire. "My position marked by IR Strobe, enemy position 70 degrees, 25 meters from my position. Engage with 2.75 rockets. Danger close."

First Sergeant popped up from inside the compound. "EVERY-ONE GET DOWN ON YOUR FACES!" I hugged the earth and buried my head into the side of the ditch, trying to get as small as possible. WHUMPH*! WHUMPH! WHUMPH! WHUMPH!* The rockets impacted farther left than I expected, almost at the low wall we had stopped at earlier. The explosions rocked the ground with impressive force.

The ditch we were in formed an L shape, which faced just short of the low wall. The compound walls followed this curvature. After the rockets hit, the three of us sat there, waiting for whatever would happen next. Suddenly, Doc Douglas jumped up, responding to a call on his radio, and sprinted to the lowest point of the compound wall, near the inner corner. He threw his gun at the nearest Ranger, and leapt over the wall in one bound, with only his medical bag in hand.

During the clearance of the building, one of 3rd Squads SAW gunners had entered a room, and stepped on a Russian PMN mine, which severed half of his foot. At the time, I had no idea what Doc Douglas was doing. I heard screaming inside the compound, and my first thought was that the Specter gunship had inadvertently caused friendly casualties. About ten minutes after Douglas went over the wall, a group of three guys from 1st Squad gathered at the low point in the wall, and began taking turns with a hooligan tool, battering the wall down to make a hole into the compound. I had taken my litterbag off by now and thrown it at the bottom of the ladder. Rose, Dale, and the sniper remained on the roof, not sure if the rockets from the Little Birds had fully suppressed the enemy. Finally, they broke through the wall, and our platoon sergeant emerged. A group of Rangers came through behind him, carrying a litter with someone wrapped up in a space blanket. One of them yelled in my direction. "Hey, get over here, grab this kit bag!" I ran to the break in the wall, and our company executive officer stood there with a bag that contained the casualty's' body armor, NODs, and any other sensitive items.

He threw the bag at me without even saying anything. I slung the bag over my shoulder, and began following the litter bearers. I didn't know if what I was doing was the right choice, since I was separating from my team leader, but sometimes you just have to say, "fuck it," and do what has to be done. We hung a right after we were clear of the compound, and our route took us into a swampy path that ran underneath low hanging trees, which made walking a nightmare. For me it wasn't so bad, but the litter bearers were having a hell of a time. Every twenty feet or so, one of them would slip off the narrow path and fall into the mud, dropping the litter and causing the casualty to scream out loudly.

The casualty was Specialist Rod, and the way he screamed was like nothing I've ever heard before. I don't know if it was the ketamine that Doc Douglas gave him or the wound, but someone who is seriously hurt screams like a wounded animal, like their mind has left them. And it was LOUD. "AHHHHHHHH! AHHHHHHHHHHH-HHHHHHHHHHHHHHH!" Each time the litter dropped, he would scream out louder. After ten minutes of walking through the quagmire of mud, we emerged into an open, tilled up field. I stayed close to the platoon sergeant, since I wasn't even really sure what to do. "Do I just drop the bag in the bird when it comes in?" The platoon sergeant responded with a calmness that was irregular for the situation. "Yep, just throw it on there, and then run back off." We waited with Rod in the middle of the field, and another squad spread out around us and pulled security outward, making sure we didn't get hit when we were most vulnerable. Rod was talking incoherently, reaching for anyone close by. He seemed to be slipping in and out of consciousness. After about five minutes the MEDEVAC bird came in, flying in low, and throwing up a large cloud of dust with it. We did our best to cover up Rod, and then the litter bearers ran him onto the bird. I ran onto the bird, threw the bag on the floor, and ran back off.

After the MEDEVAC, the rest of the platoon followed us into the field, and I linked back up with my team leader. We ended up walking to another house that, like the previous house, was completely empty and we decided not to enter. That same night, about one kilometer from us, our 1st Platoon brethren hit a pressure plate IED on a narrow path, and their EOD technician was seriously wounded. Pressure plates were a huge threat in Panjway at that time. Both platoons decided our best course of action was to consolidate at the ROD site. We took sporadic mortar, RPG, and small arms fire for the rest of the day, and ended up getting a decent amount of close air support and mortar kills.

This is one of those stories which almost every man on the ground that night would tell differently. The events of the night I describe only took about two hours, but there was so much that happened in that short time frame. It was such a chaotic situation, especially being as new as I was. I was too focused on my job to really understand how hectic the situation actually was. Everyone is "lost in the sauce" their first few times they find themselves in a combat situation, but our training usually takes over enough to get us through it all. It took me a few more missions to really start being aware of my surroundings.

–KINGSLEY
2/75

NOVEMBER 2010
"THE CAVE"

It was November, 2010. We were stationed in FOB Orgun-E, which was way up in the mountains. The FOB was just big enough for a chow hall, some little white trailers for the regular army unit that was stationed there at the time as barracks, a large, gravel HLZ big enough to fit multiple rotary wing aircraft in at one time, and a small Special Operations camp. Our camp had five long concrete barracks, which housed all of us. Each building had about five rooms that could hold up to ten or twelve men, but because we were a single platoon up there, we would only have four to six men to one room. Throughout the day and night, the sound of helicopters flying over was not uncommon. Keep in mind that it was the month of November so the weather in Paktika Province was a bitter cold. There were nights we were chilled to the bone because our rooms only had two Mitsubishi wall heaters that would barely heat the room.

At this point, we had only been in country for a few weeks, which consisted of missions almost every night. If we ever had a night off, it was due to weather. The missions that we did go on consisted of five to ten kilometers of walking through the most rugged terrain of Afghanistan's mountains. We would do elevation changes anywhere from a few hundred feet to a thousand feet a night. On a few missions we would have some Taliban fleeing the target building. These people were known as "squirters." Their course of action was usually to run up the nearest mountain, which would result in us calling for fire with any support aircraft on station at the time. We would then do a battle damage assessment (BDA) afterwards to gather information and take pictures. On a few occasions, the call for fire was not successful which would result in pursuing and eliminating the targets ourselves. On the night of November 14th, it was an ordinary routine before the mission. We would go to chow, come back to the TOC to see if we had a mission for that night, and as usual, we did. So as the routine would continue, we'd go to our rooms to put our assault uniforms on and walk to the ready-room to do pre-combat checks (PCCs) on weapons, radios and NODs. Afterwards, we would go to a mission briefing, which went into full detail of what we are going to do on target.

Once the CONOP was complete, 1st Squad, which was comprised of our squad leader Staff Sergeant Pape, Sergeant Mays, Sergeant Roberts, Sergeant Clampman, PFC Hankman and I, would go to the ready room to build porthole charges for a ROD mission that we were supposed to do that night. At that point, we were informed that the current mission had changed and we were to pack an overnight bag to go to Jalalabad, or J-bad for short. In a little less than an hour, we were on our way to J-Bad. Once we arrived, we were put in barracks with a single, plywood hallway. There were two sets of bunk beds in each room and the entire barracks smelled of mildew.

As soon as we settled in the barracks, our platoon Sergeant, SFC Falcon, and our PL, Captain Nellis, along with all of the other squad leaders left to go to the JOC to see what the situation was. Soon after, they were informed that 1-327, 101st Airborne Division ran into heavy enemy contact in the southern portion of the Wataphur Valley during Operation Bulldog Bite II. They requested support from our Task Force to clear their northernmost objective. We received a CONOP in one of J-Bad's briefing rooms. As soon as we left the CONOP, we rushed to the barracks that were about 100 meters away.

We started to put our kit on and received individual briefs from our team leaders of what was going to happen on target. As soon as we left the barracks, we were informed that one of the helicopters was broken and the mission was pushed to the right twenty-four hours. We then returned to our barracks, took off all our gear and went to chow for mid-rats, which was basically our lunch for the day. Once we ate, we returned to the barracks and relaxed. One of the guys managed to find a monopoly board, so we played that game to pass the time.

Toward the end of the game, the entire barracks shook so much that it made the bunk beds hit the wall. I never thought my first earthquake would be like that; it gave me an eerie feeling. Soon after, the squad leaders and team leaders returned from additional planning and had a better plan. Once we were handed our imagery, I was in awe of the new plan. Our entire mission was to disrupt Taliban operations against coalition forces, gather intelligence, and provide freedom of action for further operations. The goal was to clear a very large village with a platoon from 2nd Ranger Battalion.

For the rest of the night, I spent time looking at the imagery and studying it so that once I was on the ground, I would know what part of the village we were in. I finally managed to fall asleep and I slept throughout the day into the next night. Once I woke up, we put on our assault uniforms and did the usual. Shortly after, we were informed that the mission was a go, so we waited outside the barracks for the buses to take us to the airfield.

We loaded two helicopters and flew to a small combat outpost, also referred to as a COP. This COP sat in the middle of a bowl that was surrounded by mountains that had glowing lights from the houses. Immediately the helicopters took off to pick up the platoon from 2nd Battalion. We walked a long a T-barrier wall and sat down to eat MREs. We waited for our CO and first sergeant to come out of the little shack that was basically the COP's TOC. After they exited the TOC, they took the entire platoon to an even smaller concrete shack that was just big enough to fit thirty guys shoulder-to-shoulder. The shack had no light and the intelligence officer that briefed us was using a headlamp to light the white board. He basically said the terrain was the steepest we would ever climb and it was a very wooded area.

Afterwards, he went into the rules of engagement (ROE), which were simple and straightforward. One of the squad leaders immediately asked what the estimated enemy force was and the intelligence officer answered, "fifty to five hundred fighters." In pure disbelief, the squad leader asked, "Did you say fifty to five hundred?" and a quick yet blunt "Yes" followed it. Once there were no more questions, a firm "Good luck gentlemen!" was said and we were sent back out to our spot on the T-barrier wall.

Not long after that, we were loading the helicopters and flying out to the HLZ on the side of the mountain. Once we landed, the guys rushed off the helicopter into vegetation that made it feel like Vietnam. The HLZ was a dried up rice paddy, the cool air smelled of burning trash, and the night sky moved with little dots of air assets. All we could hear were the helicopters leaving the HLZ echoing off the mountains and a humming of a support aircraft overhead. My squad was the lead of the formation for the platoon. It didn't take long for Sergeant Mays to get his bearing and start moving out.

We headed straight up the mountain, through the thick vegetation and woods. Not long after that, we ran into an abandoned fighting position made of trees that were cut down and stacked like a log cabin. Immediately my heart started to pound; I could hear it in my ears it pounded so hard. Once we reached one of the false summits of the mountain, we began descending into vegetation that was no taller than my head. We followed a beaten path to an HLZ that we were to clear before continuing on to the objective. The name of the HLZ was Carolina. Once we cleared the almost 200 meter wide HLZ, we continued to one of the mountain ridges where the village was located and started the clearance of two houses.

At that time, we were informed that ten to fifteen military aged males ran from a compound as we advanced toward the area. They then split into several groups and moved west down the steep cliffs into the valley. Soon after being informed of the squirters, 1st Squad immediately took the job as "squirter interdiction team" and started the pursuit of the ones that headed west of our position. We went about 500 meters before we ran into the cliff's 400-meter drop down to the valley. The cliff was so tall the trees at the bottom did not even come close to peaking over the cliff. SSG Pape informed SFC Falcon that we'd reached the limit of advance, and could not pursue the squirters any further as an entire squad. He then directed Sergeant Mays to find a way down.

Looking across the valley, another ridge parallel from us extended about 1500 feet above our current position. While Sergeant Mays and Staff Sergeant Pape were trying to find a way down, the infrared laser from the reconnaissance assets above shined down to show the location of the two squirters at the bottom of the valley through the tall trees. The rest of the platoon was trailing behind. SFC Falcon looked down the cliff and said, "Damn." Soon after, Sergeant Mays found a way down. SSG Pape then directed the rest of the squad to stay up on the cliff. In the same instance he told SFC Falcon that he was going to take his Alpha Team leader, Sergeant Mays and the dog handler, and Sergeant Mack down the cliff and continue the pursuit of the squirters. He then looked at me and said, "Guess what I'm going to go do?". . . My reply was, "Going to go kill some mother fuckers . . . ." and in a calm whisper, he said "Damn straight!"

SSG Pape, Sergeant Mays and Sergeant Mack began climbing down, despite the fact the entire squad volunteered to go with them. After a few minutes of battling with Sergeant Roberts and Sergeant Clampman to go down with him, he still refused and went down with a three-man team. With the IR sparkle still on the squirters in the valley, they disappeared into the darkness. All we could hear was the breaking of branches while they climbed down. As soon as they reached the bottom of the cliff, SSG Pape set up an overwatch position that Sergeant Mays manned on a nearby high ground at the base of the cliff.

They made contact with one enemy rifleman who managed to squeeze one shot off before SSG Pape killed him. On top of the cliff with the rest of the platoon, all I could hear was a "tsk, tsk" sound from the suppressed weapons. After hearing the first engagement, another sparkle shined about 500 meters north and to my right. SFC Falcon asked what they were sparkling and the JTAC said it was "five to ten fighters roaming around." SFC Falcon asked for a fire mission from the air assets on station at the time and a few minutes later told us to take cover as they rained down 40mm and 105mm rounds on the fighters north of us. He then radioed down to SSG Pape to take cover until the fire mission was complete.

The AC-130 let a series of 40mm and one 105mm shells out on the mountainside where the fighters were located. The JTAC then told SFC Falcon that the fighters dispersed and were no longer a threat to us. During the fire mission, SSG Pape took contact from a second rifleman that emerged from the same area as the first rifleman. SSG Pape eliminated the second rifleman and then threw a grenade in the position of the two shooters to verify the kill. Once the grenade exploded, SSG Pape started to assault through the bodies to confirm the kills. Unknowingly exposing himself to a cave opening, an RPK machine gun opened up on SSG Pape's silhouette.

Sitting on the edge of the cliff, I could see tracers ricochet off the rocks and into the air, which gave the same appearance as fireworks. One of those rounds wounded SSG Pape. Sergeant Mack immediately realized what happened, and without hesitation, returned fire into the cave entrance. He engaged the machine gunner before he could acquire Sergeant Mack as a target. Following this engagement, Sergeant Mack was quickly joined by Sergeant Mays as six to eight fighters fled from the cave. Sergeant Mays and Sergeant Mack promptly engaged the enemies as they attempted to flee and killed at least two of them.

After this, Sergeant Mays jumped down from a six-foot rock ledge and low-crawled to Sergeant Pape's position and attempted to pull him to cover. When he was unable to pull him, Sergeant Mays moved to cover and watched over the cave until the rest of the element made their way down. During all of this, Sergeant Mays radioed to the rest of 1st Squad and the platoon that SSG Pape was down. As soon as the call was received, Sergeant Roberts, Sergeant Clampman, PFC Hankman, and I slid down the cliff to their position. Following us was SFC Falcon and SSG Arrow, the Senior Medic.

Once I made it down there with the rest of 1st Squad, I saw SSG Pape trying to sit up while pointing to his left side. Sergeant Mays at that point was already beside him working with SSG Arrow to treat his wound the best they could. It wasn't long after that Staff Sergeant Kevin Pape died from those wounds. At this time, I had no idea SSG Pape had expired because I was pulling a security position while they worked on him. The rest of the platoon made their way to us and filled gaps in the security.

The sun just started to rise behind us, making it just bright enough for everyone to put their NODs up. It was now November 16th and while all the guys switched their NODs and IR lasers off, SSG Pape was being put on a Skedco and was covered with a space blanket. SSG Victor threw several thermobaric grenades and frags into the cave opening hoping to either flush the remaining Taliban and foreign fighters out or to just kill them all together. As the rest of the platoon headed 200 meters north up a beaten path to a medical evacuation HLZ, SSG Victor's squad bounded back to a safe distance so that we could call for fire on the cave.

After arriving at the MEDEVAC HLZ, which was a plowed field on the side of the mountain overlooking the valley, Sergeant Clampman and I attempted to put another Skedco litter in its case near a rock wall no higher than my torso, separating the beaten path from the plowed field. I remember looking over and seeing SSG Pape in the larger hoistable Skedco covered up without movement. I still did not think he had died from his wounds. While working on getting the Skedco in the bag, one of the guys on the western side of the HLZ saw some of the Taliban fighters climbing their way up to the HLZ.

Without hesitation, Sergeant Clampman and I ran across the HLZ and slid in on a knee and began to engage the enemy climbing up. I could see the eyes of the enemy as they were climbing and what they were wearing; they were armed with nothing but AK-47's. I eliminated two of them before Corporal Worthington slid into the prone next to me armed with an Mk-48. One long burst of the Mk-48 pelted me with hot brass and links from the gun. It felt like lava rocks being hurled into my face. I then looked at Sergeant Clampman as he told me that we should move to SSG May's and Sergeant Roberts' position about ten meters behind us. As soon as we made our way to Sergeant May's position, he noticed fighters running into a house across the valley. He proceeded to give the command to engage with our 40mm grenades, "four-hundred meters, house in the open, twelve o'clock, two HEDP." I loaded my first round into my M-320 grenade launcher and launched the grenade.

Now remember, we were in the mountains in high elevation; thinner air means the round will fly further. Also, we were about five hundred feet above the target. I shot the first round . . . silence. Sergeant Mays looked at Sergeant Roberts and said, "Do you see where that went?" and he replied ". . . No." The correction was given to go down one hundred meters. I loaded the second grenade and shot it. The second one fell right on the house, as the same with the third round. At this point, Sergeant James, who was our FO and a former Division One football player, was about twenty feet from us against the rock wall next to the beaten path. He grabbed our attention by yelling, "You're being shot at!" and at the same time a round impacted between Sergeant Roberts' feet and myself. In a frantic voice, he turned around and yelled, "Get the fuck off the HLZ!"

He ran past me as I was turning around to get out of the line of fire. We ran to the southern portion of the HLZ where another rock wall was no higher than my torso, with two trees no more than eight feet apart. As I ran towards the wall, I could see the tree branches falling off the trees from the rounds impacting them. I watched Sergeant Roberts jump over that wall and disappear. I was not far behind him when I went to jump the wall and saw on the other side was a twelve-foot drop . . . . It was a defilade about twelve feet long and six feet wide. Sergeant Roberts was lying at the bottom with a look of pain on his face. By the time I realized that it was a drop, I was already committed to the jump and fell twelve feet and landed smack on top of Sergeant Roberts. I busted my right arm on a rock and quickly looked to see if I broke it. Sergeant Clampman was not far behind me either when he made the fall as well.

Sergeant Mays was above us standing on one of the tree roots protruding from the twelve-foot drop asking for my M-320 to engage the enemy from which we were taking cover. As I threw him the remaining 40mm rounds, SSG Shinman, CPT Nellis, Sergeant James, and PFC Ramsay made their way down to the defilade away from enemy fire, but fortunately they found a safer way. When we looked to the south toward the way we came, it was straight down about ten feet and then sloped down about another one hundred meters. The slope was nothing but shale rock and gravel with a tree line at the base. A few minutes passed by and Sergeant Mays was now taking cover down with us in the defilade.

Sergeant Roberts and Mays simultaneously yelled at everyone to shut-up. They were attempting to make out a faint voice on the radio. During a brief break in gunfire they heard a whisper over the radio, "Help Me!" Sergeant Mays looked around and wondered out loud, "Who is that and where is it coming from?"

Fifteen minutes went by without any knowledge of where it came from. At this point a CASEVAC had been called, but the HLZ was too hot to have helicopters land. We would have to drop bombs on the ridge across the valley and on the house we took contact from. Finally, Sergeant Mays spotted Sergeant Cox, one of our Snipers on the mission with us. He was about fifty meters from the tree line at the base of the slope with his helmet off and weaponless. Sergeant Mays looked at 1st Squad and ordered us to follow him with SSG Arrow right behind. I knew at the time we were in heavy contact, so did Sergeant Clampman and the rest of the squad going to help Sergeant Cox. I followed Sergeant Clampman down to the base and took cover behind a tree just as he did. Sergeant Mays, Sergeant Roberts and SSG Arrow took Sergeant Cox's arms and threw them over their shoulders and carried him all the way back up to the defilade. The rest of us were providing bounding security to allow them to climb up when Sergeant Clampman accidentally dropped Sergeant Cox's helmet and NOD's as he was engaging a target. He had to go back down to police them up before proceeding to bound back up the hill and rejoin us.

From there, PFC Ramsay and PFC Philson bounded back first, then Sergeant Clampman and I did until we reached the defilade. The entire time bounding back I watched round after round miss Sergeant Clampman and I. In some moments, if I had misplaced my footing on the rocks, I would have been wounded. When we were closer to the defilade, I could see Sergeant Mays looking back extending his arm to pull us all in. Back at our fighting position, I was gasping for air when Sergeant Mays told us to get a drink from our Camelbaks. I'd been out of water since infil, so he extended the hose from his Camelbak and I was able to drink water for the first time in over six hours. One more person joined us in the limited space we had and Specialist Taylor, a SAW gunner, provided suppression on the enemy while we bounded back. Sergeant James proceeded to use Kiowa attack helicopters for a gun-run on the slope and tree line we just came from.

As I looked over, I witnessed SSG Arrow working on Sergeant Cox's wounds. Sergeant Cox received a gunshot wound to the lower portion of his jaw. Sergeant James kept having the gun run come closer and closer to our position until he was within fifty meters from our fighting position. Danger close, the Kiowa would not shoot unless they knew our exact location. Seconds went by when CPT Nellis pulled out a VS-17 panel (a bright orange square) and set it on the outer portion of the defilade in hopes the Kiowa could see it. Knowing it would not work, Sergeant James stumbled over our legs to get to the VS-17 panel and expose himself to enemy fire. It seemed as soon as he exposed himself, the rate of fire from the enemy picked up and more of the trees fell down on us. Sergeant James held the panel extended with both arms to show the pilots where we were, despite the fact that he was completely exposed to intense enemy fire.

He then jumped down back behind cover after being notified confirmation of our position. "DANGER CLOSE! Take cover!" he yelled. I tried to stay really low to the ground in hopes of gaining cover. The gun run was close enough I could taste the dirt being thrown in the air from the impact of the rounds into the ground. In the same instant, five hundred pound bombs impacted the ridge across the valley and the house that I initially engaged. Not long after that, Sergeant Bailey was above us to receive Sergeant Cox for the CASEVAC coming to pick up any wounded.

Captain Nellis then radioed a situation report to our command. We had two wounded, Sergeant Cox and an interpreter who went by "Shotgun." After a moment of pausing, it was said that SSG Pape was "killed in action." That was the first time I realized that he was really gone. I guess it was the denial or lack of understanding of the situation and the wounds he received, but it hit us and a wave of anger came over me. As they started to push Sergeant Cox back up the twelve foot drop back to the HLZ, Sergeant Clampman and I switched positions to where we could look down the slope with Specialist Taylor and anyone else that was not helping push Sergeant Cox up the defilade.

While still under fire, two Blackhawk helicopters flew in to pick up the wounded. Sergeant Bailey laid down covering fire while running with Sergeant Cox to the helicopters. As soon as they reached the birds, Sergeant Cox pulled Sergeant Bailey in and said, "Change mags!" As Sergeant Bailey got out of the way from the birds so they could take off after they loaded the 'terp and SSG Pape's body, he looked down at the little window on the side of his P-Mag and saw he had only four rounds left and needed to change them. As that was happening, the rest of the guys and I were being helped back up to the HLZ.

Once I reached the top, I took a knee behind the trees and turned back to help the rest of the guys up. Afterward, I noticed a knee pad that I had dropped by the tree a few hours prior when we first took fire on the HLZ. I didn't even know I had dropped it, but was glad to have it back. Soon, the platoon started the grueling climb up to the original house that we were at before we began chasing squirters. Sergeant Clampman and I were dehydrated, extremely tired, and on the verge of slipping into a daze. Sergeant Roberts who was now the Alpha Team leader handed me a Cliff Shot just so I could maintain enough energy to get to the top of the cliff. When we finally got up top, we found that the 2nd Batt. guys had already established a security perimeter. All the Kiowas were still doing gun runs and Sergeant Roberts placed me in a good security position. After a few minutes, the Weapons Squad leader called for a Gustav fire mission on a single man yelling "Allah Akbar!" at them. Specialist Shale, who was our Gustav gunner, and his AG loaded up a round and shot the 84mm recoilless round at the man, and repeated twice more. After those three rounds, the threat was eliminated. Each time he fired, I could feel the pound in my chest of the round exploding, forcing air out of my lungs. I just sat there in a slight daze with my socks soaking wet from sweat and gasping for air. Sergeant Mays, who was now our squad leader, secured 1st Squad a room in the house. The house was built into a hill and had a watermill wheel on the side with an irrigation canal. The bottom floor had wooden branches holding up the stairs where we were. As soon as 1st Squad was all in the room, we realized that it had ended and a rush of emotions hit us all. Sergeant Mays said, "Staff Sergeant Pape would have been proud of what we did today . . . ."

We all managed to muster up enough strength to shed our kit and helmets. We all tried to acquire as much water as we could. Hankman and Sergeant Roberts laid down and covered up in a space blanket, falling asleep from pure exhaustion. Sergeant Clampman and I were at the other end under the blanket trying to sleep. Sergeant Mays, after handing me his extra pair of black socks, went up to the rooftop with the rest of the leadership. After we fell asleep, two loud explosions filled the valley and the overpressure hit the house with enough force to wake all of us up. Specialist Vale peeked into the room where we were and told us that it was two bombs that the fighter jets dropped on the cave where SSG Pape was killed in the hopes of destroying it.

We slept all day, although I was in and out of sleep with the Kiowa's flying overhead and people talking. Once I was fully awake, I put on my body armor with the rest of 1st Squad, and we walked out the door. A very tired Sergeant Mays, who did not sleep at all, staying awake the whole time, greeted us. While we stayed there, the rest of the platoon had found two 81mm Chinese Mortars. Inside of a giant, hollow tree stump, there were more RPGs and other weapons found as well. Our platoon sergeant took the backpack I was carrying the entire mission that contained fifteen blocks of C-4 and a satchel charge, along with other explosives. They rigged the tree stump to blow. The platoon was leaving the house as Sergeant Mays pulled the initiators to start the time fuse to the explosives, and then ran to catch up with the rest of the platoon.

Once we reached the top of the hill before going back to HLZ Carolina, the tree trunk evaporated in the air, which sent red fireballs into the air, and the house was destroyed. It clearly did not stand a chance with the amount of explosives we used, along with the RPGs and mortar rounds already being inside the tree trunk. As we continued our movement, we could hear 155mm howitzer rounds scream in and slam into the valley. Each time they impacted, it shook the ground that we stood on even though we were a great distance away. After the two-kilometer movement to reach HLZ Carolina, darkness fell on us again. We set up a large patrol base on top of a small hill overlooking the HLZ.

As the cold air crept into us, I could slowly feel the cold seep through my clothes. I went from a mild cold to freezing in less than a minute. It was so painful and my feet were so cold that standing up was excruciating. PFC Hankman, who was next to me, was as equally cold and miserable as I was. We were both shivering shoulder-to-shoulder. I managed to get a glimpse of the sky and noticed the night sky started to move again with all of the assets overhead. After a few hours, we could hear the sound of a helicopter in the distance. "Exfil birds?" I thought to myself. As it drew closer, the outline of a UH-60 Blackhawk appeared. It went over our position to hover on the other side of the hill and dropped two body bags full of water, ammo, batteries, and MREs that we requested eight hours earlier.

For the rest of that night, I faded in and out of sleep trying to stay awake, but a few times I woke up from the pain of cold settling in my bones, the brisk wind plowing through the grass to hit my side, or the sound of PFC Hankman chowing down on an MRE. The PL later came to us asking if we could empty out the water bottles and cut open the MRE's so they could not be used. When I turned around, everyone was either sleeping or under a space blanket to stay warm. Hankman and I emptied out about sixty water bottles and about the same in MREs. We kept the batteries and ammo aside to take back with us. I grabbed a duffle bag from the body bag where the water and MREs were and managed to get some hand warmers to put inside my boots to keep my feet warm and then put my legs in the duffle bag just to escape the wind.

A few more hours faded by and Sergeant Mays came by to see how Hankman and I were doing and to inform us that a call for fire was happening soon. Ten to fifteen minutes later, five hundred pound bombs smashed into the ground all the way around the HLZ's tree line. I could feel the heat from each fireball that followed the explosions; it was the best few seconds on that cold Afghanistan HLZ all night. Afterwards, the two platoons moved down to the HLZ and got in position to be picked up. Sergeant Mays and I carried the battery bag and Hankman had the ammo with Sergeant Roberts. Echoing off the mountains, you could hear the MH-47s coming to exfil us after picking up the 101st Airborne Division that we supported. Once they landed, I ran towards the back of the Chinook's warm exhaust because I was so numb in the face. As we loaded up and sat down on the bird, we snap-linked in and I leaned back to take a deep breath. As I did, I broke down. I was happy to get the fuck out of there but it was all at a great cost.

Once we arrived back in J-Bad, we sluggishly walked off the bird to the bus back to the barracks. I didn't say a word, there was dead silence. All I wanted was a bed to lie in and to fall asleep. I woke up the day we were to leave back to FOB OE while Staff Sergeant Pape's belongings that needed to go back to the States were packed up. We only had one day off before we went on our next mission.

3rd Platoon did six more missions that deployment and finally returned home for the first time since July. Of all the deployments and all the missions I've been on, that deployment hit us the hardest. I knew becoming a Ranger would entail many obstacles and endeavors that would be out of my control, but the last thing I would want to witness would be one of the greatest men I knew and fought alongside with, die within a distance so close to me, yet their fate be completely out of my or any other Rangers' control. I returned home to the United States a changed man, a better Ranger, and a stronger individual - both mentally and emotionally. RLTW!

-LOGAN A. LEWIS
1/75

NOVEMBER 2010
"THE CAVE: WOUNDED"

On or about November 14th, 2010, Team Darby out of FOB OE was preparing for another mission in the KG Pass in Afghanistan. I was a sniper attached to 3rd Platoon, C Company, 1/75. Our platoon had spent the majority of the deployment in Iraq, but as the war was nearly non-existent in that country, we were moved to Afghanistan where they were experiencing one of the most violent years of the war. While waiting for the final manifest call, a call came over the net saying our mission was cancelled and we were being pushed over to do a QRF mission. The company commander called for all of the leadership to go into the TOC and prepare for the mission brief. We were told that the 101st Airborne Division was in a serious firefight in the Kunar Valley and had a mass casualty situation. Their element was clearing through a wadi system and was ambushed by a platoon-sized element of Taliban fighters. The report was they had taken thirty casualties, ten were KIA, and they were still taking heavy enemy fire. It was not clear if we were going directly in as the QRF team, or we would be put on standby for another QRF team that was closer and could get there faster. When we arrived in J-Bad we were told that we were on standby in case another QRF element was needed, or we would possibly insert to hit a few targets. After a few hours had passed, we were stood down because the first QRF element had been inserted and provided enough support to help the 101st break contact and evacuate their wounded.

After being stood down our commander was still looking at possibly inserting our element to execute a movement to contact and set up a target line for us to clear. This at the time made sense because the enemy combatants were on the retreat and low on firepower and manpower. The decision was made that we were going to insert the next period of darkness. During the daylight hours, ISR reported seeing women and children leaving the village. This only meant one thing; the Taliban fighters knew that there was going to be an operation in that valley and they were there to fight.

While planning the mission, we were told that it was going to be a ROD and to be prepared to stay out for as many as four days! Not being at our home camp, we had to scrounge up supplies.

While going over the mission details in the TOC, I had a conversation with my good friend Staff Sergeant Ball. He had a look on his face that I could tell something was bothering him. I asked what he thought about the mission and he looked at me and said, "We should have gone in last night. Now they've had time to regroup and resupply their ammo. We are probably going to lose a few guys tonight." Hearing that from a senior Ranger staff sergeant who has been on over ten deployments really puts things into perspective. We had no idea of how hard of a battle we were in for . . .

The assault force consisted of 3rd Platoon, C Company 1/75 with attachments, and a skeleton platoon from 2/75 that had just arrived in country a few weeks prior. Our mission was to enter and clear every house or compound in that valley, which was over a hundred structures. We left J-BAD on the night of the 15th and landed in a small outpost in the middle of nowhere to do a face to face with the battle space owner. While conducting the meeting, a member of the unit that owned the battle space said they have a name for the valley we were heading to. They called it The Jungle. It was called that because of how harsh the terrain was, and how heavily wooded it was. Before we loaded the helicopters for infil, pre-mission assault fires were dropped on our intended HLZ.

After landing on a remote ridgeline outside of the Kunar Valley, we started our six-kilometer movement to the first target compound. One of the first things that came over the radio that the 'terp was monitoring for enemy chatter was, "The Americans have landed, everyone get to your positions" From that point on it was no longer *if* we will be ambushed or make contact, but *when* we are ambushed or take contact.

The terrain in the Kunar Valley is unlike anything I've ever experienced in Afghanistan. Heavily wooded is an understatement compared to the conditions we were walking in. The trees and shrubs were so thick that we had to walk in a file for most of the movement. If you fell more than a couple steps behind the man in front of you, you would no longer be able to see them. Not to mention that we would walk up then down and back up again, sometimes up rock faces and cliffs. I'm not sure how long it took us to arrive at the first target, but it seemed like four hours or so had passed and we were all sucking pretty bad. Once we finally made it to our first target and conditions were set, the main assault entered and cleared the first building. It was a dry hole. So, we went on to the second target building and it was assaulted and turned out to be another dry hole.

Making our way to the third target as security and assault was setting in, a group of fighters ran out of the back of the house and headed into the woods. The assault force entered and cleared the building and captured one fighting age male inside. When the assault was over, 1st Squad went after the squirters. Our overhead assets put an IR laser on the squirters to help 1st Squad find their location. While at the target compound, we could see the laser moving further and further away from the main element. One of the other squad leaders looked at the PL and told him that 1st Squad is moving too far from us and if they are compromised we won't be able to help them.

At this time, I remember looking at the ridge across from us and I could see hot spots along the ridge facing us. I remember thinking to myself, *those are warming fires and they probably have armed guys around them.* I told the PL this and that I thought 1st Squad was about to get ambushed. The sun was starting to crest the horizon, so our NODs and lasers were pretty much useless and the element of surprise was gone. The platoon sergeant finally came over the radio and told 1ˢᵗ Squad to hold on, they would just have a gun ship hit the squirters. SSG Pape, the 1ˢᵗ Squad leader, came back over the radio and said he followed the fighters to a cave and he was going to throw a grenade in it.

A few moments, after he said he was going to frag the cave, the ambush started. The burst of AK-47 fire rang through the valley and we knew right then that 1ˢᵗ Squad was in trouble. Everyone at the 3ʳᵈ target building immediately jumped up and started running as fast as possible to the gunfire. The platoon sergeant was trying to reach SSG Pape over the radio, but only received silence. My heart sank when there wasn't a response. While running I was saying in my head, *please say something Kevin, please say you're ok.* The platoon sergeant again tried to contact him over the radio, still no response. He tried a third time now, still nothing. Finally a call came over that I would never forget, "3-7 this is 3-1A, 3-1 IS DOWN! He's hurt pretty badly."

While running to the cave site, I radioed the dog handler, Sergeant Mack, and asked if the threat was eliminated. His response was that there was a squad-sized element that made it out of the cave. When we finally made it to the end of the trail we were following, if you went left, it headed down to the cave and if you went right, you would move up a hill that would over watch the platoon. At the intersection, I linked up with a Naval SMU Operator who was in charge of the small Afghan Partnering Unit (APU) element that was attached to us. He told me we need guys to go up this hill in case they tried to overrun us, so I went with him up the hill. When we arrived at the top of that hill, I moved behind a tree and started scanning the ridge across from us. The first thing I saw was a cave with muzzle flashes coming out of it, so I immediately started putting rounds into that cave. Almost immediately after putting rounds into the cave, I came under fire and took shelter under the same tree the operator was under.

He asked me what was wrong and I replied that enemy fire just hit all around me. A few seconds later, his 'terp was hit in the leg. He looked at me and said we need to have somebody here in case we are overrun. I told him I got it, so he left me there and took off with his APU unit. The APU, what a joke, these assholes were crying and hiding the whole time we were in the firefight. I remember yelling at them to pull security because they were crying and praying so much. Before the operator moved out with his element, he said his radio was dead. I looked at him and told him to change his battery, but he looked at me like I was crazy and said he didn't have a spare on him. Now, keep in mind that we were told we would be out here for at least a few days, and to bring extra supplies. This guy is supposed to be an elite Navy SEAL SMU Operator, yet he didn't have a spare radio battery on him? All I could say to myself was, *What the fuck . . . .*

While his element was moving out, I remember looking down the hill and into the valley and being able to see the rest of the platoon. I remember telling the platoon sergeant that I was still on that hill and could see them and had over watch for them. A few minutes went by, and I remember thinking the gunshots were starting to move a little further away. Another five minutes went by and the gunshots were now even further away.

Once I realized the platoon had moved the wounded to CASEVAC without me, it hit me like a brick in the stomach. I immediately made my way down the hill I had climbed and didn't see anyone! I realized I had been left! Completely alone now, the feeling that hit my gut was indescribable; it was so overwhelming that I dropped to a knee instantly. My anxiety was going through the roof and for some reason, I jumped up and turned around. I had a feeling that someone was watching me.

About 25 meters behind me was an enemy fighter dressed in red with his weapon at the low ready, sneaking up on me. I raised my SR-25 sniper rifle at him and shoulder fired a few times. I managed to hit him once in the stomach area and he went down. When we were making our way to Pape's element, I asked the dog handler if all of the threat was eliminated and he responded with no, there are still 7-9 guys that made it out of the cave. So, thinking I had just been walked up on by a squad-sized element, I made my way down the hill I was on. While I was running I looked over to my nine o'clock and could see the same guy in red sitting against a tree with his gun.

Still running, I heard a loud explosion and my eardrums exploded and it felt like I had gotten sucker punched on the left side of my face. My neck burned and my jaw was hurting, then I could see the blood shooting out in front of me when I was running down the hill. As I was running, I pretty much ran off the side of a cliff and started falling head over heels down this hill. My rifle flew out of my hands as I was falling, and I just kept plummeting, hitting my head off rocks, trees, and earth. During my fall, I somehow timed it and landed on my feet and ran down the rest of the way, made a right, and dove into a bush. I started feeling the left side of my neck, checking to see if I had been hit in the jugular, and made my way across my neck to the right side where it was hurting and could feel a hole and my jawbone.

Sitting in that bush, I un-holstered my Beretta M-9 and remember thinking, *damn, I'm fucked.* I tried to make a radio call and all that came out was a gargled mess. Someone responded with "Break, break, break on the net. Who the fuck is that?" Again I tried to say something and muttered out, "This is Cox, I'm hit." The next call that came over was give us a distance and direction. I didn't have a Garmin on, as they were all out when I went to pick up mine. The only thing I had was the wrist compass on my watch that I bought at the PX for ten bucks. I replied I didn't have a Garmin and asked what direction they had moved. They moved north. So I held my watch up and found north.

I began IMT'ing north, moving from tree to tree. After a few bounds I radioed the assault force to see if they could see me. They still didn't have eyes on me because they were still taking fire. I began bounding north again and after a few minutes, I stopped and radioed the assault force. They still could not see me. At this point the adrenaline was wearing off and I was getting lightheaded and dizzy. I thought to myself, this is really it. I'm going to die. At the time this event happened, my wife was six months pregnant with our first son. I kept telling myself, I'm going to make it back for the birth of my son!

I was up and bounding again and could see an embankment. Along the wall of the embankment I could see helmets going across it. I tried to yell to them and barely got anything out because of all the blood that was in my mouth. Finally I heard someone yell, "There he is!" Several of my Ranger buddies jumped down to help me. Mays, Ramsay, and Arrow, our senior medic, started performing RFR. Doc Arrow put a dressing on my neck and that little bit of pressure blocked my airway and I gasped for air. Doc Arrow grabbed for one of his Kryk kits and was about to give me a tracheotomy right there. Before he could open it I grabbed him and pulled him in close and said, "I can breathe fine if you don't press on my neck." He looked down at me and said, "Listen, if you start having trouble breathing you have to tell me so I can do this!" We made our way back to the embankment and several other guys jumped down to help and pull security for us because we were still getting shot at. Thankfully, no one else was wounded.

Once we all made it over the embankment and were under cover, we started taking a lot more gunfire. I remember lying on the ground, looking up at the second part of the embankment that was about 8-10 feet high. At the top, our FO was making his way down to our level to call in gun runs. When he jumped down, he kicked a rock off; this particular rock was about the size of a soft ball and headed straight at my face. It hit me above my left eye, and gave me a nice cut and huge bruise. Once he made it down to our level, he started calling in air support. I looked at him and mouthed, "WHAT THE FUCK!!!" Looking back, we laugh about it now. I could hear Sergeant Mays talking to someone, and what he said is something I will never forget, "We lost Pape down at that cave, and Cox got shot in the face and fell down the side of a hill." I couldn't believe what I had just heard and said, "What do you mean you lost Pape?" "He didn't make it man, he's gone." After hearing that I just lay there and tried to keep myself together but my emotions took over. A million things were running through my head. How could this have happened? We went to RIP together, were both on our sixth combat deployment, and had both gone on hundreds of combat missions.

The gun runs were really intense and lasted for almost an hour. I'm not sure how many fighters were in the Kunar that day, but it was a lot. The last few gun runs were danger close with 40mm landing right over our embankment wall. We finally received confirmation that they were sending the MEDEVAC bird. The HLZ was up on the second embankment; Bailey was at the top with a machine gun team and Captain Nellis. They decided to connect a bunch of safety lines together and try to hoist me up the wall at the three-minute call.

At the three-minute call, the assault force starting with the Mk-48 gunners, laid down some cover fire as I made my way up to the second embankment. No hoisting was needed because I climbed that wall so fast that I jumped into Bailey's arms at the top. Doc Arrow stayed by my side and used his body as a shield as we waited for the bird. Finally, the one-minute call was made and Captain Nellis pulled out a large piece of VS-17 reflective panel and started running around the HLZ for the pilots to see. He scared the shit out of us when he did that because we were still taking some fire. The bird was getting close and it finally came into view and began to land. Doc Arrow and Bailey made a shield around me and ran me out to the bird.

I loaded the bird first and the 'terp that was shot on the same hilltop I did was next. Out of the corner of my eye, I could see a litter being loaded onto the bird. Staff Sergeant Kevin M. Pape was on the litter and was loaded directly across from me. There's no training in the military that can prepare you for the death of a friend. After we were loaded, the bird picked up, and headed towards a hospital site close by. I thought for sure we were going to be shot down, but we picked up and took off without incident. When we were in the air the pilot said the flight was just over ten minutes. Sitting across from Kevin made the flight seem like it took an hour. Some of these images are forever ingrained in my memory. We finally landed at the hospital and there were a lot of people waiting for us to land. I was rushed off the bird and immediately prepped for the operating room. That was the last time I saw Kevin, and I miss him more and more as time goes on.

-ERIC COX
1/75

Chapter Eleven

"No catalogue of horrors ever kept men from war.
Before the war you always think that it's not you that dies.
But you will die, brother, if you go to it long enough."

ERNEST HEMINGWAY
"NOTES ON THE NEXT WAR," ESQUIRE, SEP. 1935

Although Rangers had transitioned out of Iraq by this point, the official end of the war in Iraq came on December 15th, 2011. This was barely noticed by the Rangers who were fully engaged in the most violent years of combat in Afghanistan. Strides were made in the war on terror though, most notable of which was the raid on Usama Bin Laden's compound in Pakistan on May 2nd, 2011, resulting in the death of the man responsible for the terror attacks almost ten years prior on 9/11. Despite this milestone, the war continued to rage in Afghanistan and Rangers continued to lead the way in the special operations task force that was hunting down the most dangerous men in the country.

2011 unfortunately was host to one of the worst losses of life in Special Operations history. In support of a Ranger platoon on the ground, a helicopter carrying a naval special warfare element was shot down, killing all 38 on board. In addition, six Rangers were killed in action that year. Staff Sergeant Jeremy Katzenberger, Sergeant Tyler Holtz, Specialist Ricardo Cerros, Jr., Sergeant First Class Kristoffer Domeij, Private First Class Christopher Horns, and Sergeant Alessandro Plutino all made the ultimate sacrifice.

SFC Kris Domeij, of 2nd Ranger Battalion, made national headlines as the most deployed Ranger to die in the war on terror. He was killed in action on his 14th combat deployment.

JUNE 2011
"SOMEWHERE IN AFGHANISTAN"

My platoon left the village under the cover of darkness. My squad was in charge of escorting the detainee to the HLZ. Although it was night, it felt just as hot as it would be during the day. We had marched about ten kilometers to reach the village and then we had to move another two kilometers to our HLZ to be picked up. As I scanned the landscape through my NODs I couldn't help but think to myself, this country and these people are so similar to my homeland - Diné Bikéyah, the Navajo Reservation.

I quickly caught myself and stopped thinking of home and focused on pulling security and scanning for the enemy. I began to run scenarios in my head; what if we take contact from the hill, looking for good cover, a rock, a dip in the ground. I looked at where my team leader moved, his signals, and if I had to I adjust with the formation, remaining vigilant at all times ready to pounce at a moment's notice. While walking I saw multiple giant holes, at least six by six and about twenty feet deep. I pointed my IR laser at them to show the trailing squad that there were enormous holes in the ground. As we reached the HLZ, the detainee began acting disgruntled, trying to break free, even yelling for help. *Shut that guy up* I thought to myself. The new guy was unsure how to handle the situation, so I quickly ran over to the detainee, grabbed him and cupped my left hand over his mouth as he began to yell. The yelling was then muffled; somehow through his facemask he grabbed hold of my pinky finger with his teeth.

With the detainee biting down on my pinky, the intense pain quickly turned into a furious rage. I raised my right hand and begin to unleash fury with my hard knuckled gloves. He stopped biting and attempted to go into the fetal position. My team leader and the senior gun team leader had to yank me off of him telling me he wasn't resisting anymore, and that the situation has been handled. "Roger that," I replied. This may seem harsh, but war is not for the faint or weak of heart. This was a bad man, and he had just attacked me. It wasn't uncommon for detainees to attack us, even reaching for our weapons at times. We had to show that we meant business; history has shown time and again, that if the tables were flipped, they would not be as kind as us.

Afterwards, we moved into position to be picked up. While waiting for the Chinook, the first rays of dawn appeared above the horizon. While in the prone position, I prayed with the dirt to the holy ones, thanking them for watching over me tonight. Off in the distance the sound of rotors from a Chinook was heard, a sound which still brings comfort to me. Putting my goggles on, I readied myself for the Chinook's landing. A "brown out" occurred as the Chinook landed to extract us, kicking up dirt and rocks in our faces. We moved to our feet, sprinted through the fog of dust to the "bird" while being barely able to see the person in front of us. I grabbed hold of a shoulder in front of me until we were aboard the bird. It all happened so fast, the bird touched the ground, the Rangers ran aboard, and then the bird was off again - less than a minute. I sat back with ease on the hard floor of the Chinook and watched the sun rise in the Afghan sky. Today was a good day.

Not long after returning from the mission, we were back in the ready room. I took off the five-pound helmet and removed the eighty-pound body armor; it's such a great feeling of relief. While cleaning our weapons and preparing equipment for the next mission, which could happen at any minute, the Alpha and Bravo Team leaders competitively argue on whose team is better. My team leader finally said, "Norcross had to step in and bust some Navajo skills because your boy couldn't handle the detainee . . .just shows . . .Alpha Team is better." Which brought the next question, "Why did you go all out on that guy?" "He bit my pinky," I said. He replied, "What the fuck!

If you would have told me that out there, I would have let you throw a few more punches in, SHIT! I may have even helped you!" We all laughed it off, and kept preparing our equipment.

After an hour had passed by, we were heading back to our rooms when our squad leader told us to head back to the ready room. Another mission. We quickly ran back in and received the mission brief. I then strapped the dusty eighty-pound body armor back on, clipped on my sweaty helmet, inserted a magazine in my faded camouflage M-4, and boarded the Stryker for the mission. I remember telling myself, *this is the life for me.*

This was my third deployment with 1st Battalion, 75th Ranger Regiment. I had one deployment to Iraq and two deployments to Afghanistan between 2008 and 2012. I am Full-blooded Diné (Navajo Indian). My clans are Kinl'ichii'nii (Red house People Clan), nishłį, Kiyaa'aanii (The Towering House Clan), báshíshchíín, Ashiihi (Salt People Clan), dashicheii doo Ashiihi (Salt People Clan), and dashinalí. I don't think anyone knew that I carried a Tádídíín pouch (corn pollen) with me. Nor do I think anyone ever saw me bless myself and pray; it's very sacred in Navajo Culture and used in many ceremonies. If Tádídíín is not accessible then ash is to be used to pray with. If that is not available, then dirt is to be used. I remember on my first deployment I did not have Tádídíín, so I was praying with dirt. Someone came up to me and asked, "What are you doing with that dirt?" "Praying," I said. "Praying with dirt? How does that help?" I honestly did not want to have a full-blown conversation with him so I said, "Mother Earth." "OH! I know what you mean, that's pretty cool."

-LEOPOLD
1/75

JULY 2011
"A MEDAL OF HONOR"

On July 12th, 2011, Sergeant First Class Leroy Petry of 2nd Battalion, 75th Ranger Regiment became only the second living service member of the war on terror to receive the Medal of Honor. SFC Petry received the nation's highest award for actions he took in Afghanistan in 2008.

His Medal of Honor citation is as follows:

For conspicuous gallantry and intrepidity at the risk of his life above and beyond the call of duty: Staff Sergeant Leroy A. Petry distinguished himself by acts of gallantry and intrepidity at the risk of his life above and beyond the call of duty in action with an armed enemy in the vicinity of Paktya Province, Afghanistan, on May 26, 2008. As a Weapons Squad Leader with D Company, 2nd Battalion, 75th Ranger Regiment, Staff Sergeant Petry moved to clear the courtyard of a house that potentially contained high-value combatants. While crossing the courtyard, Staff Sergeant Petry and another Ranger were engaged and wounded by automatic weapons fire from enemy fighters. Still under enemy fire, and wounded in both legs, Staff Sergeant Petry led the other Ranger to cover. He then reported the situation and engaged the enemy with a hand grenade, providing suppression as another Ranger moved to his position. The enemy quickly responded by maneuvering closer and throwing grenades. The first grenade explosion knocked his two fellow Rangers to the ground and wounded both with shrapnel. A second grenade then landed only a few feet away from them. Instantly realizing the danger, Staff Sergeant Petry unhesitatingly and with complete disregard for his safety, deliberately and selflessly moved forward, picked up the grenade, and in an effort to clear the immediate threat, threw the grenade away from his fellow Rangers. As he was releasing the grenade it detonated, amputating his right hand at the wrist and further injuring him with multiple shrapnel wounds. Although picking up and throwing the live grenade grievously wounded Staff Sergeant Petry, his gallant act undeniably saved his fellow Rangers from being severely wounded or killed. Despite the severity of his wounds, Staff Sergeant Petry continued to maintain the presence of mind to place a tourniquet on his right wrist before communicating the situation by radio in order to coordinate support for himself and his fellow wounded Rangers. Staff Sergeant Petry's extraordinary heroism and devotion to duty are in keeping with the highest traditions of military service, and reflect great credit upon himself, 75th Ranger Regiment, and the United States Army.

July 2011
"On Top of the Hill"

Sixteen hours in and the missiles were still coming in with a vengeance from the east. Perched atop the best vantage point in the valley, my head touched 10,000 feet and my lungs felt every inch of it. Most of us doubled over, some with exhaustion, some with mountain sickness, and practically everyone found the ground with their asses and their backs. When we started this mission, we were nocturnal creatures, sharpened by the darkness and the repetition, but now the backs of our necks and fists baked as the sun cut right through the thinning air. Had it not been for the artillery engulfing the valley below, we would have been completely out of our element.

To the south and west, our brothers fought and maneuvered around shanties of Taliban trainees. Their rounds cracked and whizzed over our heads and nearly demanded our concern, but we were too deep in this now, too near dehydration and exhaustion to waste precious energy putting a helmet back on and finding solid cover. Most of us had just finished working for this viewpoint and were enjoying our 1200 calories of processed astronaut food, the first we'd had in ten hours of sustained contact and miles of brutal terrain. Nothing short of a screaming mortar was moving these guys; we were digging in and recharging for another long night.

Nobody ever sees these days coming. I checked my watch and noted that typically my schedule dictated the next 90 minutes be spent in the gym, improving my fitness and my physique, and not on this goddamned hilltop almost two miles above sea level. This was too close to heaven for any Ranger to spend a day fighting. But here I was, next to the rest of them, rationing sips of water and squeezing chemically stabilized cheese directly into my mouth.

Last night was easy. There were only twenty-some odd fighters camping out in a cave that was probably as old as the Bible. We would drop some munitions, search the bodies, throw some chemlights and call it a night. Head back for chow and sleep as long as the air-conditioning held up. But last night became today and twenty-some odd hours became a hundred. Last night, I didn't need to save anything. Today, I couldn't afford to.

I watched the commander, leaning against the most authoritative rock he could find, talking to the voices inside of his Peltors. *Cleared to engage to phase line gold. Understood fuel bingo in fifteen mikes. Tracking all.* When Newton stated that every action had an equal and opposite reaction, he clearly hadn't anticipated the mind-bending speed at which war could travel. An obtuse flex of the thumb, air passing through vocal cords, reverberations captured in a microphone, invisible radio frequencies; these were the actions whose *re*action would be a 500 pound bomb humming along a laser guided track onto a hut made of sticks and mud. Afghanistan: the only place on Mother Earth where mountains worthy of postcards and ski resorts see more HIMARS rockets than beer lodges.

I leaned my head back and allowed myself to consider how abysmal the enemy's chances were of surviving the night. There were piles of dead bodies scattered throughout the valley and we were grumbling about the farmer's tan we were getting. This was more of a janitorial effort than a fight. We would be pushing semi-automatic brooms and open-bolt mops until higher told us the place looked clean.

The time passed, albeit slowly, and eventually, the fellows from 3rd Platoon heaved and gasped their way to the peak, less exasperated by the ten or so Taliban they had just butchered than the climb up that damned hill. Finally afforded *their* chance to rest: they happily claimed *their* 1200 calories, and *their* asses found the hilltop beneath them. Now we were one big, happy perimeter of valiant gunman, satiated by the bloodshed and tearing at airtight packages of mechanically separated chicken patties. A few took naps, soothed by the melodic percussion of explosions and the softness of the dirt beneath them, while others nervously scanned the hillside for possible reinforcements. The reinforcements weren't coming, but the night sure as hell was, creeping into the valley like the brackish water from the swamps of Fort Benning.

The hill was quiet and the mood solemn. It was becoming increasingly realistic that we were spending the coming nightfall in this valley. Nobody had slept, and nobody would. Not until this was over.

Suddenly, the platoon sergeants lumbered over with new orders, and the men of 1st Ranger Battalion steadily found their feet, undoubtedly swollen and sore. A few enemy stragglers were spotted running west, away from the valley, and the attack helicopters cut them down like stalks of Bermuda grass. The empty shells fell and echoed through the valley, conjuring the pitch and ring of church bells. It was a welcoming sound, but there was no church here. This land was not of God. This land was of the camouflaged juggernauts of the infantry. Afflicted by the miserable conditions, but in no way discouraged by the fighting, we shouldered our rifles and steadied our pace, preparing to spend the ensuing hours of darkness hunting, fixing, and finishing whatever was left in this valley to kill.

-BRYAN RIPPEE
1/75

A RANGER GOLD STAR MOTHER'S PERSPECTIVE

Dedicated to my daughter-in-love Sarah,
Kristoffer's daughters, Mikajsa, and Aalijah,
and the sacrifices of every Ranger, past, present and future.

I'll never forget my gut reaction when two planes slammed into the Twin Towers on 9/11. *We're at war. Oh no, my son is going to war. Our world changed today and will never be the same.*

My firstborn son, Kristoffer Bryan Domeij, had joined the Army in the summer of 2000 after graduating high school. When President Bush declared war on terror the next fall, knowing my son was still in Ranger training and would not immediately deploy brought me much relief.

The feelings from my teen years during the Vietnam War flooded back as I remembered how conflicted I was about the political wrangling, the anti-war movement and the treatment of returning heroes.

When my teenage patriot expressed interest in becoming a Navy SEAL, I interviewed an ex-SEAL at my work and reported to Kristoffer, "Lucky for you, I made you finish out that semester on the swim team when you wanted to quit. So . . . just how long can you hold your breath underwater these days?" In my home, I enforced only one extracurricular activity rule: Start anything you want. If you hate it, don't whine to quit. Mom's not negotiable; you will finish your commitment.

I researched the different branches' special operations forces and suggested Kristoffer consider the Air Force's Special Operations who rescue downed pilots. In my limited understanding of the military, which was nil, I figured the Air Force fights from a distance so my son would be less at risk.

The only branch of the military that I told Kristoffer I wasn't willing to compromise on were the Marines and I wasn't too thrilled about the Army, either. Olive green is just not one of my favorite colors. Kristoffer talked at length with his best friend's father, a former Special Forces Vietnam veteran, only further cementing his determination to join the Army Rangers.

When Kristoffer was seventeen, he asked his father, a Canadian, to sign permission paperwork for him to join the Army. When his dad said, "No," Kristoffer turned his charm and negotiation skills on mom. His intense patriotism reminded me of my young adult passion for my country, the United States. Kristoffer's willingness to sign away his dual citizenship surprised me. My response to his request?

"No. I can't do that." What I didn't share with my son?

If you're killed, I'll feel guilty.

I was also bothered that GI meant 'government issue' and my son was *my* son, *not* Government Issue. I shared my preference for his next step after high school graduation, "I wish you'd attend college," and added, "If you choose to join the Army when you're 18, I'll support you 3000 percent." But in my heart I hoped he'd choose college, not the Army.

Kristoffer's response? "I'm tired of studying. I'm tired of people telling me to clean my room. I'm tired of people telling me what to do."

I thought, *and you want to join the Army?*

"I want to jump out of planes and blow up stuff." As the Army's first qualified Joint Terminal Attack Controller (JTAC) evaluator, he certainly accomplished those goals. After Kristoffer's first deployment, he remarked, "I never expected us to go to war, Mom."

That's exactly why I didn't want you to join the military. As long as I can remember, we've always been involved in a 'conflict' somewhere.

Comments from both a chaplain and a general caused me to ponder. "You raised a warrior. Not everyone can raise a warrior."

How did I miss my son was born a warrior?

WHO WILL PROTECT US?

When Kristoffer was three years old, I was propelled into single parenthood. We moved into an apartment infested with creepy crawlers. One evening I walked into the bathroom and terror paralyzed every muscle in my body, except for my vocal chords. Arachnophobia, coupled with emotional brokenness, produced a shriek that probably sounded as if I was being raped.

Kristoffer rushed in. "What's wrong, Mommy?" Frozen, I pointed at a huge spider. My preschooler said, "I'll kill it for you, Mommy." His protective nature and courage stirred my mother's heart with pride.

My estrogen-drenched brain tried to nurture both my sons, Kristoffer and Kyle, into gentlemen of honor. Determined that my firstborn would never eat sugar or play with toy guns, I soon realized I'd lost both battles.

Kristoffer chewed toast into hand guns, wielded plastic Lego guns created from his imagination, drew pictures of planes and tanks, brandished kitchen knives as swords, and charged forward with his toilet plunger machine gun, proving my vast misunderstanding of testosterone.

Kristoffer and his brother, Kyle, loved watching *The A-Team* television series and then re-enacting the ex-United States Army Special Forces characters' stunts. Their pointer fingers aimed and fired, as their undulating thumbs pew-ow, pew-ow, pew-owed. Their arms liberated, simulating imaginary artillery and machine guns as they shot around the war zone, my apartment, rata-tat-ing and urh-urh-urh-urh-urh-ing.

But when they began parachuting off the top of my seven-foot tall entertainment center, I enforced my first TV parental control, "No more A-Team." And if this *Downton Abbey* gal never, ever sees another *Star Wars* movie or *Star Trek* episode, I will die happy.

In elementary school, my friends suggested that perhaps Kristoffer might have ADD, because of his high energy level and risk taking without seeming understanding of the physical consequences. Whether Kristoffer flew around on roller blades or his skateboard or sprinted across the roof of our home chasing bad guys, he seemed to lack any concern or fear for his safety.

One afternoon Kristoffer burst through the door. "Mom, John said he's gonna kill me with his dad's gun." My stomach flip-flopped. My knees turned to mush hearing my son's latest neighborhood bully report. Displaced from our safe, upscale neighborhood in Orange County, California to HUD housing near gang territory, I never felt safe. With no man to protect us, I let God know my fears. *Who will protect us?*

My just-walk-away-from-a-fight or how-to-deal-with-a-bully-speech sounded hollow. I did not understand the rules of this testosterone-drenched neighborhood. As a child, I was a tomboy, but Kristoffer's confrontational spirit mystified me. Talking to John's alcoholic, rough-looking father, who leered at my body, terrified me. I wanted to lock my two sons in our apartment and never *ever* let them play outside again.

After moving to a safe neighborhood in Colorado, a tough-talking military dad marched up to me and pointed to Kristoffer. "Who is this boy's dad?"

"I am!" Surprised by my strong response to such an intimidating man, I hurled back, "What do you want?" His whiner junior high son hid behind him. Everyone—except apparently his dad—knew Bully Boy tormented the little kids in the neighborhood.

"Your son . . ." Mr. Army Dad's gruff voice angered me.

"And your son, sir, rides around the neighborhood dispensing foul, disgusting language on the little kids via that little voice box on his bike."

Mr. Army Man swung around and marched his son home.

With an air of triumph and to my embarrassment, Kristoffer said loud enough for that dad to hear, "Way to go, Mom!" I discussed with Kristoffer the importance of not further aggravating a tense situation and humility.

WARRIOR-IN-TRAINING

In junior high, bullies accosted Kristoffer, so I enrolled him in karate. Kristoffer's moves appeared quite impressive. His arms and legs flung and flailed attacking make-believe aggressors. I drew fire from self-righteous, religious parents, when I gave Kristoffer permission to handle bullies. "Do not throw the first punch, but make sure you end it."

Kristoffer loved to camp out in the backyard in a tent, smear his handsome features with camouflage face paint, eat MREs, and attend events at the military bases in Colorado Springs where he climbed on tanks and pretended to drive jeeps and shoot machine guns.

I frequented thrift stores and garage sales, dragging the boys along. The first thing Kristoffer bought at the first garage sale we stopped at? A Navy aircraft carrier about two feet wide, two feet tall and seven feet long. He spent hours flying his planes over and around that ship and simulating explosion noises.

I purchased Army and Air Force jackets and cut off the beautiful, expensive-looking metal buttons to sew on my designer-label blazers. Kristoffer bought Army patches, lapel pins and BDUs. He marched off to junior high wearing an elegant Gucci-styled, double-breasted, full-length genuine wool Army winter dress coat that he discovered at Goodwill along with his Doc Martin-styled black leather Army boots. He also loved wearing his military-styled volunteer shirt for the Manitou Springs fire department, where he hung out with the firefighters on Tuesday nights, worked controlled burns and walked door-to-door checking on people after a flash flood.

Besides trying to relate to my sons as males, it was important to me to pass on the same spiritual legacy my father left to me. As a single mother, I relied on God to be my husband, provider, and protector. Sometimes, it seemed as if what I studied in the Bible offered little practical application to parenting my gregarious sons. How did ancient battles, blood sacrifices, circumcision, and crucifixion apply to the parenting challenges I faced? I asked God, *How do I apply biblical principles to raising sons?* The story in 1 Samuel regarding Eli, a priest, and the failures of his scoundrel sons hit me hard. God judged Eli because he "failed to restrain his sons." So I asked God, "Show me how to train my sons."

One day, Kristoffer came to me. "Here, Mommy, I found your [fake] fingernail."

"Thank you son for finding mommy's fingernail. Please put it in my hand."

"I'll put your fingernail on the dresser."

My normal response before asking God for wisdom? "Thank you so much for being a good helper. You are such a wonderful son."

However, my study in Judges 1:1-36 came to mind regarding the first battle for the Promised Land. God's people asked God, "Who will lead us in the battle against the Canaanites?"

God's order of battle? "Judah will go. I've given the land to him." Judah disobeyed God's orders when Judah turned to Simeon and said, "Fight with me." Judah fought a good fight, but failed to trust Jehovah's battle plan and promise to win the land.

Partial obedience is disobedience.

The outcome of Judah's partial obedience by deviating from God's orders? Failure to conquer the land. If Kristoffer could not obey me, he would not learn how to obey God or man. I looked Kristoffer in his charming, beautiful blue eyes.

"Kristoffer, put the fingernail in my hand."

"I'll put it on the chest, Mommy."

"Kristoffer, put the fingernail in my hand."

He slammed the fingernail into my palm. As he stormed out of the room, I prayed, "Well, God, I could use some help on how to influence Kristoffer to adjust his attitude."

After every Bible study class, I picked Kristoffer up from child-care and asked, "Guess what I learned about God today?"

My excitement stirred Kristoffer's curiosity. "What, Mommy? Tell me." He listened as I distilled God's truths from that day's lesson down to child's language.

Kristoffer challenged me with theological questions. "Mommy, who is the Holy Spirit? What does the Holy Spirit look like?"

"The Holy Spirit is God's special helper. He's like the wind. Can you see the wind, Kristoffer?

"No. I feel it."

"That's right. When the wind blows, you can feel and hear it. The Holy Spirit is like the wind. Sometimes you can feel Him. He also talks inside of you. When you choose to play with Mommy's TV, is there something that tells you 'No'?"

"Yes, Mommy."

"That, Kristoffer, is the Holy Spirit."

I wanted my sons to learn that failure is success in disguise. I never allowed two sayings in my home: "I don't know how" and "I can't." I taught the boys to say, "I'll try." I didn't care if they failed, but I expected them to try. Soon after Kristoffer started training men, I reminded him about those banned words. With passion, he replied, "Yea, that used to make me so mad when you said that."

Ten minutes later, Kristoffer expressed frustration about his trainees. "It makes me so mad when my guys say, "I don't know how" or "I can't."

I laughed and thought, *Oh really?*

THE ALIEN NATION

From the beginning, the military seemed like their own alien nation to me. My first interface with anyone in the military occurred when we moved from southern California to Colorado Springs. A colonel and lieutenant colonel in the Air Force invited me to a party. I apologized for being late because I couldn't find the apartment. I guessed the number '1530' printed on the invitation was the address, only to learn that 1530 is military time for 3:30 pm.

Military conventions mystified me. I purchased colorful Army, Navy and Air Force patches at an Army-Navy store to sew on a winter bomber jacket I sewed for Kristoffer.

As a veteran accepted the money for the mix-and-match military patches, Mr. Army-Navy man scolded, "You can't sew patches from every branch of the military on one coat."

"Why not? The colors match. I love the designs."

Scarlet flushed from his Adam's apple to his forehead. I turned to flit out the door with my matchy-patchys and his tongue lashed out. "You can't do that." I didn't know if that Vet was exhibiting a conniption fit or suffering distress from a Vietnam-related PTSD panic attack.

When I attended my first Air Force officer promotion ceremony, I observed everyone in uniform perform like marionettes on a string. I asked, "Why did everyone leap to their feet with their thumbs turned backwards?"

"A general entered the room, Ma'am."

The only thing I knew for sure about the Army and advised my son about? "Don't sign the contract unless it contains everything you want." Kristoffer attended a recruiting event. It came time to sign the contract and Kristoffer discovered the recruiter failed to include the Ranger Indoctrination Program (RIP). He employed the garage sale negotiation skills I taught him. "Well, I guess you just wasted your time. I'm not going to sign that contract." And he didn't until the recruiter added RIP.

Boot camp transformed a pudgy high school football jock into a slimmer, better-postured, proud soldier. But RIP, well, it ripped his body. I phoned my mom. "You can't believe his body, Mom. He's a hard body."

Kristoffer recoiled at my motherly observation. "Gross. That is so gross!"

I'd researched the physical training part of RIP and the requirements sounded awful. After completing a long grueling run, Kristoffer called. "Mom, I made it!"

Of course, I was proud of him and told him so, but I also inquired, "Why did you run all the way?"

"I ran and made it with only seven seconds left, Mom."

Those seven seconds changed the trajectory of Kristoffer's military career.

When my son joined the Army, I worried about my son's relationship with God. That's a mother's job. In basic training, I received a letter that made me laugh. Kristoffer decided to attend church, because staying in the barracks meant cleaning the latrines with a toothbrush. *Doesn't God work in miraculous ways?*

I can't say that I knew one iota about the Army Rangers. In a parent orientation at Fort Benning during RIP graduation weekend, I raised my hand. "Are there any women in the Rangers?" If looks could kill, I'd have been incinerated on the spot.

I sensed camaraderie among the men in that room, but had no clue what forged their fellowship. When I walked outside of that building, I stopped to read the names of fallen Rangers carved on a wooden slat fence.

I never want my son's name on that wall.

The day I finally received the dreaded letter informing me that my 'highly-trained' son was being deployed for Operation Enduring Freedom, one tidbit of information surprised me. "We can't tell you where we're sending your son."

What?! Take my firstborn son and not tell me where he is?
I will find him.

Three days after digging deep into the Internet following links on English-speaking Pakistani and Afghani websites, I emailed my son, "I think you are fighting in these mountains and you're stationed at this airbase."

Kristoffer told his commander my conclusions and his commander demanded to know how I knew these details.

My son said, "My mom's smart."

I was never quite sure what to write to Kristoffer while deployed. Compared to Kristoffer's adrenalized adventures, I figured my life seemed pretty dull. During the Cold War, I'd traveled with a missionary singing group behind the Iron Curtain. Compared to the West, the harsh living conditions, toilets and toilet paper came as a shock. I certainly didn't want to whine about frustrations about silly American extravagances.

Kristoffer said the best and funniest packet I ever sent included news articles and all the crazy comments regarding a strict vice principal at Rancho Bernardo High School accused of conducting an underwear inspection of boys and girls attending a school dance to "ensure appropriate school dress." Female thong–wearers were sent home to change into 'appropriate' underwear.

I also emailed Bible stories that occurred in Iraq. Since I love history and archeology, I wrote, "Please don't shoot at or blow up any archeological sites." Probably not on a warrior's top ten list of targets.

When U.S. tanks rolled into Baghdad and the looting began, my interest in archeology and my mothering instincts accelerated into high gear. Frustrated by angry, looting mobs shattering cases, breaking 2000-year-old statues, and stealing valuable artifacts from the National Museum, I joked with my friends. *It's time for the moms of*

America to take charge, smack some hands and tell looters to go to their rooms until they can behave and say, "I'm sorry."

Before the Iraq invasion, Kristoffer called. I'd surmised from President Bush's saber-rattling rhetoric, that an invasion of Iraq was imminent. To confirm my suspicions and Kristoffer's whereabouts, I asked, "How's the weather?"

"It's 87 degrees." Then he complained about the grit in his computer.

The same temperature as Baghdad. He's supposed to be in Afghanistan.

We hung up and I Googled the weather in Afghanistan. The high? Forty-seven degrees. By this time, I'd researched online that Army Rangers capture airports before a war begins. So I imagined Kristoffer somewhere in northern Kurdish Iraq sitting on the tarmac of a Ranger-seized airport talking to me on a satellite phone.

Kristoffer also phoned his dad. "Your mom thinks you're in Iraq." I've since found out Kristoffer was waiting in Kuwait. At least, I was right about the weather, the sand and the geographic proximity.

The next time I asked Kristoffer, "So how's the weather?"

His terse, to-the-point response? "I can't tell you that," as if the weather had become a national security secret.

So I replied, "Okay, just tell me your longitude and latitude and I'll be fine."

"I can't do that." Little did I know that longitude and latitude played a huge role in my son's job as a forward observer and a JTAC. In one of my searches to track down where Kristoffer was deployed, I even punched the call back button to obtain his phone number, but received some whacky message about the number being redirected through Hawaii.

After six or seven deployments, I lost my obsession to figure out where he was. We had our code: 'A' or 'I.' Kristoffer also assured me that the Rangers had the best equipment, best training, and was the safest place to serve in the military. He kinda failed to mention how many Rangers had already been killed in action. Yet, with every deployment, from the first until his thirteenth, I lived in a heightened state of stress. I only breathed without anxiety when he returned home—*safe.*

Deployment and My Hardest Battle

It's one thing to say, "I trust God."

It's another to entrust the warrior-child God wove together in my womb into God's hands when my government declares wars or conflicts, and repeatedly deploys soldiers to carry out dangerous missions to capture terrorists who annihilate people for whatever bizarre reasons motivate their unadulterated mayhem.

Labeled a lioness single mom by friends, I instinctively yearned to protect my risk-taker cub, even though he'd grown into a full-fledged lion with impressive skills to take care of himself and others.

The hardest thing for me, the mother of a soldier?

Releasing my son to God. My constant struggle was a seesaw between, *"I hope he doesn't die"* to *"God, I entrust him to your care."* Without question, deployments ramped up my prayer life, giving new meaning to 1 Thessalonians 5:17: *"Pray without ceasing."*

I'll never forget one particular email from Kristoffer while deployed. "Had a bad night, Mom. Will call you tomorrow. Don't ask questions."

The first words out of my mouth when he called? "Are you wounded?"

"No."

But I would soon discover he was wounded—emotionally.

At the beginning of the war, I'd subscribed to the Department of Defense (DoD) email announcing every death so I could pray for the families. At a certain point, I unsubscribed. I found it too painful to read about another death of a baby-faced soldier. After Kristoffer and I hung up, I logged on to the DoD website to read the killed in action list. I found an entry about an Army Ranger. I copied and pasted the press release into an email and clicked 'send.'

Kristoffer hit reply. "You got it, Mom."

I found out Kristoffer's deployment return date and booked a flight to Seattle. I wanted to be available, in case he needed comfort or to vent. As we waited for the plane to arrive, I cornered someone in charge to address the elephant in the room, the Ranger who'd been killed in Iraq. "When a Ranger is killed, do you get counseling for these young men?"

"Death, Ma'am, it's just business, it's just business. They can talk to a chaplain, if they want." I wanted to slap that man's stupid face off.

I worried about PTSD. I'd witnessed the effects of PTSD on Vietnam Vets and even worked for a man who'd served in the Special Forces. I never knew which bizarre personality would show up for work each day. My heart hurt for a brilliant man who'd sacrificed and served with such courage, but for whatever reasons, could not bring himself to acknowledge or seek out help.

Extreme trauma cannot be dealt with in a couple of conversations with a chaplain. And it angered me thinking the Army refused to address the issue, especially after Vietnam. I'm no dumb-dumb. I wondered if processing trauma or grief with a counselor hurt a Ranger's career. When I discussed the military suicide rate with a multiple-starred general, he said, "Yes, the DoD was taken by surprise."

That night Kristoffer wanted burritos at Taco Bell. I asked Kristoffer if he wanted to talk about the night PFC Nathan E. Stahl was killed. Kristoffer told me about driving the lead Humvee and how Nathan rode in the second Humvee when the IED exploded. My son shared his response to the horror of that night. I'll never forget the look of pain that crossed Kristoffer's face and pierced my heart. "There was so much blood. I can't talk about it, Mom." So I respected his wishes.

Kristoffer knew the risks of his job. My son went above and beyond for his country, his family *and every American*. My son appeared tough on the outside, but harbored a tender heart on the inside.

My tender warrior loved fighting for his country, but he loved his family even more. He deliberated long and hard before buying an engagement ring and asking Sarah to marry him, because he never wanted to inflict the pain of his death on her.

He called to tell me his plans to ask Sarah to marry him and then on Monday, May 28, 2007, at 8:49 am, he sent an email to family and friends with this subject line: I popped the "Q." Message: "I just wanted to tell family and friends that two nights ago I dropped down on one knee and asked Sarah to marry me. She said yes."

After their wedding ceremony, everyone celebrated at a BBQ. The women discussed breastfeeding on the right side of the deck. The Rangers drank, told stories, and laughed on the left side of the deck. Kristoffer never talked about his job and I'd only discovered Kristoffer received a promotion by Googling his name. So this was my chance to find out what he did while deployed. I pulled my chair to the middle of the deck, pretending like I was listening to the women, but I was really tuned into the Rangers' conversation.

Kristoffer shot me a move-back-to-the-women's-side-of-the-deck look. No way! Here was my chance. Hearing their war stories actually relieved some of my stress about his deployments, because my imagination was far wilder than their stories.

During my son's fourteenth deployment, for the first time, I felt relaxed, confident that he'd return home safe. I found out later that my daughter-in-love told her mom, "I have a bad feeling about this deployment." Instead of going out on dangerous missions, it was my understanding that Kristoffer was to stay in the Star Wars room to oversee the operations.

But on that fateful night, the mission was two men short.

MY WORST FEAR REALIZED

The peace and calm of the ordinary life I enjoyed about-faced on Friday, October 21st at 11:30 pm. "Who's knocking on my door?" I spoke aloud. My surprise at the sudden banging on my front door near midnight gave way to annoyance. "Probably someone with car trouble. If I ignore the knocking they'll go away."

The insistent pounding on my door continued for fifteen minutes. I finally walked down my stairs and opened the door. Two tall men in military uniforms stood on my front steps. Without asking, I knew.

"Is my son dead?"

"May we come in, Ma'am?"

Dreading their confirmation, I repeated, "Is my son dead?"

"May we come in, Ma'am?"

They followed me up my stairs and told me 'the news.' My son died, killed by an IED—an improvised explosive device—in Afghanistan on October 22nd. Bizarre, because it was still October 21st in Colorado. I asked where, but quickly forgot the name of the district. I leaned against the kind chaplain and he prayed for me. Now all I wanted was for them to leave, so I could process the explosion that had just blown up inside my brain.

"You can leave."

"Do you have someone you can call?"

"I'll be fine. I'm a single mom. I've been to hell and back. You can leave, I'll be fine." They refused to depart until I called a friend. I dialed a close friend's number and cried these horrible words, "Kristoffer's dead."

Rob and Beth drove right over. My worst, heart-crushing fear had just come true: My firstborn son . . . dead on his 14th special operations deployment. The first decision that I had to make? *Do I*

427

call Kristoffer's brother tonight? Or let Kyle get a good night's sleep? I wanted to fly to California and hold him.

Worst. Call. Of. My. Life.

After everyone left, adrenaline surged through my veins. My body shivered beneath twelve inches of two down comforters. Spasms jolted my muscles. My mind heard my heart thumping and these oddly comforting words. *"God numbers our days."* (Psalm 139:16)

All my fears about Kristoffer's emotional wounds from the past, concerns about PTSD, and my anxiety about future deployments dissipated. My son was alive, healed, whole, safe and protected in the presence of The Lord of Hosts, *Jehovah Tz'vaot*, The Commanding General over heaven and earth—and over *every* earthly and heavenly army.

Kristoffer's death in Afghanistan—however shocking to me— did not take *Jehovah*, Who Is, Who Was, and Who Is to Come, by surprise. My daughter-in-love posted this note on Facebook on October 24th, 2011: "The peace of God, which transcends under-standing, will guard your hearts and your minds in Christ Jesus.' Philippians 4:7."

> *"There is a part of the sea known as 'the cushion of the sea.' It lies beneath the surface that is agitated by storms and churned by the wind. It is so deep that it is part of the sea that is never stirred. When the ocean floor in these deep places is dredged of the remains of plant or animal life, it re-veals evidence of having remained completely undisturbed for hundreds, if not thousands of years."*

> *"'The peace of God is an eternal calm like the cushion of the sea. It lies so deeply within the human heart that no external difficulty or disturbance can reach it. Anyone who enters the presence of God becomes a partaker of that undisturbed and undisturbable calm,' Arthur Tappan Pierson."*

"I find comfort knowing that Kris is now with Jesus and his dad. I am trying to take each day and each moment as it comes and there are some really hard days to come but I am so thankful to everyone for all the love and support and prayers . . . but mostly to have peace that passes my understanding . . . knowing that God is good and that he has a plan for us. I pray you all too, can have comfort in Jesus. The Lord gave, and the Lord has taken away, Blessed be the name of the Lord,' Job 21:1."

The Army assigned me a casualty assistance officer (CAO) who showed up at my home early Saturday morning—nine hours after receiving 'the news.' I nicknamed him Sergeant Angel, because he was my on-call guardian angel who walked me through reams of paperwork, the funeral, and more paperwork. Beth came over and when my friend, Michelle, heard 'the news,' she didn't ask, she drove over and oversaw everything in my household that day.

I flew to Dover Air Force base, the morgue Air Force base that receives America's war dead and prepares them for burial. When I read my ticket and learned I was changing planes in that maze of terminals at Chicago's O-Hell Airport, I panicked. But people from the USO met me at every point on my trip. Between flying and crying, my shocked, dehydrated body felt no hunger. Before escorting me to my next plane, they fed me and made sure I was hydrated.

I met Army Ranger Charles, who accompanied Kristoffer's body back to the States. Two of Kristoffer's buddies, Jon and Jack, raced 90 mph on back roads from the DC area to arrive in time to honor Kristoffer's return. I asked Charles two questions. "Did you get the guy?"

"Yes."

"Did you flatten the place?"

"Yes."

Charles never left my son's side, even sleeping beside Kristoffer's casket on the journey home. In that one act, he touched my mother's heart deeply. The presence of these three men who knew Kristoffer provided strength and great comfort to me.

A dull, expressionless general from Washington delivered a mechanical script expressing the country's appreciation for Kristoffer's sacrifice. He flinched at my reply. "I'd have preferred you used a drone to drop a bomb and take out the Taliban commander's compound."

As shell-shocked, grieving families left Fisher House, another load checked in. The chaplain said they'd only planned on fifty deaths in 2011 and the toll was nearing 400. It was surreal watching a refrigerated coffin bearing my son's lifeless body move from the plane to the transport vehicle. As it pulled out of my sight and into the morgue, I longed to hug my son.

I needed more details from Charles. During the mission, he was on a headset and shared what he could. I can't even imagine the horror the Rangers experienced that night, because two other people also died and many others were wounded.

I agonized. *Did my son suffer?*

Charles' assurance that Kristoffer was spared any pain helped me from obsessing whether my son suffered or not. The explosion from the victim-activated IED was so powerful that Kristoffer felt nothing. I praised *El Shamayim*, The God of The Heavens, (Psalms 136:26) who whisked my son, healed and whole, away to heaven.

The target that night was a Pakistani Taliban commander with expertise as an IED maker. His booby-trapped compound contained bomb-making supplies awaiting assembly to explode and kill more people, mostly innocent Afghanis. This particular IED maker was very skilled. Most aren't. So capturing this guy was crucial to saving a lot of Afghani and American lives. I couldn't help think: *How did this Pakistani Taliban commander think that "loving your Afghani neighbor as yourself" includes blowing them up?*

Off and on over the coming months I wondered about the IED maker who I presumed was locked up in custody. *Who was he? What was his name? What about his family?* Every multi-starred General I met said, "If you need anything, let us know." I wanted to know the name of the man responsible for my son's death. I wished to meet Mr. Taliban Commander and tell him about Jesus. But I figured asking permission to visit Mr. IED in Afghanistan would never receive approval.

Somewhere I learned Mr. IED's code name, which my Teflon brain can't remember. But learning he'd been killed made me feel ill inside. His death was not satisfying. I wasn't pleased with Mr. IED's career choice, but did I hate him? No. I just kept thinking. *Did anyone ever tell him about God's heart of love toward him?*

I also wanted the longitude and latitude of the spot where my son died to look up on Google Earth. I wanted to see the spot that absorbed my son's lifeblood. It's strange that so many Afghanis and military personnel know the details of that apocalyptic night. But the family, who needs as much information as possible to help us process our heart's worst apocalypse, is redacted out of the information pool and left in the dark.

An older, mature Christian called me and read her journaling about that 'wicked horrible person who killed my son' thinking her diatribe would comfort me. It didn't. Another person thought I'd be comforted by his email condemning the war—NOT! How could that thoughtless and probably spineless idiot think I'd be comforted by political views that basically communicated—your son died in vain.

A media firestorm hit. My phone never stopped ringing. I'd answer what I thought was a business call, only to discover someone from the media wanting an interview about Kristoffer or requesting personal family pictures. As a proud mom, I felt muzzled. When a mom's child is killed, a mom needs to talk about their child. We just want everyone in the entire world to know how amazing our child is/was. Kristoffer had left orders not to talk to the media. He was just doing his job and didn't want any publicity.

I Googled Kristoffer's name and created a Google email alert. Media stories from around the world poured into my inbox. I clicked on every link and saved a PDF of every news story, until my Mac's hard drive blew up, destroying every photo I owned of Kristoffer.

As a writer, I joked that my son made the *Washington Post*, *Huffington Post*, the UK's *Daily Mail*, *Fox News* and other major networks before my writing did. His friend posted on Facebook: *Kris, you made national news . . . because you deserve national news. just wish they spelt your name right bud.*

Another comment posted on Kristoffer's Facebook wall revealed his notoriety: "They are talking about Kris in the Congress right now on CSPAN. A congressman used Kris as an example of how we need to not cut the military to retain and recruit the best in the military. Kris really is a hero in America."

Hand-written letters from generals, prototypical letters from congressmen and senators poured into my mailbox. My daughter-in-law received a hand-written note from George Bush, before we ever received letters from a more recent President that appeared signed by an automatic pen.

I received a thoughtful phone call from Senator Mark Udall. "How are you doing?" I was still flying high on shock and my faith in God. He hung up feeling inspired and promised to share my feedback regarding the budget crisis with President Obama to consider adding to his cabinet a single mom who doesn't have two nickels to rub together. We know how to juggle a monthly budget every month in a half or two and I can guarantee that single moms could identify where to cut government waste.

I'd never attended a military funeral. Sergeant Angel accompanied me and guided me every step of the way. My fried brain couldn't have navigated the trip without him. Having been a single mom for years, I was not used to anyone helping or serving me.

When Sergeant Angel drove me into the cemetery, the waving flags and Patriot Guards standing at attention awed me. I jumped out of the car and started snapping pictures. Three rows of Rangers stood at attention. I immediately loved every one of them.

Westboro Baptist church added additional, unnecessary and cruel stress to our grieving family. We worried whether the Westboro Baptist Church might find out the time and place of Kristoffer's funeral. I checked their website and kept track of their press releases and calls to protest.

But to be honest? I hoped Westboro would show up. Yep, Momma Lioness was ready to rumble. Daydreams of marching first in line as the Rangers Led the Way to confront the haters made me laugh. Kristoffer didn't come by his fighting spirit without a reason.

With tears in his eyes, one of Kristoffer's crusty commanders walked up to me. "Your son was the most stubborn man I've ever met." I was glad my son had given someone else a run for their money. Worried he'd offended me, he came back later. "No offense meant, Ma'am." I laughed so hard, because my son inherited that stubbornness from both his maternal and paternal sides of the family. I met so many wonderful Rangers that day. The moment they introduced themselves, every name slipped from my memory. Shock had Teflon-coated every shattered brain cell of my prefrontal cortex.

General Tony Thomas placed medals and a Gold Star pin in my hands. I didn't have a clue what was going on or what the pin or medals represented. My only regret? I wish I'd stayed in the viewing room to talk to my son longer, but I felt pressured thinking that others wanted to spend time with him, too. I needed my son to be buried with a tangible expression of my love. I carried a crystal angel that hung from my chandelier and slipped it in the pocket over my angel's heart.

The speakers and Chaplain Derek Murray's sermon were funny, honest, and touching. I was so thankful the Chaplain communicated a clear presentation of our family's faith. Meeting him made me so grateful that God had answered one specific prayer, to surround my son with godly influences. As a benediction, family members sang *Amazing Grace.*

After the service, I walked behind the hearse holding Mikajsa, Kristoffer's three-year-old daughter in my arms. She knew her father was in 'the box' and said, "Hurry, follow Daddy." I picked up my speed, and then noticed I'd charged ahead of General Thomas and Sarah. *That's probably not protocol.* My paced slowed to drop back in line. An Air Force plane conducted a fly over. We were handed our fallen warrior flags.

One pallbearer spoke with me at length. "Bearing your son's casket is the greatest honor of my military career. He was a great husband, a great father, a great American, a great warrior." What better tribute could a mom hear?

This Ranger didn't understand my strength. I shared my deep faith in God—in my weakness God makes me strong. Another man trained by my son was so deeply grieved he could barely share his story about my son. My heart left Seattle with a heart heavy with concern for Kristoffer's fellow Rangers.

When a soldier hurts, my heart aches. At Kristoffer's funeral, I walked past three rows of Rangers standing at attention and these words popped out of my mouth, "You are all my sons." And that's the way I feel. We're family, bonded by my son's death.

I contacted friends and asked them to please pray for the men grieving my son's death. I will never forget the pain in those Rangers' eyes. I suspected that many did not have the hope that anchors my soul or resources available to process their "It's just business, Ma'am" mourning.

Most Gold Star parents feel like I do, even though our children are dead, trust me, we're so happy for every soldier who returns alive, wounded or not. And we're here to listen or offer comfort to any of our children's buddies.

Another memorial service was planned in San Diego and the organizer booked a large auditorium, invited the press, plus important government officials to speak. I honored Kristoffer's request to avoid the media. The details of planning that memorial service are simply too traumatic to recount. Even though I was very grateful for everything that was done to organize that event, my grief perceived that the organizer did not want me to speak at my son's memorial service.

Thank God for Beth who stayed on phone standby awaiting my speed dials that week. I'd call, screaming from agony from dealing with people triggering deep pain. Beth allowed me to vent, talked me down off the ledge, and then helped me figure out how to best respond to some who wanted to silence my input at my son's memorial service and what my heart needed to share about my son with attendees. When the Chaplain and the Rangers showed up, I felt safe. They provided the rock-solid support I needed.

Kristoffer's high school also honored him that week before a football game. An honor guard marched onto the field, someone read Kristoffer's bio and everyone honored a moment of silence. I flipped the coin to decide which team got the ball, but flipped it behind my back.

A woman walked up to offer her condolences to me. I learned her husband, a Navy SEAL, was killed when a MH-47 helicopter was shot down by enemy fire, precipitating Operation Red Wings.

Kristoffer had participated in Operation Red Wings where his job as a JTAC played an integral role in that battle. He was also one of the Rangers that made it to the top of the mountain to recover the bodies of eight Navy SEALs and eight Army Night Stalkers.

Big war. Small world.

Big God. Common familial bond.

I prayed with her and wish I could remember her name.

I returned home to discover I was the neighborhood celebrity. My favorite neighbor worked to organize donations and volunteers to install a new roof and windows provided by volunteers who wanted to honor my son's sacrifice. After years of struggling as a single mom, I'd never seen or experienced this kind of generosity, caring or respect. I especially loved the screens on the windows. Kristoffer and Kyle preferred exiting out of windows in their youth, not the front door, and had broken or lost every screen in my home. Come summer, my new aluminum protectors would keep out unnerving wasps and bumblebees.

But dissent over a person who repeatedly obtained media attention without my consent to discuss our non-existent relationship almost propelled me over the edge. When I desperately needed solitude, my chest almost exploded as I refereed a heated neighborhood dispute, in addition to turning away the media knocking on my front door, calling my telephone or emailing me.

I was appalled when another Gold Star parent acted jealous and made stinging, hurtful comments to me because my son received so much media attention. In the midst of irrational grief responses wreaking havoc on my already-shredded feelings, thankfully, others stepped forward to offer support.

I felt overwhelmed by phone calls and dozens of emails from friends, family and acquaintances. Answering the same questions over and over exhausted me. I shut down, but communicated via Facebook to keep people updated, so they could pray. The prayers of friends, family, even strangers, buoyed my spirit.

A month after Kristoffer's funeral, I attended my first Gold Star Mom luncheon to be embraced by the most amazing and supportive women who understood my near heart-attack emotional pain.

The Tragedy Assistance Program for Survivors (TAPS) assigned a mentor from my Gold Star chapter to walk alongside me. Love my mentor, a volunteer "GI Granny" who works with the wounded warriors at Fort Carson. Nancy's wisdom, plus her example to reach out to encourage fellow survivors, helped me through many rough times and decisions.

After a few months my civilian friends moved on. What a relief to connect with people who shared in my journey. Early on, after meeting many other survivors, I decided that in remembering and honoring my son's sacrifice, I didn't want my entire identity to become Kristoffer's death.

I attended a GriefShare recovery support group at Fort Carson and a TAPS grief seminar. I connected with the amazing Fallen Hero Family Center at Fort Carson. Two months after Kristoffer's death, I attended the SOS Christmas party. I found it sobering to realize that every person packed into the SOS house had lost a husband, father, sibling, or child. I observed a young woman wearing her husband's wedding ring on a chain dangling from her neck. That said it all. Widow. The Ranger bond I felt with a former commander of 2/75, Fort Carson's General Joseph Anderson and his wife provided great comfort.

Because Joe had lost so many soldiers, I asked, "How do you cope with the death of so many men that you know?"

"Not very well."

The Rangers returned from their deployment and I flew to Fort Lewis for another memorial ceremony. No one prepared me for the final roll call. The moment someone called Kristoffer's name and someone answered, "He's gone, Sir." I felt an electrical shock fritz my mind. A shot of intense pain pierced my heart.

An officer announced my son was killed in action. Mikajsa, my three-year-old granddaughter placed her hands over her ears and then asked, "Is Daddy better now?"

How do I respond to that question? I sucked in deep breaths trying to hold myself together. I think I said, "Daddy is with Jesus" to which she replied, "I want my daddy. I want my daddy. I want my daddy."

I want your Daddy back, too.

Throughout the ceremony, I kept thinking, *Be strong. Hold yourself together. My son, a Ranger, would not want me to embarrass him. Stand strong. Breath deep. Make Kristoffer proud. You are a Ranger mom.* I scanned the faces of the men standing at attention in the battalions and longed to stay and talk with those who knew my son.

Later that year, Mikajsa asked, "If Jesus can take Daddy home to heaven, why can't He bring daddy back?" Speechless, I wondered how to respond to her question, when this world seems more like home than heaven and I wanted Kristoffer back too.

Heaven. Can't wait. Will be so wonderful never, ever being separated again from those we love.

Processing Loss

To process the traumatic loss of a loved one, the brain pushes everything out that it doesn't need. Unfortunately, that included my short-term memory. My "brain on stress" created many humorous moments to interrupt my grief. After visiting the Fallen Hero Family Center at Fort Carson I climbed into my GMC Jimmy, pushed the accelerator. Nothing. Dead. *Oh no, not car trouble.* My stress level escalated to stroke level. When I realized the key wasn't in the ignition, laughter plummeted my blood pressure back to normal.

Another time I stopped by Sam's Club for gas. I sidetracked myself and went into Sam's, but I couldn't remember the two items I needed, but managed to fill the basket with who knows what. As I drove into my driveway, I laughed. *I forgot to fill-up the gas tank or buy milk and bananas. How hard is it to forget milk and bananas?*

Another time, I handed a Fort Carson gate guard my ID after backing out of two gate lines, one labeled DoD registered cars only, to move to a shorter line. By this time four guards from three gates eyeballed me. *Kristoffer is dying right about now. Oh Mom.*

"Are you sure you want to give this to me, Ma'am?"

"Yes, sir."

"Are you *sure*?"

"Yes," pointing to my Army-issued, get-on-base-without-a-bomb-detector-check, family survivor sticker bonded to my windshield.

The gatekeeper flashed my credit card. We laughed as I dug out my government-issued photo ID.

Before my first *real* Memorial Day, the Army strategically scheduled the unveiling of my son's name on the Special Operations wall of remembrance that I never wanted my son's name engraved on. I was happy to hear that my Ranger escort was the man who broke his leg and who Kristoffer replaced on the mission that took his life. I worried that he might feel false guilt and I wanted him to understand that God numbers our days.

Part of the weekend I learned more about Kristoffer's job as a JTAC. I wanted to put on the 35-pound vest Kristoffer wore, but it was too heavy. My Ranger escort dressed me in a tactical vest. I pushed it close to my heart and closed my eyes, trying to imagine how Kristoffer felt wearing his vest while performing his job. It gave me joy to pick up specialized equipment Kristoffer used and to take aim through the sights of guns light enough for me to handle. The weight of some guns and a bazooka surprised me. One Gold Star attendee snarked, "Well, it looks like you're having a good time."

Yes. I was enjoying imagining my son's experiences.

While at Fort Bragg, someone mowed my knee-high grass that I'd intended to mow before I left. What a gift, mowed grass.

After returning home, I received an invitation to attend my first Special Forces military ball at Fort Carson. The commander gave me golden roses and asked me to stand in front of hundreds of soldiers and their spouses and announced, "We're your family now, Scoti."

On Veteran's Day, Kristoffer's junior high invited me to their amazing Veteran's Day program where they honored his sacrifice. When the school principal asked, "How many have parents, relatives or friends serving in the military?"

Almost every child in that auditorium stood.

MORE STARK REALIZATIONS

Kristoffer's death certificate arrived and I received another sobering shock.

Homicide.

No mother wants to read that word on her son's death certificate. And there it was. My son Kristoffer's death certificate read: homicide. No mother wants her child dead at the far-too-young-to-die-age of 29 years and 17 days. I shuttered at the un-checked box labeled 'suicide.'

Someone from Dover's morgue called to confirm if I really wanted the autopsy report and CD with pictures of Kristoffer's dead body that I'd requested. Sure did. When the package arrived, my doctor, Rob, interpreted the autopsy report, so I wouldn't draw wrong conclusions that would torture my heart. My doctor again confirmed that Kristoffer did not suffer.

I'd worried about all the alcohol I imagined Rangers consume and was relieved to hear that Kristoffer's liver was healthy. I handed Rob the autopsy CD to keep. If that autopsy CD stayed in my home, my curiosity would push me to open it and study the pictures.

Mourning the death of a loved one reminds me of an onion. Each layer that peels off stimulates tears, releasing the weight of mourning stinging the eye of the sorrowful soul. Life is so different without my son. Time is now divided between 'before' and 'after.'

I can't believe how 'before' the unimportant upset me. And isn't that how so many Americans live their lives? Pursuing unimportant significance? Stepping on people, misrepresenting others to obtain unimportant importance. Getting stuck obsessing over unimportant compulsions? Screaming about spilled water that will dry?

One benefit of mourning? The lack of energy to swim against the flow of the unimportant. Being okay with letting go of the "should's." Like one of those lazy river rides. Backside hanging in the water. Arms flopped over an inner tube. Head back, relaxed facing the warm sun. Turning my heart towards the Son and allowing myself to drift and float in the current of mourning tugging at my heart.

The unfolding process of mourning is God's gift. If my mind had to absorb the full blunt reality of this loss on the first day, week or month, I'm convinced my brain would have exploded outside my skull. The best part of raw pain? How fresh and real God's Word is. How God speaks to my heart and comforts me through His Words written in Psalms.

Those kick-me-in-the-gut days, Memorial Day, July 4, and Veteran's Day, plus spoken and sung words, the Pledge of Allegiance and the *Star Spangled Banner,* are no longer just another day or mumbled words. After 'the news,' I was too angry to sing the *Star Spangled Banner.* Now I can't sing our national anthem or say the Pledge of Allegiance or say, "I'm Kristoffer's mom" without a catch in my throat or tearing up, because my son died serving this country.

In the first few months after Kristoffer's death, I dreamed I was lost and had no way to return home. I phoned Kristoffer. "I'll come pick you up, Mom." In another dream, Kristoffer came to me. I felt joyful, delighted, excited to see him again. I asked Kristoffer a question. He began to answer. An abrupt awakening jerked me into instant consciousness—back to intense emotional pain.

After Sarah asked God to provide closure for her daughters, three-year-old Mikajsa described her daddy flying without legs (which unknown to her were blown off below the knees) in her room and playing with her. Mikajsa also told Sarah that Kristoffer also flew into 18-month-old Aalijah and Sarah's bedrooms.

God answers our prayers in the most unexpected ways.

RESILIENCE MATTERS

I will never forget the sweet look of innocence on my son's face during our last conversation via Skype. After his 14th deployment, he was to transfer to Fort Benning to his new training job. I asked, "Will you still have to be deployed?:

"Yes."

Not the answer I wanted to hear. But I was consoled by the fact that on his way to Fort Benning, he planned to stop at my home in Colorado and then at my mom's home in Mississippi. With anticipation and excitement, I could hardly wait to spend time with Kristoffer and visit his family in the South.

I did not want my son, my son's brother, my precious daughter-in-love's husband, and my adorable granddaughters' father to die. Rather than a memorial display of his medals and flag display case on my buffet, I prefer him alive. I don't want his name engraved on a beautiful tombstone or obelisk.

I miss my son.

At first, some days I could barely manage breathing. My mind raced, consumed with thoughts of Kristoffer. I wanted my son back to hug, to touch, for his wife to embrace, and for his daughters to know their dad who loved them with all his heart.

The emotional pain remains a constant. Knowing my son is in a better place does not exempt me from mourning and pain. I allow myself to ride the capricious waves of grief. On some days I can push back the reality of Kristoffer's death. Other days the finality refuses to be ignored. *This can't be true. I don't want this to be true. Oh no, it's true.* Sometimes, the emotional pain overwhelms my physical strength. With immense effort, I urge myself forward. *Just take one step, one more step.*

Sometimes I can't distinguish between whether I'm starving, even when I've just eaten, or if it's the feeling of raw emotional pain burning inside my chest —a fire that chocolate or food cannot quench.

At the end of the second year of Kristoffer's death, I chose one word to live by. Every year I select a word to focus on, instead of making resolutions, which I never keep. My word for 2014?

Resilience. Knocked down, but not knocked out.

One key to enduring this painful reality? By turning to the Man of Sorrow, to *Adonai*, my Lord, Master, Owner, and my Strong Tower. (Proverbs 18:10, Psalm 9:10, Psalm 20: 1, 7). Kristoffer grew up a common boy from Colorado Springs and San Diego, and died as the most deployed Special Operations Ranger in history.

Kristoffer spent a decade with the 2nd Ranger Battalion either preparing for war or in direct contact with the enemy in Iraq and Afghanistan. My son died so that Americans can sleep well at night. Jesus, a common boy from Nazareth, died so every person on earth can live every day with the assurance that heaven is both a reality and a possibility through Him.

Just as my heart suffered because my son died for our freedom, God's heart agonized when His son died for every person's spiritual freedom. *El Yeshuw'ah*, The God of My Salvation, and The Light of the World, sacrificed his life to save, deliver and move Kristoffer to eternal safety.

Many people spend their lives running away from difficulties or trying to sprint past them as fast as possible. My son bolted toward challenging, dangerous situations. Challenges aren't to be wished away. Just as soldiers are willing to die so Americans can be free, Jesus died on the cross to secure our spiritual freedom. Christ walked toward Jerusalem, toward the cross, toward deadly pain to bleed out and secure our eternal freedom from death.

The Army's incident report described my son's truncated body lying face down in a blast hole in the Afghan dust. All I wanted to do was to run to my son and save him. When tortuous mental images of my son bleeding out rip at my heart, I replace those pictures with God lifting my son out of that blast hole and into the reality of His eternal love, peace and life. When my mother's heart drowns in the valley of mourning and tears, my built-in homing instinct for the eternal longs for heaven—resurrection and reunion with my fallen hero, risen son.

Compared to heaven and all of eternity, the pain of grief on this earth lasts less than a nanosecond, a mere pinprick, a scar upon the heart. I look forward to the only scars in heaven—Jesus' scars. My pain, my scars, my tears will be no more. Only eternal joy and praising God alongside those I love. By the stripes torn in Christ's flesh by a barbed whip, we're healed, meaning healing comes through being united spiritually to God.

Many knew Kristoffer as a friend, a son, a brother, a husband, a warrior. Many know Jesus as a teacher, a prophet, a good person. I pray that you come to know Him as God's Son, your Savior, who longs to infuse you with hope and healing in a world filled with injustice and hurt.

Ravi Zacharias wrote in his book, *There is a Plan*, "At the end of your life one of three things will happen to your heart: it will grow hard, it will be broken, or it will be tender. Nobody escapes. Your heart will become coarse and desensitized, be crushed under the weight of disappointment, or be tender by that which makes the heart of God tender as well. God's heart is a caring heart."

The Joint Fires Observer training center at Fort Sill was named Domeij Hall in honor of my son. At the ceremony, Kristoffer's two-year-old daughter, Aaliyah, looked at Kristoffer's picture etched on the marble memorial and said, "Hi, Daddy," and then her tiny hand patted his marbleized face. My daughter-in-love and I requested that John 15:13 be engraved on the memorial plaque: *"Greater love has no one than this, that one lay down his life for his friends,"* not only to remind every soldier walking through those doors of Kristoffer's sacrifice, but more important, the message of the cross: God longs for a relationship with you and to hear you say, "Hi, Daddy." He regards you as personally worth dying for, and that your life is worth the exchange of His own.

Etched on every tombstone are two dates that belong to God, the day God planned our birth and the date God knows we'll die. Between those two dates is just one simple line—the dash—that stands for the time that's yours and mine. My son packed an awful lot of living into his dash. Have you given serious thought to your dash, your future, your hope, your legacy?

Pain, sorrow, violence, suffering, and goodbyes are the laws of earth. No more death, no more sorrow, no more crying, no more pain, and joyful reunions are the laws of heaven. My son attended death's funeral. When the law of earth played my son's *Taps*, heaven played *Reveille*—Kristoffer's wake-up call to rise and live forever.

Just as I could not ignore the insistent knocks on my door the night I received 'the news,' I cannot ignore what happened. I need *El Yeshuw'ah*, The God of My Salvation (Isaiah 12:2), who is stronger and wiser than I, who in eternity will provide meaning to my "Why's?" Meanwhile, I live by God's promises, not man's explanations. Sorrow seasons my tears and my heart as I crawl, limp, and dance towards heaven. Pain, loss, and grief drives us to what really matters in this life—authentic relationship with a sovereign God and trusting *Who God says He is.*

Even so, I still fly blind trying to navigate turbulent ups-and-downs of mourning. Unpredictable emotional loops, rolls, and spirals send me crashing. I burn with longing for my son to still be alive. I've lost all power to reclaim before-my-son-died "normal" or to control after-death's sting. Sorrow's silent, salty language runs liquid down my cheeks, releasing my heartbreak to the God of all comfort. God counts, treasures and stores every costly sacred teardrop in His bottle. (Psalms 56:8)

KEEP MOVING

In year two, agony's oppressive foot firmly planted my spirit in the nether regions of grief. I feared losing the key to escape my spiral into a deep depression. I needed to make a change, so I decided to try CrossFit for thirty days.

After the first week, the trainer gave me his pep talk about how I needed to be motivated. I was honest. "Kristoffer's death shattered my motivation, my drive. Finishing anything drains me emotionally and physically. All I can commit to is the one-minute drive to CrossFit.

I need you to push me."

"I can do that." And Josh did. I've transitioned from hating CrossFit, to a love-hate relationship, to wondering, "Am I crazy? Why am I killing myself?" to "I want an Army Ranger hard body." I wish Kristoffer were here, because he'd sure be proud of me, even though I'll never be able to complete the Hero WOD (workout of the day) named in honor of Kristoffer.

My CrossFit experience reminds me of my journey of mourning. During one difficult burpee spree between reps with barbell push and presses, my tummy laid cemented to the floor. My nose inhaled the smell of the sweaty, rubber mat as I sucked oxygen into my burning lungs.

"Keep moving, Scoti."

I bent my leg at the knee and waved it back and forth. Pretty sure that's not the movement the trainer wanted. I managed to crawl to my knees, wobble up, push butt out and heels to floor to finish a brutal round of burpees and pushing barbells over, under, here, there, and everywhere.

Even when I think I'm gaining strength, my body tells me otherwise. Some days just putting one foot in front of the other feels like I will shatter to pieces. I wear the same outfit three days in a row, three dishwasher loads of dirty dishes sit rinsed in the sink, and clean laundry breeds in the family room, but I soldier on, pushing my limits.

"Do you not know? Have you not heard? The LORD is the everlasting God, the Creator of the ends of the earth. He will not grow tired or weary, and his understanding no one can fathom. He gives strength to the weary and increases the power of the weak." (Isaiah 40:28–29)

Every day, holidays, and Kristoffer's birthdate and death date continues to come and to go. With the help of the Lord, great friends, Gold Star moms, and CrossFit, I beat back mourning's depressive pall. Still wondering what that endorphin rush feels like, though.

After one brutal week at CrossFit, my body buzzed and I asked my trainer, "Will it always be this hard?"

"It will always be a challenge. We're working on increasing your workload capacity." Then I realize I'm doing twice as much as I was several weeks before. When a trainer writes a killer warm-up and workout on the board, I think. *I can't do that.* But raw grit pushes me through the WOD, one rep at a time, and I collapse to sleep sound that night.

And that's how life and loss and grief and resilience operates—it will always challenge me to push forward—one rep at a time.

Called to Serve

Generals spoke glowing words about my son and commented how proud I must be of Kristoffer. Truth be told, I don't know who they are talking about. His ten years of service are a black hole. My son never talked about his job. And I'll be dead before I can access the Freedom of Information Act to know what part my son played.

Kristoffer told his wife, "I have stories to tell one day."

But that day never came.

Every Gold Star parent yearns to hear from their child's military friends. My heart hurts when any soldier suffers from their demons and survivor guilt, especially medics. I'm so grateful to the medics who did everything possible to save my son's life. However, God had other plans for Kristoffer.

A 6' 5" Ranger remarked, "I was afraid to contact you, a Gold Star mom," I laughed, because I think of every Ranger as a magnificent, fearless warrior. Our children's buddies know our fallen sons and daughters in a way that we will never know them. For me, it's important to understand who my son was and hear about the adventures my son experienced. I can't express how hearing from anyone who knew my son takes the sting out of the ever-persistent pain.

I am the most comforted or content when I'm visiting my

daughter-in-love, hugging or playing with my grandchildren or in the presence of Kristoffer's Ranger buddies—the closest links on earth to who my adult warrior son was.

The first month after Kristoffer was killed, I received dozens of cards from friends and strangers saying, "We'll never forget."

Yea, right. You'll get on with your lives.

A mother's love never dies. We fear people will forget our children. Death leaves a heartache no one can heal. Love leaves a memory no one can steal. Hearing our children's Ranger buddies share their memories comforts our ever-mourning hearts that our fallen children will never be forgotten. No matter how small the memory, we love hearing stories about our children or receiving pictures, no matter how much time has passed.

Please don't be afraid of us.

My son died from visible wounds inflicted by an IED. Gold Star parents are not afraid to listen to your memories, your pain, your trauma. We grieve when others, who served with honor, succumbed to death from the invisible wounds of the soul. Gold Star parents pray for opportunities to encourage those struggling with their demons that wish them dead. We'd rather shoulder the pain with you.

On September 24, 2011, less than a month before Kristoffer was killed, he wrote these words on his Facebook page: *"Then I heard the voice of the Lord, saying, "Whom shall I send, and who will go for us?" Then I said, "Here am I. Send me!"—Isaiah 6:8. Thank you for all the love. If I don't get back to you anytime soon . . . sorry."*

Kristoffer felt truly called by God to be a Ranger. Before a deployment, he'd often shoot me an email. "I'm off to do the Lord's work." I confess . . . Army Ranger never appeared on my top ten list of "called by God."

How and where we live out our calling looks different for each person. I'm awed by how my son lived out his high calling. Fully aware of the risks, he wanted to make a difference, and like a missionary, he was willing to lay down his life for his values, his family, his friends, even strangers. How many people can say they live from the heart with that kind of passion and integrity?

Those who fought alongside my son reveal the results of my prayers for God to fulfill "a future and a hope" (Jeremiah 29:11-13) that my son would become a faithful husband, father, and friend. Rangers tell me about my son's example and commitment to his family and faithfulness to his wife. Before Kristoffer left on his final deployment, he told Sarah, "I love you and want to spend the rest of my life with you and I'll do whatever it takes."

On TDY's, Kristoffer lost respect for married men who walked from the bar to a hotel room with a one-night stand. When one Ranger wanted to quit his marriage, Kristoffer encouraged him, which saved his marriage. Another Ranger told me that on one deployment, Kristoffer walked up to him on the plane that was waiting for takeoff, "We're two guys over the limit. Go home and spend the time with your family."

Kristoffer was invited to the White House to attend a Medal of Honor ceremony honoring Leroy Petry. Kristoffer said, "Thank you. I'd rather stay home with my family."

The national and international media quoted his commanders. "Sergeant First Class Domeij was the prototypical special operations NCO—a technically and tactically competent Joint Terminal Attack Controller and veteran of a decade of deployments to both Iraq and Afghanistan and hundreds of combat missions. His ability to employ fire support platforms made him a game changer on the battlefield—an operator who in real terms had the value of an entire strike force on the battlefield," said Col. Mark W. Odom, commander of the 75th Ranger Regiment.

"Sergeant First Class Kris Domeij will be dearly missed by the men of 2nd Ranger Battalion He was one of those men who was known by all as much for his humor, enthusiasm, and loyal friendship, as he was for his unparalleled skill and bravery under fire," said Lt. Col. David Hodne, commander of 2nd Battalion, 75th Ranger Regiment.

"This was a Ranger you wanted at your side when the chips were down. He and his family are very much part of the fabric that defines 2nd Ranger Battalion. He is irreplaceable . . .in our formation . . . and in our hearts."

Other comments were also posted on Facebook.

"Kris Domeij, you set the standard for fire support in the Regiment and then exceeded that standard every time you hit the ground."

"You were truly a master of your craft, and I always felt better knowing you were with us anytime we were outside the wire. Thanks for everything you did, and everything you stood for."

"You were a man among men. I learned a lot from you every time we spoke, and those things that I learned from you I implemented regularly to teach my men."

"When I needed a few quals just before my second deployment, I couldn't get them through my own unit so Kris invited me on two training exercises with him. I took leave and just met up with him in Arizona and then again in Arkansas. He had never met me in his life, and I wasn't even in the Army. He didn't care, he did whatever he could to help as many people as he could. If a couple of Marines needed some specific training before they launched on their next deployment, and he could help, he was willing to do whatever it took. Long story short, he took me under his wing, invited my Marines & me out on a couple of exercises, and taught us stuff that saved our lives."

What meant the most to me when I learned of my son's death? When the Chaplain told me he witnessed my son reading his Bible while deployed and when the Chaplain told those who attended his funeral, "Kristoffer had rock solid values."

Even though my world has changed and nothing will ever be the same again, as I look back on my baby, the boy, the man, the warrior; Kristoffer now experiences the truths of these ancient, timeless texts in 1 Corinthians and 1 Peter 1:23-24: *"All people are like grass, and all their glory is like the flowers of the field; the grass withers and the flowers fall, but the word of the Lord endures forever. Our life is but a temporary tent and if that tent is destroyed, we have a home in heaven.* Kristoffer lived knowing that faith in the death and resurrection of Christ is *"to be absent from the body is to be present with the Lord."*

–SCOTI SPRINGFIELD DOMEIJ
PROUD 2/75 GOLD STAR MOTHER OF SFC KRISTOFFER DOMEIJ
KIA OCTOBER 22, 2011 ON HIS 14TH DEPLOYMENT

August 2011
"Extortion 17"

On the night of August 5th – 6th, 2011 one of the worst tragedies in modern special operations history occurred. By this point in the war, the men who made up the special operations community were some of the most proficient, combat hardened warriors that the world had ever seen. Despite that, the enemy always has a vote.

1st Platoon, Bravo Company, 2/75 was on a longer than normal deployment as the rest of the company was rotated to be on Team Merrill, and they surged ahead with them. Their platoon had a mission to conduct yet another raid in pursuit of a high value target in the Tangi Valley, which was in Wardak Province, on the night of August 5th. The mission was not easy, as the Rangers took contact not only during their movement to the target but also on the target. Despite the tough fight that left some wounded, the enemy combatants were no match for the Ranger platoon. They had secured the target and were finishing up gathering anything of intelligence value, when it was suggested by the Joint Operations Center (JOC) back at the FOB to launch a platoon of SEALs from a Naval Special Mission Unit to chase down the 3-4 combatants that ran, or "squirted" from the target.

This was a notoriously bad area to be in, and the Ranger platoon sergeant responded that they did not want the aerial containment that was offered at that time. The decision was made to launch anyway. The platoon sized element boarded a CH-47D Chinook helicopter, "Extortion 17" for the flight out as no SOF air assets were available on that short of notice. As Extortion 17 moved into their final approach of the target area at approximately 0238 local time, the Rangers on the ground watched in horror as it took effective RPG fire. The helicopter was shot down, killing all 38 on board. The call came over the radio that they had a helicopter down, and the platoon immediately stopped what they were doing to move to the crash site as fast as possible. Because of the urgency of the situation, they had to leave the detainees they fought hard to capture behind.

The platoon moved as fast as possible, covering 6-7 kilometers of the rugged terrain at a running pace, arriving in under an hour. They risked further danger by moving on roads that were known to have IEDs planted on them in order to arrive at the crash site as fast as they could, as they were receiving real time intelligence that the enemy was moving to the crash site to set up an ambush. Upon their arrival, they found a crash site still on fire. Some of those on board did not have their safety lines attached and were thrown from the helicopter, which scattered them away from the crash site, so the platoon's medical personnel went to them first to check for any signs of life. With no luck, they then began gathering the remains of the fallen and their sensitive items.

Similar to the Jessica Lynch rescue mission almost a decade prior, the Rangers on the ground decided to push as many guys as possible out on security to spare them from the gruesome task. Approximately six Rangers took on the lion's share of the work. They attempted to bring down two of the attached cultural support team (CST) members, but had to send them back as they quickly lost their composure at the site of it all. On top of that, the crashed aircraft had a secondary explosion that sent shrapnel into two of the Ranger medical personnel who were helping gather the bodies. Despite their injuries, they kept working. Later in the day they had to deal with a "flash flood," which was the enemy fighters releasing dammed water into the irrigation canal that went through the crash site in an attempt to separate the Ranger platoon, cutting them in half. Luckily, because of the sheer amount of water coming their way, they heard it before they saw it and were able to move out of the way before anyone was hurt. If that wasn't enough, there was also an afternoon lightning storm that was so intense it left some of their equipment inoperable, and their platoon without aerial fire support.

Meanwhile, 3rd Platoon, Delta Company from 1/75 was alerted after coming off a mission of their own. They took a small break to get some sleep before they flew out to replace the other platoon, which would hold the site through the day. Once they awoke, they were told to prepare to stay out for a few days. They rode out and landed at the nearest HLZ, which was seven kilometers away from the crash site, and made their way in with an Air Force CSAR team in tow.

After arriving, the platoon from 2/75 then had to make the seven-kilometer trek back out to the HLZ, as that was the nearest place for a helicopter to land in the rugged terrain. The men were exhausted at this point, having walked to their objective the night before, fighting all night, then running to the crash site, securing it through the day only to be told to do another long movement to exfil.

New to the scene, the platoon from 1/75 began doing what they could to disassemble the helicopter and prepare it to be moved. The last platoon had already evacuated all the bodies that had perished in the crash as well as the sensitive items on board, so now the only thing left was the large pieces of the aircraft that were spread out through three different locations. They were out for three straight days, using demolitions as well as torches to cut the aircraft into moveable sections, and then loading them on to vehicles that the conventional Army unit that owned the battle space brought in.

Despite the gruesome and sobering task, the Rangers worked until the mission was accomplished. The third stanza of the Ranger Creed states that you will never fail your comrades, and that you will shoulder more than your fair share of the task, *whatever it may be*, one hundred percent and then some. The Rangers of these two platoons more than lived the Creed in response to the Extortion 17 tragedy.

SEPTEMBER 2011
"GRENADE"

In July of 2011, I was on my way to conduct my third combat deployment as a Ranger in 3rd Platoon, B Company, 2/75 as a tabbed SAW gunner. We were to be extended this trip since it was our turn to be Team Merrill. This meant we would be extended by two months and would be bouncing around all over Afghanistan from FOB to FOB. The first place we were headed was Kandahar, the only base in Afghanistan where the sewage pond is right in the middle of the base. So you can imagine what that smells like every day. If you know anything about Afghanistan, you know that Kandahar and the surrounding provinces are littered with IEDs. It was pretty stressful to go out on missions there due to the fact that we were scared shitless to step on one. At least I was. Not exactly how I want to go out.

Being there in the summertime we were able to experience Ramadan. It's a month long holiday where Muslims basically don't do anything for the entire month. Not even eat. So considering that they had no energy, the chance of guys running away on target was rare. Which was good for us, as nobody wants to take off running after a guy with 60-80 pounds of gear on in the middle of July.

We busted our ass in Kandahar for a month, going out almost every night. Then we were told we were going up north to the Logar province to FOB Shank. The upside was that it was a little cooler, the downside was most of our missions would be in the mountains. You can't land on the target all the time in the mountains like you can in the south so there was a lot of walking.

FOB Shank could be a pretty stressful place. We took indirect fire minimum once a week, and lived in tents surrounded by sand bags and mortar shelters. It was a pretty cool looking place actually,

I felt like I was at war there. I liked it there, but also anything was better than Kandahar. The first few missions in Logar were pretty good. We took contact two or three times and actually had some good mission successes. After about two weeks of being in Logar, we went on another mission.

We were to land at a small COP about 3-5 kilometers from the target and walk in. The walk sucked. We started out at the COP, and then went through what seemed like an abandoned town, through muddy fields, over about six walls, across a river, and through some more urban area and fields. When we finally reached the target compound, the walls were about 15-20 feet high and the gate was proving to be difficult to get into. The plan was once we entered, my squad and I would go right with the rest of the platoon, and 3rd Squad would go left to one tiny room in the corner.

Well, that didn't happen. I ended up being pushed left with Frank from 2nd Squad and Oskar from 3rd Squad. Plans sometimes don't work like you want them to. I was the number one man lead-ing up to this small room that was up some stairs through a door that was open. I shined my laser into a window that was facing us and saw nothing, so I continued. I came up the stairs, peaked in the room and saw a man sleeping and some messed up sheets next to him. I thought either someone else is up and moving in here or they left the room before we arrived. As I button hooked the corner fed room, there was a man in my face literally screaming like a girl, so I pushed him up against the wall and the team leader from 2nd Squad attempted to subdue him. This guy was oddly tough, which seemed ironic for the way he reacted when we came in the room.

The squad leader from 3rd Squad had the other guy locked down as we tried to cuff this guy. Then he yelled "Pipitt switch me!" So we switched and I walked over to flex cuff the other guy. I put one zip tie around his wrist then all the sudden there was a loud explosion and I was on my ass. Smoke filled the room along with the unforgiving smell of an explosive device.

We laid there screaming for help over the radio for what seemed like longer than it should have been for the rest of the platoon to get to us. I lay there feeling like my entire body was on fire, literally. My hands curled into fists without me having any control of it, my mouth went instantly dry and I felt the true meaning of the word panic. I watched Frank and Oskar lie there as helpless as I was, calling for help. I'll never forget the wave of emotions that hit me all at that moment. Watching two brothers of mine lay there, one bleeding out and there was nothing I could do. Something I will never forget is the hopelessness of that moment. To even fathom the thought of one of them dying right there is unbearable. I give serious credit to any Ranger that has had to witness such things and be as helpless as I was.

After about a minute of screaming for help the rest of the platoon finally arrived. The other guy that I was in the process of flex cuffing was still alive and sat in the corner next to me in a panic. My platoon sergeant came through the door and put about 10-15 rounds into his face. Blood was flying all over. Some of it got on my helmet, which I still have today sitting on my bookcase. That was justice at its finest for me. By this time both medics were in the room working on us. I remember telling one of them to work on Oskar and Frank first because I knew I wasn't dying after my platoon sergeant had already looked at me and made the call that I was fine. But the pain overcame me and I was screaming for pain medication. I finally received an IV and was off to ketamine land.

The next thing I remember is waking up in the FOB Shank "hospital" they had set up. All the NCOs were around me as well as the PL. One of my best friends was holding my hand, something else I will never forget. My PL handed me the phone and said call your mom and let her know you're ok. So I called my girlfriend instead. I let her know, then called my mom and by that time my girlfriend had already told her so she was a wreck once she answered the phone. That wasn't something I needed at the time, but it was understandable. Everything from then on was a blur until I arrived in Germany and came to my senses. However I do remember all the guys laughing at the hilarious things I was saying.

I ended up having multiple shrapnel wounds to both legs, left arm, and both feet. I had compartment syndrome on my right lower leg and a fasciotomy was performed on both sides to relieve the pressure so I had two giant holes in my leg for about twelve days until they were closed. If I told you this occurrence had not affected me mentally, I would be lying. It has been a rough two years since this happened. I have had PTSD shoved down my throat, and it has made me grow to hate the term. It's not a disorder. Of course, someone is going to be affected by an incident like this. All three of us were, but that's a whole other story. I am fully recovered now with minor pain here and there that limits me from some things, but for the most part I am functional and I would go back to Afghanistan and wreak havoc on those individuals again and again if I could. Oskar, Frank, and I are all alive and well thanks to the men of 3-B and all attachments.

-KASEY PIPITT
2/75

Epilogue

You may have noticed that this book ended rather abruptly and without much of a conclusion. That was very much on purpose, as the story is not over. Rangers are still going out on target, still fighting our nation's enemies, still being wounded or killed in action. At the time of this book being written, four more Rangers have been killed in action; Sergeant Tanner Higgins, Sergeant Thomas MacPherson, Sergeant Patrick Hawkins, and Specialist Cody Patterson. A career Ranger, Command Sergeant Major Martin R. Barreras was killed from wounds sustained in action while serving in the 1st Armored Division. Many more have been wounded, most notably on October 6th, 2013 when B Company, 3/75 sustained nearly thirty wounded in action in a mass casualty event. Since 9/11, The Regiment has had 64 Rangers make the ultimate sacrifice, and another 672 wounded in action. Rangers have been awarded a Medal of Honor, a Distinguished Service Cross, 49 Silver Stars, 303 Bronze Star Medals for Valor, and more than 600 Purple Hearts.

The men of the 75th Ranger Regiment rose to the occasion when their country needed them most. They have executed every mission that they were assigned to the very highest standard, setting the bar high for future generations. My hope is that every person who reads this book has an immense amount of respect for the sacrifice and contributions that Rangers and their enablers have made in the war on terror. It is cliché to say that 'Freedom is not free', but that statement speaks volumes. Blood, sweat, and tears have been given on behalf of the American public; the men who shed these precious liquids have not asked for anything in return, except maybe to remember the fallen Rangers who made the ultimate sacrifice.

Rangers will continue to energetically meet the enemies of our country on the field of battle, moving further, faster, and fighting harder than any other soldier. Rest assured that no matter the challenge, Rangers will be there on behalf of the American people taking the jobs nobody else can or will do. Rangers Lead the Way!

A Word On Transition

"Warriors gather together because they long to be with men who once acted their best; men who suffered and sacrificed, men who were stripped of their humanity, men who were willing to die for one another."

CSM Martin R. Barreras
Inspired by *"These Good Men"* by Michael Norman

As you read this unparalleled collection of stories of Rangers in the War on Terror, you may have re-experienced some events of your own. This is common and totally normal. What's also totally normal is for a Ranger to squash feelings and emotions that arise deep within – sometimes using alcohol, a killer workout, or some other way so that externally no one can see he is affected. The problem with this is it will surface at some point in time and could result in something bad happening – the end of a relationship, a losing encounter with law enforcement, a lost job, even worse.

But there's a secret. The secret is that virtually every other Ranger feels exactly the same way. Externally we all look like we are hard as nails, that nothing bothers us – but when you unpeel the layers of our lives you'll find broken relationships, lost jobs and opportunities and more. Add to that an injury or wound that forces us to depart active duty, and we start to feel the best thing we ever did in our life is now past.

It doesn't have to be that way. In 2010 a group of Ranger veterans formed Gallant Few, Inc., a 501(c)3 nonprofit with a priority focus on US Army Ranger veterans that also helps any other veteran as resources permit. Our core belief is that a Ranger should never transition alone, without another Ranger buddy close by. The Gallant Few Ranger network is nationwide, and there is a Ranger in the network either in or near you now. We also need more Rangers (and veterans of all eras, branches of service and experience) that have already successfully transitioned to join us to mentor Rangers and other veterans leaving active duty.

While we say we will "fight on to the Ranger objective though I be the lone survivor," the reality is active duty Rangers very rarely operate alone. You always have a Ranger buddy. Don't walk that transition patrol alone.

Join us at www.gallantfew.org,
email us at ranger@gallantfew.org,
or call 316-249-0218.

KARL MONGER
1/75 1990-1993, RANGER CLASS 14-83

Acknowledgements

The one thing that any reader of this book needs to realize is that this book absolutely would not have been possible if it were not for the support and hard work of dozens of people who believed in this project.

My wife Lauren, as usual, has provided me with nothing but support and encouragement through out this project, and many others. She has listened to my frustrations, understood when I needed to step away to gather myself, and shared with me the hope of accomplishing something truly special even at the sacrifice of our family and relationship at times. I couldn't ask for a better friend and partner in life than her. One of the strongest women I know, I am lucky to have her in my life.

My parents, Marty Sr. and Marie Skovlund and Robert and Arleen Wall have provided support and encouragement in so many ways. They have understood the magnitude of this project from the beginning, and made it possible for me to continue on this book to completion when it seemed unfeasible to do so at times. Their constant guidance and advice, even though I may not always show it, was a major factor in staying motivated and seeing this through.

The contributors to this book made *Violence of Action* possible, and with out them there wouldn't be a book in your hands right now. They put themselves out there in a way few are willing to do, and in the course of their courage have made the recording of Ranger history possible. Some of them are now working on books of their own, I encourage anyone reading this to keep a look out for them and support them.

If it were not for the men of C Company, 1st Ranger Battalion, I would not be the man I am today. From the day I showed up as a young, new Ranger, they established a standard of excellence that I continue to strive for, and I don't think any of them will truly understand the impact they had on me ever since. As I worked through this book, I couldn't help but think of previous Ranger buddies, team leaders, squad leaders, and platoon sergeants that I had who could end up reading this. It was that thought that drove me through over ten rounds of editing, long nights of research, and the nearly unbearable weight of making sure this book was done correctly.

The 75th Ranger Regiments Public Affairs shop was truly exceptional in helping me complete this project with out delay or worry of compromising the Regiment's mission. Tracy in particular went out of her way for this project, and I can't thank her enough for her help.

A lot of research and interviews with subject matter experts went into the making of this book. I won't name most of them by name, they know who they are, but I appreciate them taking the time to talk over periods of Regiments history with me, and making sure that I was telling our story as accurately as possible. I only served for a portion of the time this book covers, so having these Rangers as reference made all the difference in the world. Major Andrew Fisher and Master Sergeant Harold Montgomery put a lot of work into the section about Ranger Medics. They are legends in their own right, known for the work they have done in the medical field for the 75th Ranger Regiment specifically, and the military in general. Their contribution to this book explains how much impact the Regiment has had on medical advances and the implementation of them in the unit – something I had neither the knowledge nor experience to accurately portray alone.

This book went through several (more than ten) rounds of editing. Charlie Faint and his wonderful wife Lilla, Leo Jenkins, Matt Sanders, Jenna Evans, Scoti Domeij, Mike Wall, and Jack Murphy took a significant amount of time out of their schedule to help perfect this book. Their efforts in both the content editing and copy editing phase of this project truly made the difference in the pursuit of excellence for this book.

It's a thankless job, but I would be remiss if I did not mention Lorie DeWorken, who did the cover and interior design of the book. It's a detail that is often overlooked, but if it's not done right then it distracts from the words in the book in the worst way. Her patience as well as understanding of what we needed was appreciated, and I would recommend her services to anyone else looking for top quality work on their book.

There have been a few organizations that played a large role in the development of this book. Namely, SOFREP.com and Shadowspear. com provided a lot of resources and guidance on this project. Both organizations have a crack staff that will bend over backwards to help fellow veterans out, and I encourage anyone reading this book to check their work out as well. I would also like to mention Nick, Kerry, Jack, Dale, and Gary for not only providing reviews for the book, but their honest feedback on what we had written and compiled. All five of these men have done amazing things both in the military and out, and continue to support their fellow veterans in any way they can.

We had a few last minute struggles with the completion of this book. One of which was regarding the foreword. Mat Best, the man who has brought more than a few smiles and laughs to the veteran community through his YouTube videos, stepped up big time. He is an excellent representative of the Ranger community, both during his time in uniform as well as his time since separating from the service. When choosing someone to write a foreword for a work such as this, we wanted someone who could accurately represent the men in this book. He more than fit the bill, and we were thankful to have him aboard this project.

Finally, I would like to thank God. I am a man of faith, and He has carried me through both the good and bad times. My prayers have been answered on many occasions, and His comfort and guidance have made a significant impact in my life – and on this book.

Acronyms

1SG	First Sergeant. The senior enlisted soldier in a company, and principle advisor to the company commander.
A-10	The only jet engine aircraft designed solely for close air support. It's primary weapon is a 30mm rotary cannon, which is the heaviest automatic cannon mounted on any aircraft.
AA	Assembly Area. References the area that paratroopers meet at on the drop zone after an airborne operation.
AC-130	A ground attack aircraft that is primarily used for close air support of troops on the ground.
AAA	Anti-Aircraft Artillery
AAR	After Action Review. This is a debrief after every mission, to go over what was supposed to happen, what actually happened, and any improvements for next time.
AFO	Advanced Force Operations. Refers to the early special operations teams that operated in Afghanistan.
AG	Assistant Gunner
AO	Area of Operation
APC	Armored Personnel Carrier
ARSOF	Army Special Operations Forces
AT	Anti-Tank

BAF   Boat Assault Force. References an infil to an objective from a boat platform.

BDA   Battle Damage Assessment. Usually performed to confirm the results of an air strike.

BIAP   Baghdad International Airport

"Birds"   Term used to reference helicopters or other air mobility platforms.

BP   Blocking Position. Elements that provide security around an objective so that enemy forces cannot get in or out.

CCP   Casualty Collection Point

Chalk   A group of paratroopers or other soldiers that deploy from a single aircraft. The size of a chalk depends on what aircraft is being used.

CO   Commanding Officer. Usually references a company commander.

Combat Scroll   References the units "Deployment Patch" that is worn on the right shoulder after a soldier has deployed. In the 75th Ranger Regiment it is called a "Combat Scroll."

CP   Command Post

CPT   Captain. In the 75th Ranger Regiment, typically this rank will control a platoon or if a senior Captain, will control a company.

CQB/CQC   Close Quarters Battle/ Close Quarters Combat

CSAR   Combat Search and Rescue

CCT   Combat Controller Technician. Refers to Air Force special operations personnel who are both JTAC's and air traffic controllers.

CASEVAC   The movement of a patient from the point of injury or casualty collection point with no en route medical care or medical equipment on board.

CONOP   Concept of the Operation. An abbreviated version of an Operations Order that is most often used by special operations because of the shortened planning process.

CONUS   Continental United States

COP   Combat Outpost. A military presence that is smaller than a Forward Operating Base but larger than a patrol base.

DoD   Department of Defense

DZ   Drop Zone

EMT   Emergency Medical Technician

EOD   Explosive Ordnance Disposal

ETAC   Enlisted Terminal Attack Controller

Exfil   The removal of an element from the objective, usually to return to base.

FARP   Forward Aerial Refuel Point

FOB   Forward Operating Base. The most common military installation in the deployed environment.

F3EAD   Find, Fix, Finish, Exploit, Analyze, and Disseminate. Targeting system built on close coordination between operations and intelligence functions, intended to drive friendly operations at a pace faster than the enemy can withstand.

FMC	Final Manifest Call
FSO	Fire Support Officer
FO	Forward Observer. In the 75th Ranger Regiment, may or may not be JTAC qualified depending on experience level. The FO controls air assets and conducts call for fire missions.
FIST	Fire Support Team
FRAGO	Fragmentary Order. References a change to the mission.
GAF	Ground Assault Force. References an infil to an objective from a ground vehicle.
GWOT	Global War on Terrorism
GMV	Ground Mobility Vehicle. The special operations version of a Humvee.
GP	General Purpose
GFC	Ground Force Commander
HAF	Helicopter Assault Force. References an infil to an objective from a helicopter.
HHC	Headquarters and Headquarters Company. The command and support element in every battalion.
HLZ	Helicopter Landing Zone
HUMINT	Human Intelligence.
HVT	High Value Target
Infil	The movement of an element to the objective, whether by air, land, water, or a combination.
IR	Infra Red. References the lasers on Rangers' rifles that can only be seen with night vision devices.

ISR — Intelligence, Surveillance, Reconnaissance. Typically refers to aviation platforms that serve those functions.

IMT — Individual Movement Technique. References the 3-5 second bounds that troops perform under fire.

J-2 — The intelligence directorate of a joint staff; intelligence staff section.

JSOC — Joint Special Operations Command. An elite organization that is a sub-unified command of SOCOM and oversees the Special Mission Units.

JLIST — The full body suit that is worn for protection against WMD threats.

JTAC — Joint Terminal Attack Controller. Controls air assets and conducts call for fire missions.

JMAU — Joint Medical Augmentation Unit

JDAM — Joint Direct Attack Munition. References "smart bombs" that can be guided to a specific target.

"Kanked" — Slang for something being cancelled.

KIA/WIA — Killed in Action / Wounded in Action

LP/OP — Listening point/ Observation Point

LOA — Limit of Advance

LZ — Landing Zone

LAW — Light Anti-Tank Weapon

MBITR — Multi Band Inter/Intra Team Radio. This is the common radio carried by most Rangers.

MRE — Meals, Ready to Eat. The high calorie field rations given to troops.

MEF   Marine Expeditionary Force.

MICH   The helmet that was issued to Rangers through much of the GWOT.

MOLLE   The pouch system that was issued to Rangers early in the GWOT.

MPC   Multi-Purpose Canine

MEDEVAC The movement of a patient either from the point of injury, or a casualty collection point, to a medical facility with en route medical care.

MWR   Morale, Welfare, and Recreation. Generally, MWR is the term used to reference the place service members can access the phone or internet to communicate with loved ones back home.

"Mid-Rats" Midnight Rations. Refers to the meal that is served at midnight as lunch for those who work on a 'reverse' schedule.

NSW   Naval Special Warfare. Encompasses all of the Navy's special operations units.

NCO   Non Commissioned Officer

NLT   No Later Than

NVG/NOD Night Vision Goggles/Night Observation Devices. One and the same.

NBC/CBRN Nuclear, Biological, Chemical/Chemical, Biological, Radioactive, Nuclear.

NAI   Named Area of Interest

OCONUS Outside of the Continental United States

OP	Can refer to either an 'observation post' or may be short for 'operation'.
OPSEC	Operational Security. References the information that is not for public release.
PA	Physicians Assistant.
PMCS	Preventative Maintenance Checks and Services
PUC	Person Under Control
PT	Physical Training
POW	Prisoner of War
Pro-Mask	The "gas mask" that is issued to troops for protection against WMD threats.
PX	Post Exchange. References the shopping center on military bases.
PCI	Pre-Combat Inspection
PL	Platoon Leader. In the Ranger Regiment it is usually a Captain or a First Lieutenant promotable.
PFC	Private First Class. A soldier that is generally a rifleman and is typically inexperienced.
PKM	A Russian or Chinese built 7.62mm machine gun that is similar to the M-240B.
QRF	Quick Reaction Force
RBA	Ranger Body Armor
Recce	Short hand for "reconnaissance.'
RFR	Ranger First Responder. References the minimum medical qualification all Rangers must be certified in annually.

RTB   Return to Base

RFS   Release for Standards. Refers to the process that a Ranger is separated from the Regiment for sub-standard performance.

RRD/RRC   Regimental Reconnaissance Detachment / Regimental Reconnaissance Company. Both the same unit, but when the Regiment stood up the RSTB, RRD became RRC.

RRF   Ranger Readiness Force. References the level of alert that a Ranger unit is on.

RTO   Radio-Telephone Operator. References the communications specialist in each element.

RIP   Ranger Indoctrination Program. The 75th Ranger Regiments 3-4 week selection process until it was replaced with the eight week Ranger Assessment and Selection Program (RASP).

RPG   Rocket Propelled Grenade

ROD   Remain Over Day. References a mission that extends past one period of darkness.

ROE   Rules of Engagement. The rules that dictate what actions troops can take in combat.

SAW   Squad Automatic Weapon

SSE   Sensitive Site Exploitation. The search for intelligence after an objective has been cleared.

SOP   Standard Operating Procedure

SOCOM   Special Operations Command. Oversees all special operations units from all branches.

SEAL	Refers to the Navy's elite special operations force, short for 'Sea, Air, Land'.
SMU	Special Missions Unit. Refers to units that fall solely under the Joint Special Operations Command. Commonly referred to as "Tier One" units in the media.
SOAR	Special Operations Aviation Regiment. References the 160th SOAR, which provides special operations aviation platforms for all SOF.
SOF	Special Operations Forces. The general term for all special operations units.
SF	Special Forces. Refers specifically to the 1st Special Forces Regiment, an Army special operations unit. They are also commonly known as Green Berets, for their distinctive head gear.
"Squirter"	Term used for any enemy personnel that run from an objective.
SBF	Support by Fire
Skedco	A litter that is used to transport wounded troops.
SSG	Staff Sergeant. Usually controls a six to nine man element.
SGT	Sergeant. Usually controls a three to four man element.
SFC	Sergeant First Class. Usually controls a platoon.
SPC	Specialist. Usually a member of a fire team.
Sarn't, Sarnt	Abbreviation for "sergeant."

Stryker   An armored troop carrying vehicle that has wheels instead of tracks, commonly used for ground movement of combat forces.

TST   Time Sensitive Target. A target that comes up on short notice and must be acted upon quickly.

TSAF   "This Shit Ain't Free" – a saying in the Ranger community, made popular by a 3/75 Ranger who started a company by the same name.

TOT   Time on Target. The time that the element will arrive at the objective.

TF   Task Force

USASOC   United States Army Special Operations Command. Refers to the branch that oversees all Army special operations units.

XO   Executive Officer. The second in command in a military unit.

The Ranger Creed

Recognizing that I volunteered as a Ranger, fully knowing the hazards of my chosen profession, I will always endeavor to uphold the prestige, honor, and high esprit de corps of my Ranger Regiment.

Acknowledging the fact that a Ranger is a more elite soldier, who arrives at the cutting edge of battle by land, sea, or air, I accept the fact that as a Ranger, my country expects me to move further, faster, and fight harder than any other soldier.

Never shall I fail my comrades. I will always keep myself mentally alert, physically strong, and morally straight, and I will shoulder more than my share of the task, whatever it may be, one hundred percent and then some.

Gallantly will I show the world that I am a specially selected and well trained soldier. My courtesy to superior officers, neatness of dress, and care of equipment shall set the example for others to follow.

Energetically will I meet the enemies of my country. I shall defeat them on the field of battle for I am better trained and will fight with all my might. Surrender is not a Ranger word. I will never leave a fallen comrade to fall into the hands of the enemy and under no circumstances will I ever embarrass my country.

Readily will I display the intestinal fortitude required to fight on to the Ranger objective and complete the mission, though I be the lone survivor.

RANGERS LEAD THE WAY!

-CSM Neal R. Gentry

Coming Soon
from Other Ranger Authors

On Assimilation
By Leo Jenkins – November 2014

Voices from the Shadows
By LTC Charles Faint with Marty Skovlund, Jr. – 2015

Two Charlie
By Grant McGarry – Fall 2014

The Bearded Conservative
By Marty Skovlund, Jr. – 2014

No Tomorrow: The End of Days Series
By Iassen Donov – Spring 2015

Back to Babylon
By Jonathan Baxter

Sons of the North Star: A Maine Family At War 1861-1865
By Pete Huston

Curmudgeonism: A Surly Man's Guide to Midlife
By Kelly Crigger
Graybeard Books
2014

About the Author

Marty Skovlund, Jr. was born and raised in Huron, South Dakota, where he enlisted in the U.S. Army immediately after high school. His first assignment was to the 1st Battalion, 75th Ranger Regiment. While at 1/75, he served in a variety of roles and deployed to both Iraq and Afghanistan on multiple occasions. After his fifth deployment, he volunteered for recruiting duty and was assigned to the Syracuse Recruiting Battalion as a recruiting NCO. In 2012 he founded Blackside Concepts, and separated from the Army after eight years of service in June 2013 to run his business full time. He is happily married with his wife of five years, and is father to a new baby girl – their first. He currently resides in Colorado Springs, Colorado.

CPSIA information can be obtained at www.ICGtesting.com
Printed in the USA
BVOW06*1347120715

408373BV00006B/204/P